The Race Controversy in American Education

Recent Titles in
Racism in American Institutions
Brian D. Behnken, Series Editor

The Color of Politics: Racism in the American Political Arena Today
Chris Danielson

How Do Hurricane Katrina's Winds Blow?: Racism in
21st-Century New Orleans
Liza Lugo, JD

Out of Bounds: Racism and the Black Athlete
Lori Latrice Martin, Editor

Color behind Bars: Racism in the U.S. Prison System
Volume 1: Historical and Contemporary Issues of Race and
Ethnicity in the American Prison System
Volume 2: Public Policy Influence(s) toward a Racial/Ethnic
American Prison System
Scott Wm. Bowman, Editor

White Sports/Black Sports: Racial Disparities in Athletic Programs
Lori Latrice Martin

Racism in American Popular Media: From Aunt Jemima
to the Frito Bandito
Brian D. Behnken and Gregory D. Smithers

Voting Rights under Fire: The Continuing Struggle for People of Color
Donathan L. Brown and Michael Clemons

The Race Controversy in American Education

Volume 2

LILLIAN DOWDELL DRAKEFORD, PhD, EDITOR

Racism in American Institutions
Brian D. Behnken, Series Editor

 PRAEGER™

An Imprint of ABC-CLIO, LLC
Santa Barbara, California • Denver, Colorado

Library of Congress Cataloging-in-Publication Data

The race controversy in American education / Lillian Dowdell Drakeford, editor.
    pages cm. — (Racism in American institutions)
Includes bibliographical references and index.
ISBN 978-1-4408-3263-5 (alk. paper) — ISBN 978-1-4408-3264-2
1. Critical pedagogy—United States.   2. Minorities—Education—United States.
3. Children with social disabilities—Education—United States.   I. Drakeford, Lillian Dowdell.
  LC196.5.U6R33   2015
  379.2'6—dc23   2015001775

ISBN: 978-1-4408-3263-5
EISBN: 978-1-4408-3264-2

19 18 17 16 15   1 2 3 4 5

This book is also available on the World Wide Web as an eBook.
Visit www.abc-clio.com for details.

Praeger
An Imprint of ABC-CLIO, LLC

ABC-CLIO, LLC
130 Cremona Drive, P.O. Box 1911
Santa Barbara, California 93116-1911

This book is printed on acid-free paper (∞)

Manufactured in the United States of America

Contents

III. Moving toward an Antiracist Education

Series Foreword

Brian D. Behnken

The Race Controversy in American Education is the second two-volume collection to be published in Praeger Publisher's series, Racism in American Institutions (RAI). The RAI series focuses on the ways in which racism has become, and remains, a part of the fabric of many American institutions. For example, while the United States may have done away with overtly racist acts such as extralegal lynching, racism still affects many of America's established institutions from public schools to corporate offices. While the media discarded many of its most racist practices and characters years ago, stereotypical depictions of people of color remain with us. Schools were supposed to be integrated after 1954, yet today many American schools remain one-race schools. This open-ended series of one-volume works examines the problem of racism in established American institutions. Each book in the RAI Series traces the prevalence of racism within a particular institution throughout the history of the U.S. and explores the problem in that institution today, looking at ways in which the institution has attempted to rectify racism, but also the ways in which it has not.

The Race Controversy in American Education explores the critically important subject of racism in American schools. Institutional racism within schools should surprise no one, given the long history of school segregation and educational inequities in the U.S. The multiple scholars in 33 well crafted, analytical chapters expand our viewpoint by looking at many of the historic and contemporary manifestations of racism in education. Take for instance zero tolerance policies, which unfortunately tend to target and affect students of color, debilitating young learners and, in some ugly cases, criminalizing them for relatively minor infractions. Those zero tolerance policies have also led to another problem in American education, the school or cradle to prison pipeline. In an oddly reminiscent policy move, educators have in essence enacted a new form of "tracking," one that tracks students of color from schools to prisons.

The authors in these two volumes do not simply address problems in the American educational arena. They also offer novel and important recommendations for how we might work to solve these problems. One solution that education experts have advanced for decades is the restructuring of the curriculum to more fully reflect the diversity of the U.S. That restructuring could also work to target specific groups who are underrepresented in certain fields, from students of color is science or engineering to female students in math. Other authors in this volume seek to correct problems in leadership in schools or emphasize the ways unrecognized groups, or focus on management issues as a corrective measure.

Taken together, these 33 chapters go far in explaining institutionalized racism in education and offering solutions to these problems. This is the goal of the RAI series. Editor Lillian Dowdell Drakeford has skillfully brought these volumes together. As a lifelong educator she is well suited and uniquely experienced for this project. *The Race Controversy in American Education* touches on not just an important subject, but one that profoundly impacts the lives of millions of young Americans on daily basis.

Brian D. Behnken
Iowa State University
Ames, Iowa

Preface

Still Troubled after All These Years

Not everything that is faced will change, but nothing will change until it is faced.[1]

Ever since I grew old enough to reflect, I have been deeply troubled by the insidious persistence of racism and inequality of opportunity in America's public schools. At various junctures throughout my life, I have had the occasion to contemplate the impact of growing up black in America.

I Remember . . .

In 1962, I was one of 60 black children crammed into a partitioned second-grade classroom. There were two teachers, Mrs. Hart and Mrs. Lyle. My teacher was Mrs. Lyle. We did not know we were overcrowded because everybody acted like they had good sense, for the most part, so there were no major distractions, of which we were aware, to teaching and learning. We all knew one another from the neighborhood, we were sure that our teachers loved us, and we learned what we needed to learn to be ready for third grade. That was all that mattered. It was not until I became old enough to reflect on the situation that I realized the inequity of our circumstances. I later learned that our school was overcrowded, but across town, classes in the all-white schools had only 20 students.

It was not until I became a teacher that I realized that there had to have been numerous caveats to teaching and learning from Mrs. Hart and Mrs. Lyle's perspective: caveats like not being able to give individual attention to those students who probably needed it most; having to insist on absolute order, discipline, and control when a little unorthodox active learning might have occasionally better suited the learning environment; and being forced to teach to the middle in deference to the infamous bell curve, which automatically discounts children who appear as outliers in the larger spectrum. In retrospect, I wondered what happened to the much-anticipated reform that was supposed to follow the *Brown v. Board of Education* (1954) victory. At the time, however, in my innocence, I knew nothing of the *Brown* decision, segregation, or the interest that fueled. My world was black and it felt and looked pretty good to me.

I first felt the sting of racism in the seventh grade. I was one of a select group of African American students bused across town to integrate an all-white middle school in Gary, Indiana. While some students were unfriendly, it was not their unfriendliness that bothered me the most. It was not a personal prejudice that I felt; it was more of systematic, institutionalized, collusion of lifelong perceptions of being marginalized because of my color. What troubled me most was a nagging sense of self-doubt. It was a self-doubt borne out of being ignored and feeling diminished in the white environment—ignored at lunch, ignored in class, and rarely asked for my opinion. It was a feeling of doubt that my dad may have unknowingly nurtured as I often heard him lament "if you're black, you have to be perfect and then improve." What a tall order! I doubt that it is possible.

At any rate, I began to second-guess my intellect and ability alongside the majority population of white students. Suddenly, everybody seemed smarter than I was just because they were not black. It was a very unfamiliar feeling because I was accustomed to being one of the smartest students in the class. I did not realize that I still may have been one of the smartest students in the class even if the class was full of white people. Despite loving parents, both of whom were career educators, and numerous positive black role models within my family, church, and neighborhood, the ravaging effects of institutional racism in American society had managed to teach me that white was naturally right and better and that being black made me not quite good enough.

I came home and announced that I just did not feel as smart as the white kids. "They're smarter than I am," I cried. It took a stern talking from my father, one I will never forget, to jolt me out of this destructive self-talk. His words hit me like a splash of cold water on the face. "Don't ever doubt yourself or what you can do. You are just as good, just as smart as anybody else. Keep your eyes on the prize." I took his words to heart, consecrating them in my memory, and have, since then, often culled great strength from their remembrance at critical junctures throughout my life. In one sense, I have never looked back, that is to say, I rarely doubt my capacity to achieve great things. Yet, in another vein, I am constantly reflecting on the why of that lived experience. Several niggling questions come to mind.

How is it that such effects are learned and through what everyday mechanisms? How do the pedagogical dimensions of overt white supremacy differ from the more covert expressions of white dominance in the alleged raceless or color-blind contemporary era, and what effect do they have on black youth? Do children of color still learn from school and society that they are inept and if so, to what degree? Do they learn this differently and if so, how? What happens to children who rarely hear positively affirming words? What happens to children who accept the negative identity frequently ascribed to them? What happens to them?

I fear that many children die inside, and our whole society, even if unknowingly, dies a little bit right along with them. Without a language of hopeful possibility, children become fatalistic about their future, grow cynical, and become what society tells them they are. They become low achievers. All too often, in the midst of progress in more privileged school districts and wealthy suburbs, many African Americans attend substandard schools with substandard resources and substandard teachers who race to beat the children out of the doors at the close of the school day. Of course, this is not the case everywhere, but if it is the case anywhere, that is one case too many.

Some Time in 1979 . . .

Still troubled, I found myself struggling to explain the how and why of racism and naively contemplated what might be done to get rid of the irksome problem once and for all. I wrote an essay back in 1979 on racism and whether black history courses can eradicate racism. I did not believe then (and do not believe now) that racism has much at all to do with ignorance. To the contrary, I argued that racism is caused by insecurities inherent to the human experience and exacerbated to varying degrees by unfulfilled yearnings for security and belonging wrought by society. I wrote:

> All of us, at birth, become detached from our original oneness with nature and truth. We are forced to attune ourselves to a foreign and contradictory human existence. Thus, each step we take into this new existence brings with it fear, insecurity, and the challenge to fuse the perfection of our pre-birth existence with the imperfection of our lived experiences. If we succeed in meeting this challenge, we find truth and become productive and creative individuals. If we fail, we find deception and remain insecure and afraid. The extent to which we fail or succeed in this endeavor is largely determined by the nature of the society into which we are born.

I have since learned that I was not alone in these views. Author and scholar, James Baldwin expressed a similar stance:

> Everyone really knows how long the Blacks have been here. Everyone knows on what level Blacks are involved with the American people and in American life. These are not secrets. It is not a question even of the ignorance of White people. It is a question of the fears of White people. . . . So that's what makes it all so hysterical, so unwieldy, and so completely irretrievable. Reason cannot reach it. It is as though some great, great wound is in the whole body, and no one dares to operate: to close it, to examine it, to stitch it.[2]

In my not so scholarly treatise, I also pondered an unsettling connection between racism, inequality, education, and the larger society:

> Our society, because of its capitalistic and highly industrialized nature, makes it difficult for us to meet this challenge [winning the battle over insecurity during separation from the womb]. The ideals of capitalism and industrialization negate the value of truth and existence. These ideals of merciless competition, technological progress, efficiency, and material accumulation negate the value of truth because they encourage us to outsmart each other and nature. We are rewarded for giving the appearance of truth. These ideals negate the value of our existence because they remind us that we can always be replaced by machines. . . . Thus, we are constantly afraid and insecure. . . . We make technology, efficiency, and the almighty dollar our means, our ends, and our gods. . . . Our passivity has resulted in a number of deceptions. . . . Justice has become the interest of the wealthy. . . . White Americans, who came to this country in search of its traditional values and a new identity, have lost sight of who they are or where their lives are headed. They are sure of nothing except their contrived superiority over black people. . . . Therefore, if the schools are to actively debase racism, then we, as educators, must restore the traditional ideals upon which our country was founded. We must revitalize the quest for truth and our bond with nature. . . . We must determine, for ourselves, what ideals we will teach. Foremost among these ideals must be high intellectual standards, balance and harmony, and truth and justice.

While today, I might pick some parts of this passage apart, it demonstrates my enduring interest in what schools should teach, the role of racism in school and society, and the negative impact of a capitalistic society more concerned with money and human efficiency than basic human worth and dignity. I continue to ponder how schools might function differently to unseat the arrogance of power, perception, and privilege in education.

Over the Next 30 Years . . .

Still deeply troubled, it seemed that I was at my wits end after years of teaching in a public urban school district and watching reform after reform fail to appreciably effect sustained change or eradicate persistent racial inequality of educational opportunities and outcomes. Between 1976 and 2006, I saw a number of educational reforms come and go, some more than once. Across the United States and in my district, I witnessed a myriad of educational reforms, all of which aimed to close the racial achievement gap, raise standards for all students, and promote excellence with equity. In every case, the unspoken impetus behind reform revolved around the controversy of race.

I remember the popular magnet school reform of the late 1970s and early 1980s. The overt appeal of magnet schools stemmed from the assertion that magnet schools provided parents and students with curricular choices while also providing a more diverse student population. "These schools emphasized the performing arts, math or science, or other curricular themes or approaches in an attempt to attract students voluntarily, without coercion from school boards or court edicts."[3] Promoted as a means of democratizing opportunity, magnet schools aimed to subtly maintain integration without mentioning race and also appease both the lower and middle classes. Unfortunately, there are at least two historical problems with increasing democracy in education. First, serving two masters—the interests of the privileged and the interests of the marginalized—has yet to work. Those in power rarely give up power and when they do, it is almost never without struggle. Second, throughout America's history whenever schools have become more inclusive and democratic, traditionally privileged Americans have rushed to the assumption that "more equality meant more mediocrity."[4] Hence, magnet schools ended up serving the privileged, for example, the children most likely to succeed anyway, without magnet schools. In my district, the magnet schools of real quality and in the greatest demand grew increasingly selective by establishing exclusionary admission criteria. Very few of the most needy children reaped the benefits of attending quality magnet schools. In time, the magnet movement waned as it became pretty obvious that magnet schools neither effectively stopped whites from leaving the city and abandoning public schools nor closed the racial achievement/opportunity gap.

Amid the push for magnet schools, I recall a brief resurgence of counterculturals who argued in favor of reforms such as "schools without walls, open classrooms, and more learning pods, electives, and student freedom."[5] Like other schools across the United States, we tried things like "schools without walls, open classrooms, and more learning pods, electives, and student freedom,"[6] but when these gimmicks failed to bring about change, they were replaced with calls for back-to-basics curricula, increased accountability, and a myriad of reform plans, such as performance contract learning, behavioral objectives, and other schemes.

By the 1980s, in fact, mainstream legislators, lawmakers, parents, and educators had grown very anxious about the perceived democratization of schools. They were alarmed by the alleged rise of low standards, soft curriculum, social promotion, and lack of discipline, all of which were covertly attributed to integration and the democratization of schools. I remember parents and teachers lamenting that schools were no longer fulfilling the "old republican promise that America was a land of opportunity where merit alone conferred distinction in a fluid social order."[7] In response to the call for change, schools spent the next decade trying some of everything to increase excellence in the schools, hence came the dawning of minimum competency-based testing.

It caught on like wildfire everywhere, and my district was no exception. Many of the early competency-based tests were quite rigorous. I remember, however, when it became apparent that the wrong students (e.g., the historically *good* students) would not be able to pass the tests, the tests got less rigorous, which, of course, defeated the original purpose of the minimum competency testing. More important, the tests did little, if anything, to address racial inequality or inequity. In fact, because students of color and poverty fared even more poorly than their white counterparts on the exams, the tests actually exacerbated racialized assumptions about their ability and desire to learn. Lackluster improvement in student achievement and persistence of the "achievement gap" between advantaged and disadvantaged youngsters prompted educators and policy makers to shift their focus away from the big picture to little picture reform. Schools set their sites on restructuring schools and making classroom improvements.

Reforms emphasized quality improvement at the school sites. Increasingly, problems confronting schools were seen as a systems problem; consequently, reformers believed a bottom-up approach to change might be more effective. My district tried employing Baldrige to promote and improve the classroom learning system as well as the system at the district level. Grounded in the business principles of Total Quality Management, Baldrige in education views change as a planned event.[8,9] It is a way of doing things and a mind-set that has the potential to transform a stagnant, learning-impoverished school culture into an adaptive, continuously improving, learning-enriched school culture. When Baldrige works as it should, whole school systems align their goals and objectives across and within every subsystem involved in the processes of educating and schooling, teaching and learning. I actually became a Baldrige trainer for the district, and I still strongly assert that it has great merit for facilitating continuous improvement. But, in time for reasons too complex to explain in this discussion, support for Baldrige almost disappeared, except for the proven Plan-Do-Study-Act improvement cycle. What followed across the country and in my district was a myriad of reforms, all of which aimed to close the racial achievement gap, raise standards for all students, and promote excellence with equity.

I taught through a parade of reforms that included Effective Schools, Success for All, specialized academies, smaller learning communities, schools-within-a-school, site-based administration, professional learning communities, academic teams, coaching teams, NCLB, high-stakes testing and increased accountability, design teams, and a lot of "Working on the Work."[10] Heck, I frequently led the band! Through it all, I found this much to be true. Racial inequality of opportunity and outcomes persists. The system fights to stay the same. It protects the privileged. And testing is here to stay.

June 2006 . . .

Still troubled, I enrolled in the PhD in Leadership and Change Program at Antioch University. Convinced that the persistent problem of inequality in education stemmed from the absence of the ethic of care in teachers and school leaders, I hoped to better understand how I might emulate the ethic of care in my profession, live and inspire the moral obligation of education, and help others understand the power of caring in the change process. Decisions grounded in the ethic of care require us to *know* those we teach and serve them well. We must love the children not only for who they are but also for who they can and want to be. Carol Noddings postulated that "the first job of schools is to care for our children."[11] Hence, I devoted a lot of time to reading the literature on the ethic of caring but found myself continually drawn to the haunting problem of race in America. At the root of the reason for a lack of caring and moral obligation was race. Simply put, what I discovered was that race and racialized assumptions determine how deeply and sincerely teachers and leaders care about how *some* children learn. If each of us is honest with ourselves, we don't care the same for everyone. I took a good look at myself, and the role of race in my own consciousness.

I examined the eye through which I process information, the lens through which I construct reality, the means by which I determine my actions, and the possible consequences of those actions. I learned that I am irrevocably influenced by my lived experiences, and growing up black in America is first and foremost among them. I discovered that I, too, must strive to function within an anti-oppressive framework.

We all are a product of our lived experiences, and each of us grapples with making sense of our humanity. When one adds the stain of the proverbial color line, the pernicious race question in America, and the determinative power associated with race to the extant trials of the human condition, the result is a mutually imprisoning human dilemma. "Who is the slave and who is free?"[12] Indeed, it is difficult to discern. We all suffer from the human construction of race and the bondage of racism. I wrestled with questions about the role schools play in perpetuating the bondage, and the role schools should play in eradicating it. I asked:

What ideologies and epistemologies dictate the order of modern society? What do schools teach? What should schools teach? What do we learn and why? Who benefits from the order of society and education today? What are the possibilities for fruitful intervention in contemporary conflicts? How can education change the nature of society?

I looked for answers from scholars, philosophers, and theorists and became intrigued with critical pedagogy, resistance theory, and critical race theory. Everything I read led me to want to explore the concept of allegedly color-blind, raceless educational reform and its historical significance in the ongoing struggle to provide equity in education. Hence, the central question of my dissertation was, how have allegedly race-less, color-blind educational reform agendas in the post-*Brown* era, intentionally or unintentionally, affected racial inequality of educational opportunity and outcomes in America's public schools? The answers were both simple and complex.

Let it suffice to say that I grew even more convinced that race matters, racism endures, and, to the extent that schools are training grounds for how people view themselves and the world, if we ever intend to achieve equity and equality in schools and society, we must not feign blindness to that which ails us.

October 2013

Still troubled, I was recently retired from my district but eager to effect change, and make a difference. Lo and behold, an old contact to a new opportunity! I was blessed with the chance to plan, edit, and contribute to this amazing two-volume collection: *The Race Controversy in American Education.*

I believe in the transformational power of education, intellectualism, and writing. I see this work as a change agent. As the seminal author, James Baldwin explained: "The paradox of education is precisely this—that as one begins to become conscious one begins to examine the society in which he is being educated. . . . You write in order to change the world . . . if you alter, even by a millimeter, the way people look at reality, then you can change it."[13]

Notes

1. http://www.goodreads.com/author/quotes/10427.James_Baldwin.
2. Mead and Baldwin 1971, p. 1.
3. Reese 2005, p. 248.
4. Ibid., p. 219.
5. Ibid., p. 309.
6. Ibid.
7. Ibid., p. 287.
8. Mukhopadhyay 2005.
9. Maurer and Pedersen 2004.
10. Schlechty 2002.
11. Noddings 1992, p. xiv.
12. Conklin 2013, p. 127.
13. http://www.goodreads.com/author/quotes/10427.James_Baldwin.

Bibliography

Conklin, T. 2013. *The House Girl.* New York: HarperCollins Publishers.

Edmonds, R. 1982. "Programs of School Improvement: An Overview." http://www.eric.ed.gov/ERICWebPortal/search/detailmini.jsp?_nfpb=true&_&ERICExtSearch_SearchValue_0=ED221536&ERICExtSearch_SearchType_0=no&accno=ED221536.

Maurer, R.E., and S.C. Pedersen 2004. *Malcolm & Me: How to Use the Baldrige Process to Improve Your School.* Lanham, MD: Scarecrow Education.

Mead, M., and J. Baldwin. 1971. *A Rap on Race.* Philadelphia, PA: J.B. Lippincott.

Mukhopadhyay, Marmar. 2005. *Total Quality Management.* 2nd ed. Thousand Oaks, CA: Sage Publications.

Noddings, C. 1992. *The Challenge to Care in Schools: An Alternative Approach to Education.* New York: Teachers College Press.

Reese, W.J. 2005. *America's Public Schools: From the Common School to "No Child Left Behind."* Baltimore, MD: Johns Hopkins University Press.

Schlechty, P.A. 2002. *Working on the Work: An Action Plan for Teachers, Principals, and Superintendents.* San Francisco, CA: Jossey-Bass.

Success for All. 1993. Number 5, August 1993. https://www2.ed.gov/pubs/OR/ConsumerGuides/success.html.

Introduction to Volume 2

The discussion around the controversy of race in American education continues in Volume 2. Chapters in this volume are divided into three sections: (1) Students on the Margins (Section I), (2) Answers Inside the Arts and the Extracurriculum (Section II), and (3) Moving toward an Antiracist Education (Section III).

The chapters in Section I, Students on the Margins, examine the role race and racism play in the marginalization of students frequently sidelined by mainstream society. In Chapter 1, Christine Brigid Malsbary begins with a discussion of schooling as a contested and political site within the political landscape of the post-1965 immigration era in America. Through the lens of a race-critical, historical perspective, Malsbary identifies four battlegrounds of cultural identity that confront immigrant youth and children of color in America and proposes ways educators can disrupt the "battle fatigue" many of these children experience in school. Steve Grineski and Julie Landsman in Chapter 2 provide further insight into the many ways in which schools and teachers marginalize children of color and poverty in American schools. They share the voices of school-age young people and offer concrete suggestions of ways teachers can bring students from the margins to the center of educational policy and practice. The last chapter in Section I (Chapter 3) examines African American teen mothers. Authors Christine Stroble, Melissa Pearson, and Greg Wiggan use black feminist theory and qualitative research data to initiate a new conversation about the unique educational experiences of black teen mothers. They discuss the historical sexual politics of black women and motherhood. By sharing the voices and lived experiences of black teen moms, the authors seek to debunk historical myths and unidimensional characterizations of black single women and uncover the racialized policies and practices that affect these mothers and their schooling.

Section II, Answers Inside the Arts and the Extracurriculum, investigates the role that art education and the extracurriculum may play in addressing the race controversy in American education. In Chapter 4, written by M. Francine Jennings, explores how arts integration curriculum may combat racism and social injustice in the 21st century. She examines the impact that teachers' attitudes have on teaching about race, class, and culture, and offers practical strategies for reducing teacher resistance to talking about race and racism. Jennings also provides practical examples of arts-based lessons that are aligned to social justice aims and the Common Core Standards. In the second chapter of this section (Chapter 5), Jeffrey O. Sacha investigates how youth culture, school resources, and student–teacher mentorship contribute to the marginalization of low-income students of color and argues that the extracurriculum is both product and producer of the racial order of any given school. He presents a variety of methodological advantages to using extracurricular activities as a window through which to study race, class, and gender among high school students.

The final section in this volume (Section III), "Moving toward an Antiracist Education," includes a variety of chapters, each of which presents a counterhegemonic educational strategy aimed at providing a more democratic, inclusive, antiracist education. The first chapter in this section (Chapter 6), written by Anthony Ash and Greg Wiggan, explores the utility of science as a transdisciplinary, critical method to teach about diversity issues such as race, ethnicity, and culture in teacher education programs. They discuss implications for the role that science may play in promoting meaningful discussions of human diversity that will encourage inclusive and transformative results in science education. In Chapter 7, Cheryl P. Talley et al. acknowledge the impact of long-term, pervasive, and intransigent racial distinctions imposed on children of color and poverty. They present empirical evidence and promising intervention strategies, however, that suggest students can be provided cognitive and emotional tools that develop resilience, bolster positive self-images, and enhance the overall quality of their educational experience. Next, Laura M. Harrison in Chapter 8 asks, What makes talking about race so difficult? Why do certain conversations about race feel threatening to some students? Harrison asserts in the third chapter of this section that moving toward an antiracist educational agenda requires understanding racism on a systemic level. She explains how the tenets of Critical Management Studies can provide a framework for interrogating racialized hierarchies that have been accepted as the natural order of societal structures and helping students and educators engage in transformative conversations about racism. In Chapter 9 Anthony Collatos calls attention to the need to re-frame how knowledge is valued in educational reform. He posits that youth, parents, and educators must be empowered to form partnerships that recognize the impact of race, privilege, and access and challenge poli-cies and practices that foster racial inequality within schools. Collatos docu-ments the work of two strategic university-led initiatives aimed at building university–community partnerships that dismantle historical patterns of racial inequality and educational inequity. Chapter 10, written by Carolyn M. Shields, discusses the role of transformative leadership as a means of effect-ing change in assumptions and beliefs, policies and curriculum, pedago-gies and practices that will move schools toward learning places that are inclusive, inviting, and equitable for all students. She explains how school leaders can create and maintain environments that nurture antiracist edu-cation, social justice, inclusion, and democracy.

The next two chapters in this section (Chapters 11 and 12) view the chal-lenge of moving toward an antiracist education from a slightly different perspective. Each positions hope and responsibility for moving toward an-tiracist education largely within the black community. Duane L. Davis ex-plores the U.S. educational system as a tool of cultural imperialism and draws attention to a need for a positive collective identity among African American youth and a trusting intra-community relationship within the larger African American community. He suggests that developing indepen-dent schools within the African American community may be the best way to achieve those goals. Candice Jimerson-Johnson asserts that in some ways African Americans of the post–civil rights era have unwittingly contrib-uted to the continuation of racial inequities in America's public schools. She alleges that the restoration of African American racial solidarity, shared common values, and a resurgence of the collaborative efforts among Afri-can American leaders in politics, religion, education, and communities will yield the greatest gains for African American children.

The last four chapters in this section (Chapters 13, 14, 15, and 16) explore remedies to the race controversy in American education in a broader context. Tema Okun begins by exploring education within the context of social jus-tice. She maintains that education must be repurposed to encompass teach-ing in ways that encourage students to navigate, think, and act consciously and critically; recognize and challenge misinformation that perpetuates structural inequity; and realize their full capacity to flourish through access to resources and skill-building, and the building of cultural capital. Next, Margo Okazawa-Rey extends the notion of repurposing education within the context of Critical Ethnic Studies and Women and Gender Studies. She discusses the social-justice origins of these studies and uses critical theory of intersectionality and a materialist analysis to make the case for their continuation and advancement in the education of not only the historically marginalized but also all undergraduate students in U.S. academies. George J. Sefa Dei further expands the debate on race and racism beyond the confines of U.S. education, and highlights the need to transform anti-racism education to include broader questions of colonialism and colonial settlerhood in the context of the North American experience. He presents Indigeneity and decolonization as international categories and makes the case for reframing antiracist practice for a global context. The last chapter (Chapter 16) written by Joan T. Wynne discusses her personal lifelong journey to unlearn racism. She talks openly about living with unearned privilege and shares what she has learned about the negative consequences of the dominant cultures' institutions on black students. She also provides strategies that she has found effective in creating environments that support the intellectual achievements of black students. Wynne encourages herself and others to undertake what may arguably be the most difficult transformation of all: a desire to recognize and unlearn the wrong in what seems right and normal about the controversy of race in American education, so much so as to bring about a change of heart.

Part I
Students on the Margins

Chapter 1

Waiting for the World to Change: Racism and Immigrant Education since 1965

Christine Brigid Malsbary

Children of immigrants are the fastest-growing sector of the children and youth population in many postindustrial nations, including Australia, Canada, Sweden, the United States, and France.[1] But schools in many countries have been slow to respond to the urgent needs of immigrant children and young people. In the United States, when we think about schools, we tend to conjure up images of a neatly kept schoolhouse and a plump, matronly, apple-toting schoolteacher. But for many students, schools may feel more like protest sites, evoking images of frustrated protestors squaring off against police protected by tactical equipment and riot shields. School as battleground is a more apt metaphor for immigrant youth attending schools in communities under siege in the current warfare that is immigration politics. These battles are the lineage of centuries of race-centered immigration and education issues, surfacing in controversies over education programs.

Globalization and education scholar Marcelo Suarez-Orozco argues that schooling in the global era is no longer so simple as the one-way assimilation models of the past according to which ethnic, racial, linguistic, and religious minorities learn the codes of the majority society. In order to move to a new model of bilingual and bicultural education, we must first expose, process, and record the ways in which schooling of immigrant children has been an extension of the racialized exclusion of immigrants in U.S. society. Excavating the racism that has driven controversies engendered in the past 50 years around the schooling and learning of immigrant children and youth in U.S. schools means decentering issues of their "failure." Rather, a race-centered approach to the politics of immigrant schooling means understanding how programs, laws, and institutions are implemented for immigrant children in ways that maintain *whiteness.*

Whiteness is not static, and through immigration over time people from a variety of national origins and ethnic roots have moved in and out of whiteness. Rather, "whiteness" and "white supremacy" are terms that refer to a collective U.S. consciousness that maintains a social structure that economically, politically, and educationally disadvantages certain groups. For immigrants, racism has a hydra-head, surfacing in and through educational controversies around language, culture, and citizenship status. Racism engages across a myriad of issues to maintain whiteness through debased educational opportunities for immigrants. Excavating racism in immigrant education is a primary step toward social justice action and reparation.

Race and Immigration: A Brief History

Over 40 million immigrants live in the United States, representing 13 percent of the U.S. population and up from 5 percent in 1970.[2] We are in the midst of one of the largest immigration periods of U.S. history. Immigration is the inevitable result of economic push–pull factors and political and cultural global shifts. It is extremely divisive in the United States—and always has been. Schools are implicated in this battle, as the immigrant (foreign born) and immigrant-origin (those who reside in an immigrant household where one or more parent is foreign-born) school-aged population grows. One-quarter of all the children under 18 have at least one immigrant parent ("immigrant-origin"), and of that number 12 percent of children were born outside the United States themselves ("immigrant").[3]

During the last major immigration peak, immigrant restrictionists drew new racial boundaries sharply defining who was white and who was not. This legacy effects racial consciousness today. During the last major immigration period, "between 1880 and 1930, over 27 million new immigrants arrived, mainly from Italy, Germany, Eastern Europe, Russia, Britain, Canada, Ireland, and Sweden." In an expansion of racial exclusion, "Congress passed the 1917 Immigration Act which prohibited immigration from a newly drawn 'Asiatic barred zone' covering British India, most of Southeast Asia, and nearly all of the Middle East."[4] Racist restrictionist sentiment continued through the 1920s, and in 1924 laws were passed that established national origins quotas that set limits around who could come to the United States. These laws heavily favored northern Europeans. W.W. Husband, the immigration commissioner general who helped to design the laws, believed that some nationalities "resisted assimilation" and organized quotas to favor those groups who were more likely to "contribute to the advancement of the nation."[5]

In other words, immigration has always been inextricably tied to race and racism. The 1924 quota was 2 percent of each nationality already represented in the United States among naturalized citizens. The quota didn't only restrict certain nationalities—it excluded some. This carefully designed number excluded blacks, nearly all immigrants from East and South Asia, and many Mexicans. In fact, whether or not Mexicans should be included in the quota was hotly contested and had much to do with race. Some racialized them as white, and others as Indian, and therefore dirty, indolent, and prone to criminality.[6] U.S. consuls in Mexico began to enforce visas, cutting what had been free flow in the Southwest area and Mexican migration by 76.7 percent. In essence, this created a large undocumented immigrant population as laborers continued to work throughout the Southwest according to demands of the binational market.

In the end, 84 percent of the quota was reserved for northern and western Europeans. Mae Ngai, author of *Impossible Subjects: Illegal Aliens and the Making of Modern America,* writes:

> The national origins quota system involved a complex and subtle process in which race and nationality disaggregated and realigned in new and uneven ways. At one level, the new immigration law differentiated Europeans according to nationality and ranked them in a hierarchy of desirability. At another level, the law constructed a white American race, in which persons of European descent shared a common whiteness, the legal boundaries of both white and nonwhite acquired sharper definition.[7]

Immigration law constructed a white American race by drawing boundaries for who was white and who was not white.

The Changing Face of Immigration: 1965 Reform

During the civil rights era, immigration law had become an embarrassment internationally and hotly contested at home. The government had received pushback from southern Europeans who were separated from their families, like the Portuguese and Italians, who said that the quotas discriminated against them. A system of family reunification was posed as the answer to the maldistribution of quotas that favored white European immigration.

In 1965 immigration law was reformed, initiated by John F. Kennedy, and signed into law by Dwight Eisenhower. The *1965 Immigration and Nationality Act* permanently ended the quota system and began a system of (1) family reunification and (2) skilled labor—a provision that professionals with exceptional skills could enter the United States.

Unexpectedly for the reformers, family reunification led to the most profound demographic transformation in U.S. history, changing the cultural, ethnic, and linguistic face of America. Immigrants from Northern and Western Europe were replaced by immigrants from Mexico, China, India, and the Philippines. After 2000, only 15.9 percent of immigrants were white. Simultaneously, color-blind racism emerged as the dominant ideology of the post–civil rights era. Rather than Jim Crow era racism that permitted the open expression of direct racial expression, such as Husband's view that immigrants of color did not "Americanize" well, post–civil rights color-blind racism uses cultural rather than biological explanations for minorities' inferior behavior and performance and silently naturalizes racial phenomena like segregation in schools and other institutions—among other aspects. The transformation of immigrant education into the schooling of (primarily) racial minorities combined with a color-blind racial mentality has led to explosive treatment of educational issues in schools and communities that serve immigrant students. Due to the repression of open expressions of racism in schools, racism has surfaced in other ways and around other issues, like bilingualism, learning English, cultural exclusion in curriculum, and undocumented students' access to public funds.

Race Controversies: Four Battles in Immigrant Education

White supremacy manifests itself in education such that all curriculum and pedagogies are about White culture and pejorative White perspectives of people of color. These programs finally give students of color a space to learn about themselves in non-pejorative ways.[8]

Battle #1: The Life and Death of Bilingual Education

Language of instruction and the rights of children to speak their native languages in schools have always been political and contested. There is a rich, deep history of bilingual education in U.S., from the language rights movement among indigenous communities to Japanese schools in Hawai'i and California. The kinds of bilingual programs we think of today originate with

Cuban migration to Miami. Intent on retaining cultural heritage, Cuban communities established bilingual programs. These programs began to spread around the nation as researchers began to see the benefit of it for learning. In 1968, Lyndon B. Johnson signed *Bilingual Education Act,* Title VII of the *Elementary and Secondary Education Act,* into effect. While states like California and Texas already had provisions for students whose primary language was one other than Spanish, the Bilingual Education Act provided federal funds for innovative bilingual education programs nationally.

While bilingual education flourished for a period, the conservative Reagan era witnessed backlash. At this juncture, much of the controversy around bilingual education was presented in race-neutral ways. Peter Duignan, a Fellow at Stanford's Hoover Institute, voiced the resentment and fear of many when he criticized students for not learning enough English in bilingual education programs. He argued, in a way that progressive educational philosopher Paulo Freire might term paternalistic that immigrant children of color purposefully resisted "americanization" by enrolling in bilingual programs. The perspective recycled a century-old restrictionist immigration perspective that excluded certain nationalities on the basis that they would "resist Americanization," that is, were not white enough.

In the 1990s, a series of propositions effectively ended state funds for bilingual education, despite decades of strong research that irrevocably demonstrated that language-minority children learned best when provided with native language pedagogies and bilingual curriculum. While nations as different as Finland, South Africa, and Taiwan emphasized the importance of learning in two languages to educate a globally prepared workforce, white racial consciousness in the United States overrode concerns about engaging in a global economy. Resolutions like Proposition 227 in California in 1998, Proposition 203 in Arizona in 2000, and Question 2 in Massachusetts in 2002 ended the flexibility of families to choose programs for themselves and for their children.

The pressure on immigrants to quickly learn English is itself racialized. As I argued based on findings of a study I did of immigrant youth in a multiethnic and multilingual high school in Los Angeles, racism surfaces in concerns around language. In other words, race was an acceptable argument for exclusion and restriction when W.W. Husband, the restrictionist immigration commissioner, was alive. In a color-blind society, racism must latch onto other domains to do its work—like language. The subordinated status of Latinos and other immigrants of color is circulated through a pervasive discourse of linguistic otherness that denies the origins of multilingualism and bilingual education in the United States, and how much our students would benefit from retaining their native languages in order to participate in global linguistic diversity. As sociolinguists Samy H. Alim and Geneva Smitherman argue, that work of integrating more effectively into U.S. society through Standard English acquisition is a specific burden relegated to the bodies of brown and black immigrants.[9]

The red herring argument that immigrants must learn English (at the expense of their native languages) ignores the multilingual origins of the United States. Uncovering our multilingual heritage shows that underneath beliefs that we only speak English, there have been many different languages spoken throughout our history. There are speakers of many indigenous languages in the heartlands, Alaska and Hawai'i, German speakers, French and African creoles originating from the communities of early settler-colonialists and slaves, and the continuous presence of Spanish in the Southwest as lands passed hands. Looking at our history clearly tells us that positioning English as the dominant language into which all immigrants must socialize has always been a major controversy in schools, from Italian-language education in Chicago and New York City to the ending of German-English bilingual education during World War I, and battles around Japanese-language schooling during World War II.

First, with the ending of bilingual education post-1965, children and youth *unlearn* their native languages, often meaning increased challenge to their ability to converse with family, community, and usually a loss of identity. Language is about family ties, cultural affiliation, heritage and continuity. When immigrants and the children of immigrants are painted as less intelligent due to their emerging English skills, Herbert Kohl's (1994) seminal piece on "assent to learn" comes to mind. Kohl narrates the story of a Spanish-speaking grandfather who refuses to learn English because he believes that "learning what others want you to learn can sometimes destroy you."[10] In his case, the loss of Spanish signaled the loss of community, family, and history. Kohl differentiates between failure to learn and not learning. Not learning is withholding one's assent because one doesn't believe that the learning that is emphasized is a good choice for you or your community. Not learning in a hostile society can be a healthy, well-reasoned choice, and Kohl writes, "Sometimes you have to work very hard at it."[11]

Learning English at the expense of one's native language has come to signify a willingness to be "American" (i.e., white, middle-class, and Christian Protestant). Immigrants are often of color, poor (class status may change as they cross borders and their professional credentials are invalidated), and Christian Catholic or Muslim. As a primary site of the battle to maintain whiteness, the controversies surrounding bilingual education have spread even to states where bilingual education still occurs. For example, in 2007 the first dual language English-Arabic school in the country opened in post-9/11 New York landscape. The move brought widespread protest. The principal, a moderate Muslim woman, was called a radical jihadist and a 9/11 denier. The school was called a *madrassa*—a center of Islamic learning. Scholars and immigration rights activists called the criticism racist, pointing out how Arabic language and culture were being conflated with terrorism.[12] The case demonstrates how racism is persistently enacted through language controversies in schools. Language becomes a proxy for being American, which is itself a proxy for maintaining whiteness and economic and cultural power despite an increasingly multiracial, multicultural, multireligious society.

Battle #2: Are ESL Programs Segregation?

In 2009, a *New York Times* article publically questioned how education assimilates immigrants.

The journalist who wrote the story, described her experience:

Walk with immigrant students, and the rest of Hylton feels a world apart. By design, they attend classes almost exclusively with one another. They take separate field trips. And they organize separate clubs.

"I am thankful to my teachers because the little bit of English I am able to speak, I speak because of them," Amalia Raymundo, from Guatemala, said during a break between classes. But, she added, "I feel they hold me back by isolating me."

Her best friend, Jhosselin Guevara, also from Guatemala, joined in. "Maybe the teachers are trying to protect us," she said. "There are people who do not want us here at all."

Hylton's faculty has been torn over how to educate its immigrant population. Some say the students are unfairly coddled and should be forced more quickly into the mainstream. And even those who support segregating students admit to soul-searching over whether the program serves the school's needs at the expense of immigrant students, who are relentlessly drilled and tutored on material that appears on state tests but get rare exposure to the kinds of courses, demands or experiences that might better prepare them to move up in American society.[13]

English as a Second Language (ESL) programs were designed to quickly teach immigrants English before they integrated into the English-speaking population. They emerged from the genuinely good intentions of reformers to avoid *sink or swim* schooling, the colloquial term for previous placing immigrant language learners in classes without any support. The battle for integrated schooling started back in the early 1970s in San Francisco, when the district integrated Chinese students who had been previously barred from public schools. Resulting legislation, *Lau v. Nichols* in 1974, mandated that linguistic minority students receive equal educational services and linguistically appropriate accommodations but did not suggest how, leaving room for segregated schooling. As bilingual education was ejected from our institutional repertoires, most schools have adopted some form of ESL programs. Researchers on a variety of ESL programs argue that they are tracking immigrant students academically, culturally, and linguistically.

As Jeanie Oakes, a researcher with the Ford Foundation, argued in her classic study of tracking *Keeping Track,* students in lower tracks receive reduced curriculum, thereby limiting their opportunity to meet the same kinds of academic challenges over time and keeping them intellectually behind.[14] Laurie Olsen, one of the foremost immigrant education scholars in the country, recently published a report on ESL programs in California. Her report found that in one of three districts in California, 75 percent of students in ESL programs have been there for six years or more. These students received no or weak language development program, many of them had been switched from school to school through inconsistent programs, they received curriculum she described as "narrow" or "partial," and they experienced extreme social and linguistic isolation.[15]

While the original intention of *Lau v. Nichols* was to give students language support as they integrated into the school system, "extra support" has become a form of racial sorting. Eduardo, an immigrant-origin student in an ESL program in Los Angeles, was one of my participants in a study I conducted in 2008. He is an example of the kind of student described by Laurie Olsen's report. He said:

> I was born here. And I feel that just because English isn't spoken in your home, "oh, you should be in ESL" or "oh, this kid he doesn't know English at all, and look at his last name". . . . Just because of the color of our skin or by our last name or by the language that we're speaking at home! We can do anything that we can put our minds to and that's what we do.[16]

Eduardo pointed out that the "color of our skin" and "our last names" and "the language that we speak at home" were the reasons he and his fellow U.S.-born Latinos were sitting in ESL classes. Being brown, being Latino, and speaking Spanish meant that he was culturally, racially, and academically tracked into a program he considered inferior and that he was tired of it. His comments mirror findings by researchers that brown-skinned, Spanish-speaking students are hyper-segregated in ESL "ghettos" in secondary schools.[17] What is also striking about this data is how deeply aware young people are of the way they are positioned by adults and society. We tend to make decisions for young people, without really asking them how they feel about it.

There are many fine programs that teach English-language skills and academic content simultaneously. I worked for such a school in New York City as a teacher when I first started working in immigrant education. The issue of ESL programs is not one of learning. Professors at the Graduate School of Education at Stanford University have done extraordinary work on language, literacy, and learning in the content areas at their *Understanding Language* Institute, and in my own research I have documented many fine teachers who can do, and enjoy, the complex and fascinating work of making the language of content transparent. In other words, we *could* integrate immigrant students if we wanted to. The issue of ESL programs is one of continuing to segregate the "other" so they won't impact the classes of students who we believe need to get ahead academically.

Whiteness provides rationalizations that suppress the contradiction between democratic ideals and the existence of people of color under white supremacy, and define and privilege membership in the white community. The embattled education space of ESL programs separates and segregates immigrants of color with a tired red herring argument that they must learn English. The red herring argument means that lawmakers, education policy makers, and school employees do not need to confront their own racism, advocate for reform, and truly meet the needs of a 21st-century global society.

Battle #3: Curriculum and Cultural Exclusion

It is impossible to discuss the politics of immigrant education without addressing the education of immigrant Mexican and immigrant-origin Mexican Americans. It is important to clarify that not all Mexican-origin (Chicanos) are *immigrants*, given that large swathes of the Southwest were once Mexico. Post-1965 Mexican immigrants are the largest single group of immigrants to come to the United States in history proportionately.[18] Both immigrant Mexican and Chicano children and youth have consistently received inferior schooling conditions, including segregation, high and harmful levels of stress, severe underrepresentation of Chicano and other Latino teachers, and subjection to unfavorable teacher–student interactions. In their book, *The Latino Education Crisis: The Consequences of Failed Social Policy,* researchers Patricia Gandara and Frances Contreras outline the scope of the problem:

> Latinos are the largest and most rapidly growing ethnic minority in the country, but academically they are lagging dangerously far behind. As has been thoroughly documented, a college degree is increasingly a prerequisite for a middle-class job and middle-class income; the gaps in earnings and opportunity between those with college degrees and those without have widened dramatically since 1983. But about half of all Latino students fail to even graduate from high school, and while all other ethnic groups—including African Americans—have gradually increased their college graduation rates, Latinos have seen almost no such progress in three decades.[19]

A primary adverse schooling condition for Mexican/Chicano students is cultural exclusion through the school curricula. Multiple studies have found that, despite the rich bicultural history of the Southwest, little is offered to Mexican American children about their roots, histories, and contributions to the United States in textbooks, social studies courses, or language classes.[20] As Mexican immigrants move increasingly to the Southeast and the heartlands, areas of the United States newly experiencing Latino presence, these issues proliferate.

The battle over the removal of the Mexican American Studies (MAS) curriculum from the Tucson, Arizona, school district in 2010 brought Mexican cultural exclusion in education to the public light. Arizona's then superintendent of schools, Tom Horne, led the fight against MAS in the Tucson Unified School District, the biggest school district in southern Arizona with a 60 percent Latino student population, because he said the program taught students to resent Anglos.[21] The Arizona legislature instated House Bill 2281, ordering the district to shut down the program or lose $14 million, nearly 10 percent of its funding. He removed seven books from the shelves of schools in a widely criticized modern-day censorship case. Teachers, students, and activists argued that the Mexican American program emphasized critical thinking, which led to their increased graduation rates and high student achievement. They argued that curriculum that supports an ethnic identity supports marginalized youth. On the other hand, the administration and the lawmakers argued that an ethnic studies program fostered racial resentment, that it was designed for students of a particular ethnic group and therefore racist, and that advocating for ethnic solidarity is separatist and divisive.

The removal of MAS occurred in the context of a state that has become well known for its anti-immigrant sentiment and actions. For example, the anti-immigrant law, S.B. 1070, passed in 2010, requires police to determine the immigration status of someone arrested or detained when there is "reasonable suspicion" they are not in the United States legally. The American Civil Liberties Union, along with a coalition of civil rights organizations, and international figures like the pope who compared the law to life under Nazi Germany, challenged the Arizona law on constitutional grounds. Students, community members, and faculty from Arizona State University protested the removal of the program. In one instance, students taped their mouths shut and walked out of a governmental officials' speech, claiming that they hadn't been allowed to ask the representative questions, nor were they allowed to say anything to her. In another, students took over a school board meeting and declared that they were instating a "Youth School Board," reading the UN convention of human rights as their guiding principles. Their actions were rooted in decades of youth protest in the Southwest and California designed to change the system to allow their full cultural expression.

Cheryl Matias, a professor and author at the University of Colorado-Denver, writes that the emotional and psychological aspects of whiteness must be examined to investigate how whites emotionally and mentally invest in whiteness, an investment that hinders their ability to become . . . culturally responsive.[22] Her remarks help us to understand the implicit racial bias in Horne's ideology. For instance, at a school board meeting Horne read aloud a section from one of the banned books. The section of the text he read was attempting to define "white privilege," the concept that whites do not see the privilege with which they walk through the world. Horne responded emotionally and defensively:

> White people are individuals. Some of them think as individuals, others think collectively. You cannot tell how somebody thinks . . . by race. . . . You don't know anything about somebody by their race. And this curriculum is propagating a racist philosophy that tells you what's important about people is not their individuality, but their race.[23]

Horne's argument is indicative of thinking that uses color-blind meritocracy to argue that stereotypes or prejudicial attitudes toward whites—by people of color—is the same thing as racism. He incorrectly equated a stereotype (when a universalist term is applied to a group of people ["all" white people, "every" black person]), with racism. Unwilling to sit uncomfortably with a characterization that (most) white people do not recognize that they receive privilege from a racialized society that actively subordinates (some) people of color, he emotionally rationalized that the *MAS* program should be dismantled. Racism is an act of systematic institutional brutality that maintains schooling conditions that fail generations of specific students based on their phenotypes, languages, and cultural-historical affiliations. Racism defies decades of research that demonstrates that culturally responsive curriculum helps students of color access institutions that are normed to dominant American culture. As such, white lawmakers dismantling a successful educational program invested in the cultural inclusion and empowerment of a specific group of children and youth who have been violently separated from their rights to a meaningful education *is a clear act of racism*.

As Eduardo Bonilla-Silva explains in his book *Racism without Racists: Color-Blind Racism and the Persistence of Racial Inequality in America,* color-blind racism is a strategy taken by whites to claim that people of color are playing the race card and that if minorities would stop thinking about the past, work hard, and complain less, than everyone could just get along.[24] Color-blind racism is different to the Jim Crow era racism, he writes. Since the 1960s, most whites no longer post signs reading "No Niggers Welcomed Here."[25] Rather, many whites create a system of supremacy though subtle, almost invisible institutional practices: not showing all available units in an apartment building, advertising jobs either in all-white networks or in ethnic newspapers, or suggesting that people of color are behind because they don't work hard enough. In education, excluding entire cultural groups from school curriculum and then passing a law banning curriculum that attempts to fill in the silence is a form of color-blind racism. Matias discusses,

> Focusing on educational gaps, dropout rates, and low test scores are symptoms of the problem. The problem itself lies in the systemic racist practices that allow white supremacy and whiteness to reign supreme in education; and while maintaining white supremacy, the root cause of this condition also hurts students of color.[26]

The Mexican American studies battle illuminates the ways in which the crisis of Latino education is directly related to the question of who controls the curriculum, that is, white supremacy.

Battle #4: Access to Public Schools: The Case of Undocumented Students

In Jose Antonio Vargas's beautiful film, *Documented,* he details his journey of discovering he was undocumented in high school, entering the workforce, and his subsequent challenges to disclose/hide his status. In the film, Vargas celebrates as his friends discover they are eligible for a memo signed by the Obama administration called *Deferred Action for Childhood Arrivals.* The memo permits temporary relief for undocumented young people who are in the process of being deported. While not providing a pathway to citizenship, it allows young people to be eligible for employment while they wait (for the world to change). Vargas, in his late twenties, is ineligible for the amnesty and remains undocumented.

Vargas's film attempts to bring a social justice issue to light that remains mired in political acrimony. The issue of amnesty for children and youth without citizenship papers is of utmost urgency. In 2014, as this chapter was written, some 47,000 children were being held on the U.S.-Mexico border in detention camps, waiting to be deported back to the violent cities in Central America that they fled hoping to join their parents in the United States. International outrage over the situation has not deterred the Obama administration from their work to block the children from seeking refuge in the United States.

There are an estimated 2.1 million undocumented students, noncitizen youth who were brought as babies to the United States by their parents. Of those, 1.1 million undocumented are under the age of 18.[27] The word "undocumented" has been chosen by many as a more apt descriptor of immigrants who are unauthorized. By framing people as "illegal," issues are ignored, like the reality of economic push–pull factors that create global migration, the ways in which we have constructed a closed nation-state (given that passports and visas were an invention of the World War I era) with borders, and the reality of our broken immigration system. In the United States it can take up to 16 years to receive correct documentation and residency status. By the "mid-1980s, an estimated 3 to 5 million noncitizens were living unlawfully in the country.[28] Prior periods of large-scale immigration, before visas, were subject to numerical ceilings, so the phenomenon of 'illegal immigration' is a relatively recent element of immigration policy history and debates."[29] The language of undocumented tries to reframe and reposition the debate to look at documentation as something that is fluid.

Just as racism surfaced in debates around language, cultural inclusion, and integration, it also surfaces in economic perspectives undergirding the question of political citizenship. A race-centered analysis of the battle around undocumented students in the United States must illuminate the political-economic heart of the matter. In other words, the battle for undocumented students' access to schooling is a battle for resources—a primary motivator of racism since the early times of slavery. Given the United States' shift toward a *neoliberal economy,* an economy oriented toward the private sector, schools have become mechanisms of the market. "Neoliberalism" refers to the merging of the market and the state. Schools as state-sponsored institutions increasingly oriented toward capitalism in ways that benefit the economic elite, who are usually also white. The goal of neoliberal education reformers is to promote human performance in order to respond to the demand for labor. Within this context, immigrants are seen as problems that are a drain on resources. In this way, racism engages neoliberalism in schools, supporting the widely held belief that "illegal" immigrants are stealing public resources like education and are not worth investing in as they don't contribute to U.S. economy.

The question of whether immigrants are worth investing requires that we shift from a neoliberal perspective in education to a democratic vision of what is the *public.* Public schools can be sites to foster multicultural democratic citizenship, and there are many fine schools that are doing that in a difficult educational climate. We can think about schools as fostering ethical virtues, critical thinking, and human freedom. When we consider the thinking of John Dewey, Marie Montessori, or Socrates, one wonders if they would have been welcome in today's environment. Both Western philosophers and educational philosophers from indigenous traditions, Chinese philosophies, and beyond privilege a different kind of education question: what are our *responsibilities* toward the young? A race-centered approach might elaborate this question: what are our *responsibilities* toward the most vulnerable among us given that U.S. citizens are beneficiaries of imperialism and the labor of the impoverished all over the world? Given this orientation and reconceptualization of the purpose of schooling—from schools as places to prepare students to satisfy the vagaries of the market that only certain students can enter, to asking ourselves what kinds of responsibilities we have to young people in our midst—the battle around schooling access for undocumented youth takes on new light.

There is precedence of social justice legislation on behalf of undocumented students as a way to protect the democratic impulses of public education. In 1982, the U.S. Supreme Court held in *Plyer v. DOE* that undocumented schoolchildren could attend public schools without regard to their immigration status. *Plyer v. DOE* began in 1975 when the state of Texas started charging tuition to undocumented students because they were not state residents and therefore not eligible for public services. As Michael Olivas, Distinguished Chair of Law at the University of Houston Law Center, explains in his book, *No Undocumented Student Left Behind,* Texas argued that establishing a subclass of Mexican American children as illegal was necessary to preserve limited resources of education for residents.[30] Texas stated that the legislation would protect the state from what they termed "an influx" of illegal aliens, arguing that the unlawful presence of undocumented children made it less likely that they would remain in the United States. Texas reasoned "illegal" children would not use the *free* education they received to contribute to the social and political goals of the United States.[31] The economic argument that substantiated their argument was also racialized, given that the children who brought the lawsuit were Mexican in a region, the Southwest, previously discussed as failing to provide adequate educational conditions.

When the case reached the Supreme Court, Justice Brennan ruled that children are not responsible for their citizenship status, and treating them as such would "not comport with fundamental conceptions of justice." He further argued that while public education is not a "fundamental right" it does maintain a "fundamental role" in maintaining the fabric of our society.[32] Brennan admonished Texas for promoting the creation of a subclass of illiterates that would add to the problems and costs of unemployment, welfare, and crime. In other words, Brennan took the economic argument being made and turned it on its head.

In the aftermath of *Plyler v. DOE,* there has been only one direct attack on the case: Proposition 187 in California in 1994. Prop. 187 was part of the campaign of the governor to limit access to all forms of resources for hospitals and various social services. It was overturned at the federal level, partially due to *Plyler v. DOE. Plyler v. DOE* asks certain questions: what kind of country are we? How are we going to treat the most vulnerable among us—undocumented children? While the case of *Plyler v. DOE* is mostly about educational justice, it is also viewed as an apex case that is a preservative for other rights as well given the overall frame of immigration law. Olivas writes that the case begins to move us away from notions of national sovereignty based on nation-state land ownership to more humanitarian principles of nationality as participation.[33]

Still there are many indirect attacks on *Plyler v. DOE* in our current educational climate. Olivas recounts these indirect attacks which include police coming onto school campuses and arresting children who "look" like they're undocumented, meaning the police arrest children who have stereotypically Mexican features and phenotypes. Schools, in anticipation of police raids, send home notes to parents telling them not to bring their children to school in anticipation of the day's police raid.[34] This racial battle is the most virulent of all of today's warfare on our children and one of the most hidden. That undocumented children are permitted to be hunted down by the police on school campuses ignores several things. First, the hysteria over "illegal immigration" ignores how the global political economy that creates economic push–pull factors necessitates the movement of human labor across borders. Convoluted immigration law and how hysterical rhetoric hinders true immigration reform is also ignored. In all, the racialized neoliberal agenda defeats its own purposes: if we are educating students for a global economy, then bilingual, bicultural children and youth are our greatest asset.

Conclusion: Racial Battle Fatigue and Critical Race Counseling

There are very real lives implicated in each of the four battles discussed. These accounts are not just historical details but summaries of how racism works in the schooling experiences of children and youth who attend schools every day. To conclude the brief history I have shared in this chapter, I will discuss a practical method that may be of help to youth attending school in educational battlefields. I call this method "critical race counseling": this goal of this counseling is to work with children and youth to name the tools of their oppression and identify the cultural strength and assets of immigrant communities in which they participate.

In my own research I have interviewed some 50 immigrant high school students formally and spoken with hundreds more informally as a teacher, teacher educator, and anthropologist. All the students I have spoken with want to have access to college and a good life and, even more basically, would like to enjoy their everyday experiences in school, feel welcomed, and learn something. Unfortunately, what many of them learn is that going to school every day is a painful experience that must be endured. Several students I've spoken with have spoken about their desire to drop out of school. One student I interviewed did leave school. Only weeks prior she told her teachers that English was "too hard" and that she didn't think she could succeed. On the other hand, interviews, which I've conducted with youth who attend schools that support their bilingual, transnational lives and connect them with their heritage cultures and communities, indicate that they are mostly eager to work hard, see bright futures ahead of themselves, and want to contribute to the multicultural, multilingual American Dream.

In research that talks about *racial battle fatigue,* a term describing the social-psychological effects of living with racism on school campuses, students of color reported psychological stress factors like frustration, shock, anger, disappointment, anxiety, helplessness, and fear.[35] As research on racial battle fatigue relates, exposure to race-related stressors at the interpersonal, societal, institutional, and individual levels can lead to the same kinds of traumatic psychological and physiological stress conditions of soldiers in combat and posttraumatic stress disorder.[36] Given that immigrant students already are vulnerable to stressors that native-born children are not, including separation from parents and siblings, cultural adjustment, learning a new language, and possibly deportation, adding racially toxic schooling environments is potential disaster. It clarifies, in part, reasons why immigrant, bilingual students of color may leave school before high school graduation. As my first school principal used to say when I was a young teacher, "Students vote with their feet."

The remedies for injuries caused by racism are complex. Reparations must be made at all levels of the education system, including law, educational policy, teacher education, funding, language of instruction, and organization of the school day. In addition to these, we need avenues for young people to vocalize and name their experience in ways that are safe. Naming oppression can provide options to avoid youth internalizing that the reason their schooling experiences are harmful is due to personal failure. In other words, youth must be aided to see that their school-based lives occur in a historical moment of which racism has always been a part. What I term "critical race counseling," or critically counseling youth to understand the effects of racial battle fatigue and identify how their experiences in schools are racialized, could be one such avenue. Critical race counseling could continue the work of excavating—exposing, processing, and recording—the sites of battle.

Critical race theory in education is a framework that has been used by legal and education scholars to "theorize, examine and challenge the ways that race and racism implicitly and explicitly impact on social structures, practices, and discourses."[37] Critical race counseling is counseling that employs critical race theory in ways that help youth to make sense out of their experiences—both by naming tools of oppression and by identifying community strengths and assets. Critical race counseling might take the shape of counseling forums, dialogues, teach-ins, or other community forums during which immigrant children and youth can come together to learn about racial battle fatigue, share their experiences with racism in a safe space with allies, and identify the tools of oppression.

Critical race counseling could be organized to do the following sorts of things: first, identifying tools of oppression. When identifying, youth could learn about the history of school programs designed for and against them, learn about linguistic and cultural exclusion in educational policy, and learn how to respond to color-blind racism in order to manage their own racial battle fatigue. In other words, youth could engage their own race-critical excavation of schools and education in their local communities. Second, critical race counseling could identify community cultural strengths and assets that come out of the immigrant experience. Forum leaders and counselors can learn how to help youth identify cultural assets by using theoretical tools developed by critical race scholars and Chicana feminists. These theoretical tools include, for example, Tara Yosso's (2005) work on "community cultural wealth," Delores Delgado Bernal's work on "pedagogies of the home" and "cultural intuition" (1998), and Gloria Anzaldúa's (1999) border-crossing and mestiza consciousness. While we are waiting for the world to change, critical race counseling could mean the difference between losing one more immigrant student and helping a young person survive the trauma that is schooling in the United States today.

Notes

1. Suárez-Orozco and Sattin 2007.
2. Migration Policy Institute Data Hub.
3. Ibid.
4. Hipsman and Meissner 2014.
5. Ngai 2014, p. 22.
6. Ibid.
7. Ngai 2014, p. 25.
8. Matias 2013, p. 72.
9. Alim and Smitherman 2012.
10. Kohl 1994.
11. Ibid.
12. Ghattas 2007.

13. Thompson 2009.
14. Oakes 2005.
15. Olsen 2010.
16. Focus Group Interview, April 19, 2010.
17. Faltis and Arias 2007.
18. Migration Policy Institute Data Hub.
19. Gandara and Contreras 2009, pp. 2–3.
20. Valencia 2002.
21. Planas 2013.
22. Matias 2013, p. 76.
23. Three Sonorans News 2011.
24. Bonilla-Silva 2002.
25. Ibid.
26. Matias 2013, p. 72.
27. Educators for Fair Consideration.
28. Migration Policy Institute.
29. Hipsman and Meissner 2014.
30. Olivas 2012.
31. Ibid.
32. Ibid.
33. Ibid.
34. Ibid.
35. Smith, Allen, and Danley 2007.
36. Ibid.
37. Yosso 2005.

Bibliography

Alim, H. Samy, and Geneva Smitherman. 2012. *Articulate While Black: Barack Obama, Language and Race in the U.S.* New York: Oxford University Press.

Allen, Ricky Lee. 2004. "Whiteness and Critical Pedagogy." *Educational Philosophy and Theory* 36 (2):121–136.

Anzaldua, G. 1987. *La frontera. Borderlands.* San Francisco: Aunt Lute Books.

Bernal, D. D. 1998. "Using a Chicana Feminist Epistemology in Educational Research." *Harvard Educational Review* 68 (4): 555–583.

Bernal, D. D. 2001. "Learning and Living Pedagogies of the Home: The Mestiza Consciousness of Chicana Students." *International Journal of Qualitative Studies in Education* 14 (5): 623–639.

Bonilla-Silva, Eduardo. 2002. "The Linguistics of Color Blind Racism: How to Talk Nasty about Blacks without Sounding 'Racist.'" *Critical Sociology* 28 (1–2): 41–64.

Callahan, Rebecca M. 2005. "Tracking and High School English Learners: Limiting Opportunity to Learn." *American Educational Research Journal* 2 (42): 305–328.

Crenshaw, Kimberlé. 1998. "Race, Reform, and Retrenchment: Transformation and Legitimation in Antidiscrimination Law." *Harvard Law Review* 101 (7): 1331–1387.

Duignan, Peter. 1998. *Bilingual Education: A Critique.* Stanford, CA: Hoover Institution Press.

Educators for Fair Consideration Fact Sheet. Educators for Fair Consideration. 2012. *Fact Sheet: An Overview of College-bound Undocumented Students.* http://www.e4fc.org/images/Fact_Sheet.pdf.

Faltis, C., and B. Arias. 2007. "Coming Out of the ESL Ghetto: Promising Practices for Latino Immigrant Students and English Learners in Hypersegregated Secondary Schools." *Journal of Border Educational Research* 6 (2): 19–35.

Freire, Paulo. 2000. *Pedagogy of the Oppressed.* New York: Herder and Herder.

Gandara, Patricia, and Frances Contreras. 2009. *The Latino Education Crisis: The Consequences of Failed Social Policy.* Cambridge, MA: Harvard University Press.

Ghattas, Kim. 2007. "New York Arabic School Sparks Row." BBC News.

Goldenberg, Claude. 2008. "Teaching English Language Learners." *American Educator*: 8–44.

Hipsman, Faye, and Doris Meissner. "Immigration in the United States: New Economic, Social, Political Landscapes with Legislative Reform on the Horizon." Migration Policy Institute. April 16, 2014. http://www.migrationpolicy.org/article/immigration-united-states-new-economic-social-political-landscapes-legislative-reform.

Jacobson, Matthew Frye. 1999. *Whiteness of a Different Color.* Cambridge, MA: Harvard University Press.

Jasso, Guillermina, Douglas S. Massey, Mark R. Rosenweig, and James P. Smith. 2003. "Exploring the Religious Preference of Recent Immigrants to the United States: Evidence from the New Immigrant Survey Pilot." In *Becoming American: Immigration and Religious Life in the United States,* eds. Yvonne Yazbeck Haddad, Jane Smith, and John Esposito. Maryland: Alta Mira Press. http://nis.princeton.edu/downloads/papers/jmrsrel.pdf.

Kohl, Herbert. 1994. "*I Won't Learn from You*": And Other Thoughts on Creative Maladjustment. Rethinking Schools. New York: New Press.

Malsbary, Christine. 2012. "Pedagogy of Belonging: The Social, Cultural and Academic Lives of Recently-Arrived Immigrant Youth in a Multilingual, Multiethnic High School." ProQuest Dissertation and Thesis Database.

Malsbary, Christine. 2014. "'Will This Hell Never End?': Substantiating and Resisting Race-Language Policies in a High School." *Anthropology and Education Quarterly* 45 (4): 373–390.

Matias, Cheryl. 2013. "Check Yo'self before You Wreck Yo'self and Our Kids. Counterstories from Culturally-Responsive White Teachers . . . to Culturally-Responsive White Teachers!" *Interdisciplinary Journal of Teaching and Learning* 3 (2): 68–81.

Migration Policy Institute Data Hub. 2001–2015. *Data Hub*. Washington, DC: Migration Policy Institute.

Ngai, Mae M. 2014. *Impossible Subjects: Illegal Aliens and the Making of Modern America*. Princeton, NJ: Princeton University Press.

Oakes, Jeannie. 2005. *Keeping Track: How Schools Structure Inequality*. New Haven and London: Yale University Press.

Olivas, Michael A. 2012. *No Undocumented Child Left Behind: Plyler v. Doe and the Education of Undocumented Schoolchildren*. New York: New York University Press.

Olsen, Laurie. 2010. "Reparable Harm Fulfilling the Unkept Promise of Educational Opportunity for California's Long Term English Learners." *Californians Together*.

Planas, Roque. 2013. "Arizona's Law Banning Mexican-American Studies Program Is Constitutional, Judge Rules." *The Huffington Post* (March 11).

Rosenzweig, Mark R., and James P. Smith. 2003. "Exploring the Religious Preferences of Recent Immigrants to the United States: Evidence from the New Immigrant Survey Pilot." *Religion and Immigration: Christian, Jewish, and Muslim Experiences in the United States*. Walnut Creek, CA: AltaMira Press.

Smith, William A., Walter R. Allen, and Lynette L. Danley. 2007. "'Assume the Position . . . You Fit the Description' Psychosocial Experiences and Racial Battle Fatigue among African American Male College Students." *American Behavioral Scientist* 51 (4): 551–578.

Suárez-Orozco, Marcelo, and Carolyn Sattin. 2007. "Introduction: Learning in the Global Era." In *Learning in the Global Era,* ed. Marcelo Suárez-Orozco (pp. 1–46). Los Angeles: University of California Press.

Thompson, Ginger. 2009. "Where Education and Assimilation Collide." *New York Times*.

Three Sonorans News. "Tom Horne-Richard Martinez Ethnic Studies Debate." YouTube video, 12:07. March 22, 2011. https://www.youtube.com/watch?v=It0mw_bAhXg.

Valencia, Richard R. 2002. "The Plight of Chicano Students: An Overview of Schooling Conditions and Outcomes." In *Chicano School Failure and Success: Past, Present and Future,* ed. Richard R. Valencia (pp. 3–51). London and New York: Routledge.

Valenzuela, Angela. 1999. *Subtractive Schooling: U.S.-Mexican Youth and the Politics of Caring*. Edited by Christine F. Sleeter, *SUNY Series, The Social Context of Education*. Albany: State University of New York Press.

Yosso, Tara. 2005. "Whose Culture has Capital? A Critical Race Theory Discussion of Community Cultural Wealth." *Race, Ethnicity and Education* 8 (1): 69–91.

Chapter 2

Bringing Students Back from the Margin

Steve Grineski and Julie Landsman

Introduction

Racism and classism are alive and well in our public schools. Difference from a white, middle-class norm is often viewed as *oppositional—either or, good* or *bad*. The marching orders are—If you are not *my way,* you are the *other* and ultimately *you are disappeared.* When teachers dismiss students' home and culture as unimportant to necessary knowledge, they ignore the very essence of a child's attempt to make meaning of his or her life. By centering their classrooms on white European curricula and materials, they are denying students of color what is basic to human understanding: the search for identity. Students who are marginalized are pushed from central positions of inclusion and sent to where exclusion and invisibility reside.

An official definition of marginalized reads: *acute and persistent disadvantages rooted in social inequalities.*[1] In many of our schools, we have participated in the creation and perpetuation of such social inequalities.

Students who are marginalized are viewed through the lens of deficit thinking. This means they are seen as deficient, maladjusted, and cited as problem children and youth. Deficit thinking encourages teachers to see some students only for what they do *not* have: be it money, access, white skin, European culture, or college-educated parents. Being African American alone can trigger implicit bias and lower expectations from teachers. Often teachers are not even aware they are thinking in deficit terms about their black students. Based on racist assumptions about their ability, students of color are often not encouraged to take challenging, college-oriented classes. Hopelessness, anxiety, fear, and anger can become each student's constant companion. It is only by the sheer strength of their resilience in the face of such alienation that black and brown students survive, let alone thrive in many of our schools.

As educators, we have seen superficial attempts to provide equitable education over many years. Many call it "Reinventing Education." Some want to increase the attendance of students in Advanced Placement (AP) courses while others feel the answer is adopting the Common Core, a national system of grade-level goals required for graduation. Still others think the remedy is to have frequent professional development sessions in multicultural education.

We have seen these programs and standards come and go. In our combined careers in education totaling 60 years, we have experienced many attempts to revamp and reorganize public schooling. Steve originally taught elementary school and has been a professor in education at Minnesota State University Moorhead for the past 30 years. His experience is working with students who are rural, poor, Native American, and white. Julie was a public school teacher in Minneapolis for 25 years and has written many books on education from her experience in urban schools. In all this time, we have come to believe in the importance of the human connection and contend that the relationship between student and teacher, student and principal, student and social worker, and student and counselor is at the core of what we do in education.

We also contend that we will not satisfy our moral imperative as educators: "first do no harm" if we, as a country, fail to recognize and change the power relationship between students who are marginalized and those who control our basic system of schooling. Any change in this power dynamic must include reimagining what subjects and materials students will study and what part students will have in deciding the content of the materials they will use. Truly reinventing education involves reenvisioning how we connect to students, fund our schools, train our teachers, and hire administrators.

In the first section, The Problem, we look at marginalization and race. We examine those conditions that bring about the marginalization of students of color. Many strong black students experience a lack of control when they are rarely given a voice or when they are not heard, encouraged, or recognized for their innate intelligence and grit. Schools that continually suspend students of color refuse them entry to certain high-level courses, and schools that belittle their contribution to class discussion can exacerbate feelings of stress, anxiety, and depression in their students of color. Ultimately, these students will avoid the place that makes them feel this way. We see, in the statistics of failure rates, low graduation rates, higher numbers of suspensions of black males, and higher rates of referrals of black students to special education, the complicity of the public education system in the ongoing racism of our society. Given the continuing intersection of race, segregation, and poverty and the fact that our schools are funded according to the wealth of individual districts and even neighborhoods, poor students of color often attend schools with far fewer resources than their white counterparts who live in tax-rich suburbs. Consequently, many students of color are limited in their life chances and opportunities. Our schools are perpetuating a system that is inequitable at its very core.

In this section we include marginalization from the students' point of view. How does it feel to be left out of history, literature, science, art, music, and even math in one's daily school experience?

In the second section, Solutions, we explore ways to base what we teach in the concerns, histories, and interests of the students who arrive at our school doors. From them we can find the keys to ensure that students of color succeed in public education. Many schools and classrooms are making the connections to students that are necessary for success. Teachers are often teaching effectively *in spite of* what they are told they must do: in spite of the regimented one-size-fits-all district curriculum; in spite of the *teaching for the test* mania present today. Many teachers are reaching our kids. They are asking the questions that require them to connect to students in a deep and constructive way; understanding the whole universe of his or her culture, personality, and unique ability to learn. There are places that believe all children are "our children" as Lisa Delpit describes in her book *Other People's Children*.[2] They are demanding and working toward antiracist, social justice curriculum and pedagogy, well aware of the intersection of race and poverty in our country and in our schools. They are activists.

The Problem: Systemic Trauma and Marginalization

Researchers, Elizabeth Dutro and Andrea C. Bien state in their AERA paper:

> We contend that some students' positioning within the racist, classist, sexist, and homophobic discourses that permeate the institution of public schooling in the United States, as well as the material impacts of social inequities in communities, constitutes a trauma, a wound, as we are defining such experiences in our work, and must be heard. Thus, conceptualizations of trauma in literary trauma studies intertwine with key arguments from scholars of race and post colonialism across disciplines around the traumatic individual, institutional, and systemic consequences of racism.[3]

Many of our students, be they poor, of color, or a combination of the two, may suffer from traumatic stress as described earlier. It is our belief that schools have always been complicit in this trauma. At the same time schools must also play a part in rectifying the collusion of our education system in the racism that causes such trauma.

There is evidence that children in poverty also may suffer from *fiscal trauma*. Vanessa Jackson, licensed clinical social worker, defines this trauma as "an intense emotional reaction, characterized by depression, anxiety/worry, a profound sense of shame and a fear for survival in response to inadequate financial resources."[4] When fiscal trauma intersects with racial oppression, the stresses under which our students live are overwhelming. What is remarkable is the fact that students and their families are able to flourish and thrive despite their situation.

Parents of students of color frequently feel marginalized as well. Because the history of white supremacy in the United States is long and deep and because this history has resulted in discrimination and prejudice over centuries, jobs, housing, and health care for many people of color have been denied. In this denial we see how race and poverty are inexorably linked. In failing to recognize this history when working with parents and students, schools are complicit in perpetuating its racist consequences.

America's Report Card once again reminded us that over 20 percent of U.S. children live in poverty, while the national study *Housing Costs, Zoning and Access to High-Scoring Schools* reinforced what has been known for decades: low home values and less-equitable communities translate to lack of access to high-quality schools and the transformative opportunities they offer. On average, families need an income of about twice the poverty level to cover basic expenses. Using this standard, 45 percent of children live in low-income families. *Child poverty rates are highest among African American, Latino, and American Indian children.*[5]

Students of color and students who are poor are full of promise. Unfortunately, many teachers and staff do not truly believe the preceding statement. They do not affirm that their black, brown, poor, and homeless students are multidimensional, ever changing, and unfinished with "hopes, dreams, and aspirations . . . passions and commitments . . . [and] skills, abilities, and capacities."[6]

It is clear too that many public school teachers, administrators, and the regimented programs used to govern numerous schools for students in poverty can actually exacerbate any trauma students may be experiencing. This idea has been well documented by Jonathon Kozol for over 30 years in books that include *The Shame of a Nation, Amazing Grace,* and *Savage Inequalities.* Whether it be the "savage inequalities" of school funding, limited enrichment classes, too much behavior modification and robot-like teaching or militarized classroom management, and a lifeless and standardized curriculum with its matching punitive and high-stakes testing regimes—children in urban schools get the message that their struggles to find meaning in their lives are irrelevant and unimportant. Yet, even in the face of this, Kozol describes how many students, loved by their families and communities, carry with them badges of resilience. They overcome marginalization to succeed.

Conservative writers often criticize Kozol as presenting exaggerated claims of oppressive schooling and mean-spirited and racist systems. However, those who "walk next" to students attending low-income and segregated schools know that Kozol's stories still ring true. Beverly Tatum in her 2006 book, *Can We Talk about Race and Other Conversations in an Era of School Resegregation,* argues that racism and segregation is alive and well within U.S. schools. Gorski's 2013 *Reaching and Teaching Students in Poverty: Strategies for Erasing the Opportunity Gap* recognizes that the "savage inequalities" Kozol described over 20 years ago continue to educationally limit many students today. Because of a history of real estate discrimination, red lining, and housing and bank discrimination, black students find themselves living in segregated areas of our cities and in tax-poor neighborhoods. Because of the current regressive and geographically based school funding formula and resulting unequal per pupil spending, they receive an education with few resources and poor conditions. Kozol, Tatum, and Gorski, like so many others who spend time with students, know firsthand that schools are not, and have never been, the "great social equalizer."

Response to Intervention (RTI) and the Common Core are just two examples of systems claiming to reinvent education. Like many other concepts these simplistic solutions are mistakenly applied to the complex situations faced by students, teachers, and administrators. RTI utilizes a seductive branding of well-designed and early instruction to convince teachers that this approach will assist struggling learners and solve their behavior problems, while neglecting the all-important social skills. The Common Core State Standards Initiative is an educational initiative in the United States that details what K-12 students should know in English, language arts, and mathematics at the end of each grade. The initiative is sponsored by the National Governors Association and the Council of Chief

State School Officers and seeks to establish consistent educational standards across the states. While it may be beneficial for schools to recognize
certain essential skills, those who espouse the Common Core neglect the
real cause for "achievement gaps": poverty, racial segregation, and white supremacy. A number of states have chosen not to adopt the Common Core,
while others may adopt it but use varying methods of assessment to measure progress. Thus, there is little national uniformity in standards-based
education.[7]

Adding to student marginalization is the narrow and limiting curriculum mandated in many states. Even those with Common Core can design their own materials and content to go along with the standards. This
can leave many students of color experiencing a lack of connection to history, literature, and the arts in their districts. One example of this is can be
found in the recent Mexican American Studies Program controversy in the
Tucson Public Schools. It illustrates what happens to those educators who
try to counter the marginalization of students of color. Although criticized
for teaching anti-Americanism, communism, terrorism, and reverse racism
by conservative policy makers, this social justice curriculum actually taught
Mexican and American history and Central and South American literature
and culture through a critical lens. Despite the criticisms the program was
transformative: 93 percent of its students graduated from high school and
85 percent attended college, pushing back against a much lower statewide
statistic of 48 percent of Arizona Latino/Latina students who graduate from
high school. Yet in 2011 educational decision makers, including state legislators, the state superintendent, the Tucson superintendent, opted to dis-
continue the program. Even when something is proven to work, powerful
forces can disregard the rights and achievements of students of color, imposing racist values on our schools. The fight continues to reestablish this
ethnic studies curriculum that places students at the center of their own
education.[8]

In many states disciplinary educational decisions and policies marginalize students of color. Zero tolerance policies affect students of color
in larger numbers than their white classmates. The over-referral of students of color to special education programs for behavior, along with
disproportionate suspension rates for these students, creates a system-
wide oppression that limits the possibilities for millions of young people.
Too often these practices set students of color on a school-to-prison
pipeline.

In 2013, the Children's Defense Fund emphatically concluded that

a black boy born in 2001 [has a]one-in three chance of going to prison in his lifetime, more than five times the odds for a White boy born in the same year. The Cradle to Prison Pipeline is a trajectory that leads to marginalized lives [and] imprisonment. . . . Zero tolerance school discipline policies are a key feeder into the pipeline to prison and play a significant role in fueling the dropout crisis.[9]

In the landmark report, "Brown fades: The end of court-ordered school desegregation and the re-segregation of American public schools," the authors provide overwhelming evidence that students of color are increasingly attending schools with fewer white students—American schools are indeed more and more racially segregated.[10] Staggering numbers speak to this crisis: Every 26 seconds a student drops out of school or 1.3 million students every year. When students were asked why they dropped out, the top reasons included the following: school was boring and not relevant to their lives; teachers and schools had low expectations for them, even though they had high personal expectations; lack of needed supports; and outside of school factors (e.g., help support family) took priority.[11]

The resegregation within our schools, where whole floors are set aside for advanced classes which are filled with white and middle-class to upper-class students while other floors are filled with black and brown students who take the least challenging course work, is perpetuating the marginalization of our children. When curriculum in U.S. schools includes primarily windows for students of color into white European cultures and contains no mirrors that reflect their lives and cultures, such students feel invisible within their schools. In addition to such invisibility within instruction, when schools are too large to provide appropriate support services and real connection to students' lives, such spaces become empty of meaning and dignity for students of color. They feel they have no place in the system.

Taken together, resegregation, culturally insensitive curricula, disengaged students, and disproportionate and extreme discipline and punishment lead to students of color who feel school is not a place for them and that school is in fact a place of intimidation and unfair disciplinary practices. This leads students of color to drop out. Black and brown students are heartbreakingly overrepresented in the nation's dropout numbers. The dropout rate for African American students is 37 percent, for American Indian students is 35 percent, for Hispanic students is 34 percent, while for white students 18 percent. Students living in families in the bottom 20 percent of income levels are five times more likely to drop out of school when compared to students living in the top 20 percent of income levels. In 11 states the white student graduation rate is 89 percent or over, while in no state is this true for African American, American Indian, Hispanic, or poor students.[12]

And lest we not forget—teacher education is at fault here too. It is a well-established fact that many schools of education offer narrow and simplistic approaches to learning about the economic, social, political, racial, and educational contexts that shape and surround the lives of students and their families. As a result, many preservice and in-service teachers are miseducated when it comes to teaching for social justice. David Stovall concludes emphatically that "the vast majority of White women who graduate from teacher preparation programs and populate the majority of the teaching force remain underprepared to engage the realities of marginalization, racialization, and criminalization in schools."[13]

Students are placed at great risk when underprepared teachers enter the classroom. These new teachers are not trained to consider their students' as holistic beings. Resistance to considering the power of their privilege and a righteous belief in deficit thinking about the very children they are assigned to teach are additional tragic outcomes of this lack of preparation. Sadly, noncontroversial curricula; field placements that do not challenge existing beliefs about students, families, schools, and communities; and faculty who mirror demographics of the programs' dominant groups are common practices that add to teachers' inability to humanely and expertly teach students with life stories different from their own. Kincheloe, writing in Spring's *The American School: A Global Context from the Puritans to the Obama Era*, captured the silencing supporting these practices: "Teacher education programs assume schooling is unequivocally a good thing serving the best interests of individual students, marginalized students, and the culture in general."[14] Teacher education students have much to "unlearn" when it comes to how they have been socialized to think about students of color who come under their care.

How Do Students Respond?

Some students are helped by their teachers and families to learn methods that enable them to survive the day-to-day inhumanity of their school lives. Other students survive by "closing their ears and eyes" to school, in order to "not hear" and "not see" denigrating messages given to them as they go through their day. Without support or without means of resisting toxic messages, others come to believe in their own inferiority. Consequences for these student groups are at best that they lead passive and unengaged school lives or at worst they drop out.

It is a deep-rooted reality that living in poverty makes it more difficult for some students to engage in school. And because poverty happens to students outside of school, where students spend most of their time, the reasons for students' disengagement can lie outside the school walls. Lack of appropriate health care, food insecurity, chronic and acute stress, housing instability, and extreme mobility are some of the negative realities for the more than 20 million students living in poverty. Because of racist policies and a history of continuing discrimination and prejudice, poor students of color experience not only the difficult reality of food insecurity, housing instability, and lack of health care but also racist police practices, job discrimination, and housing segregation based on the color of their skin. This adds an additional layer of oppression to their economic situation.

As mentioned earlier, one of the ways students of color respond to feeling marginalized is to resist what school wants to teach them. In *I won't learn from you*, Herbert Kohl suggests that the only rational response to marginalization is resistance. One form of resistance is not-learning. This is a responsive action to classroom and school affronts made to family and culture and personal integrity and identity. It is an

active, often ingenious, willful rejection of . . . teaching. It subverts attempts at remediation as much as it rejects learning in the first place . . . I've [Kohl] come to side with them [students] in their refusal to be molded by a hostile society and have come to look upon not-learning as positive and healthy in many situations.[15]

Teachers may believe that students are simply failing because they don't care about or don't understand the subject matter. This is a common, *mis*interpretation of students who choose to not-learn. While making this choice leads to negative classroom outcomes for students, it does offer them a chance to hold tight to their identities. The danger is that teachers will view this resistance as negative and push students further out to the margins by referring them for disciplinary consequences or even referring them to special education for behavioral problems.

Teachers who do want their students to resist being "molded by a hostile society" realize students must learn to operate within systems leading to high school graduation, postsecondary education, and meaningful employment. Master teachers know their students at deep levels and engage them in honest and realistic conversations about what it takes to succeed, while keeping one's self-respect. The task before both teachers and students is to claim identity, think creatively, and work together toward students' graduation. Students and educators must walk a fine line. Walking this line means teaching in a way that reaches and connects to all—allowing students time to claim their identities. It means students working to connect to curriculum and to engage in heated discussions. It means being fearless, both as a teacher and as a student.

What Does It Feel Like to Be on the Margins?

We know the facts. We are aware of the problem. Here, we share the lived experiences of students on the margins.

Michael

He was a slim African American eighth grader. His blue shirt hung loosely on his shoulders; his face revealed an open, yet troubled expression. In one year he had experienced the death of the grandmother who partially raised him, and the arrest of his brother for a brutal beating and who now was awaiting trial as an adult. Yet Michael had decided he wanted to graduate high school in four years and maybe go to college. His individual determination combined with his mentoring, speaking, writing, and collaborating in a class for African American males in his middle school had made this dream appear possible. Michael wrote:

> I am Devastation and Demolition
> I am trusting and loving,
> Finding that most men can't even be half that.
> I need help while time is frozen. . . .
> I am stronger than I set out to be.
> I started being a man when I reached out and grabbed hold of the hand that reached out for me.
> Looking up to someone that passed away, but never showing pain and hurt upon my face.
> Now I am where I have enough time to tell what I have bottled up.
> Read me as I am but know I am a page less book

Michael was struggling with his African American identity. He had heard the negative messages about black males all his life. He was not sure how his skin color, his culture, and his particular black story fit into his school experience. He was on the margins. The African American male class was filled with men of color who were doing well, who mentored and spoke and instructed students in their heritage. The teacher in this class, Kristy, says that Michael has been telling his story over the year, slowly, in parts, amid days of silence and withdrawal. Gradually, Michael says he has come around, because of those in the class and other teachers connected to it. They "take one step forward, two steps back" with him. The class was a consistent, unfailingly supportive environment, with high expectations and reasonable structure.

"When I learned about James Baldwin I learned that I come from greatness." Michael told Julie. Michael and his black classmates had not experienced such a pride in their heritage in all their previous seven years of their schooling.

By providing a safe space, patience, and consistency while acknowledging their feelings that "I bear the weight of the world" this African American men class supported Michael and his classmates through the year. From how to tie a tie to the history of the Harlem Renaissance to the contributions of black scientists, Michael and his classmates developed pride and confidence in themselves and hope for their own futures. At the same time his teachers continued to challenge them to get their work done. "They don't need you to feel sorry. They need you to listen," said Kristy.

Mithson

Mithson is a 14-year-old Haitian American young man staying at a local emergency homeless shelter. His marginalization was from unequal opportunity. He was not encouraged to take advanced classes. He told Steve. "You know, it's not fair for kids like me . . . you know poor kids, we just don't get the same opportunities as other kids." Mithson elaborated on his interests in American history, "I am really interested in the Civil Rights Movement, the 1968 Olympics, black athletes, and Muhammad Ali." He never studied this history in his high school. Completing college so he can manage and then own an NBA team is his life goal—"There should be more owners of color."

This unequal opportunity also played out in the way his gifts and potential were not tapped by his teachers. Steve asked Mithson, "If I asked your teachers about you, what would they tell me?" Without missing a beat Mithson said, "He is really quiet." This is from a young man who speaks three languages: English, Creole, and French.

Sarah

Sarah, a Somali American first-year college student experienced cultural dislocation and complete disconnection from her school experience. She remembered her high school as years of being patronized, ignored, and discriminated against, to the point where she was told she would have to surrender her head covering or hijab, because of a no-hat rule in her particular high school. Her male Somali counterparts fared worse, she said, because they were also considered unintelligent *as a group.* Many of these males drop out and even Sarah considered her high school years as "The Hell Years."

Dyani, an enrolled member of the White Earth Nation in northwestern Minnesota and student in Steve's class, shared a generational example of the alienation she feels in the same public school attended by her mother, herself, and her children. This sense of alienation has driven whole generations of Native Americans to the margins.

> They are excluding our students' needs and not considering their feelings in the curriculum . . . the teaching is limited . . . never Social Studies lessons about the 11 nations in Minnesota and the special relationships they have with the United States government . . . never information that we have tribal councils and a chairperson which is like having a city council and a governor . . . and never lessons questioning Columbus Day or sports mascots. . . . We even report to the state that our school district is not meeting our students' needs . . . but nothing changes . . . so our students feel like outsiders and are less able to learn and be successful . . . they'll disengage, become rebellious, or just leave.

Devalued identity, unequal learning opportunities, cultural disconnect, and a sense of alienation have driven these students to the margins. These young men and women are told in many ways that they will not, *cannot,* measure up. Even if they are working-class or middle-class black and brown children, they are given subtle and not so subtle messages about their inadequacy. Students of color are often not given the same consideration as white students either when they are walking down the hall without a pass or cannot make it to a meeting, or a practice because of problems at home. As a gifted basketball player, Mithson was very excited to try out for his ninth-grade high school team. However, he was sick on try-out day and the coach would not let him try out on another day. Because he was excluded from an opportunity to try out for the team, Mithson received another message that he was just not that important.

Michael is a deep thinker, a young man who has been lucky enough to be in a class where he has learned that he can make it in school without sacrificing his African American identity. How many have we abandoned when such identity is lost or denied? Will Mithson be able to hold onto his identity given the marginalizing messages he receives? How many of Sarah's Somali brothers or her Latina friends' sisters and cousins have given up and are relegated to lives of desperation?

Solutions: Teaching toward Dignity

Hutchinson asks those of us who believe in our students: "What would education look like that took seriously the claim that we must pay attention to the dignity of the child?" and then reminds us that "the concern of dignity must be one that directs all activities of the teacher and school . . . concern for the dignity of children should become a cogent part of the discussions . . . in school reform efforts today." "When school relationships result in compromised student dignity the logical, yet destructive outcome is marginalization . . . the antithesis of dignity."[16] Teaching in the way Hutchinson demands runs counter to the alienation, lack of cultural identity, and educational opportunity that all students require to succeed.

Rethinking how we educate is more than ill-advised attempts to legislate what is wrong in schools. Rather this work requires that we consider the moral basis for the relationships students and teachers have at school. This morality is grounded in believing that all humans are complex, incomplete, and taking shape. It is a morality the respects the complicated, multifaceted dignity of each human being in our school, our classroom. Such a moral commitment to dignity involves an unconditional belief in the best of each individual *and* an acknowledgment of the human need for caring, belonging, and community. Here are some ideas teachers can use to better connect with students and honor their stories.

Disruptive Pedagogies

Paul Gorski suggests ways of thinking about teaching that would go a long way in helping teacher educators, practicing teachers, and preservice teachers to eliminate marginalization. He asks teachers to consider working at the intersections of equity and justice and to realize that schooling has a profound sociopolitical context.

Gorski challenges teachers to resist simple solutions to complex problems. He wants teachers to commit to seeing *systems* as sources of problems and not individuals affected by the problems. Darren Lund and Paul Carr write about how this kind of thinking can be realized through "disruptive pedagogies" that challenge teacher education students and in-service teachers to reconsider existing beliefs so they can act on the world in more critical ways. Disruptive pedagogies challenge students to critically reflect on how they have been socially constructed to think about race and racism, privilege and oppression, and poverty and wealth. All the while this pedagogy does not alienate or silence the voices of student teachers. When trying to "disrupt" the status quo of remaining silent about race and racism in K-12 schools, an insightful senior teacher education student made this important in-class observation, "How can we create curriculum that connects with students who are of color and poor, if we cannot even talk about race [and class]?"[17]

Become Fearless in Talking about Race and Cultural Biases. Make This a Part of the Conversation with Colleagues and Students

It is essential in doing the work of education that time is given for teachers to learn about white privilege, cultural competence, and white supremacy. To do this they need to be encouraged to have discussions about race, class, behavior, language, and any issues that arise each day. Since the teaching force in this country is over 80 percent white, many teachers arrive in our classrooms with assumptions and misperceptions that come from seeing the world through a white lens. They make assumptions about the ability of students of color, often expecting less of those students. They believe they are objective observers of the world while also believing that adults of color have subjective views of events and policies. They often do not even consider the effect statements, requirements, and historical assumptions might have on students of color. These well-meaning teachers often communicate in condescending, patronizing ways without realizing it. One way to counter misperceptions and false assumptions is to make sure teachers form alliances with parents and community leaders. Classrooms then become places where cultures intersect. For this connection to happen white teachers need to become comfortable being uncomfortable. They need to be willing to talk about implicit bias and race and privilege. In order to put a halt to the marginalization of students of color, such work of self-reflection and examination have to happen.

In order that a white supremacist curriculum is eliminated and replaced with an inclusive, multiperspective, and challenging one, every teacher and administrator has to redo and re-create what and how he or she teaches. This work of re-creation and true reinvention encourages the exploration of terms like "classics" or "great literature" or what comprises United States History, World History, Music, and Art. It involves questioning what is referred to as "the canon." We are then doing what is best for white students as well as those of color when we rethink the content of our classrooms.

The Arts

The arts may also serve as a means of teaching toward dignity. Joanne Kohler works with students experiencing homelessness and has created films around this situation. She believes that in some cases students cannot find language to talk about their trauma.

> They are trying to open up when they do not have the words for what is going on in their lives. They need time to talk. They need ways to articulate what is happening to them, with them: this includes painting, sculpture, music, drama, poetry, photography, filming and dance. Artistic expression is often especially powerful when they work on story telling or performance or painting—any way of articulating their situation—in groups.[18]

Such advice applies to all students marginalized because of their race or because they are poor. In addition to classes in their regular day, art, music, and poetry can be part of affinity groups after school, such as African American culture clubs, Latino performance groups, or student-led meetings around issues such as racism, gay/straight alliances, neighborhood challenges. Artistic expression can result in public performances, community meetings, publications, or films. Advocating for after-school support for students can be anything from finding ways to provide bus service to get students home after the regular hours to directing a play, building sets, and organizing parents to bring families to performances. It is nitty-gritty work. Teachers must fight to keep arts within the school day. This crucial outlet for all students has been eliminated in many schools. We lose students when we do this.

Storytelling

In addition to finding space for art and music, teachers can clear out a psychic and physical space for storytelling. By exchanging stories, students come to know each other. It is during this time that students find themselves at the center of the class. Whether in morning circle time, as part of a check-in at the end of the day, or as part of a class project, stories engage and motivate students. Done with skill and compassion teachers can create thematic units of study around what they hear in the stories their students tell. Linda Christenson has created some remarkable books, published by *Rethinking Schools,* on using story and student voices to bring students in from the margins. Time set aside for story pays off in lack of discipline problems as the year goes on. When an entire school participates in giving students a voice, whether in writing or talking, students experience school as a community. One math teacher in a Minneapolis high school had her students keep math journals. She found that while the topic was to observe ways they used math during the week, the real benefit of these journals was that she got to know what was going on in her students' lives and established trusting relationships with them.

Building trust takes time. Some students of color may have felt the sting of assumptions in the ways teachers respond to them. The more teachers reveal that they too are learning, that they too are trying to understand a culture, dialect, or language not their own, the more their students will trust them and the more the class will coalesce.

Teachers who tell their own stories create a place of trust, respect, and modeling. When a teacher in one Minneapolis middle school was going through the serious illness of her father, she let her students know this. They were able to see her come in each day to teach, all the while understanding that while she was there for them, she was struggling with his last illness. When he passed, they felt a part of her grieving. They did not grieve her father, as they had not met him, yet they understood that she was gone for a few days and needed their support in her absence and on her return. The teacher, who reveals to students when she is dealing with pain or loss, without asking anything from them, provides a model of how to survive such life events. And when she is feeling joyful—at the birth of her first child, a marathon run, a master's degree completed, she asks students to join her in celebration. Teachers do not have to be automatons to teach well. Students of color are impressed to learn that white teachers have their own challenges. Revelation does not imply weakness; it implies trust, strength, and a willingness to risk.

One teacher in an alternative high school in Minneapolis asked black students, who made up 95 percent of her class, for the meaning of some of the words they used. She noticed they arrived each September with a new set of terms and phrases. By the end of the year her students had created a "Glossary for White People" comprising these words and their meanings.

It was the occasion for much laughter, some additions from parents, and a sense of real accomplishment when the glossary was completed.

Being Available

Teachers who spend time forming ties with individual students, be it with after-school help or early morning conversations before the first bus arrives, connect with their students on a deeper level. A teacher in a middle school in Minneapolis makes her room available at two or three lunch times during the week. Students can come and play board games, eat at her small tables, and talk with her one on one. She sets rules (eight as the maximum number of students) and guidelines for respectful behavior. Students often reveal what is going on in their lives over a chessboard more easily than in face-to-face conversations. The more teachers stand in the hall while students are passing or greet them at the door with a handshake, or mention a debate tournament, sports match, school newspaper story a student participated in, the more students understand that they are *seen*. These occasional comments require keeping track of what is going on with students outside of class. Teachers have to be ready to defend their decision to add time with students. Forming alliances with other like-minded teachers is essential.

Schools are set up to make relationship building difficult: it is not unusual to see class sizes of 40 in many middle and high schools, while elementary schools can reach 28 to 30 in one room. *The Small Schools Workshop,* cofounded by Mike Klonsky and Bill Ayers, provides consulting support for teachers wanting to create more personalized learning communities by pushing back against the movement to create bigger and bigger schools.[19] While it may seem overwhelming to be asked to know about over 150 students in depth, teachers can use an after-school homework help time, a before-school book club once a month, to reach as many young people as possible.

Center Learning in Student Experiences

Lisa Delpit, a noted scholar and writer about education, in her book *The Skin That We Speak* has a wonderful discussion of centering student concerns and interests as the driver of curriculum. One year her 12-year-old African American daughter came home from school talking about the different styles of African American hair, how the boys looked with their fades, and the girls' braids or weaves. Delpit helped create a multidisciplinary thematic unit centered on the subject of hair. She collaborated with teachers to put together a course around the history of hairstyles, the chemicals in products students used on their hair, and what was involved in being a cosmetologist. She lists the things involved in being a successful hair dresser: "bookkeeping; record keeping; marketing; small business operation and entrepreneurship; chemistry; anatomy; physiology; basic psychology; public speaking; interpersonal communication and computer operations." Add on to this art and poetry and music, short stories, all around the subject of hair, you have a student-centered course grounded in student interests. Delpit goes on to say:

> With some attention and thought, any teacher should be able to create a curriculum for many school-based subjects from a spectrum of topics. The object is not to lower standards or just teach what is interesting to the students, but to find the students' interests and build an academic program around them.[20]

One high school in St. Paul has developed a course called "The Literature of Love" which includes Shakespeare, poetry through the ages, contemporary novels, short stories, and song lyrics. It is an Honors Course. Another school developed a semester-long course on the Harlem Renaissance. These are two of the courses most in demand at these schools and include students who are rich, poor, white, black, Asian, and Latino. What tapping into these interests does is to center the student who may feel marginalized by placing his or her culture or interests or concerns at the center of the course. Bringing in speakers who look like the students and who know about the topic in all its variations can break down that barrier between student and school. Again, Delpit states:

> We have not fully realized the extent to which the media and general American belief systems have permeated the consciousness of African American children. Many have internalized the belief of the larger society that they and people who look like them are less than the intellectual norm. If schools [focus on] slavery rather than on the brilliance of the African intellectual legacy, children come to believe that there is nothing in their heritage to connect to schooling and academic success. . . . When we know the real history of Africa—the Egyptian wonders of technology and mathematics, the astronomical genius of the Mali Dogon, the libraries of Timbuktu—then we can teach our children that if they do not feel they are brilliant, then it is only because they do not know whence they came.[21]

By using surveys and questionnaires and listening to students talk about their lives, rigorous courses can be designed around any subject students are motivated to learn about. By questioning often white, mandated, top-down curriculums, including those of AP and International Baccalaureate (IB), teachers can provide the impetus to reinvent education. A unit simply called HOME could bring in literature, art, science math, and history in a dizzying array of incarnations. A unit on WATER could also do the same thing, including geography units and research on safe drinking water in neighborhoods. It takes teachers who are willing to explore what is not in their "expertise," to innovate, to delegate, and to even question the status quo to make the radical change that is essential if we are to reach equity in education. A wonderful resource for the study of math is the *Rethinking Schools* publication*, Rethinking Mathematics: Teaching Social Justice by the Numbers* by Eric Gustein.[22]

By asking the simple question "What do you want to know more about?" teachers can create a curriculum. They can revamp science, rethink literature, and reenvision history.

Teachers as Advocates

If changes are to occur, teacher education must play a major role in helping future teachers join those veteran teachers who are social justice educators. The cost is great if schools do not bring all students, including those on the margins, into the fight for racial equity. Unless black and brown students and their parents have a say, our schools will not be inclusive. If we lose these students, we lose our democracy and our ability to tap into the collective brilliance of our children. Even if they are not used to the role of advocate, teachers and administrators can assume it, accept it, and challenge the status quo.

Parental Connection

For all students the teacher/parent or guardian connection is essential. This means finding ways to meet with adults at times and in places that are convenient for them. It may mean that conferences take place in the neighborhoods and communities from which students come: in a library instead of in school and visiting homes before school starts in the fall. In some cases, parents' experiences in school were not always positive. Bringing school to them can go a long way toward developing trust. By asking the question "What do you want for your child this year in school?" teachers can emphasize that their child's education will be done in partnership. Together teacher and parent/guardian will provide a caring, challenging, and positive year for their child. One of the biggest mistakes school personnel make in interacting with communities of color is to assume those who live in poorer neighborhoods are not concerned or do not value education. Nothing could be further from the truth. From separate times for African American Parent Teacher Organization groups to meet, or phone calls home when a child is doing well, to inviting parents who are musicians or artists or doctors into the building to interact with students, teachers, and staff can create communities within their buildings. In one St. Paul School, in August, teachers walked the neighborhoods where their students lived and interviewed parents. They said later that this was the most valuable experience they had had in understanding their students—better than workshops with "experts," or time in their classrooms.

Schools as Community Centers

Schools that work well become community centers, including after-school activities, parent support groups, and night-time classes for adults with child care provided. The boundary between school and community is made porous, so that parents coming to pick up their child are welcomed and encouraged to stay awhile, to sit in the library and read a book to their child, or to grab a cup of coffee.

At a high school in a suburb in Minnesota, teachers noticed that the black and brown students who were bused out to school from the city were demoralized by the door they entered from the bus parking lot. While the suburban students who drove or walked or carpooled to school came in by the elaborate entryway at the front of the building, the city students entered in the back by the loading dock. The situation was somewhat remedied when teachers wrote and received grants to have someone redesign the back entry to the building. In addition, students became involved in creating a mural, a garden, and a new doorway.

The ways to make school feel open and welcoming are limitless: Who is standing at the doorway or at the admissions desk at the front of the entrance? How are parents greeted? What languages are present on the walls and in the hallways? Is the front office staff receptive to all cultures and children who are black or brown? Has the entire staff received ongoing staff development as new immigrant groups move into the city neighborhood or small town where school is located?

Embracing Cultures

Pao Yang, a young man who came to the United States from a refugee camp in Thailand, and who is Hmong, says that the hardest thing he had to learn when adapting to the schools in the United States was the way that individualism—each one for oneself—was encouraged. His culture emphasizes community, support for each other above all. Being aware of the worldviews of the students who enter your doors means your building becomes a place that centers each student within his or her culture, family, or struggle. It also means that you can accept a way of being in the world without judging, without assuming yours is superior. Schools that embrace many perspectives are places that provide dignity.

Authentic Assessments

There is no more damaging development in education these last 15 years than the obsession with standardized testing and scoring. The preponderance of tests, be they state tests, district tests, or national tests, takes time from demanding and rich curricula. The more these tests demand hours of drill and regimented lessons, the more students and teachers become frustrated, demoralized, or exhausted. Many such tests are biased and are useless as evaluative tools for teachers, and their purchase takes valuable funds needed for technology, small class sizes, and enrichment activities. On the other hand, evaluations that measure students' ability to understand concepts, to wrestle with complex questions, and to form critical thinking abilities require tools of assessment that differ entirely from standardized tests. Constructing assessments that measure such skills can give all involved a true picture of how students are doing. Teacher observation of student ability must be given weight in evaluations. By making any form of assessment culturally inclusive students will feel more confident in the assessment process.

Unit- or Theme-Based Instruction

The finest teachers look at the students in front of them and plan from there. It is possible to take standards that are assigned to each grade level or subject area and which may seem arbitrary and adapt them to the interests and requirements of a student-centered classroom. It takes some daring, careful wording, and belief in the dignity of children to do this. We have seen teachers create amazing units around Heritage, or Courage, or Immigration/Emigration, or Journeys, using the guidelines assigned to them by their district. They make sure they are ready to explain how their plans satisfy specified requirements. This kind of work may sometimes mean being subversive in a way that benefits students.

If teachers do not have autonomy in meeting their district's state standards, but are assigned a rigid curriculum, they can build in short, 10-minute, 5-minute, discussions, prompts, writing exercises to get students thinking and expressing themselves. Often students look forward to those first moments if there is some inclusive activity, a quick freewrite on the subject of music or an entry from the African American Registry about famous people born on the day the class meets. Much can be done at the beginning or end of the class period or school day to enliven a class even in the most dictatorial building.

Create Spaces for Laughter, Exploration, Dreaming, and Humor

Classrooms can be full of life, joy, confusion, consternation, and love. When teachers, administrators, hall guards, and staff recognize their students' emotional lives, they acknowledge and celebrate their classrooms as spaces where varied and complex human beings can exist with each other. In good schools students are thought of as "our kids." The more boys and girls and teens are considered in all their variety and dignity, the more educators feel compelled to reject prepackaged, highly regimented education that is found primarily in schools for students of color. There are books that have silly questions in the "Do fish have eyebrows?"; there are Brain Teasers, Minute Mysteries, riddles, and word origins that can humanize a classroom. Making classrooms fun and active does not have to sacrifice high academic expectations; creating such classrooms may even challenge a racist and limited perception of what is needed to teach "those kids." Human connection allows noise and giggling, tears, and wonder to be part of the atmosphere. There is nothing that says that an alive and vibrant classroom cannot be also one that demands and challenges students to the utmost.

Professional Learning Communities That Empower Teachers of Color

Teachers of color often become frustrated by white colleagues who may agree with them in private, while at department or all school meetings these same colleagues are nowhere to be heard when support is needed. White teachers may agree with their colleagues of color over lunch that there is a necessity to examine changes to curriculum or the way students are disciplined but when the topic comes up with the entire staff, these white teachers are silent. This basic lack of support for substantive change and lack of courage to join colleagues can drive the best teachers of color and even their white allies out of U.S. schools. To change this requires tough conversations.

Often students of color will go to the few teachers who look like them for advice. If they are elementary students, they literally cling to teachers or teacher aides of color. They stop by for hugs or jokes. Older students linger in the rooms of black teachers to talk before and after school; they even call or e-mail them at home. The chance to be with an African American math teacher or a Native American English teacher is essential for these students, not to mention how important it is for white students to see teachers of color in front of their classrooms. What white teachers often do not understand is the extra time, emotional involvement, and parent contact this entails for teachers of color. The few teachers of color in a building often become defacto counselors and social workers for students of color, this on top of their regular teaching load. There must be space and time provided for open and honest, if uncomfortable, discussions about the racial dynamic in each building. Learning from those white teachers who do connect with students of color is also key to changing how marginalized students are treated. The alliances between black and brown teachers with white teachers can reach deep, turning around schools that are struggling.

Encourage Students to Become Engaged in Service Learning

Through projects that tap into the energy of students who want to improve their neighborhoods, small towns, or suburbs, students experience themselves as change agents. This sense of agency is essential for them to feel in control, in the center, brought in from the margins. Mentorships grow from community connections. Projects to lessen violence, be they electives, part of the regular curriculum, or after school, are often initiated by students when the atmosphere is right. Providing students with the reflection and planning time to structure their own words and their own actions is tapping into powerful human motivation: knowing what they want to change and then acting on this knowledge. Playgrounds have been cleaned up, buildings have been cleared of asbestos, music teachers have been hired—all based on student motivation and inclusion. It is the most relevant and meaningful curriculum we can provide when we give students, be they 7 or 17, the belief in their own power.

Conclusion

In this chapter we have exposed the myriad ways in which students are marginalized. We have offered strategies to repurpose education and teach toward dignity. We see from the statistics on dropout rates and from studies of lack of student engagement that what is now the status quo has not worked for students of color. We can safely assume continuing to educate in this way will not work in the future. Students of color will continue to feel disengaged and hopeless in U.S. schools.

Our system is entrenched in a white supremacist curriculum. White authors are featured in many literature classes, and history is viewed through a white lens in many textbooks. Inequitable funding and resources combined with individual biases and assumptions cause students of color to be left out: tracked into less demanding courses and marginalized. Our system, as it stands now, perpetuates segregation and lowered expectations for black and brown children. Teachers are not being prepared to change this: they come from institutions with little understanding of race and economic privilege. They arrive in our schools without any deep awareness of the intersection of race and poverty and the part this plays in relegating black and brown students to dismal futures. Institutional racism, through universities and public schools, places whole groups of students on the margins, making our education system complicit in the trauma and the despair that accompanies many students of color who enter our classrooms each day. What is remarkable is how these very students not only survive but flourish on their own, not always because of school, but despite it.

We know that through pedagogies that demand new and veteran teachers to understand the place of racism in educational institutions and the part that schools play in perpetuating entrenched racism within larger economic and social contexts, we can begin to create schools that are change agents. The need to view the context of schooling by rethinking curriculum, connecting in deep ways to communities of color, if met head-on, offers great possibility for changing the very structure of education. We see change and hope even now, in individual districts, in schools, and in classrooms all over the country. Educators alone cannot end poverty or racism, redlining or homelessness. Yet educators *can* be part of a radical, progressive, and humane shift toward equity in our country. Students have the energy to join their teachers to make schools into places where no individual is left on the margins—where all are treated with dignity.

This radical work on the part of educators requires constant awareness, respect, reaching out to community, and belief in the brilliance of students like Michael, Mithson, Sarah, and Dyani. In this way we address the search for identity, the need for equal opportunity, the cultural adaptation, and the need to be free of alienation on the part of our students of color. The best teachers listen. Many teachers and mentors cross over the boundary between school life and community life.

Ultimately, providing education that stems from a belief in the dignity of all students involves working in ways small and private but no less revolutionary. It also means working in public, political, and policymaking arenas—to dismantle white privilege. All our voices are needed in whatever context we work. They are needed because our schools continue to fail those students whom they marginalize: be they middle-class black students or Latino students who live in poverty or be they Hmong students whose parents work double shifts or Native American students whose mothers put in long hours as social workers.

The most inclusive, equitable curriculum we can provide is to center our work with students in what they bring: their strengths, their culture, and their desire to learn. These students come from a rich history of educational achievement, persistence, literature, the arts, and ingenuity. Yet this very history and brilliance is absent in much of what they are taught or even encouraged to think about, research, or study during their years in school. Leaving students of color out of the center of our educational pedagogies and content is relegating them to outsider status. We are not educating with a concern for the dignity of each human being before us.

In order to bring students in from the margins we must challenge our educational system in its entirety. We must come armed with the knowledge of racism and white supremacy—the world from which our students come. We must teach from a position of advocacy and belief in the assets and resilience of whole communities that go unrecognized in our schools. Be it through political campaigns, school board elections, adoption of authentic and engaging curricula, or questioning suspension rates, in every context and arena, we must push toward teaching for dignity. It is up to us to have the moral courage to act.

Notes

1. "Reaching the Marginalized" 2014.
2. Delpit 2008.
3. Dutro and Bien 2014.
4. Jackson, p. 2.
5. National Center for Law and Economic Justice.
6. Ayers 2004, p. 40; Ayers 1998, p. xvii.
7. Ravitch.
8. Precious Knowledge 2014.
9. "Dismantling the Cradle to Prison Pipeline: Preventing Pushouts in Mississippi Schools" 2014.
10. Reardon et al. in press.
11. Bridgeland, Dilulio, and Morison 2006.
12. "The Drop Out Crisis" 2014.
13. Stoval 2013, p. x.
14. Spring 2011, p. 4.
15. Kohl 1994, p. 2.
16. Hutchinson 1999.
17. Lund and Carr 2013.
18. Joanna Kohler Productions.
19. Small Schools Workshop 2014.
20. Delpit 2008, p. 45.
21. Ibid., p. 46.
22. Gustein 2005.

Bibliography

"America's Report Card." Children's Hunger Alliance. Accessed May 8, 2014. http://www.Childrenshungeralliance.org/. . ./childrenshunger/. . .1666.pdf.

Ayers, William. 1998. "Popular Education: Teaching for Social Justice." In *Teaching for Social Justice,* eds. William Ayers and Jean Ann Hunt. New York: The New Press, Teachers College Press, p. xvii.

Ayers, William. 2004. *Teaching toward Freedom: Moral Commitment and Ethical Action in the Classroom.* Boston, MA: Beacon Press, p. 40.

Bridgeland, John, John Dilulio, and Karen Burke Morison. 2006. "The Silent Epidemic: Perspectives of High School Dropouts." *The Bill and Melinda Gates Foundation and the Civic Enterprise.*

Christenson, Linda. 2003. Reading, Writing, and Rising Up: Teaching about Social Justice and the Power of the Written Word. Milwaukee, WI: Rethinking Schools.

Christenson, Linda. 2009. *Teaching for Joy and Justice: Re-imagining the Language Arts Classroom.* Milwaukee, WI: Rethinking Schools.

Delpit, Lisa. 2008. "No Kinda Sense" (Chapter 3). *The Skin That We Speak*. New York: The New Press, pp. 45–46.

"Dismantling the Cradle to Prison Pipeline: Preventing Pushouts in Mississippi Schools." Children's Defense Fund. 2013. Accessed July 13, 2014. www.childrens defense.org/. . ./dismantling-the-cradle-to.html.

"The Drop Out Crisis." Raise Up Project. Accessed June 1, 2014. http://www.raise upproject.org/crisis.

Dutro, Elizabeth, and Bin, Andrea C. Bien. 2014. "Listening to the Speaking Wound: A Trauma Studies Perspective on Student Positioning in Schools." *American Education Research Journal* 51 (1): 7–35. Accessed July 15. http://aerj.aera.net.

"Equity and Social Justice from Inside-Out: Ten Commitments of a Multicultural— Educator." *Educating for Equity and Social Justice*. Accessed May 10, 2014. www.sevenhillscharter.org/wpup/2011/07/10commitmentsof. . .

Gorski, Paul. 2013. *Reaching and Teaching Students in Poverty for Erasing the Opportunity Gap*. New York: Teachers College Press.

Grant, Carl, and Vonzell Agosto. "Teacher Capacity and Social Justice in Teacher Education." Accessed May 1, 2014. http://www.works.bepress.com/cgi/viewcon tent.cgi?article=1002&. . .

Gustein, Eric. 2005. *Rethinking Mathematics: Teaching Social Justice by the Numbers*. Milwaukee, WI: Rethinking Schools.

"Housing Costs, Zoning and Access to High-Scoring Schools." Brookings Institution. Accessed May 8, 2014. http://www.brookings.edu?. . .19-school-inequality-rothwe.

Hutchinson, Jaylynne. 1999. *Students on the Margins: Education, Stories, and Dignity*. Albany: State University of New York Press. 10, 65, 27.

Jackson, Vanessa. "Poverty as Trauma: Understanding the Impact of Fiscal Trauma on Individual and Family Life." Accessed May 1. http://www.Academia .edu/3994418/Povertyastrauma, 2.

Jensen, Eric. 2013. "How Poverty Affects Classroom Engagement." *Educational Leadership* 70 (8): 24–30.

Kohl, Herbert. 1994. *I Won't Learn from You and Other Thoughts on Creative Maladjustment*. New York: The New Press, p. 2.

Kozol, Jonathon. 1991. *Savage Inequalities: Children in America's Schools*. New York: Harper.

Kozol, Jonathon. 1995. *Amazing Grace: The Lives of Children Lives and the Conscience of a Nation*. New York: Crown Publishing.

Kozol, Jonathon. 2005. *The Shame of a Nation: The Restoration of Apartheid Schooling in America*. New York: Crown Publishing.

Lund, Darren, and Paul Carr. 2013. "Disrupting Denial and White Privilege in Teacher Education." In *Cultivating Social Justice Teachers*, eds. Paul Gorski, Kristen Zenkov, Nana Osei-Kofi, and Jeff Sapp (p. 111). Sterling, VA: Stylus Press, pp. 108–125.

National Center for Law and Economic Justice. "Poverty in the United States: A Snapshot." Accessed March 10, 2014. http://www.nclej.org/poverty-in-the-use.php.

Precious Knowledge. Public Broadcasting Service. Accessed April 7, 2014. http://www.pbs.org/.../precious-knowledge/film.htp.

Ravitch, Diane Blog. "AFT-Yes to Common Core, Remediation Needed by Arne Duncan" and "Pearson Errors: Would You Trust Your Child to This Corporation." Accessed July 15, 2014. http://www.dianeravitch.net/category/common-core/.

Ravitch, Diane Blog. "Pearson Likely to Get 1 Billion PARCC Contract Despite Checkered Past." Accessed July 15, 2014. http://www. dianeravitch.net/category/pearson/.

"Reaching the Marginalized." Education for All: Global Monitoring Report, Chapter 3. Accessed July 15, 2014. www.unesco.org/.../efareport/reports/2010-marginalization.

Reardon, Sean, Elena Grewal, Demetra Kalogrides, and E. Erica Greenberg. 2012. "Brown Fades: The End of Court-Ordered School Desegregation and the Resegregation of American Public Schools." *Journal of Policy Analysis and Management.*

Small Schools Workshop. Accessed March 30, 2014. http://www.smallschools workshop.wordpress.com.

Spring, Joel. 2011. *The American School: A Global Context from the Puritans to the Obama Era.* 8th ed. New York: McGraw Hill, p. 4.

Stoval, David. 2013. "Foreword: Into the Messiness: Struggle, Defeat, and the Victory Condition in Troubling Times." In *Cultivating Social Justice Teachers,* eds. Paul Gorski, Kristen Zenkow, Nana Osei-Kofi, and Jeff Sapp (p. x). Sterling, VA: Stylus Press.

Tatum, Beverly. 2006. *Can We Talk about Race and Other Conversations in an Era of School Resegregation.* Boston, MA: Beacon Press.

Winter, Marcus. 2006. "Savage Exaggerations." *Education Next* 6 (2): 71–75.

Chapter 3

The Other Story: The Truth about Black Teen Mothers in Education

Christine Stroble, Melissa Pearson, and Greg Wiggan

Notions about black women and motherhood are cast in glorious tales of strength, resilience, and unconditional love. Often when we think of black mothers, it is through a stereotyped image of the chaste and strong matriarch or the independent superwoman. While many in the black community might see these images as positive, the problem, among many, with these stereotypes, is the absence of sexuality, what it actually takes to become a mother. To recognize sex as a means to motherhood is to also recognize the horrendous sexual oppression that black women have suffered. The sexual politics of black women and motherhood has been an enduring issue since the rise of western patriarchy and the paradigm of slavery.

Black women's bodies became property of slaveholders to serve both their recreational and procreational desires. He, the enslaver, degraded, dehumanized, and humiliated black women so egregiously that she became a mere object. Often black women were subjected to forced public nudity and banned from legal marriage. This disposition left black women vulnerable to the double bind of racial and sexual oppression. Furthermore, in early 18th century, Sara Baartman, otherwise known as the Hottentot Venus, was dissected physically and metaphorically to berate the sexuality of black women. Baartman was enslaved and paraded in front of audiences of sideshow seekers who concluded that black women must be predisposed to sexual promiscuity.[1] In addition, in 1765, in Thomas Jefferson's scathing *Notes on Virginia*, he characterizes black women as "Vile seductresses who lured white men away from their chaste female counterparts."[2] He also described them as "animalistic" and "aggressive." These notions became embedded in the psyche of America and black women as antithetical to the Victorian notions of modesty, purity, and fragility, "True Womanhood."

For centuries, black feminist scholars pushed back against and worked ferociously to refute the accusations. Just one example among many is Mary Church Terrell, a 19th-century club woman who wrote that "foul aspersions upon the character of colored women are assiduously circulated by the press of certain sections and especially by the direct descendants of those who in years past were responsible for the moral degradation of their female slaves."[3] In a speech called "The Progress of Colored Women" she argues, "To-day [1937] in each and every section of the country there are hundreds of homes among colored people, the mental and moral tone of which is and high and as pure as can be found among the best people of any land."[4] Despite the efforts of black feminist scholars to deconstruct pejorative claims about the black woman's intellectual gifts and talents, the myth of promiscuity has become a systemic lie which has colored the ways in which black women and girls are viewed in socioeconomic, political, and educational institutions. In the case of teenage pregnancy, the myth of promiscuity supports reasons not to empathize with the plight of young black mothers and see them as one-dimensional human beings who leech on federal programs and nourish the social ills that threaten American ideology.

To further understand the struggle for black single mothers is to understand the pernicious indictment of matriarchy by Daniel Patrick Moynihan in 1965.[5] The Moynihan Report attempts to explain why "Negroes" struggle to "fit in" to American ways of life after the proclamation of the Civil Rights Act of 1964. He points out that reasons for much of the "Negro" problem can be found in the circumstances of Negro children born out of wedlock and the number of Negro households led by women. The report quotes statistics about the disparities in education, employment, and poverty between "Negroes" and whites. It also characterizes the homes of single black mothers as broken, and the children as delinquent. All of these ills are blamed on Negro women. He posits, "In every index of family pathology—divorce, separation, and desertion, female family head, children in broken home, and illegitimacy . . . for Negro families is unmistakable."[6] The reversal of roles in black families where females dominate and males lack power is to blame. While the report points out that many of pathologies are derived from systemic racism in America; the emphasis on black matriarchy's role in crippling the family structure and progress of black men is striking. The infamous Moynihan Report succeeded in making the word "matriarchy" a pejorative term. Black feminist Mary Ann Weathers responds vehemently to the misnomer as she proclaims in an essay of liberation:

> Don't allow yourselves to be intimidated any longer with this nonsense about the "Matriarch" of Black women. Black women are not matriarchs, but we have been forced to live in abandonment and been used and abused. The myth of the matriarch must stop, and we must not allow ourselves to be sledgehammered by it any longer.[7]

Weathers and many other black feminists are deconstructing the myth of a nefarious mother-figure who rules her house so fiercely that it damages her children and runs her man away. The skewed message that this sends to both black men and women is that young, black mothers are destined for a self-fulfilling prophesy. However, it also detracts from the real problem confronting young, black mothers: inequality. The talk of sexual anomaly, promiscuity, and matriarchy is red herrings in the dialogue about recognizing a young mother as a human being first. It compounds and reinforces aspects of shaming single black mothers, which has far-reaching debilitating effects on their self-esteem, and deeper implications for success. Even more, there is much more to the story of black teen mothers that refutes arguments of promiscuity and does not cast her or her offspring as social pathologies.

Undoubtedly, the lore, myths, and unidimensional characterizations of black women have drawn the ire of black feminists and create an exigency to raise flawed consciousness. If black women are going to be liberated from centuries of aspersions and misrecognition, their lives in all realms must be acknowledged and validated. Therefore, we look at black teen mothers through a black feminist lens with black feminist thought.

Black feminist scholar Patricia Hill Collins explains the significance of black feminist thought as "a second level of knowledge, the more specialized knowledge furnished by experts who are part of a group and who express the group's standpoint."[8] She "encourages all Black women to create new self-definitions that validate a Black women's standpoint." In Collins's thought model, when black teen mothers tell their stories, they are engaging epistemology, creating new understanding and ways for others to acknowledge their existence. The aim is to resist and depart from the "Eurocentric masculinist process of knowledge-validation," which she defines as "the institutions, paradigms, and any elements of the knowledge-validations procedure controlled by white males and whose purpose is to represent a white male standpoint."[9] To frame a discussion about black, single mothers without the input of black single mothers is to validate the destructive myths which limit their freedom and possibilities in the world.

Subsequently, our attempt to lend voice to young, black mothers is not an attempt to condone or condemn black teenage pregnancy. Instead, it is an attempt to create space for another story to be told about young black mothers, her story. It is important to understand how notions about single motherhood among black women are perceived as reasons for her marginalization and misrecognition. For example, often in educational institutions, young, black single mothers suffer a public shame which renders them virtually invisible to be recognized as citizens fully capable of public participation, while simultaneously making them exposed and vulnerable to the myth of promiscuity, which may indeed place them on a track of academic failure.

In her book *Sister Citizen: Shame, Stereotypes, and Black Women in America,* Melissa Harris-Perry argues that recognition is key to full access to participation in American society and warns that misrecognition "in the form of stereotype and stigma" marginalizes and denies "social possibilities." She contends that "African American women lack opportunities for accurate, affirming recognition of the self and yet must contend with hypervisibility imposed by their lower social status."[10] Harris-Perry also asserts that in their efforts to confront racism and gender oppression black women find themselves trying to stand up straight in a crooked room.[11] She claims, "They have to figure out which way is up. Bombarded with warped images of their humanity, some Black women tilt and bend themselves to fit the distortion."[12] In educational institutions, policies and behaviors regarding black teen pregnancy cause young women to suffer great bouts of depression and in extreme cases they resort to suicide. A new conversation must be had to tell another story about black teenage mothers, which may contribute to the knowledge about black women through recognition of their lived experiences.[13] The impetus for the discussion is to implore educational institutions to recognize the implications of racism in policies and practices regarding teen pregnancy and schooling.

Educational System's Reaction to Teen Pregnancy

The educational system has in large part remained silent with regard to teenage pregnancy.[14] Wanda Pillow in "Teen Pregnancy and Education: Politics of Knowledge, Research, and Practice" writes:

> Between 1972 and 2002, *Educational Researcher* failed to print any articles on the education of pregnant or mothering students, a silence echoed in other

major educational journals. By comparison, a cursory search on teen pregnancy will generate a plethora of research about teen pregnancy and teen parenting from psychological, sociological, health, public policy, and social welfare viewpoints. Furthermore, although there is a wealth of evaluation research on teen pregnancy prevention and teen parenting programs, this research is most often conducted by researchers outside the arena of education and largely ignores the educational experiences of school-aged mothers.[15]

As a result,

education policy affecting teen mothers has effectively been removed from the education arena. Although they are the front-line service providers to pregnant and mothering students, educators are situated as "low-profile service providers." Consequently, although teen mothers have long been the topic of national debate, we know very little about how pregnant and mothering students are being educated. In fact, many school districts historically have not and currently do not collect data specifically tracking teen mothers.[16]

Pillow argues that "these educational gaps and silences are even more shocking when we consider that under Title IX, passed in 1972 and implemented in 1975, public schools are explicitly charged with providing equal educational access and opportunity to pregnant and mothering students."[17] She contends further that "this silence—the low profile surrounding teen pregnancy in educational research, policy, and practice—is neither natural nor neutral. Rather, the gaping data holes are a constructed and highly politicized silence."[18]

This silence creates a space where teen mothers are not recognized in public education—indeed some educators (administrators, teachers, counselors) do not feel teen mothers belong or "fit" in public schools—and thus, teen mothers' access to full participation in school is hindered. Recently, many individuals and groups, including Erin Prangley, the associate director for Government Relations of the American Association of University Women (AAUW) in Washington, D.C., have been urging the U.S. Department of Education, Office for Civil Rights (OCR), to monitor treatment of teen mothers in public school.[19] In fact, Prangley has been asking the OCR to collect data about teen mothers and how schools serve them.[20] Prangley wants the OCR to, "ask the schools point blank: Does your school provide child care, transportation, or tutoring? Does your school track data on girls who become pregnant?" Prangley's request speaks to the need for data on teen mothers. Pillow concurs that until teen pregnancy is researched and studied as an educational issue, teen mothers will not receive the education they deserve and are entitled to.[21]

The U.S. Department of Education, Office for Civil Rights, did issue guidance on treatment of teen mothers in a letter dated June 25, 2013, written by acting assistant secretary for Civil Rights, Seth Galanter, urging colleagues to "support pregnant and parenting students so that they can stay in school and complete their education and thereby build better lives for themselves and their children."[22] Furthermore, in recent years, a few scholars have investigated teen pregnancy from an educational perspective and found that although teen mothers have a renewed interest in furthering their education after motherhood, schools fails to capitalize on their renewed interest.[23,24] Rigid school policies and practices make it difficult and create great challenges and obstacles for these students to stay in school. SmithBattle in "I Wanna Have a Good Future: Teen Mothers' Rise in Educational Aspirations, Competing Demands, and Limited School Support" illustrates how school barriers often disrupted the educational progress of her participants and led some students to leave school reluctantly.[25] Three of the young women in her study faced "cumbersome enrollment processes, stringent attendance policies, lack of educational options, and bureaucratic mismanagement."[26] As a counterexample, SmithBattle offered the unique story of one student, Pam, who attended "a school that fostered her connection to school, reinforced her motivation to succeed academically, and provided college advisement."[27] Pam's school capitalized on her renewed interest in her education. She received homebound instruction near the end of her pregnancy, gave birth over the summer, and returned to school her junior year without interruption while her son attended subsidized day care.[28] Pam also continued cheerleading with the help of a teacher who drove her and her son home after practice. Pam also attended a parenting class. Furthermore, Pam was advised to consider the community college and was informed free tuition was available for her because of her grades. Pam's story illustrates the impact support of teachers and school staff can have in helping teen mothers stay in school and graduate.

In "Getting My Education: Teen Mothers' Experiences in School before and after Motherhood," Zachary found that "teen pregnancy and its links to educational achievement centers on the importance of a supportive and organized school environment in helping individuals achieve."[29] All the young mothers in Zachary's study "discussed how her current school was helping her to build a more positive future and increase her confidence in herself and her intellectual abilities. The women emphasized that the support and encouragement they received from their teachers was an important factor helping them to remain in school."[30]

The Implication for Black Girls

In light of the sexual politics of black women and the educational system's silence in regard to teen pregnancy, there are serious implications for black girls whose gender, race, and class status place them at an even greater disadvantage. As discussed in the first section, black teen mothers are perceived as loose/promiscuous. This lack of respect for black single mothers is another form of oppression they must overcome in addition to the obstacles and challenges teen mothers in general face in public schools, as discussed earlier. Furthermore, Venus E. Evans-Winters in *Teaching Black Girls: Resiliency in Urban Classrooms* explains how race, class, and gender oppression embedded in school practices and policies put black girls at an even greater risk of school failure:

> African American girls are more likely to experience social barriers, in a society that values White over Black, men over women, and wealth over poverty. Also, African American students are more likely than their White male and female peers to encounter race, class, and gender discrimination in the classrooms, curriculum and pedagogy, putting them at higher risk of school failure.[31]

Part of the reason why is in the field of education the research has been either on black male students or on white students. Evans Winters in noting why African American females are missing from the resiliency literature argues:

> There are several reasons why Black female adolescents are absent from the literature. Compared to Black males, Black females have fewer behavior problems. African American girls' behaviors are least likely to affect others; thus research and the resulting reform efforts tend to focus on Black males. Another factor is that White women have dominated the women's movement, which means their research is conducted on themselves or white adolescents. Last, researchers tend to assume that white females and Black females have similar socialization processes. . . . By ignoring or subsuming Black girls' experiences within White girls' or Black boys experiences; we overlook the imitable experience of the Black girl.[32]

Their Stories

The heart of our chapter is the narrative of the experiences of a select group of teen mothers. Their stories are drawn interviews which took place in the Southeastern region of the United States between 2012 and 2013 with 10 young women, all who had become mothers between ages 15 and 19; yet at the time of our interview, each young adult was between ages 18 and 33 years. Each young mother was either enrolled in or had recently graduated from college.

In this space we share the stories of four young mothers beginning with Laura, age 27, a recent pharmacy school graduate, and ending with Quincy, age 18 and a college freshman. We share each mother's educational experience, how she was able to graduate from high school and go to college as a teen mother, and what factors contributed to her success. In all their stories, there is a demonstration of perseverance; resilience; and the presence of school, home, and community supports and resources.

Laura—A 27-Year-Old Recent Pharmacy School Graduate

Laura and I sat down at the kitchen table in my apartment to begin our interview. After admonishing Laura to relax and explaining that there were no right or wrong answers—she was there just to share her story—I began asking Laura about her educational experience. I asked her to recall her elementary school experience and to rate her overall elementary school experience on a scale of 1 to 5, with 1 being Bad and 5 being Excellent. Laura's response was a 4. She explained that she had great teachers throughout elementary school. She then rated middle school a 4, noting that she was always in the higher-level classes which she really didn't like. Laura explained why, "I was in the higher classes, which honestly, I didn't really like being in the higher classes. I was just like singled out. There wouldn't be any Black people in the classes, of course." Laura further explained how the classes were divided:

> There weren't many Black people in the classes. They were based on grades, basically, so there weren't really many Black students in those classes, and even through my three years of middle school, it was the same.
>
> If there were other Black students in the class with me, they were the same ones in each grade, sixth, seventh, and eighth grade, the same Black people that were in the classes together, in those type of classes, the same ones the whole time. But I mean, I still had a good educational experience.

I asked Laura "How did that make you feel, being one of only a few Black people in the class?" She responded that she really didn't like it:

> I didn't really like it. You don't feel like you can—I don't want to be yourself, because I was myself, but it's still like you don't feel like they have the same background as you. You don't have that type of connection with them, because they don't necessarily come from where you come from.
>
> Actually, like a lot of those, the other white people that were in my class, they were from better socioeconomic background statuses and things like that, where I wasn't, honestly. I didn't come from—they had their parents that bought them whatever and all of that other stuff, and I didn't come from that, so it was just different, which I wasn't at the lower, lower end. We weren't just truly poor, but they had the families, they had everything.

Then we discussed high school, which Laura rated a 3, partially because she had to go to two different high schools as a result of rezoning. Being rezone to a new high school created a problem with Laura's class ranking even though she had a 3.8 grade point average. The new school for some reason said it couldn't provide Laura her ranking and the reason she was given was that she went to a different high school in ninth grade. For that reason—something beyond her control—Laura was told she could not be part of the ranking. Laura didn't believe that rational and suspected there was another reason (her pregnancy) why she was not given a ranking or could not be in the top 10. Laura's response to the school explanation was:

> That's what they said. I don't know what my ranking is, but yes, that's supposedly why I couldn't. I have no clue of my ranking. I never found out where I ranked, or I couldn't be in the top ten. I won't say I couldn't be ranked.
>
> I probably was ranked. I honestly think I probably was in the top ten, but I couldn't get put in the top ten, so I probably was ranked, but I don't know my ranking. It wasn't an award, but as far as the student body, my class, senior superlatives, I was voted Most Intellectual.

All along, Laura knew she wanted to be a pharmacist and when she got pregnant at age 17 at the beginning of her senior year, she didn't let her teen pregnancy stop her from pursuing her dream. Because Laura had earned most of her high school credits by first semester of her senior year, she got permission from the superintendent to graduate early—in December of her senior year. It wasn't until spring semester, however, in May that she participated in the graduation ceremony with her class. Consequently, second semester of high school, before and after she had her baby, Laura worked in a plant and saved up some money in preparation for starting college in August.

In college, Laura started off at a two-year, community college in her hometown just taking her prerequisite courses. She lived with her parents and they helped her with her daughter. After two years, in order to take full advantage of financial aid, Laura transferred 50 miles away from her hometown to a four-year college. She says,

> Getting my undergraduate degree, it was a struggle at times also, because when I moved to finish up at the four-year college, I was only fifty miles away from home, but still. I needed someone to watch my daughter at one point in time, which just so happened that I remember when I was trying to look for apartments to move there, I was looking for daycares as well, and I really couldn't find the daycares that I was looking for.

Fortunately Laura was able to find a day care and the "woman who ran the daycare, she ended up watching my daughter for me sometimes, when I needed her, some evenings when I was working late. She would just take my daughter home with her after school and she would stay over there until I got off work. She helped out quite a bit."

At the age of 22, Laura earned her bachelor's degree in chemistry with a minor in biology. She received her acceptance letter to pharmacy school before she graduated so she knew she would be going to pharmacy school the following August. In August, Laura enrolled in pharmacy school. It wasn't easy, Laura explained:

> Pharmacy school? It was pretty tough. When you're in high school, they're like, "When you get to college, it's a whole other world. You'll have to study." I got to the community college and I did not really study at all, and I had A's and B's all through those first two years, but then honestly, when I went to the four year college, it was that jump that they had claimed you have, from high school to college.
>
> But really, it was just with certain classes. Some of my prerequisites for pharmacy school, I would say just those classes, not all of my classes. Some of them were still like I didn't study for them. I just did my work and went on about my business.
>
> It was just a couple of classes, I'll say, in undergrad, in the four year college that I had to focus on. But then, when I got to pharmacy school, I promise you, I made up all the years I didn't study. I studied in pharmacy school. I studied a lot—like, a lot. . . .

Yes, a whole lot. Yes, it was different. It requires a whole lot of hard work and studying. It was different. It was a lot of work.

Laura was able to complete the work, however, and just seven months before our interview, she graduated from pharmacy school. At the time of our interview Laura and her daughter were living in the apartment complex where I was living and she was employed as a pharmacist with one to the largest U.S. drug retail stores. Laura later commented on how much she enjoyed sharing her story, and she and I still remain in contact.

Toni—A 24-Year-Old Graduate of an Historically Black College and University

I arrived at Toni's apartment to conduct our interview. As Toni warmly welcomed me and directed me to the kitchen table to set up my laptop, I thanked her for graciously opening her home to me. We began with the same initial question that I asked Laura: How would you rate your overall elementary school experience, on a scale of 1 to 5, with 1 being Bad and 5 being Excellent? Toni rated her elementary school experience a 5, explaining that she grew up as a normal child. She admired and gravitated to her teachers in elementary school. For middle school, she rated that experience a 5, in part because she attended two very different middle schools: one "white," the other more "black." I asked Toni if the difference in the racial make-up of her school impacted her. She explained going to the black school where she had black teachers significantly impacted her:

> It definitely did play a part because I was identifying more so with the people that were more like me. You know, it was a lot growing up. In middle school, boys are coming into the picture. Females are learning to interact with each other, but I definitely gravitated to a couple of teachers, one in particular, who played a part in my life going up into high school. I still keep in touch with her to this day.

Toni also rated her high school experience as a 5. She elaborated on how much she learned and enjoyed going to her magnet high school. Laura explained:

> I didn't have anything against my home school, but they actually had a medical academy at the magnet school that I went to, and at that time, I wanted

to be into pediatrics, so that was definitely like, "Yes! That's where I want to go." I didn't even think about what other schools were there. That's the school that I wanted to go to.

Toni found out she was pregnant near the end of her junior year in high school. She had just finished playing basketball for the season. She gave birth at the beginning of her senior year. Toni talked a great deal about struggling internally with being a teenage mother. It was her dream to be a pediatrician and in her mind after getting pregnant she couldn't still do that; yet Toni says she was still able to graduate high school and college because she had support.

> The struggle was more internal for me because it's my reality. And yes, I'm doing this, but in the back of my mind it's like, "How am I doing this?" Literally. I don't—how am I still waking up every day, going to school, having a child at this point?
>
> Yes. High school. I was a teen mom, so even if I didn't want that to show on the outside that I was struggling, it was a struggle for me. Almost still a disappointment in myself, but this is my reality, this is what I'm going to have to do at this point.
>
> Everything that I was or wanted to be had changed at this point, so everything went smoothly, but inside, I didn't know what the next step was for me. I didn't know how my college experience was going to be. I just hoped for the best, and I had so much support even if I wanted to crawl up in a ball, I couldn't.

I asked Toni if there was anything (i.e., counseling, a mentor) that would have helped her with her internal struggle and she responded that she did have help and that's how she was able to keep going:

> I think I did have that help, and that's how I was able to keep going. I don't think that anybody's going to wake up and say, "Oh it's fine!" You're going to have that within yourself, when there's a life-altering situation going on. You now have a child. Regardless of what kind of help, you're going to have your own internal things that you deal with on a day-to-day.
>
> Even somebody that doesn't have a child, they're still dealing with their own situations. So the support that I had was necessary for me between the family support, the support at school, the programs that are geared specifically toward teenage mothers—the support that I would've needed, I had.

Toni feels she was able to graduate high school and college because of the support of her family, teachers, and the adolescents parenting program that she participated in, especially the adolescent parenting program:

> With the same support of my family, teachers, and these adolescent parenting programs because—the programs specifically—because everyone in the room is just like you. Now you no longer feel alone. You no longer are wondering, by yourself, how you're going to do it because they would often bring other girls who were like two steps ahead. When you see somebody that's just like you, that played basketball just like you, that was very popular just like you, and now they have a child, and now they're in college, and now they're about to graduate. You say, "Well, if she can do it, why can't I?" Why would I crawl up and say, "Now I can't do it."
> Because I'm looking at somebody that has, and that is, and that will.

Toni told me that if she hadn't had the support of the adolescent parenting program through the partnership between her school and the community agency, she's not sure if her life would have turned out as it has:

> If I didn't have that [adolescent parenting program] in place, I don't know how my situation would have turned out, and that's through—because your mother, she's there. She's going to support you. But identifying who I am, and having that support system of other females who are just like me, as well as targeted parenting skills to understand exactly what we're supposed to do, why is my child is doing this, is he supposed to be here, is he not supposed to be here, as well as the support and encouragement to go on to go to college. That was their main goal. That's their mission. That's all that they do. So without that, I don't know where I would be, if my situation would have turned out as well as it did.

Thankfully, Toni had the support she needed and now she is a college graduate. I asked Toni what it means to be a college graduate and she explained it means everything. It means redemption. It means "there's no shame here":

> It definitely means a lot. And so when I say that I have a child—you know some people—because they'll ask, "How old's your son?" And when I say, "Six." They go, "Well, how old are you?" I say, "Well, Twenty-four." So you do the math in your head, and it's not anything daunting for me because I still did everything I was supposed to do.
> I still went to school, I was able to finish school on-time. I was going to finish early, and I did what I had to do. Now I'm taking care of what I have

to do. If not, I would possibly feel some kind of weight if I knew that I was struggling or knew that I hadn't properly prepared myself to care for him, but there's no shame here.

Xiomara—A 22-Year-Old Recent Graduate of Local Community College: Recently Accepted at Four-Year Research One Institution

Xiomara and I lived on opposite ends of town and we agreed I would come to her apartment. I was running a little behind our scheduled time and ended up in rush hour traffic, in the dark, struggling to find her apartment complex. After missing my turn, I finally arrived and Xiomara, as did Toni, graciously welcomed me into her home. After a brief exchange with her boyfriend and her daughter, Xiomara and I settled in at her kitchen table to conduct our interview. We started with our first question: How would you rate your elementary school experience on a scale of 1 to 5, with 1 being Bad and 5 being Excellent? Xiomara rated her elementary school experience a 3 because she went to five or six different elementary schools. Xiomara stated that every time she got settled in, she felt uprooted and had to make new friends. Also, her dad died and she had to move with her mom, whom she didn't know that well:

> Yes, so I felt like every time I got settled, I had to be uprooted and had to make all new friends, and my dad died when I was in the fifth grade, so yeah. It was just like the continuous moving from place to place. Then my dad died and I had to move in with my mom who I didn't really know that well.

Xiomara rated her middle school experience a 5. She went on to say:

> Middle school was great. I cheered. Me and my best friend were the cheer-leader captains. We were like the most popular, we were like the most pretty. It was just all fun. Everybody was our friends. I just had so many friends and so much fun. On the weekends, we would meet everybody at our school at the mall.
>
> That was when Waverly Place (pseudonym) first opened. We would all go there to the Raceway and to the movies and just hang out, and carpool. Somebody's mom would drop us off, and then somebody's mom would pick us up and drop us all off at home. It was just fun. All I remember is fun from middle school.
>
> Yes, all of my classes were great. I loved all of my teachers. And I've always been like a honors student, so I took algebra in the seventh grade and geometry in the eighth grade, so.

High school was just average for Xiomara. She rated it a 3. Xiomara got pregnant in the middle of her 11th grade year. She explained that she wanted to remain at her home high school but because the girls in her school wanted to fight her, out of fear for her safety, she transferred to the alternative/nontraditional school for teen mothers. I asked if she ever shared her concerns regarding fearing her safety to the principal and she brushed off my suggestion explaining that the administration wouldn't have addressed her concerns. Why not? I asked, and she explained that it would have just been her word against the other girls. That's how her high school operated. Xiomara explained that it was her intent to go to the alternative school until she had her daughter and then return to her home high school but, "I got there and they gave me the option to graduate in January, and I had all my classes. All I needed was like, one class, so I just took that option."

Even though Xiomara says she regretted staying at the alternative school because "It's an alternative school, and I was so smart, and I just never felt like I belonged there . . . I just didn't feel like I belonged there." Xiomara graduated Salutatorian from the alternative high school.

After graduating from high school, Xiomara enrolled in the local community college, and on the day of our interview, she received her acceptance letter to the local research one urban institution where she would earn her four-year degree.

Xiomara and I wrapped up our interview with her sharing with me how attending college is going to open doors for her and her daughter and how graduating from college will feel like redemption:

> I feel great about attending college because I know that it's going to open up doors for us in the future, and I feel that all the people who are disappointed and are let down, I feel like some way this would make—. . . . Yeah, like reaffirm me and let them know that even though I did make a mistake—not saying Lisa (pseudonym) is a mistake, but teenage pregnancy was a mistake—that I'm still the same Xiomara that y'all are used to. I'm still smart, I'm still going to finish school like y'all expected me to from the beginning, so.

Sensing Xiomara was still struggling with self-confidence, I asked if her teen pregnancy hurt her self-esteem. As she burst into tears, she responded:

> Yeah, in a way because I—my family—well, my dad's side of the family—they always put me on a pedestal. And even on my mom's side of the family, they always put me on a pedestal just because I was different from them, and

because I was so smart, and because I always got straight A's. They always put me up there, so then I felt like—when I got pregnant—like everybody just—I guess looked at me a different type of way, like I was looked at like I was one of them. And I know—I want to cry.

But I know that I'm like the same—the same Xiomara that they're used to—but I care a lot about what my family thinks about me, and I just feel like I let them down so much by getting pregnant, and I just ruined their whole perception of me. I want to get that back. I want them to look at me the same way.

. . . Yeah, I feel like at my college graduation is when they're going to say, "She really did it. She really didn't let this hold her back."

I spent the next few minutes encouraging Xiomara and telling her what a great job she was already going. I really wanted her to know her worth and that she didn't need to wait on the validation from other. She must know her own self-worth.

Quincy—An 18-Year-Old Freshman in College

Quincy and I met in a cubicle at the local branch library to conduct our interview. I began this interview as I had all the others by asking Quincy to rate her elementary school experience on a scale of 1 to 5, with 1 being Bad and 5 being Excellent. Quincy rated her elementary school a 4. She said school was wonderful but there were some things outside of school that were problematic. Quincy explained that her mother was an alcoholic and drug addict:

Problems in my home, like with my mother, and—because my mother—not to get personal, but it bothered me, so I'd rather just get it out. My mother was actually on drugs. She did crack cocaine, she smoked marijuana, and she was an alcoholic. So that had an impact on me, but going to school was a motivation for me—for me just to get out of the house.

I was never abused physically, but of course, there's some mental abuse, so me just getting out the house, going to school, and being able to see my friends, staying in after-school programs was a way for me to get away. And she didn't do those drugs every day.

She drunk more than she did any of the crack or whatever, but it was, I would say, once a week she would probably do crack. So she'd wake me up in the middle of the night, and she was very, very—like, how would I say—petrified, because she would always say, "Well, somebody's after me Quincy, somebody's after me. Get up, let's go, let's got." Waking me up in the middle of the night on the days that I would have school, so that was an issue for me.

Quincy remembers this kind of behavior from her mother happening from when she was about 4 years old until she was 12 and in the sixth grade when she moved out and in with her grandmother. So for Quincy, school was a safe place and in elementary school she was involved in the Beta Club and other advanced programs.

On a scale of 1 to 5, 1 being the Bad and 5 being Excellent, Quincy rated her middle school experience as a 5: Excellent. Quincy explained that she played basketball and was captain of the team her seventh and eighth grade years. Quincy also started dating in eighth grade and had a boyfriend. Our conversation then turned to high school and Quincy rated it a 3. She said she still played basketball but she got pregnant the summer going into her tenth grade year. She was 15 years old. Quincy says that having her child made her want to be successful: "It made me want to be successful because now, it wasn't just me living my life for me. It was me living my life for me and my child."

And, that's what Quincy did: After having a child at age 15, she stayed in school and graduated. She was on homebound for over two months having her son, but she stayed up to date on all assignments. Quincy says,

> I made sure I came to school and got all my assignments, I took all my tests, and things like that because I didn't want to fall behind in school.
>
> I refused to take all that time out to fall behind, and then when you get in school, you've got to be like—you tell the teachers, "Well, how was I supposed to—they call this work up, and you all did this months ago, or weeks ago, and I'm just now trying—" no, I did not want to do that. I just wanted to get my stuff done.

Quincy says she believes she was able to graduate from high school mainly because of her grandmother who was there for her and who pushed her. Quincy says if she was giving out an award, it would be to her grandmother:

> I wanted—if I was handing out awards, I would give the all-star award to my grandmother. I really would. She's been there for me no matter how upset she's been when she first found out I was pregnant until today, me sitting in this seat. She's provided everything for me. If I needed it, it was there. If my child needed it, it was there.
>
> . . . . Exactly. And she pushed me. She was the reason why I never gave up. She always tell me, "You give up, then you getting out my house."
>
> So, I didn't want to go back home. Of course, there's no way in the world I wanted to go back home, so in order for me to keep going, it was all her.

"Don't come in my house with any Fs, don't come in my house with any Ds. If the class is too hard, you can C your way out, but you're not going to D and F your way out."

So that was always her motto, and even for her—she even went back to school because I was in school. She told me that if she can go back to school and pass some classes, I can stay in school and pass my classes. So she went back to school to take the algebra class, just so that I—she can be supportive of me, and, you know, her point was, "If I can do it, you can do it."

And for Quincy, being a high school graduate, after becoming a teen mother at such a young age means so much because as she said, she had so many people telling her she'd never graduate:

I feel successful, I feel great. I feel like I did something that a lot of parents don't do, and it makes me feel good. And it makes you look good. It makes you look wonderful because people get so excited when you tell them that you graduated from high school as a teenage parent. So it makes you feel good. It—I mean, it's speechless. Like, I can barely get it out of how wonderful I feel just because I graduated.

Oh man. I feel I got—I mean, it means—I don't know, because I feel like I just accomplished something, and the thing is, you have people that tell you, "You'll never do it. You'll never do it." And now I'm looking back at them like, "Ha. I told you so." So, I mean, it makes you feel good. And it means a lot to me.

In summary, this narrative described the educational experiences of four young women who began pregnant while still in high school. Each was able to persevere through her struggles and with the help of home, school, and community supports and resources was able to graduate from high school and go to college. At the time of our interview, some had graduated from college.

What Needs to Happen with Education Policy, Curriculum, and Pedagogy?

Clearly, the first step that needs to happen is that the educational system needs to be held accountable—something that has yet to be done in spite of Title IX. Title IX lays accountability for equitable education for teen mothers with public schools but 40 years after the passage of Title IX, the educational system has not been accountable to and for the education of teen mothers. *Education Week* noted such in a June 2012 article titled, "Title IX Promise Unmet for Pregnant Students."[33] Pillow argues that "a severe lack of data and research tracking the education and educational experiences of the pregnant and mothering students has allowed arena of education to remain uninvolved and unchallenged in the provision of education to pregnant and mothering students."[34] Laura's experience of not being ranked and possibly not being part of the top 10 because of her teen pregnancy is but one example of how schools must be held accountable for their treatment of teen mothers.

Second, the curriculum needs to be inclusive of the needs of pregnant and parenting students, black teen mothers in particular. Topics and course offerings should include racism and sexism, sexual politics of black women and teen pregnancy, and cultural/gender/racial attitudes about teen pregnancy. All the young women interviewed would have benefited from courses mentioned about. From the interviews, it was evident that all the young black mothers experienced racism and sexism and many were not aware of what they were fighting against. Courses such as those mentioned earlier would have empowered them.

Finally, black teen mothers need a gender- and cultural-specific pedagogy. Evans-Winters in *Teaching Black Girls* writes that a gender- and cultural-specific pedagogy

> requires that the teacher be totally committed to the eradication of sexism and racism in all of its forms. The assignments and discussions serve to inform and demonstrate to the students and others in the school building that the teacher's classroom is a safe space for such a discussion. However, the teacher should not just talk about it; she also must be "about it." She should be constantly challenging and deconstructing traditional gender roles and sexist practices. Simultaneously, she is responsible for interweaving discussions about gender and cultural inequality into lessons on a daily basis. The teacher must be comfortable with accepting gender- and cultural-specific pedagogy a political project.[35]

The black teen mothers interviewed here would likely have greatly benefited from an opportunity to discuss some of the aforementioned topics with another black female. Unfortunately, such opportunities are all too rare in the current educational system. We must do a better job to reach out in meaningful ways to black teen mothers.

No longer can we sit by and allow the educational system to remain silent or turn a blind eye to the educational needs of black teen mothers. It is imperative that we push for educational policy that holds schools accountable. We must mandate a more inclusive curriculum and more gender- and cultural- specific pedagogy for our girls.

Notes

1. Quoted in Harris-Perry 2011, p. 57.
2. Ibid., pp. 55–56.
3. Terrell 1995, p. 65.
4. Ibid.
5. Moynihan 2014.
6. Ibid.
7. Weathers 1995, p. 158.
8. Collins 1989, pp. 745–772.
9. Ibid.
10. Harris-Perry 2011, p. 39.
11. Ibid., p. 28.
12. Ibid., p. 29.
13. Collins 1989. p. 751.
14. Pillow 2006, pp. 59–84.
15. Ibid.
16. Ibid., p. 60.
17. Ibid.
18. Ibid.
19. Shah 2012.
20. Ibid.
21. Pillow 2006, pp. 59–84.
22. U.S. Department of Education.
23. SmithBattle 2007.
24. Zachry 2005, pp. 2566–2598.
25. SmithBattle 2007.
26. Ibid., p. 361.
27. Ibid., p. 354.
28. Ibid., p. 363.
29. Zachry 2005.
30. Ibid., p. 2594.
31. Evans-Winters 2011, p. 20.
32. Ibid., p. 13.
33. Shah 2012.
34. Pillow 2006.
35. Evans-Winters 2011, p. 156.

Bibliography

Collins, Patricia Hill. 1989. "The Social Construction of Black Feminist Thought." *Signs: Journal of Women in Culture and Society* 14 (4): 745–772.

Evans-Winters, Venus E. 2011. *Teaching Black Girls: Resiliency in Urban Classrooms.* New York: Peter Lang.

Harris-Perry, Melissa. 2011. *Sister Citizen: Shame, Stereotypes and Black Women in America*. New Haven: Yale University Press.

Moynihan, Daniel Patrick. "The Negro Family: The Case for National Action of Policy Planning and Research United States Department of Labor March 1965." Accessed October 1, 2014. http://web.stanford.edu/~mrosenfe/Moynihan's%20The%20Negro%20Family.pdf.

Pillow, Wanda S. 2004. *Unfit Subjects: Unfit subjects: Educational policy and the Teen Mother*. New York: RoutledgeFalmer.

Pillow, Wanda S. 2006. "Teen Pregnancy and Education: Politics of Knowledge, Research and Practice." *Educational Policy* 20 (1): 59–84. doi:10.1177/089590 4805285289.

Shah, Nirvi. 2012. "Title IX Promise Unmet for Pregnant Students." *Education Week* (June). http://www.edweek.org/ew/articles/2012/06/13/35titleixsocial .h31.html.

SmithBattle, Lee. 2007. "I Wanna Have a Good Future: Teen Mothers' Rise in Educational Aspirations, Competing Demands, and Limited School Support." *Youth and Society* 38 (3): 348–371. doi:10.1177/0044118X06287962.

Terrell, M. C. 1898. "The Progress of Colored Women." In *Words of Fire: An Anthology of African American Feminist Thought 1995*, ed. B. Guy-Sheftall (pp. 64–68). New York: The New Press.

U. S. Department of Education, Office for Civil Rights, "Dear Colleague Letter: Supporting the Academic Success of Pregnant and Parenting Students," Accessed October 1, 2014. http://www2.ed.gov/about/offices/list/ocr/letters/colleague-201306-title-ix.pdf.

Weathers, M. A. 1970. "An Argument for Black Women's Liberation as a Revolutionary Force." In *Words of Fire: An Anthology of African American Feminist Thought 1995*, ed. B. Guy-Sheftall (pp. 158–161). New York: New Press.

Zachry, Elizabeth M. 2005. "Getting My Education: Teen Mothers' Experiences in School before and after Motherhood." *Teachers College Record* 107 (12): 2566–2598.

Part II

Answers Inside the Arts and the Extracurriculum

Chapter 4

Confronting Social Justice Issues through the Lens of Arts Integration

M. Francine Jennings

The purpose of this chapter is to address K-12 arts integration strategies that might be employed to address social justice issues related to discrediting the exacerbation of racial inequality. Although arts integration and social justice will reside as the topical centerpieces of this document, the chapter's ancillary ideas will include discourse around (1) teacher resistance to exploring matters of race and (2) the natural alignment of teaching arts-based social justice lessons with Common Core Standards, academic achievement, and the development of 21st-century skills.

Prior to addressing practical arts integration strategies for consideration, theoretical frameworks and definitions for both arts integration and social justice will be addressed, followed by exemplars of specific ways the arts might confront issues associated with racial disparity, racial identity, and racial discrimination across grade levels. In tandem with this discussion, possible and probable reactions, negative and positive, will be presented via anecdotal and narrative examples. Throughout this discussion, there will be an examination of (1) educators' attitudes related to teaching matters of race, class, and culture and (2) the relevance and appropriateness of relating arts integration and social justice to Common Core Standards, academic achievement, and 21st-century skills. In conclusion, the reader is expected to take away the following ideas: (1) Social justice pertaining to racial issues can be purposefully and successfully addressed using arts integration strategies; (2) teacher attitudes are important indicators in addressing social justice; and (3) the use of arts integration to address social justice issues has relevance to Common Core Standards, academic achievement, and preparation for 21st-century skills, thus leveling the playing field for all learners.

Who I Am and What I Do

Over the past 10 years, I have functioned in the capacity of National Faculty at Lesley University, a private university in Cambridge, Massachusetts. This position has afforded me the distinct pleasure of being assigned to teach courses across the United States for the division of Creative Arts in Learning as a part of Lesley's Graduate School of Education. As a professor of arts integration, I teach practicing K-12 educators to incorporate a variety of arts disciplines into core curriculum areas. While the focus of this unique program resides in integrating the arts, a number of required ancillary themes emerge within the scope of each course, including (1) culturally responsive teaching, (2) critical pedagogy/social justice teaching, (3) common core connections, (4) technology-based teaching, and (5) cross-curricular teaching. The sole program of its kind in the United States, the Lesley program embraces a cohort configuration which allows students to begin and end as a supportive learning community. The 22-month program enables students to complete a master's degree in curriculum and instruction, with an emphasis on arts integration.

The majority of Lesley's cohorts are located in Southern, Midwestern, Northeastern, and Western states where students' ages range from 25 to 55, with an average age of about 32. Mirroring current national teacher demographics, students tend to be white, middle class, and female.

As a female professor of color from the South, undoubtedly, my teaching assignments have been and continue to be nothing less than interesting and gratifying, offering opportunities for meeting new people, exploring new geographical territories, and expanding my teaching into new dimensions. In particular, however, because of my charge to undergird my teaching in matters of social justice and culturally responsive teaching, I have come to view arts integration as a valuable, nonthreatening tool to discuss, confront, and investigate matters of race, culture, and class.

The Landscape of Arts Integration

First Encounters

It was at a time when we were still able to say Christmas rather than Winter Holiday. Excitement and anticipation permeated the air at this semi-suburban middle school in southeastern Virginia. I had been charged with teaching English and language arts skills to 20 nonnative speakers from more than 10 different countries. Since this would be the last class for the day, students enthusiastically anticipated my arrival, and furthermore, they knew we were going to have fun while we were learning. My idea of having fun always seemed to manifest itself through the use of music, movement, drama, poetry, and storytelling. I wasn't sure why, but these were modalities that naturally poured out of me. On this unusually cold, snowy day, I planned to teach the kids new vocabulary by having them to perform holiday songs through lip syncing. After showing the class a humorous lip sync presentation and explaining expectations of the activity, copiously and carefully, I reviewed a word wall of phrases and expressions they would need. Following that, I placed students in groups, gave them a written copy of a song to learn, handed them a list of key words from the song with definitions, pulled out picture dictionaries to reinforce the meanings of selected words, and distributed tape recorders. My last step was to dispense tapes of the songs the students would be learning to lip sync. I still recall the feelings of exhilaration as I floated around the tables while students made one discovery after another through reading, moving, singing, observing, researching, talking, and listening. Alas, it was time for the final lip sync performances, and I could tell that these students had truly captured the meanings of their words! Once class was over, this cute little boy from Ecuador shouted, "Miss Teacher, I learn so many words today. This is the great thing we do. It's so fun!" I had no idea that I was using a strategy called arts integration. I had used the art forms of music, drama, and movement to teach vocabulary to my English as a Second Language students.

Definitions and Theoretical Considerations

Arts integration, sometimes referred to as arts in learning,[1] arts infusion,[2] and learning through the arts,[3] at its very core, invites students, educators, artists, parents, and the greater community into an innovative learning space that fosters individuality, mutual respect, and often spirituality. As I have continually immersed myself into the rudimentary essentials of this work, I have constructed a personal definition which I tend to convey to educational professionals as well as laypeople who I find to be extremely curious about what I do. That said, my interpretation of arts integration can be articulated as a process or method that pairs selected arts modalities with content for the sake of deepening, enhancing, and enriching curricular and artistic concepts. I prefer to dub this as my base definition, since more often than not, questions relative to how arts integration is done, what it looks like, and how it benefits the learner are generally not far behind. In order to satisfy these curiosities, I usually extend my base definition through adding that the arts integration process begets opportunities for collaboration, exploration, observation, inquiry, practice, and reflection to work together.

In comparing my "base" definition of arts integration to those submitted by some of the forerunners in the field, the similarities are startling. Pascale and Donovan, practicing professors of arts integration at Lesley University, assert, "Arts integration is the investigation of curricular content through artistic explorations. In this process, the arts provide an avenue for rigorous investigation, representation, expression and reflection of both curricular content and the art form itself."[4] These authors envision arts integration as an investigative process, as well as a vehicle providing linkages to curricular content. The second part of the definition delineates functional components and benefits of arts integration. Changing Education through the Arts (CETA), the educational arm of the Washington, D.C.–based Kennedy Center, focuses on training teachers to incorporate the arts into the core curriculum. CETA's definition is expressed as follows: "Arts integration is an approach to teaching in which students construct and demonstrate understanding through an art form. Students engage in a creative process which connects an art form and another subject and meets evolving objectives."[5] The definition implies that students will be building knowledge and showing what they know through an arts modality. Authors of the definition have left the term "creative process" open-ended, thereby offering it as an object for discovery. Merryl Goldberg, professor of visual and performing arts at California State University, San Marcos, portrays arts integration as "a method that encourages students to grapple with and express their understandings of subject matter through an art form."[6] Goldberg further contends that arts integration can be manifested in three distinct ways: (1) learning with the arts which enables one to learn subject matter with the aid of an art form (i.e., learning about slavery through songs from the Underground Railroad); (2) learning through the arts which allows one to express understanding through an art form (i.e., students dramatize dangers associated with the Underground Railroad; and (3) learning about the arts which often comes as a result of learning with and through the arts (i.e., as a result of dramatizing the Underground Railroad experience, students may become more interested in learning more about the art form of drama).[7]

In considering arts integration theoretically, John Dewey, father of the experiential education movement, emerged as one the most notable predecessors of arts integration.[8] His progressive education theory stressed that education should be deliberately active and should provide real-life experiences as a hallmark for learning;[9] moreover, Dewey recognized and embraced the idea that art occupies an inescapable space in deepening our instruction and ultimately our personal lives. In *Art as Experience*, he explains that "the work of art operates to deepen and raise great clarity."[10] The beauty in Dewey's thinking extends not only from his views on the way learning is constructed but from his ground-breaking views about the arts, for in his eyes, the individual brings experience to art while art brings experience to the individual.[11] Such views are indisputably in line with principles of arts integration signifying that this discipline should not only be experiential but also serve to add depth to instruction.[12]

The constructivist theoretical framework examines how cognitive structures add insight to meaning and organization through learning experiences.[13] Similar to the pronouncements of Dewey, constructivist theory embraces the idea that learning must be grounded in an experiential, activity-based environment. In addition, constructivism highlights a crucial element of arts integration in advocating that students should have the opportunity to construct their own learning, thereby allowing cognitive development to become more transformative.[14] As a consequence of this series of actions, students have greater opportunities to make personal connections to obtained knowledge.[15]

Gardner's theory of multiple intelligences defines the word "intelligence" as "the capacity to solve a problem or fashion a product valued within one or more cultural settings."[16] Put simply, the theory implies that intelligence is an ability to solve a problem or create something in a naturalistic setting. Practically, if I need to solve the problem of giving someone directions, I would be able to do it within a given context and setting. Gardner elucidates the idea that educators have gravitated toward narrowly assessing student knowledge through the overutilization of verbal and mathematical means; however, Gardner's beliefs have ignited the idea that everyone has the capacity to demonstrate what he or she knows through eight distinct modalities. These modalities are specified as follows:

(1) verbal-linguistic—demonstrating knowledge through means associated with words and phrases;
(2) logical-mathematical—demonstrating knowledge through means associated with numbers, patterns;
(3) visual-spatial—demonstrating knowledge through visual or spatial means;

(4) bodily kinesthetic—demonstrating knowledge through bodily or tactile means;

(5) interpersonal—demonstrating knowledge through activities that promote work with others;

(6) intrapersonal—demonstrating knowledge through activities that promote self-awareness;

(7) musical-rhythmic—demonstrating knowledge through musical or rhythmic means; and

(8) naturalist—demonstrating knowledge through activities associated with nature or the environment.[17]

The multiple intelligences operate as a logical intersection with arts integration given that the vast majority of arts experiences converge with several of the designated intelligence modalities. For example, if a student is asked to work within a small group to learn syllables through creative movement, he or she would be demonstrating knowledge through the kinesthetic intelligence while using the body, the interpersonal intelligence while working with others, the intrapersonal intelligence while making decisions about his or own movements, the logical intelligence while making tangible connections to the language arts content, and the visual-spatial intelligence while determining his or her position in space. As a consequence, the process provides a practical inroad for learners to express multiple cognitive abilities, ultimately increasing opportunities for success.[18]

In summary, it is safe to say that those who practice in the field of arts integration share the following beliefs:

- Arts integration fosters experiential learning.
- Arts integration engages critical thinking, problem solving, and decision making.
- Arts integration encourages collaborative learning structures.
- Arts integration promotes inquiry, discovery, and student-centered learning.
- Arts integration requires that objectives are met in the content area and in the art forms.[19]

Critical Pedagogy as Social Justice Teaching

A Practical Look

The arts integration program at Lesley University boasts several themes that run across each course, one of which is critical pedagogy. When I was first trained in critical pedagogy, I felt a bit intimidated and overwhelmed regarding its intentions, but once I studied and began to analyze its applicability to the world, I began to accept it. To go a step further, I confess that I began to embrace it. I was grateful for my original lack of understanding as this led me to think of how my adult learners may want to steer away from teaching with the lens of critical pedagogy. After all, critical pedagogy, in practice, demands that we do something to "save the world."[20] I thought to myself, since I'd found myself struggling with such a burden, surely my students would struggle as well, but once I convinced myself that I could successfully sell my students on the idea of critical pedagogy as a viable approach to teaching, I decided to focus on how I might best present the concept in a nonthreatening manner. Then, the light bulb came on! Why not use an arts integration strategy? This *was* my area of expertise, so why not implement it? I, therefore, took a position of inquiry-based learning, starting with an activity that would enable students to discover aspects of the term and its coexistence with social justice. I began by having a student to sit on an imaginary wall. My students and I recited the Humpty Dumpty nursery rhyme, but when we came to the part where Humpty fell, the student was instructed to fall and remain in the fallen position throughout the discussion. I then posed the question: What issues could have possibly contributed to Humpty Dumpty falling off the wall? As with most activities contextualized in this structure, there was no way to foresee subsequent responses, but I was thrilled by the quality of problem-posing submitted by my students. Maybe the wall wasn't constructed for people who were shaped like Humpty. Maybe Humpty had a problem with his balance? Maybe Humpty's parents weren't available for guidance. Maybe Humpty had cried for help, and no one heard him? Maybe Humpty's parents couldn't afford to send him to a place that accommodated him? In observing the problems that students posed, I recognized that inherent in each was an issue of disenfranchisement pertaining to Humpty. For example, if the wall was constructed only for people of a particular shape, this would become a handicapping condition for Humpty. If Humpty's parents couldn't afford to send him to another "wall," his socioeconomic condition would limit his options. After a rather lengthy discussion, I then asked: What could we possibly do to improve Humpty's situation based on each problem you posed? Again, the responses were outstanding but at that moment, I heard several students passionately admit that they hated seeing our student continually lying on the floor and wanted to help her to get up. Bingo! The big idea that critical pedagogy requires us to look at problems and take action for the sake of the disenfranchised had taken hold. It became clear that I could now introduce a more academic-friendly definition of critical pedagogy. From there, I summoned students to construct a definition of critical pedagogy based on the problem-posing activity. They knew that *pedagogy* had to do with the way we teach, and *critical* may have something to do with critical theory, which encompasses analyzing, critiquing, and submitting ideas for changing society. One brave soul finally blurted out, "I've got it. It's like teaching so that we bring up problems in society to see how we can do something about them! We just did that with Humpty Dumpty!" Other students agreed and chimed in with more information. I expressed my excitement with their thinking and offered to go a step further by introducing some of the ideas of Paulo Freire, the father of critical pedagogy.

Freire sets up a framework for teaching social justice in schools by advocating teaching that would promote the demise of oppressive behaviors toward the disenfranchised.[21] Freire persisted in the belief that issues of oppression should be addressed within a classroom context so that students could confront and challenge the realities of an inequitable society. Although critical pedagogy's definition is not static, Freire's ideas, often hailed as too political for classroom instruction,[22] encompasses teaching expectations that foster the expansion of social justice thinking and action. These expectations, several of which intersect directly with tenets of arts integration teaching, include the following:

(1) Raise consciousness of a possible social condition through problem-posing. (Have you ever thought about why Humpty might have fallen off the wall? What problems may have contributed to Humpty falling off the wall?)

(2) Ground new knowledge in the experiences of students and teachers alike. This is produced through meaningful dialogue. (Have you ever fallen down or failed at something? What happened? Why did this happen? How did you feel?)

(3) Approach learning as an active process allowing everyone an opportunity to speak and give examples (having someone to act in the role of Humpty and allowing others to react).

(4) Set up opportunities for students to engage in social action. (Can we come up with specific ways to address Humpty's fall? Can we think of a group of people who may have fallen "off the wall" and suggest ways to assist them?)

(5) Empower learners to critique and challenge oppressive social conditions and to envision and work toward a more just society. (Why didn't the builders of the wall think about individuals shaped like Humpty Dumpty?)

(6) Rally around one or more disenfranchised groups identified via race, class, gender, and so on. (In Humpty's case, the disenfranchised group would be individuals shaped a particular way.)

Onward to Social Justice

Nieto and Bode's (2008) definition of social justice affirms it as a "philosophy, approach, actions that embody treating all people with fairness, respect, dignity, and generosity,"[23] which mirrors Freire's ideas and thoughts exactly; therefore, teaching for social justice is critical pedagogy and critical pedagogy becomes teaching to promote social justice. In elaborating on their definition, Nieto and Bode proclaim that social justice teaching "challenges, confronts and disrupts misconceptions, untruths, and stereotypes that lead to structural inequality and discrimination based on race, social class, gender, and other social and human conditions."[24] Indeed, this sounds like an overwhelming responsibility for teachers, but the implication here is twofold: (1) Structural inequalities and discrimination in schools do exist; and (2) if teachers are to be engaged in social justice teaching, they have a charge to deflect these kinds of inequalities. Nieto and Bode further declare that social justice teaching requires the provision of necessary resources to all children, including emotional resources that lead to high expectations, the reinforcement of student strengths, and creation of an environment for social change.[25]

Teacher Reluctance to Confront Social Justice Issues

Wearing the Cloak of Color Blindness

A Color Blind Anthem
I don't see color. We're all the same.
Race doesn't matter. What a lovely refrain.
I don't see color. Such a waste of time!
What's the big deal? As long as I'm kind.
I don't see color. Can that really be true?
If I don't see color, do I really see you?

—M. Francine Jennings

Over the past five years, I have heard an increasing number of my students making references to being color-blind. In fact, statements associated with color blindness, heard only among my white students, occur so often that it sometimes appears as if they have taken an undercover *oath of color blindness* to fend off any and all references to race and, in some cases, culture. My experience has been that once the pronouncement of color blindness goes into effect, I begin to see a brand of passive-aggressive resistance to participating fully in specific kinds of activities. For example, in conjunction with a unit on planets, I asked students to draw an image of a Utopian planet and to describe the people on the planet. As I moved around the room, I noticed that the students of color included all races of people in their descriptions, whereas the white students either reassigned their people to animals or designed their people to be translucent or semitransparent. The avoidance of and resistance to race identification among all the white students were profoundly evident, as if to say, "You can't make us talk about race or color!" Case and Hemmings argue that this kind of resistance is often used as a distancing strategy to avoid topics of race and racism.[26] In keeping with Case and Hemmings's lines of reasoning, Scruggs describes color-blind behaviors as avenues to ignore or overlook racial and ethnic differences for the sake of promoting racial harmony, when, in actuality, we see more of a demotion of racial harmony resulting from these assertions.[27] This brings to mind an encounter I had with a middle-aged white student who continually pledged her allegiance of color blindness to the class. She proceeded to say that color and race should never be factored into how a person sees a child. Afterward, I asked her to describe me. She described everything about me except my skin color and my race. I proceeded to tell her she had done a wonderful job of describing me but had left out a couple of critical points. She responded that nothing else was really important to the description. She didn't know it, but she had brought forth a striking revelation—the revelation that she was making the omnipotent decision of what was important in my description. It never occurred to her that, maybe, just perhaps, I should have a voice in what was important to my description and that her ultimate determination not to describe my skin color or to include my race was an overt determination not to see me. Once I explained how overlooking my skin color and race was in essence denying part of my identity and culture, I noticed a major transformation in her facial expressions. I could also tell that she had become deeply affected because she began to weep. This very well-intentioned student was grounded in the idea that it was much safer not to acknowledge differences and "assumed that the mere perception of difference is a problem."[28] More important, however, here was one more teacher who was awakened to the potential damage that could be inflicted on the identities of her students in the wake of previous ill-conceived notions. If, as Scruggs suggests, the trend among white teachers to distance themselves from conversations about race continues to persist, authentic opportunities for social justice teaching will be continually negated.

Accessorized under the Umbrella of Kindness

Teacher Quote #1

I saw this big, dark-skinned 4th grader coming down the hall wearing a hat and listening to something through his headphones. I knew this was going against school policy, but what if he thought I was picking on him. So, I just smiled at him, hoping he would think I was a nice person.

Teacher Quote #2

My black students have wonderful ideas when they write. I realize that I'm supposed to be helping them to write correctly, but feel like I might be insulting them if I make too many corrections. It's much better to be kind than to be too critical.

As a single mother who worked two jobs while attending graduate school, like many other parents, I wanted the assurance that my child would be entrusted to teachers who were knowledgeable, kind, and fair. Having teachers with these attributes, coupled with my child's brains and talents, served to enhance my belief that successful experiences would follow. Then, something happened. One day, my daughter, a gifted high school musician and performing artist, approached me with a very perplexed look on her face. She mentioned that her drama teacher told her something that she didn't understand. Upon hearing the confusion in her voice, I asked her to tell me about the situation. Her response shocked me. "My teacher told me that since I was so talented in the arts, I don't really need to go to college." I asked my daughter if she was sure about the statement, and she was. In our home, college was an expectation, so the statement gave my daughter a disappointing jolt to anticipations she held for her future hopes and desires. Upon assuring my daughter that there would be no changes to her original college plans, I promptly made an appointment to speak with her drama teacher. I had experienced very pleasant encounters with her in the past and didn't expect this one to be any different. After a period of light conversation, I ventured into my reason for our meeting. "Why did you tell my daughter she didn't need to go to college?" I had asked the question before I knew it. She explained to me that many of her African American students, like my daughter, already possess the natural skills to make it in the industry. She also mentioned that my daughter had the fortitude and determination to be successful without college. Finally, she stated that she felt like she was being kind by relieving us of the burden of thinking about college. Furious, I explained to her that my family didn't need her brand of kindness. In an afterthought, I began to ponder a long list of the "what if's, the main one being" what if I had allowed this teacher's act of kindness to propel my daughter's future into another direction?

The scenario invites discussion of assumed innocent acts of kindness and "good intentions" by well-intentioned teachers who lack cultural sensitivity. Very similar to my daughter's drama teacher, white preservice teachers in Marx and Pennington's study demonstrated a pervasive attitude that the students they were teaching needed their help and guidance based on deficiencies and deficits that existed in their lives.[29] My daughter's teacher, as well as the preservice teachers in the study, honestly felt that being kind and nice were sufficient qualities to teach all children; however, Picower points out that the embodiment of being nice acts as yet another tool to divert and escape the need for preparation to become effective while teaching in diverse environments. Picower goes a step further in revealing that the tool of "just be nice" functioned to "maintain white innocence while keeping the focus of urban educational failure on students rather than on their own willful lack of preparation to teach in communities unfamiliar to them."[30] That being said, in looking back at the two teacher quotes I used to open this section, in both instances, students were placed in positions which could result in eventual failure. For example, in teacher quote #1, if the fourth grade boy happened to receive a suspension later that day, the teacher who wanted to "be nice" can absolve herself or himself of all responsibility. In like manner, in teacher quote # 2, if the student happened not to fare well on her writing test, the teacher can convince herself or himself that everything possible had been done to help the student. Finally, if my daughter had not gone to college and subsequently dropped out of life, her drama teacher could have blamed my daughter for not applying herself.

I have highlighted only two major factors contributing to teachers' reluctance when it comes to confronting social justice issues. For certain, there are dozens more, but if our current generation of diverse students is to take its respective place in society as marketable citizens, the work of social justice teaching must be not only encouraged but also required. The following poem summarizes why we must continue to move forward in the social justice initiative.

Stalemate
So what do we do with these harsh realities?
So many fear to face blunt actualities,
Hidden shame and guilt and blame
Will only produce more of the same
Safe ways of teaching . . .
Nothing far-reaching . . .
Week after week
Turning the other cheek
Then nobody knows . . .
And nobody grows . . .
                    —M. Francine Jennings

Social Justice in Action: Arts Integrated Lessons

Although, I have infused arts integration pieces throughout this discussion, this section offers more detailed insights into the dramatic dynamics of using arts integration as a tool to address matters of social justice. For each of the two activities that follow, I have included common core objectives, artistic objectives, social justice objectives, and 21st-century skills employed. The decision to include 21st-century skills was twofold: First, it is no longer a matter of choice for students to be taught the necessary skills to function in an increasingly globalized society and economy. Tony Wagner listed seven survival skills for the 21st century, which included (1) critical thinking and problem solving, (2) collaboration across networks and leading by influence, (3) adaptability and agility, (4) initiative and entrepreneurialism, (5) effective oral and written communication, (6) accessing and analyzing information, and (7) imagination and curiosity.[31] In addition, the Partnership for 21st Century Skills, in describing the skills and expertise needed to be successful in today's economy, placed an emphasis on the 4 Cs which stand for creativity, collaboration, communication, and critical thinking.[32] Second, I wanted to demonstrate how arts integration activities are seamlessly interwoven into 21st-century skills. In presenting my each arts integration lesson, I have also included a description of each activity, a script of dialogues, and my reaction to the power of the activity as a mechanism to address social justice.

Lesson I.
Title: A Night in the Park—Music, Visual Arts, Drama, and Creative Writing

Cognitive Common Core Objectives—English and Language Arts—(Grade 6)

Presenting claims and findings, sequencing ideas logically and using pertinent descriptions, facts, and details to accentuate main ideas or themes; using appropriate eye contact, adequate volume, and clear pronunciation.[33]

Artistic Objectives—(Grade 6)

Music (Grade 6)—Analyzing the uses of elements of music in aural examples representing diverse genres and cultures.[34]

Visual Arts (Grade 6)—Choosing and evaluating a range of subject matter, symbols, and ideas.[35]

Drama (Grade 6)—Acting by developing basic acting skills to portray characters who interact in improvised and scripted scenes.[36]

Social Justice Objective—Examining issues of race, culture, identity, and socioeconomic class.[37]

21st-Century Skills Addressed—Creativity, Critical Thinking, Communication, Collaboration.[38]

A Night in the Park is an arts integrated activity I conceived originally for sixth grade African American middle school students enrolled in a program called Project Nobility. Under the auspices of Atlanta Public Schools' Century 21 initiative and Spelman College's Continuing Education department, Project Nobility's focus was to employ the use of fine and performing arts to reinforce language arts, social studies, math, and science skills. A few months after introducing the lesson to the middle school students, I incorporated the identical lesson into one of my classes at Lesley University. I was curious about comparing the responses of sixth-grade African American students from urban Atlanta with those of middle class white teachers from the Midwest. A description of the activity and subsequent response comparisons follow:

Activity Description

(1) I placed students into groups of four or five students and assigned each group a number.

(2) I asked students to close their eyes to visualize themselves walking around in a large park on a hot summer night. I had them to imagine that in the well-lit park, some park visitors were listening to music through their headphones while others were playing music through speakers for everyone to hear, and as a consequence, they would be exposed to many kinds of music.

(3) I told students that I would be playing 60 seconds of five musical pieces of diverse genres and would be assigning each group to one musical piece. I, then, gave each group a set of directions to be followed after I played their designated music. The directions were to (a) decide on the race, gender, age, socioeconomic background, and occupation of the person that might be listening to the music, (b) draw a picture of the person and give the person a name, (c) write a creative narrative about the person in the park, and (d) prepare a short skit to accompany the narrative.

(4) I then played 60 seconds of various genres of music. I played classical music for group 1, blues for group 2, house music for group 3, rock music for group 4, and Native American flute music for group 5.

(5) I allowed each group 15–20 minutes to complete the entire assignment offering them an additional 3 minutes to present their pieces.

In both groups, members worked meticulously to ensure that all aspects of the assignment were covered, leaving no dearth of collaboration or cooperation. As I gravitated from one group to another, I sensed a refreshing sense of intragroup community, as well as a spirited eagerness to share final products. As each presentation came to a close, students were exceptionally forthcoming as they offered comments, compliments, and inquiries relative to the presenting group's choices. In like manner, the presenting groups displayed an aura of pride, dignity, and accomplishment. Indeed, I was no less than ecstatic about what we had accomplished thus far, but now it was time to move beyond the surface of the experience and yield to the underlying truths. The time had arrived to observe how the arts had served as a catalyst to engage in "reflection about what they learned, how they learned it, and what it means to them."[39] With that in mind, I posed the following question: You came up with a tremendous amount of information about your fictional character, based on a mere 60 seconds of music, can you believe that? Now, I am curious about how you came up with your end products and what you got out of this. Here are the middle school students' group 1 narrative and dialogues.

Narrative

Her name is Mrs. Annie Norrell. She has mixed gray hair and is almost 60 years old. She is a little bit fat. She has a big house with two dogs and five cats. She is sitting in the park fanning because it is hot, but she is swaying from side to side listening to her opera. It is loud and she is singing with the music. She has traveled around the world.

Student 1: Well, my grandmama plays classical piano and she got a nice house. That's how we started out.

Student 2: Yeah, and I got a auntie that sings that opera stuff and she says (pointing to student 3) she went to the opera with her class and saw this black lady singing the same song you played. I told my counselor that my auntie could sing opera, but she didn't believe me.

Teacher: Hmmm. . . . So far, three of you know African Americans that sing opera.

Student 3: Yeah, so if they sing it, they have to listen to it.

Student 4: I never seen no black people sing that kinda music, but, I know a black guy who came to my school and he was playing it on the piano.

Student 1: So, we wanted to represent! We could a just drew a white dude, but they always getting' props.

Teacher: So, are you saying that white people get more credit for performing classical music than black people?

Student 2: Yeah, they get more credit for everything! This was cool because we can let people know what our people can do. Sometimes, our teachers think all we can do is rap.

Teacher: Oh, I see. I get the feeling that you felt pretty good about this activity. Well, who did the drawing?

Student 2: I did the drawing. . . I wanted make her look like she had done something for herself. She (pointing to student 3) made up the narrative cause she can write good and talk

	good, and he say he wanted to act like the lady. We had fun . . . can we do this again?
Teacher:	Maybe! So, what did you learn?
Student 1:	We want people to learn more about us!
Student 2:	Black people got a lot of talent . . . and all us can work together.
Student 3:	We can draw and act out our feelings.
Teacher:	You guys did an incredible job!
All:	Thank you!!!

The middle school students referenced in the preceding dialogue welcomed the opportunity to showcase the fact that African Americans not only listen to classical music but are also performers in the genre. When placed in perspective, I saw the activity as a vehicle for the students to shamelessly release feelings that they might have otherwise internalized. "We coulda just drew a white dude, but they always getting props" was probably one of the most salient statements in the script. I interpreted this to mean that these students were keenly sensitive to society's propensity to deny certain extensions of identity where African Americans and other people of color are concerned. This interpretation quickly reminded me of the hidden curriculum which Giroux and Penna define as the "unstated norms, values and beliefs that are transmitted to students through the underlying structure and meaning in the social relations of the school and classroom life."[40] Moreover, the statement that "white people get credit for everything" came across as a pronouncement of outrage and disappointment about the oppressive state of African Americans, yet this moment was quickly upstaged by a gentle message of empowerment and hope: "This was cool because we can let people know what our people can do." These students met common core objectives and arts objectives and played a critical role in assessing their own learning. I surmised that they must have also felt successful, because they asked if they could do the activity again.

In comparison to the urban middle school students who threw caution to the wind, my adult students from the Midwest approached the assignment with significantly more rigidity. Although I assured them that there were no right or wrong methods, answers, or thinking points, several of the teachers continually asked "Is this what you're looking for?" or "do you want it like this?" or "are we doing this right?" I surmised that there may have been at least two reasons for this riveting trepidation. First, in my years of working with teachers, I have discovered that there is usually a glaring need to be in possession of a prototype, exemplar, or template to ensure that they know exactly how to proceed and where they should end up. Unfortunately, for those with a heightened propensity for this kind of order, arts-based explorations can be extremely frustrating. I have also found that many of the teachers want certain kinds of information to be outlined so they can make early decisions about outcomes and can avoid any problems or unwanted conflicts that might arise; however, working with the arts can be much like going on a road trip without a map or GPS; arts-based investigations have the tendency to take the individual into unchartered territories demanding more than a moderate degree of risk-taking, transparency, and spontaneity. Second, I have discovered that an overwhelming number of white teachers embody a genuine fear that they will reveal themselves as racist or biased if their words or actions are misinterpreted.[41] Given that this assignment openly called for opinions pertaining to race, gender, and class, the teachers became a bit anxious. This was in no way surprising; however, I continually wonder how teachers can lead their students through vital dialogues about racism and bias if they miss opportunities to address their own feelings. Landsman notes that white teachers are in need of in-depth inquiry of their own racial and cultural identities, which often generates considerable fear and discomfort, largely derived from fears of their own racism.[42] As a matter of fact, I actually overheard one group in deep conversation about not appearing biased before getting started with the activity. The teachers' classical group created the following narrative and responses:

Narrative

His name is Diamond Valentino, but he prefers to be called Diamond. He has lived on six continents and claims a mixed heritage.

At 65, he is semiretired and occasionally performs with high-profile groups, if called. He has lived well and is still attractive, but now he must watch his weight. Diamond is looking to slow down even more and finds that relaxing in the park helps him to move in that direction.

Student 1: We didn't want to designate a particular race to our person, because we wanted him to be considered exotic.

Teacher: What an interesting twist!

Student 2: Yes, and we figured if he was relaxing in the park, he was probably comfortably retired, maybe around 65, or so.

Student 1: We agreed that a lot of people who listen to classical people are older people and are probably more settled, so that's why we drew a grey-haired male with a rather stout figure.

Teacher: Any particular reason why you made the person male?

Student 2: So many of the prominent opera singers are male and we figured a guy would most likely be listening to the music.

Student 3: We felt it would be safer to make the gentleman mixed race, so we wouldn't have him boxed into being white or black.

Teacher 1: I really like your thinking in solidifying this character, but could you explain exactly what you mean by safe?

Student 4: The way we analyzed the activity, we felt as though you really wanted to see if we would associate a person listening to classical music with being black, Mexican, or white or something like that. We figured it may make us look biased if we said the guy was white, but we've never seen a black or Mexican person listening to classical music.

Teacher: So what I hear you saying is that your fictionalized character's race was assigned based upon suspicions that I might think you were biased if you said what you really felt?

Student 2: Yeah, we don't want you to think we're biased toward our own race.

Teacher: Don't get me wrong, I love your character, but what does that do to the authenticity of your true feelings? Perhaps you *have* been exposed solely to white men who listen to classical music, and it would have been okay to say that.

Student 1: Well, I've been accused of being prejudice and racist, and I didn't want to take the chance. But I see what you mean.

Teacher: We all have prejudices and biases, but it's important to face them and discuss them. Actually this is a great start and I'm happy we talked about this.

Student 3: We really enjoyed the activity. I could easily see my kids loving the creative component just as we did . . . but it made me think about our perceptions of people.

Student 1: We need to loosen up and not be so uptight and worried about what others think. I'm terrible with that.

Teacher: Think about it this way. People generally bring their own experiences to interpretations of their identities and if your kids were to do this activity you would find out quite a bit about them. Super job on your presentation!

Student 2: Now, I'm curious about the interpretations of some of your other groups!

Teacher: I'll be more than happy to share those!

I must say that I was a bit suspicious about this group's authenticity as they breathed artistic life into their classical character. I wondered if there would be a kind of attempt to sidestep the truth in an effort to mask something that might attract shame or embarrassment to their group. The crux of the matter was embedded within the context of a blatant reality: The only person of color in the room happened to be me, the teacher. To that end, how much were they willing to divulge at the risk of getting me upset? And if they were to upset me, how might that affect their grades? As I listened carefully to comments in the script, it was fair to say that my suppositions were confirmed. Their drawings were extraordinary, their descriptive narratives were metaphorically poetic, and their dramas were accurately aligned with the character's formation. The interconnectedness between the art forms was as strong as it was deep, and much to my contentment, the dialogue was motivated by their own insecurities and hesitations. These teachers squirmed, struggled, and fought to unveil individual truths around matters of race and bias. Once again the arts had succeeded in providing an entrance to what could have been a taboo discussion.

Lesson II.
Title: Akeelah and the Bee

Cognitive Common Core ELA Objectives (Ninth grade)
Use precise words and phrases, telling details, and sensory language to convey a vivid picture of the experiences, events, setting, and/ or characters.[43]
Artistic Objectives (Ninth grade)
Theater—Analyzing, critiquing, and constructing meanings from informal and formal theater, film, television, and electronic media productions.[44]
Social Justice Objectives—Analyzing racial and cultural disparities; framing messages of empowerment and hope.[45]
21st-Century Skills—Communication, Critical Thinking, Accessing, and Analyzing.[46]

Back in 2006, I was introduced to a delightful movie entitled *Akeelah and the Bee*. I had heard that it was a *good* movie and that I should probably add it to my list of films to see. The movie unfolds the delightful story of 11-year-old Akeelah, an African American girl, whose gift of spelling propels her into winning the national spelling bee. While watching the movie, I recall how impressed I was with the tasteful treatment of such delicate themes as disparity in school resources, racial identity, student learning styles, and teacher expectations. Upon reviewing the movie at least four more times, I decided to use specific clips from "the bee" as writing prompts for the eighth and ninth graders at an after-school program in northeast Georgia. My contract stipulated that I would use arts integration to enhance student curricular skills in writing and language arts. My students, all Mexican American and African American, were brilliant, inquisitive, and energetic and hated to write, but I remained confident that the incorporation of Akeelah's story would inspire them to be encouraged to write. I also desired to utilize this form of media to "produce a genuine synergy between the content areas"[47] while creating an environment of discovery and inquiry.

Activity Description

(1) After setting the stage for the clip, I instructed students to jot down notes on anything they saw, heard, thought, or felt. I was cautious not to make suggestions; however, I made mention that their comments should revolve directly around matters pertaining to the story.

(2) I asked them to write to complete the following:
In this clip, I learned_____. I also found out_____. The best thing about this clip was_____.

(3) Given these points, I explained that we would begin to write once we had engaged in a discussion of their ideas. The following dialogue exemplifies several of the exchanges.

Narrative

Student 1: That black girl was smart. It made me feel good because people don't think you can be smart if you come from a poor neighborhood. My neighborhood, it's mostly Blacks and Mexicans and people act like we're supposed to be dummies.

Teacher: So, it sounds like you can identify with the main character and you were proud of her.

Student 1: Yeah, and it's not fair that people make up their minds about you because of what race you might be or where you live.

Student 2: and especially the people in this school. It's the teachers mostly that act like you stupid or something.

Teacher: Hmmm . . . so what kinds of things have you experienced?

Student 2: Well, first . . . I like the movie, but it made me kinda mad, because at least they let her give the answers her way, but around here, the teachers don't care . . . they want everybody to answer the same way. Like I can draw stuff and do stuff with music, but don nobody care about that. If I can't answer their way, they think I'm dumb.

Teacher: So right now I've heard several ideas come to focus. The movie clip made you feel proud that Akeelah was successful, but parts of the clip remind you that sometimes there are people who doubt your ability to be successful because of your race and where you live. You also think you should have the opportunity to demonstrate what

	you know in more than one way. I get the sense that you think there's a lot of unfairness.
Student 1:	Right!
Student 3:	Sometimes, it makes you wanna give up, like Akeelah almost did. She had good coach. That's wussup!
Student 4:	Can I read my thing you give us?
Teacher:	Of course, let's hear it?
Student 4:	In this clip, I learned all people can do great things. I also found out I can show the world what I can do if somebody gives me a chance. The best thing about this clip was watching Akeelah win the spelling bee.
Teacher:	Wow, that's amazing. See, you've got a great start to your writing! Akeelah's story has helped us to think about some really important feelings. As we begin to write, some of you may want to develop some of the points you've made. You also may want to think about what we can do to make some changes at your school. I would love to hear some of your suggestions. Maybe we can make things better.

This activity brought forth a generous supply of emotional dialogue. The eighth and ninth graders respectfully and tactfully shared how important it was for people, particularly, their teachers, to value their unique gifts, abilities, and experiences, rather than to make assumptions based on race or socioeconomic background. Unfortunately, deficit theory, the belief that students of color or from low socioeconomic backgrounds can't achieve due to their environments, took center stage as students described its existence in their own voices. Equally important were the students' robust calls for teachers to not only value their abilities but acknowledge their individual strengths, an approach that has proven to foster high levels of academic success among all students. Yvette Jackson acknowledges that in identifying and activating student strengths, we reinforce the idea that success is, indeed, possible. In addition, Jackson contends that activating student strengths has the potential to transform relationships between students and teachers.[48] The young man who read his short cloze piece beamed with pride as he shared his responses. His most telling statement "I can show the world what I can do if someone gives me a chance" brought about internal feelings of ambivalence. On one hand, I was elated to know that he wanted to show the world what he could do, and on the other hand, I cringed at the thought that his success was based on *if* someone gives him a chance. All in all, the experience of watching and reacting to the video clip seemed to empower my students to see themselves in a different light and transfer the richness of their spoken ideas into writing. Then they wrote with conviction, compassion, and truth.

Conclusion

My journey through arts integration has been filled with memorable teaching and learning treasures. It has been a wonderland toppled with fantastical mysteries and magical moments. It has been a memorable voyage reminiscent of deep waters and wide rivers. Indeed, my journey through the arts has taken me to heights, widths, and depths unimaginable. Arts integration is what I do!

I am called to make a difference in the lives of children, youth, and adults, and in so doing, it is my undeniable responsibility and obligation, through my teaching, to ensure that every person I touch feels honored, respected, and safe. This calling requires that I create an environment where hopes become realities and achievement becomes more than a wish.

This chapter has touched only the surface on the topic of arts integration and social justice, but I am convinced that the arts have the kind of transformative impact on people that endures—the kind of transformative power that lifts individuals out of feelings of bondage, discrimination, failure, and despair into feelings of freedom, equality, success, and hope.

Notes

1. Changing Education through the Arts (CETA) 2012.
2. Tunks and Grady 2003.
3. Goldberg 2012.
4. Pascale and Donovan 2013, p. 14.
5. CETA 2013, p. 1.

6. Goldberg 2012, p. 25.
7. Ibid., pp. 25–28.
8. Dewey 1997.
9. Ibid.
10. Dewey 1934.
11. Jackson 1998.
12. Burnaford et al. 2001.
13. Piaget 1969.
14. Ibid.
15. Goldberg 2012.
16. Gardner 1983.
17. Armstrong 2006.
18. Ibid.
19. CETA 2013.
20. Monchinski 2008.
21. Freire 1970.
22. George 2014.
23. Nieto and Bode 2008, p. 11.
24. Ibid., p. 11.
25. Ibid.
26. Case and Hemmings 2005, p. 57.
27. Howard 2006.
28. Ibid.
29. Marx and Pennington 2003.
30. Picower 2007.
31. Wagner 2008.
32. The Partnership for 21st Century Skills 2014.
33. National Governors Association Center for Best Practices and Council of Chief State School Officers, 2010a, p.33.
34. Consortium of National Arts Education Association 1994a, p. 16.
35. Ibid., p. 4.
36. Ibid., p. 6.
37. Nieto and Bode 2008, pp. 11–12.
38. Wagner 2008, pp. 14, 34, 36.
39. CETA 2012, p. 2.
40. Giroux and Penna 1979.
41. Howard 2006.
42. Landsman 2001.
43. National Governors Association Center for Best Practices and Council of Chief State School Officers, 2010b, p. 43.
44. Consortium of National Arts Education Association 1994a, p. 10.
45. Nieto and Bode 2008, pp. 11–12.

46. Wagner 2008, pp. 14, 34, 36.
47. Burnaford et al. 2001, p. 10.
48. Jackson 2011.

Bibliography

Armstrong, Thomas. 2006. *Multiple Intelligences in the Classroom*. 3rd ed. Alexandria: Association for Supervision and Curriculum Development.

Burnaford, Gail, Arnold Aprill, Cynthia Weiss, and Chicago Arts Partnership in Education. 2001. *Renaissance in the Classroom and Meaningful Learning*. Mahwah, NJ: Lawrence Erlbaum Associates.

Case, Kim, and Annette Hemmings. 2005. "Distancing Strategies: White Women Preservice Teachers and Anti-racist Curriculum." *Urban Education* 40 (6): 606–626.

Changing Education through the Arts (CETA). 2012. *Arts Integration Conference: Exploring an Approach to Teaching*. Washington, DC.

Consortium of National Arts Education Association. 1994a. "National Education Standards for Visual Arts: Grades 5–8." http://www.nacdnet.org/education/contests/poster/2009/National_Standards_for_Visual_Art_Link_To_State_Dept_of_Ed.pdf.

Consortium of National Arts Education Association. 1994b. "National Education Standards for Theater Education: Grades 5–8." http://www.aate.com/?page=nationalstandards58.

Consortium of National Arts Education Association. 1994c. "National Education Standards for Theater Education: Grades 9–12." http://www.aate.com/?page=nationalstandards58.

Dewey, John. 1934. *Art as Experience*. New York: Capricorn Books.

Dewey, John. 1997. *Experience in Education*. New York: MacMillan Publishing.

Freire, Paulo. 1970. *Pedagogy of the Oppressed*. New York: Herder and Herder.

Gardner, Howard. 1983. *Frames of Mind: The Theory of Multiple Intelligences*. New York: Basic Books.

George, Ann. 2014. "Critical Pedagogies: Dreaming of Democracy." In *A Guide to Composition Pedagogies*, eds. G. Tate, A.R. Taggart, K. Schick, and H.B. Hessler (pp. 92–109). New York: Oxford University Press.

Giroux, Henry, and Anthony Penna. 1979. "Social Education in the Classroom: The Dynamics of the Hidden Curriculum." *Theory and Research in Social Education* 7 (1): 21–42.

Goldberg, Merryl. 2012. *Arts Integration: Teaching Subject Matter through the Arts in Multicultural Settings*. 4th ed. Boston, MA: Pearson Education.

Howard, Gary. 2006. *We Can't Teach What We Don't Know: White Teachers, Multiracial Schools*. 2nd ed. New York: Teachers College Press.

Jackson, Phillip W. 1998. *John Dewey and the Lessons of Art.* New Haven, CT: Yale University Press.

Jackson, Yvette. 2011. *The Pedagogy of Confidence: Inspiring High Intellectual Performances in Urban Schools.* New York: Teachers College Press.

Landsman, Julie. 2001. *White Teacher Talks about Race.* London: Scarecrow Press.

Marx, Sherry, and Julie Pennington. 2003. "Pedagogies of Critical Race Theory: Experimentation with White Preservice Teachers." *International Journal of Qualitative Studies in Education* 16 (7): 91–110.

Monchinski, Tony. 2008. *Critical Pedagogy and the Everyday Classroom.* New York: Springer.

National Governors Association Center for Best Practices, and Council of Chief State School Officers. 2010a. "Common Core Standards for Speaking and Listening: Grade 6." http://www.corestandards.org/ELA-Literacy/SL/6/.

National Governors Association Center for Best Practices, and Council of Chief State School Officers. 2010b. "Common Core Standards for Literacy: Grades 9–10." http://www.corestandards.org/ELA-Literacy/W/9–10/.

Nieto, Sonia, and Patty Bode. 2008. *Affirming Diversity: The Sociopolitical Context of Multicultural Education.* 5th ed. Boston, MA: Pearson Education.

Pascale, Louise, and Lisa Donovan. 2013. *Arts Integration across the Content Areas.* Huntington Beach, CA: Shell Education.

Piaget, Jean. 1969. *The Psychology of the Child.* New York: Basic Books.

Picower, Bree. 2007. *The Unexamined Whiteness of Teaching: Will the Circle Be Unbroken?* New York: New York University. Doctoral dissertation.

"Press Kit." *Partnership for 21st Century Skills.* Accessed March 28, 2015. http://www.p21.org/about-us/press_kit.

Tunks, Jeanne, and Patricia Moseley Grady. 2003. "Arts Integration in University Courses." *Curriculum & Teaching* 5 (4): 61–70.

Wagner, Tony. 2008. *The Global Achievement Gap.* New York: Basic Books.

Chapter 5

How Race Mediates the Predictors and Impacts of School-Based Activity Participation

Jeffrey O. Sacha

Educators, policy makers, and increasingly philanthropic organizations are turning to extracurricular activity participation as a way to address persistent racial inequality in schools.[1] Compared to other interventions aimed at reducing racial gaps in school achievement—such as out-of-district student busing, school vouchers, and charter school creation—the provision of quality extracurricular opportunities is not a contentious political issue. For progressive audiences, the extracurriculum empowers young people by providing outlets for a variety of cultural expression and skill development. Conservative audiences see school-based activities as a means of social control for "at-risk," potentially deviant students. Extracurricular participation squares with the myth of American meritocracy by appearing to offer all participants the chance to overcome structural inequality and disadvantage through individual effort and determination.

Academic research on extracurricular involvement has resoundingly found that participation is associated with benefits for students.[2] Students who participate in extracurricular activities evince better academic outcomes, less externalizing behavior, and stronger school engagement than nonparticipants.[3] The outcomes of extracurricular involvement are well documented in the literature, but some aspects of student participation remain under-explored.[4] Extracurricular experiences are influenced by contextual, school-level factors, but these influences have yet to be studied qualitatively.[5] The lack of qualitative research has left the relationship between race and extracurricular participation speculative. Do extracurricular activities benefit all students in the same way? What role do race, class, and gender play in structuring extracurricular activity participation for students?

Critical race theory (CRT) is an interdisciplinary epistemological framework that locates and interrogates race and racism as a structural, historic, and political force that limits access to opportunity and resources for nonwhite people. Applying this theoretical lens in educational research means taking racism and race-based inequality as a foundational element of the schooling process.[6] The generally optimistic findings and conclusions from extracurricular activity scholars run counter to the work of other critical race theorists who have studied other aspects of school. Other aspects of the school context, such as punitive disciplinary structures, systems of academic tracking, and student social life, have been studied qualitatively by educational researchers. Notable educational ethnographers have centered race in their analyses of these aspects of school and have argued convincingly that race is an irreducible, institutionalized aspect of schools that often works to the disadvantage of male black and Latino students.[7] The persistent racial gaps in both academic achievement and punitive school disciplinary experiences are not the result of cultural deficiency or individual-level behaviors but are driven by racial ideologies that are institutionalized via systems of academic tracking and school discipline policy/enforcement.[8] Qualitative, race-focused educational research has recognized the importance of extracurricular participation for students but has not yet theorized how the extracurriculum interacts with disciplinary and academic aspects of school. Unlike these aspects of the school context, extracurricular participation has largely been found to benefit students across race, class, and gender. What is it about this school context that sets it apart from other aspects that have been shown to replicate social inequality and impede post–high school social mobility for black and Latino students? What might a CRT lens add to future studies of extracurricular involvement?

This chapter starts with a summary of educational research that has examined the relationship between school-based extracurricular participation and race. The prominent theoretical frameworks and methodological approaches used in this field document several ways that extracurricular participation impacts students. However, the processes through which these outcomes are produced are less clear. In the absence of causal theories or contextual details, the influence of race as a structuring factor in school-based activity participation remains unclear. To help better theorize the relationship between race and extracurricular participation, this chapter looks to high school sports as a particular form of extracurricular involvement where race and gender are more salient. Sociology of sport research has argued that sports are a powerful product and producer of race and masculinity.[9] This chapter presents the *racialized extracurriculum* as a way to approach the study of school-based activity participation. This concept incorporates elements of CRT to better interrogate the relationship between race and extracurricular participation for students. The racial order of any school context moderates the ways that extracurricular activities impact or fail to impact participants. Finally, this chapter discusses four key aspects of the extracurriculum that are illuminated by the racialized extracurriculum: recruitment/retention processes for participants, student–teacher mentorship, participation decisions among students, and punitive school discipline experience.

Extracurricular Activity Participation

Since its inception, the field of school-based extracurricular activity research has generally found that extracurricular participation benefits students. This field of study was initiated by sociologists during the 1960s, but the vast majority of recent scholarship has come from psychologists.[10] This disciplinary shift is reflected in contemporary methodological and theoretical approaches used to study school-based activity participation. Terms such as "prosocial behavior," "risk factors," "resilience," and "externalizing behavior" are often used to explain adolescent development in extracurricular contexts; the individual participant, rather than the context of participation, is often the unit of analysis. Methodologically, the vast majority of research on extracurricular activities over the past 15 years has been quantitative.[11] The outcomes associated with participation can be grouped into three related developmental categories: academic, attitudinal, and behavioral.

Extracurricular participation is associated with beneficial academic outcomes for students, such as higher graduation rates, greater postsecondary educational attainment, and higher grade point averages.[12] However, the academic benefits of participation do not accrue uniformly for students. Differences in outcomes for students vary across race, gender, family income background, and type of extracurricular activity.[13] Participation in school-based activities has been found to especially improve academic outcomes for low-income students.[14] Participation in school-based activities bolster "at-risk" students' commitment to the learning process and attaches them to the school context through peers and school-based adults. Like academic outcomes such as grade point average, graduation rates, and college enrollment, extracurricular participation also impacts student attitudes about school and educational aspirations. In general, extracurricular participants are more likely than nonparticipants to value school, see themselves as popular, and expect to earn a college degree.[15]

While participation in school activities generally benefits academic outcomes for participants, its impact on student delinquency and risky behavior is less consistent.[16] The heightened popularity that comes with extracurricular involvement—most noticeably via sports participation—makes participants more likely to attend parties, be sexually active, and drink alcohol in high school.[17]

The abundance of quantitative research on extracurricular activity participation has produced somewhat consistent findings on the outcomes of and predictors for participation. However, the *process* through which participation comes to impact students is less consistent across studies. Several studies use variations of social capital theory to explain the apparent benefit of extracurricular participation.[18] According to these theories, the quantity and the quality of a student's social networks are improved through participation in school-based groups and activities. Larger social networks improve a student's access to information and make them more likely to conform to the rules and expectations of the school setting.[19] Other researchers believe that the influence of social capital is mediated through family influences, high school quality, neighborhood characteristics, and relationships with school-based adults.[20] These explanations see the extracurriculum as acting and being acted upon by other developmental contexts.[21]

While they support the quantitative findings, social capital theories struggle to account for the qualitative experiences of historically marginalized groups. For some high school students, high school success and post–high school social mobility is not hindered by a *lack* of social capital but the *presence* of structural disadvantages associated with poverty and racially discriminatory systems within schools. Thus, the school-based racialization that low-income students of color experience may preclude them from acquiring and exchanging social capital through extracurricular participation in the same way that their white peers do.

Participation rates in certain activities differ significantly among students across race, class, and gender. Recruitment and encouragement from family, friends, and school-based adults play an important role in the recruitment and retention students for activities.[22] In 1997, Mahoney and

Cairns speculated that students deemed "at risk" by teachers and peers would be systematically excluded from participation in school-based activities.[23] Low-income students of color are more likely than affluent white peers to be excluded from extracurricular participation because some activities require teacher or peer nomination, a minimum grade point average, or financial investment by the student's family. The uneven ability for students to access some extracurricular spaces challenges the notion that all students can develop skills at school through hard work and individual determination. Thus, the social processes that track certain groups of students into particular extracurricular activities come to resemble the academic tracking pipelines that place some students in college-preparatory tracks and others into remedial tracks. Research has shown that Latino and black male high school students are more likely than their peers to be seen by teachers as academically delayed and placed into remedial educational tracks that impede or disallow the pursuit of postsecondary education.[24]

The tracking processes of the extracurriculum are important to investigate, in light of previous research that argues for the positive influence of school-based activity involvement. Might the extracurriculum play a compensatory role for students tracked into remedial or special education tracks? Are students in these remedial academic tracks allowed or encouraged to participate in activities? Do certain types of extracurricular activities—such as high school sports—act as the extracurricular analog to special education classes in the formal curriculum? These questions are important to answer given the high rates of participation in sports among low-income young men of color and the potential for high school sports to promote or hinder high school outcomes and postsecondary social mobility.

Extracurricular participation is far from a homogeneous collection of activities. Academic clubs, student government, volunteering, art clubs, theater, music, and sports have been shown to produce different outcomes and experiences for participants.[25] The identities, skills, and friendship networks developed in these contexts are believed to drive these differences in outcomes.[26] For the purposes of this chapter, school-based sport is a particularly interesting space in which to examine how race and gender are potentially shaped by participation. Interscholastic sport has several qualities that mark it as unique, compared to other forms of extracurricular participation. More high school students participate in interscholastic sport than any other extracurricular activity.[27] It is also one of the last forms of extracurricular activity where students of color participate at equal or greater rates than their white peers.[28] In the face of declining participation rates in non-sports extracurricular activities, young men of color in particular continue to participate in school-based sports at high rates. In addition, relative to other school-based activities, high school sports often enjoy greater financial support from schools and heightened visibility and coverage among the student body. Thus, high school sports are a useful space in which to study the connections between race, gender, and the impacts of participation.

Race and Gender in Sociology of Sport Research

Sport sociologists have found that sport is a uniquely gendered and racialized social space within which people construct their identities, friendship groups, and worldviews.[29] The centrality of bodies in sports emphasizes physical differences among athletes and often results in the privileging of the male body and subordination of the female body as physically inferior. The subordination of femininity to masculinity is a foundational element of gender ideology. In fact, team sports participation in the United States emerged at the end of the 19th century and was justified as a way to train young men to both conform to a group and compete against one another in a controlled environment.[30] This logic promoted the utility of sports as a means of creating "the ideal man" and contributed to a popular commonsense attachment of boyhood to sports participation that justified the exclusion of young women and girls from sports, both inside and outside of schools. It was not until the passage of Title IX in 1972 that schools were required to provide equal sports opportunities for male and female students. Title IX shifted popular understandings of gender and sports participation. Since its passage, the participation rates of young women have reached historically high levels.

Michael Messner uses the term "soft essentialism" to describe post-Title IX sports experiences for young women.[31] Traditional hard gender essentialism argues that young men are naturally aggressive, competitive, and predisposed to want to play and excel at sports. According to hard gender essentialism, young men who do not want to participate in sports are "sissies" who are acting against their nature. This logic was used by early proponents of team sports to defend the utility of sports for young men and, shockingly, persists today. Soft essentialism, on the other hand, views gender performance and development as more choice-driven, rather than nature-driven. Soft essentialism sees young women who *choose* to participate in sports as showing initiative and commitment but does not view female nonparticipants as outliers. The shift toward a soft essentialist understanding of young women has not challenged the privilege of masculinity in sports spaces. By and large, men's sports continue to be the gold standard of athletic performance, and school resources dedicated to men's sports continue to outstrip those dedicated to women's sports.

Race is an equally salient feature of contemporary interscholastic sports. Where the gender order in sports privileges the bodies and experiences of men over women, white athletes enjoy a wider range of athletic experiences than nonwhite athletes. Compared to whites, athletes of color are disproportionately seen as "overly physical" and undisciplined by coaches and fans. Phrases in the evaluation of athletes such as "freak athlete" or "naturally gifted" are disproportionately applied to black athletes, which undermines the hard work and discipline required to excel in sports. Whites, on the other hand, are more often evaluated by coaches and commentators based on the nonphysical, cognitive aspects of sports performance. The failure of white athletes to excel in their athletic performance does not exclude them from receiving praise for being "good sports."[32] This racialized assessment of athletic performance supports racist logics of white supremacy that see whites as "natural leaders" or as intellectually superior to nonwhites.[33]

While educational research has generally confirmed that school-based sports benefit participants, sport sociologists have reached mixed conclusions about the benefits of sports on young people. Emotional and physical investment in sports by young men of color has been characterized as both beneficial and detrimental. In his early work, Harry Edwards critiqued what he saw as an over-investment in sports—a "treadmill to oblivion"—among young black men, their families, and communities.[34] Edwards's "playbooks over textbooks" argument posited that investment in sports often comes at the expense of more productive, mobility-enhancing pursuits such as academic training and professional development. He also contended that sports generally bolsters male privilege but marginalizes black male athletes, in particular, by situating black athletes as physically superior but intellectually inferior to whites.[35] Many researchers agree that sports continue to reinforce racist beliefs about black men.[36] Still, others acknowledge the problematic history of race and sports but highlight the agency of athletes in reshaping popular understandings of race.

Ben Carrington (2010) builds upon Michael Omi and Howard Winant's concept of *racial projects* through his concept of *sporting racial projects*. He writes:

> Sports [is] a particular racial project . . . that has effects in changing racial discourse more generally and that therefore reshapes wider social structures.

Sports become productive, and not merely receptive, of racial discourse and this discourse has material effect both within sport and beyond. *Sport helps to make race make sense and sport then works to reshape race.*[37]

Carrington cites historic examples of professional and Olympic athletes who channeled the cultural purchase of athletic stardom into shifts in popular notions of race. These shifts do not necessarily mean progress, however. Sporting racial projects can consist of both progressive *and* conservative attempts to define the significance of race. Carrington suggests further that the popularity of certain sports and the visibility of student-athletes position sports within a prime context for changing the discourse of race in the school setting. Indeed, interventions directed at improving graduation rates, test performance, and college enrollment have not been particularly successful in altering the racial discourse in the school setting. Changing the way that students of color feel about themselves and are perceived by school-based adults and their peers in the school setting requires a massive cultural shift. Carrington's work may provide a contextual framework for a different kind of conversation about race, but the potential for change cuts both ways. Existing notions of race may be reified or challenged.

On the one hand, participation and success in interscholastic sports might be seen as evidence of discipline and dedication on the part of student-athletes. However, the racial undertones of the "dumb jock" stereotype potentially limit the impact of school-sports participation for young men of color. If black and Latino young men are channeled into high school sports because they are seen as unteachable or unworthy of intellectual development, then the benefits that other students glean from sports will likely evade them. Each avenue of extracurricular involvement has a unique connection to a set of racialized and gendered logics that mediate the experiences and outcomes of participants. The next section outlines four school-based processes that are implicated in the racialization of extracurricular activities.

The Racialized Extracurriculum

The predominance of quantitative, outcome-focused research on extracurricular activities has produced causal theories that conceptualize race as an individual-level characteristic of participants, rather than an institutionalized aspect of schools. Conversely, sociological theories argue that race is an institutionalized aspect of schools that shapes student experiences with the formal curriculum and school-based discipline experiences.[38] This framework has not been widely applied to the study of school-based activities, however, despite being cited by several ethnographic studies as being an important space for young people to craft their identities.[39] More qualitative approaches to studying extracurricular activities might help shift race from an individual-level mediator of extracurricular outcomes to an institutionalized force that shapes how the extracurriculum functions within particular schools. Extracurricular spaces may offer more freedom, relative to curricular spaces, for nonwhite students to connect to school and develop skills. Conversely, extracurricular spaces may operate as an extension of repressive school practices that criminalize students of color.

To supplement the individual-level, developmental focus of past studies of extracurricular activities, this chapter develops the analytic concept of the *racialized extracurriculum,* which uses elements of CRT to suggest areas of future research on school-based activities. CRT in educational research refutes race-neutral presumptions about the forces and processes that impact students. This approach assumes that contemporary institutional racism in schools often operates in invisible, color-blind ways that can make it hard to locate if assuming that schools are race-neutral, meritocratic institutions.[40] CRT frameworks have been used to study other aspects of school (i.e., punitive disciplinary structures, academic tracking, and social hierarchies), but school-based activities have only been peripherally explored through these frameworks.

The concept of the racialized extracurriculum encourages researchers to approach school-based activities critically. Rather than an inclusive and universally accessible space, the extracurriculum might discourage or disallow certain groups of students from participating or participating fully. The following sections discuss four aspects of extracurricular experiences that future research could explore by using the racialized extracurriculum concept.

Activity Recruitment and Retention

The lack of qualitative research on extracurricular involvement presents opportunities for future educational scholars and practitioners to explore why and how students come to be involved in activities. To be sure, students do not come to high school as blank slates ready to be pushed or pulled into clubs and activities. By their early teens, a person's activity preferences, peer groups, cultural dispositions, and self-perceived talents are well formed.

Thus, some activities may not appeal to students. Along with self-selection or opting out of certain activities, some extracurricular activities actively exclude student from participating because they require significant financial investment from a student's school or family.[41] Thus, students from low-income families are excluded from participation and schools with high concentrations of low-income students may not be able to offer such clubs and activities.

Somewhere between the elective aspect (individual student activity preference) and the structural aspect (activity availability and provision) of participation in extracurricular activity exists the social process of activity recruitment and retention. This process may encourage or discourage students from participating in the available forms of extracurricular activities. Occasionally, willing participants are disallowed from participation because of a lack of skill, a perceived incompatibility with the activity, or a failure to meet requirements like a minimum grade point average. Family, friends, and school-based adults also play important roles in student recruitment and retention for extracurricular activities.[42] In her 2002 ethnographic study of U.S.-born children of Caribbean immigrants, Nancy Lopez found that young women reported much more nurturing relationships with teachers than their male peers and that young women were also much more engaged in school-based extracurricular activities and clubs.[43] Understanding the potentially discriminatory processes of activity encouragement and discouragement requires additional ethnographic or interview-based research.

The social processes that encourage or discourage certain groups of students to participate in particular extracurricular activities resemble those that track students into academic pipelines. Along with objective measures such as test scores and grade point averages, perceived academic aptitude of students plays a huge role in whether students are sorted into college-prep or remedial academic tracks in schools.[44] Research has shown that Latino and black male high school students are more likely than their peers to be placed in special education courses and educational tracks that impede or disallow the pursuit of postsecondary education.[45] The potential tracking processes of the extracurriculum are important to investigate, given the simultaneous benefits to and racial gaps in participation.

Deciding to Participate

Race plays an influential role in shaping how students perceive social boundaries, desirable behavior, and appropriate cultural comportment.[46]

In her ethnography of a New York high school, Prudence Carter (2007) found that students creatively crafted and presented identities based on individual "racial and ethnic ideology, cultural styles, access to resources, and treatment within school and family."[47] The attachment and investment that some students appeared to have in school was based largely on the rewards and validations meted out by institutional agents such as peers and school-based adults. According to Carter, students play a key role in enforcing ethnoracial boundaries within a school. Students are sometimes chastised by one another for behaving outside these boundaries and can be accused of "acting white," "acting black," or "acting Hispanic." The decisions that some students make about academic and social engagement in school are in part informed by their individual understandings of these boundaries.[48]

The relationship between race, student cultural disposition, and school behavior is well documented in social science research. Researchers who support the theory of oppositional culture attribute the persistent racial academic achievement to an aversion to "acting white" among low-income students of color. According to this theory, historically oppressed groups develop an aversion to mainstream school values and adopt a confrontational culture that establishes unique prescriptions for status and success.[49] Critics of this theory argue that, despite having a critical view of white, middle-class models of behavior, black and Latino students still very much aspire to success. In his 2011 book *Kids Don't Want to Fail*, Angel Harris argued that "black cultural deficiency models" among educators and policy makers inappropriately assume apathy or hostility to exist among students of color.[50] Harris counters these claims by presenting robust data, which show that post–high school mobility and success are very much a priority for youth of color. Student dissatisfaction with under-funded schools or discriminatory punitive discipline policies does not mean students do not care about school and learning. Harris's findings have important significance for the relationship between race and the extracurriculum.

A relative lack of extracurricular participation among students of color should not be attributed solely to apathy or disengagement from the schooling process. Students are much more likely to participate in activities that appeal to their interests and self-perceptions of ability. Race plays an important role in how students assess the value of participating in specific extracurricular activities. In order to understand student perceptions of extracurricular activities, the racial meanings associated with these activities need to be taken into account. With the exception of interscholastic sports, little is known about the racial significance that students attach to extracurricular activities. Interviewing participants, as well as nonparticipants, would help to illuminate the relationship between school-based activities and the racial boundaries that previous scholars have discussed. What are the racial connotations that students and teachers attach to extracurricular activities like performing arts, music, community service groups, or academic clubs? How is race constructed and potentially reconstructed in these spaces? What barriers or motivations keep nonparticipants from engaging with extracurricular activities?

Extracurricular Teacher–Student Mentorship

Black and Latino youth have fewer mentoring opportunities outside of the family than their white peers. The flight of the middle class from U.S. urban centers during the late 1980s and 1990s weakened the institutional resource base of the inner city and changed the kinds of social networks available to residents.[51] Increased joblessness and weakening of community institutions like churches, political organizations, and recreational centers created a crisis of mentorship for low-income youth of color. Middle-class flight changed the demographic of the workforce in urban schools. Thus, fewer teachers and administrators working in urban schools were living in the communities in which they worked. This resulted in not only a geographical distance but a cultural disconnect as well. This distance has important implications for the willingness of teachers and staff to mentor low-income students of color in both curricular and extracurricular settings. Limited access to mentorship can be associated with negative educational and social outcomes for adolescents. Conversely, mentorship has been strongly linked to the quality of a student's school engagement.[52] School-based adults provide both practical and psychological assistance to students. As discussed earlier, social capital theorists found mentorship in extracurricular activities to be of great benefit to students. Thus, sources of school-based mentors are important to study, especially in the context of schools that serve students from low-income families.

More research is needed in this area. Very little is known about the relationship between race, extracurricular involvement, and mentorship experiences for students. Major contributions might be made to the field of extracurricular research if the unit of analysis is shifted from the participant to the school-based adult charged with supervising the activity, that is, coaches, faculty advisors, and other nonfaculty adults. The motivations and strategies that these adults bring to school-based activities can hugely impact student experiences. What strategies do activity facilitators use to connect with student participants? How do mentoring approaches differ among activity facilitators across race?

Punitive School Discipline

During the early 1990s, laws and policies were created in schools that drew hard lines regarding the classification of offenses and how these infractions were to be managed. *Zero tolerance* discipline policies required mandatory out-of-school suspension or expulsion for school-based violations related to drugs, weapons, or fighting.[53] During this time, the disciplinary structures of inner-city high schools became increasingly intertwined with formal law enforcement apparatuses.[54] The use of formal legal sanctions has accompanied the passage of zero tolerance discipline policies. Both of these trends have produced high rates of punishment for low-income young men of color in inner-city schools.[55]

Experiencing school-based discipline is negatively associated with high school degree attainment, post–high school job acquisition, and other outcomes related to social mobility in the transition to young adulthood.[56] Conversely, extracurricular involvement has been shown to benefit several school-based outcomes for students. Participants in extracurricular activities have higher graduation rates, greater postsecondary educational attainment, and more productive social networks than nonparticipant peers.[57] Despite extensive research showing the general benefits of extracurricular participation, little research has explored its association with experiencing school-based discipline.

The increased frequency and severity of school-based punishment for young men of color since the early 1990s have emerged concurrently with their lower participation rates in most extracurricular activities.[58] The exception to this trend of disengagement is male participation in high school sports.[59] Thus, exploration of the impacts of certain types of extracurricular involvement, such as sports participation, on punitive disciplinary experiences among black and Latino males would be fruitful. Like other forms of school involvement, high school sports participation significantly improves the likelihood of high school graduation and postsecondary educational enrollment for low-income young men.[60] The results of high school sports participation for young men are not all positive, however. Male high school athletes have been found more likely to participate in deviant or risky behaviors.[61] While we know that male student-athletes participate in these behaviors more often than their nonathlete peers, it is unclear whether this translates into experiences of school-based discipline like suspension, expulsion, or classroom removal. Qualitative research, especially ethnography, would be especially useful for illuminating the link between high school sports participation and formal school-based discipline. This approach would allow researchers to explore how structural forces and context-specific experiences shape experiences with interscholastic sports.

Conclusion

Making sense of race and racism in our schools requires going beyond the level of the individual student. Racism and racial inequality in school are often manifested in individual-level experiences, feelings, and relationships but are rooted in institutionalized policies and social structures. Improving the provision of curricular and extracurricular aspects of school requires investigating these institutionalized and structured elements of racial inequality. The age-old myth of meritocracy obfuscates this structural analysis. Meritocratic understandings of school life and extracurricular activities focus on the individual experiences of student participants and posit that every student can participate and thrive in any school-based activity. This ignores or renders insignificant the structuring role that gender, class background, and race play in shaping extracurricular experiences for students. The playing field is not level.

Historic rulings such as *Brown v. Board of Education* (1954) and Title IX (1972) have shown that equality of *opportunity* does not necessarily produce equality of *outcome* for historically marginalized groups. The removal of de jure exclusions based on gender and race does not prevent de facto inequality and achievement gaps from persisting. Changes to exclusionary policies and laws are a necessary first step toward equality, but these changes do not eradicate the more subtle, institutionalized forms of inequality. This chapter has discussed some aspects of the extracurriculum for future research to illuminate by using the concept of the racialized extracurriculum.

The concept of the racialized extracurriculum pushes educational researchers and practitioners to explore some of the subtle or invisible ways that race and racism shape school-based activities for students. Using the racialized extracurriculum approach follows the work of previous educational scholars who have used CRT to interrogate academic tracking and punitive school discipline policy. It is an analytic concept aimed at located sources of institutional racism within schools and crafting interventions aimed at reducing racial achievement gaps.

Indeed, the call for more research is great, but this chapter is more than a call for a shift in educational theory and research. School-based adults who oversee extracurricular activities could also benefit from viewing race as a key factor in the how the extracurriculum is structured. School-based adults do a great disservice to students of color by adopting color-blind attitudes in how they interact with their students, particularly in how they encourage or discourage students to cultivate skills within extracurricular spaces. Teachers and administrators are not impervious to the deleterious effects of racism and need to monitor themselves and one another in their mentoring practices with students. A safe and nonjudgmental environment needs to be created among faculty so that conversations can be had about race and the encouragement of student engagement within the extracurriculum. A concerted effort must be made to recruit students *and* faculty advisors/facilitators of all races and genders.

Notes

1. Eccles and Templeton 2002; Feldman and Matjasko 2005; Kahne et al. 2001.

2. Fredricks and Eccles 2006; Holland and Andre 1987; Mahoney, Cairns, and Farmer 2003; McNeal 1995.

3. Broh 2002; Fredricks, Blumenfeld, and Paris 2004; Marsh 1992; Marsh and Kleitman 2002.

4. Eccles and Templeton 2002; Feldman and Matjasko 2005.

5. Glennie and Stearns 2012; McNeal 1999.

6. Solórzano 1998.

7. Barajas and Ronnkvist 2007; Conchas 2006; Lewis 2003; Lopez 2002; Nolan 2011.

8. Alexander, Entwisle, and Horsey 1997; Ferguson 2000; Harris 2011; Morris 2005; Oakes 2005.

9. Carrington 2010; Hartmann 2004, 2012; Messner 1995.

10. Farb and Matjasko 2012.

11. Fredricks et al. 2002 for examples of qualitative research in the field. See McLaughlin 2000; McLaughlin et al. 1994.

12. Eccles and Templeton 2002; Feldman and Matjasko 2005; Fredricks and Eccles 2006; Mahoney, Cairns, and Farmer 2003; McNeal 1995;.

13. Broh 2002; Eccles and Barber 1999; Mahoney, Larson, and Eccles 2005; Marsh and Kleitman 2002; Sabo et al. 1993;.

14. Broh 2002; Kahne et al. 2001; Mahoney and Cairns 1997; Marsh and Kleitman 2002; Peck et al. 2008.

15. Darling 2005; Fredricks and Eccles 2008; Marsh 1993.

16. Broh 2002; Eccles and Barber 1999.

17. Eccles et al. 2003.

18. Broh 2002; Coleman 1987; Eitle and Eitle 2002; McNeal 1999; Ream and Rumberger 2008.

19. Portes 1998.

20. Bohnert et al. 2009; Farb and Matjasko 2012; Lopez 2002; McNeal 1999; Portes 1998; Stearns and Glennie 2010; White and Gager 2007.

21. Fredricks and Eccles 2008; Luthar, Shoum, and Brown 2006.

22. Quiroz et al. 1996.

23. Mahoney and Cairns 1997.

24. Cammarota 2004; Noguera 2003; Pollard 1993.

25. Eccles and Barber 1999; Rose-Krasnor, Willoughby, and Chalmers 2006.

26. Eccles and Barber 1999.

27. Feldman and Matjasko 2005; Holland and Andre 1987.

28. Eitle and Eitle 2002; Mahoney and Cairns 1997.

29. Carrington 2010; Hartmann 2003; Messner 1995; Shakib et al. 2011.

30. Cavallo 1981.

31. Messner 2009.

32. Stone, Perry, and Darley 1997; Stone et al. 1999; Wiggins 1997.

33. Carrington 2010.

34. Edwards 1969, 1984, 1994.

35. Carrington 2010; Edwards 1969; Harrison et al. 2011.

36. Hoberman 1997.

37. Carrington 2010, p. 68 (emphasis in original, Omi and Winant 1994).

38. Ferguson 2000; Lewis 2003; Lopez 2002; Morris 2005; Oakes 2005.

39. See Carter 2007; Lopez 2002.

40. Harper, Patton, and Wooden 2009.

41. Mahoney and Cairns 1997.

42. Quiroz et al. 1996.

43. Lopez 2002.

44. Oakes 2005.

45. Cammarota 2004; Noguera 2003; Pollard 1993.

46. Carter 2007.

47. Ibid., p. 12.

48. Lewis 2003.

49. Ogbu 1978.

50. Harris 2011.

51. Putnam 2000; Wilson 1996.

52. roh 2002; Eccles et al. 2003; Feliciano and Rumbaut 2005; Rhodes and DuBois 2008.

53. Hirschfield 2008; Reynolds et al. 2008.

54. Nolan 2011.

55. Gregory, Skiba, and Noguera 2010; Kim et al. 2010; Skiba et al. 2011.

56. Kirk and Sampson 2013; Losen and Gillespie 2012; Gregory, Skiba, and Noguera 2010.

57. Fredricks and Eccles 2006; Mahoney, Cairns, and Farmer 2003; McNeal 1995.

58. Feliciano and Rumbaut 2005.

59. Eccles et al. 2003; Eitle and Eitle 2002; Lopez 2003; McNeal 1998.

60. Mahoney, Larson, and Eccles 2005; McNeal 1995.

61. Eccles et al. 2003; Eccles and Barber 1999; Fejgin 1994; Hartmann and Massoglia 2007; Miller et al. 1999.

Bibliography

Alexander, Karl L., Doris R. Entwisle, and Carrie S. Horsey. 1997. "From First Grade Forward: Early Foundations of High School Dropout." *Sociology of Education* 70 (2): 87–107.

Barajas, Heidi Lasley, and Amy Ronnkvist. 2007. "Racialized Space: Framing Latino and Latina Experience in Public Schools." *Teachers College Record* 109 (6): 1517–1538.

Bohnert, Amy M., Maryse Richards, Krista Kohl, and Edin Randall. 2009. "Relationships between Discretionary Time Activities, Emotional Experiences, Delinquency and Depressive Symptoms among Urban African American Adolescents." *Journal of Youth and Adolescence* 38 (4): 587–601.

Broh, B.A. 2002. "Linking Extracurricular Programming to Academic Achievement: Who Benefits and Why?" *Sociology of Education* 75 (1): 69–95.

Cammarota, Julio. 2004. "The Gendered and Racialized Pathways of Latina and Latino Youth: Different Struggles, Different Resistances in the Urban Context." *Anthropology & Education Quarterly* 35 (1): 53–74.

Carrington, Ben. 2010. *Race, Sport and Politics: The Sporting Black Diaspora.* 1st ed. New York: Sage Publications Ltd.

Carter, Prudence L. 2007. *Keepin' It Real: School Success beyond Black and White.* New York: Oxford University Press.

Cavallo, Domincik. 1981. *Muscles and Morals: Organized Playgrounds and Urban Reform, 1880–1920.* Philadelphia: University of Pennsylvania Press.

Coleman, J.S. 1987. "Families and Schools." *Educational Researcher* 16 (6): 32–38.

Conchas, Gilberto Q. 2006. *The Color of Success: Race and High-Achieving Urban Youth.* New York: Teachers College Press.

Darling, N. 2005. "Participation in Extracurricular Activities and Adolescent Adjustment: Cross-Sectional and Longitudinal Findings." *Journal of Youth and Adolescence* 34 (5): 493–505.

Duncan-Andrade, Jeffrey M.R. 2010. *What a Coach Can Teach a Teacher.* First printing. New York: Peter Lang Publishing.

Eccles, J.S., and B.L. Barber. 1999. "Student Council, Volunteering, Basketball, or Marching Band: What Kind of Extracurricular Involvement Matters?" *Journal of Adolescent Research* 14 (1): 10–43.

Eccles, Jacquelynne S., and Janice Templeton. 2002. "Chapter 4: Extracurricular and Other After-School Activities for Youth." *Review of Research in Education* 26 (1): 113–180.

Eccles, Jacquelynne, B.L. Barber, Margaret Stone, and James Hunt. 2003. "Extra-curricular Activities and Adolescent Development." *Journal of Social Issues* 59 (4): 865–889.

Edwards, Harry. 1969. *The Revolt of the Black Athlete*. New York, NY: MacMillan Publishing Company.

Edwards, Harry. 1984. "The Black 'Dumb Jock': An American Sports Tragedy." College Board Review 131 (Spring): 8–13.

Edwards, Harry. 1994. "Black Youths' Commitment to Sports Achievement: A Virtue-Turned-Tragic-Turned-Virtue." *Sport* 7 (July): 86.

Eitle, T.M., and D.J. Eitle. 2002. "Race, Cultural Capital, and the Educational Effects of Participation in Sports." *Sociology of Education* 75 (2): 123–146.

Farb, Amy Feldman, and Jennifer L. Matjasko. 2012. "Recent Advances in Research on School-Based Extracurricular Activities and Adolescent Development." *Developmental Review* 32 (1): 1–48.

Fejgin, N. 1994. "Participation in High-School Competitive Sports—A Subversion of School Mission or Contribution to Academic Goals." *Sociology of Sport Journal* 11 (3): 211–230.

Feldman, A.F., and J.L. Matjasko. 2005. "The Role of School-Based Extracurricular Activities in Adolescent Development: A Comprehensive Review and Future Directions." *Review of Educational Research* 75 (2): 159–210.

Feliciano, Cynthia, and Rubén G. Rumbaut. 2005. "Gendered Paths: Educational and Occupational Expectations and Outcomes among Adult Children of Immigrants." *Ethnic and Racial Studies* 28 (6): 1087–1118.

Ferguson, Ann A. 2000. *Bad Boys: Public Schools in the Making of Black Masculinity.* Ann Arbor, MI: The University of Michigan Press.

Fredricks, J.A., P.C. Blumenfeld, and A.H. Paris. 2004. "School Engagement: Potential of the Concept, State of the Evidence." *Review of Educational Research* 74 (1): 59–109.

Fredricks, Jennifer A., Corinne J. Alfeld-Liro, Ludmila Z. Hruda, Jacquelynne S. Eccles, Helen Patrick, and Allison M. Ryan. 2002. "A Qualitative Exploration of Adolescents' Commitment to Athletics and the Arts." *Journal of Adolescent Research* 17 (1): 68–97.

Fredricks, Jennifer A., and Jacquelynne S. Eccles. 2006. "Is Extracurricular Participation Associated With Beneficial Outcomes? Concurrent and Longitudinal Relations." *Developmental Psychology* 42 (4): 698–713.

Fredricks, Jennifer A., and Jacquelynne S. Eccles. 2008. "Participation in Extracurricular Activities in the Middle School Years: Are There Developmental Benefits for African American and European American Youth?" *Journal of Youth and Adolescence* 37 (9): 1029–1043.

Glennie, Elizabeth J., and Elizabeth Stearns. 2012. "Opportunities to Play the Game: The Effect of Individual and School Attributes on Participation in Sports." *Sociological Spectrum* 32 (6): 532–557.

Gregory, Anne, Russell J. Skiba, and Pedro A. Noguera. 2010. "The Achievement Gap and the Discipline Gap: Two Sides of the Same Coin?" *Educational Researcher* 39 (1): 59–68.

Harper, Shaun R., Lori D. Patton, and Ontario S. Wooden. 2009. "Access and Equity for African American Students in Higher Education: A Critical Race Historical Analysis of Policy Efforts." *Journal of Higher Education* 80 (4): 389–414.

Harris, Angel L. 2011. *Kids Don't Want to Fail: Oppositional Culture and the Black-White Achievement Gap*. Cambridge, MA: Harvard University Press.

Harrison, Louis, Gary Sailes, Willy K. Rotich, and Albert Y. Bimper. 2011. "Living the Dream or Awakening from the Nightmare: Race and Athletic Identity." *Race, Ethnicity and Education* 14 (1): 91–103.

Hartmann, Douglas. 2004. *Race, Culture, and the Revolt of the Black Athlete: The 1968 Olympic Protests and Their Aftermath* (1st ed.). Chicago: University of Chicago Press.

Hartmann, Douglas. 2012. "Beyond the Sporting Boundary: The Racial Significance of Sport through Midnight Basketball." *Ethnic and Racial Studies* 35 (6): 1007–1022.

Hartmann, Douglas, and Michael Massoglia. 2007. "Reassessing the Relationship between High School Sports Participation and Deviance: Evidence of Enduring, Bifurcated Effects." *Sociological Quarterly* 48 (3): 485–505.

Hirschfield, Paul J. 2008. "Preparing for Prison? The Criminalization of School Discipline in the USA." *Theoretical Criminology* 12 (1): 79–101.

Hoberman, John. 1997. *Darwin's Athletes: How Sport Has Damaged Black America and Preserved the Myth of Race*. New York: Mariner Books.

Holland, A., and T. Andre. 1987. "Participation in Extracurricular Activities in Secondary-School—What." *Review of Educational Research* 57 (4): 437–466.

Kahne, J., J. Nagaoka, A. Brown, J. O'Brien, T. Quinn, and K. Thiede. 2001. "Assessing After-School Programs as Contexts for Youth Development." *Youth & Society* 32 (4): 421–446.

Kim, Catherine Y., Daniel J. Losen, and Damon T. Hewitt. 2010. *The School-to-Prison Pipeline: Structuring Legal Reform*. New York: New York University Press.

Kirk, David S., and Robert J. Sampson. 2013. "Juvenile Arrest and Collateral Educational Damage in the Transition to Adulthood." *Sociology of Education* 86 (1): 36–62.

Lewis, Amanda E. 2003. *Race in the Schoolyard: Negotiating the Color Line in Classrooms and Communities.* New Brunswick, NJ: Rutgers University Press.

Lleras, Christy. 2008. "Do Skills and Behaviors in High School Matter? The Contribution of Noncognitive Factors in Explaining Differences in Educational Attainment and Earnings." *Social Science Research* 37 (3): 888–902.

Lopez, Nancy. 2002. *Hopeful Girls, Troubled Boys: Race and Gender Disparity in Urban Education.* 1st ed. New York: Routledge.

Losen, Daniel J., and Jonathan Gillespie. 2012. "Opportunities Suspended: The Disparate Impact of Disciplinary Exclusion from School." http://escholarship.org/uc/item/3g36n0c3.pdf.

Luthar, S.S., K.A. Shoum, and P.J. Brown. 2006. "Extracurricular Involvement among Affluent Youth: A Scapegoat for 'Ubiquitous Achievement Pressures'?" *Developmental Psychology* 42 (3): 583–597.

Mahiri, Jabari. 1998. *Shooting for Excellence: African American and Youth Culture in New Century Schools.* Urbana, IL: National Council of Teachers.

Mahoney, J.L., B.D. Cairns, and T.W. Farmer. 2003. "Promoting Interpersonal Competence and Educational Success through Extracurricular Activity Participation." *Journal of Educational Psychology* 95 (2): 409–418.

Mahoney, J.L., and R.B. Cairns. 1997. "Do Extracurricular Activities Protect Against Early School Dropout?" *Developmental Psychology* 33 (2): 241–53.

Mahoney, Joseph L., Reed Larson, and Jacquelynne S. Eccles. 2005. *Organized Activities as Contexts of Development: Extracurricular Activities, After-School, and Community Programs.* Mahwah, NJ: Lawrence Erlbaum.

Marsh, H.W. 1992. "Extracurricular Activities—Beneficial Extension of the Traditional Curriculum or Subversion of Academic Goals." *Journal of Educational Psychology* 84 (4): 553–562.

Marsh, H.W. 1993. "The Effects of Participation in Sport during the Last 2 Years of High-School." *Sociology of Sport Journal* 10 (1): 18–43.

Marsh, H.W., and S. Kleitman. 2002. "Extracurricular School Activities: The Good, the Bad, and the Nonlinear." *Harvard Educational Review* 72 (4): 464–514.

McLaughlin, Milbrey W. 2000. "Community Counts: How Youth Organizations Matter for Youth Development." January. http://eric.ed.gov/?id=ED442900.

McLaughlin, Milbrey W., Merita A. Irby, and Juliet Langman. 2001. *Urban Sanctuaries: Neighborhood Organizations in the Lives and Futures of Inner City Youth.* 1st ed. San Francisco: Jossey-Bass.

McLaughlin, Milbrey Wallin, Merita A. Irby, and Juliet Langman. 1994. *Urban Sanctuaries: Neighborhood Organizations in the Lives and Futures of Inner-city Youth.* San Francisco, CA: Jossey-Bass Publishers.

McNeal, R.B. 1999. "Participation in High School Extracurricular Activities: Investigating School Effects." *Social Science Quarterly* 80 (2): 291–309.

McNeal, R.B. 1995. "Extracurricular Activities and High-School Dropouts." *Sociology of Education* 68 (1): 62–80.

Melnick, M. J., D. F. Sabo, and B. Vanfossen. 1992. "Educational-Effects of Interscholastic Athletic Participation on African-American and Hispanic Youth." *Adolescence* 27 (106): 295–308.

Melnick, M. J., and B. E. Vanfossen. 1993. "High-School Athletic Participation and Postsecondary Educational and Occupational-Mobility—A Focus on Race and Gender." *Sociology of Sport Journal* 10 (1): 44–56.

Messner, Michael. 1995. *Power at Play: Sports and the Problem of Masculinity.* Boston, MA: Beacon Press.

Messner, Michael. 2009. *It's All for the Kids: Gender, Families, and Youth Sports.* Berkeley: University of California Press.

Morris, Edward W. 2005. "'Tuck in That Shirt!' Race, Class, Gender, and Discipline in an Urban School." *Sociological Perspectives* 48 (1): 25–48.

Noguera, Pedro A. 2003. "The Trouble with Black Boys: The Role and Influence of Environmental and Cultural Factors on the Academic Performance of African American Males." *Urban Education* 38 (4): 431–459.

Nolan, Kathleen. 2011. *Police in the Hallways: Discipline in an Urban High School.* Minneapolis: University of Minnesota Press.

Oakes, Jeannie. 2005. *Keeping Track: How Schools Structure Inequality.* 2nd ed. New Haven, CT; London: Yale University Press.

Ogbu, John U. 1978. *Minority Education and Caste: The American System in Cross-Cultural Perspective.* 1st ed. New York: Academic Press.

Omi, Michael, and Howard Winant. 1994. *Racial Formation in the United States: From the 1960s to the 1990s.* 2nd ed. New York: Routledge.

Peck, Stephen C., Robert W. Roeser, Nicole Zarrett, and Jacquelynne S. Eccles. 2008. "Exploring the Roles of Extracurricular Activity Quantity and Quality in the Educational Resilience of Vulnerable Adolescents: Variable- and Pattern-Centered Approaches." *Journal of Social Issues* 64 (1): 135–155.

Pollard, D. S. 1993. "Gender, Achievement, and African-American Students Perceptions of Their School Experience." *Educational Psychologist* 28 (4): 341–356.

Portes, A. 1998. "Social Capital: Its Origins and Applications in Modern Sociology." *Annual Review of Sociology* 24: 1–24.

Putnam, Robert. 2000. *Bowling Alone: The Collapse and Revival of American Community.* New York: Simon & Schuster.

Quiroz, P. A., N. F. Gonzales, and K. A. Frank. 1996. "Carving a Niche in the High School Social Structure: Formal and Informal Constraints on Participation in the Extra Curriculum." In *Sociology of Education and Socialization*, ed. Pallas (vol. 11). London: JAI Press.

Ream, Robert K., and Russell W. Rumberger. 2008. "Student Engagement, Peer Social Capital, and School Dropout among Mexican American and Non-Latino White Students." *Sociology of Education* 81 (2): 109–139.

Reynolds, Cecil R., Russell J. Skiba, Sandra Graham, Peter Sheras, Jane Close Conoley, and Enedina Garcia-Vazquez. 2008. "Are Zero Tolerance Policies

Effective in the Schools? An Evidentiary Review and Recommendations." *American Psychologist* 63 (9): 852–862.

Rhodes, Jean E., and David L. DuBois. 2008. "Mentoring Relationships and Programs for Youth." *Current Directions in Psychological Science* 17 (4): 254–258.

Rhodes, J.E., and R. Spencer. 2005. "Someone to Watch over Me: Mentoring Programs in the After-School Lives of Youth." In *Organized Activities as Contexts of Development: Extracurricular Activities, After-School and Community Programs,* eds. J.L. Mahoney, R.W. Larson, and J.S. Eccles (pp. 419–435). Mahwah, NJ: Erlbaum.

Rose-Krasnor, L., M.A. Busseri, T. Willoughby, and H. Chalmers. 2006. "Breadth and Intensity of Youth Activity Involvement as Contexts for Positive Development." *Journal of Youth and Adolescence* 35: 385–399.

Sabo, D., Mj Melnick, and Be Vanfossen. 1993. "High-School Athletic Participation and Postsecondary Educational and Occupational-Mobility—A Focus on Race and Gender." *Sociology of Sport Journal* 10 (1): 44–56.

Shakib, Sohaila, Philip Veliz, Michele D. Dunbar, and Don Sabo. 2011. "Athletics as a Source for Social Status among Youth: Examining Variation by Gender, Race/Ethnicity, and Socioeconomic Status." *Sociology of Sport Journal* 28 (3): 303–328.

Skiba, Russell J., Robert H. Horner, Choong-Geun Chung, M. Karega Rausch, Seth L. May, and Tary Tobin. 2011. "Race Is Not Neutral: A National Investigation of African American and Latino Disproportionality in School Discipline." *School Psychology Review* 40 (1): 85–107.

Solórzano, D. 1998. "Critical Race Theory, Racial and Gender Microaggressions, and the Experiences of Chicana and Chicano Scholars." *International Journal of Qualitative Studies in Education* 11: 121–136.

Stearns, Elizabeth, and Elizabeth J. Glennie. 2010. "Opportunities to Participate: Extracurricular Activities' Distribution Across and Academic Correlates in High Schools." *Social Science Research* 39 (2): 296–309.

Stone, J., Z.W. Perry, and J.M. Darley. 1997. "'White Men Can't Jump': Evidence for the Perceptual Confirmation of Racial Stereotypes Following a Basketball Game." *Basic and Applied Social Psychology* 19: 291–306.

Stone, J., C.I. Lynch, M. Sjomeling, and J.M. Darley. 1999. "Stereotype Threat Effects on Black and White Athletic Performance." *Journal of Personality and Social Psychology* 77: 1213–1227.

White, Amanda M., and Constance T. Gager. 2007. "Idle Hands and Empty Pockets? Youth Involvement in Extracurricular Activities, Social Capital, and Economic Status." *Youth & Society* 39 (1): 75–111.

Wiggins, D.K. 1997. "'Great Speed but Little Stamina': The Historical Debate over Black Athletic Superiority." In *The New American Sport History: Recent Approaches and Perspectives,* ed. S.W. Pope (pp. 158–185). Urbana, IL, University of Illinois Press.

Wilson, William J. 1996. *When Work Disappears: The World of the New Urban Poor.* New York: Random House, Inc.

Part III

Moving toward an Antiracist Education

Chapter 6

Science as a Critical Method for Deconstructing Diversity Discourse: Toward an Antiracist Teacher Education

Anthony Ash and Greg Wiggan

In the seven decades following World War II, scientific innovation and population diversity emerged as two of the most remarkable sociopolitical issues in the United States. Since the Soviet launch of Sputnik in 1957, science has permeated nearly every aspect of contemporary society. Alongside then extant Cold War tensions, the Space Race demonstrated that economic and military sustainability in the new knowledge-based political economy would require a workforce trained in science, technology, engineering, and mathematics (STEM) disciplines. The rapid expansion of scientific innovation also provided the means for increased global migration. In conjunction with the slow but sure dissolution of institutional barriers during the 1950s and 1960s, an influx of immigrants to the United States stimulated a rise in interracial unions over the next several decades. The subsequent explosion of demographic heterogeneity indicated that the global efficacy of the United States would rely on individuals from a variety of different racial, ethnic, and cultural backgrounds, which prompted a still-growing body of research and public policy aimed raising STEM achievement and supporting the entry and persistence of underrepresented minorities in STEM areas. In the ostensible pursuit of national security, economic sustainability, and high quality of life, the combined influence of science and diversity has made a profound impact on 21st-century public education.

As schools and society grow more diverse, the onus for preparing a democratic and critically thinking workforce falls on the future educators of the United States. Compounding the difficulty of this task is an education system in which the sordid legacy of racial discrimination and social exclusion in this country persists. The juxtaposition of students from a diverse array of intersecting cultural and linguistic backgrounds with a homogeneous teaching force unprepared to teach them has prompted debates about teaching in more equitable ways. Further, the demonstrable ability of scientific innovation to address environmental concerns, stimulate new industries, and support advancements in health care suggests that scientific knowledge will continue to be a significant aspect of schools and society in years to come. Thus, preparing a diverse workforce is often centralized in research related to (science) education. Given the national focus on science for its role in addressing present and future concerns of humanity, along with issues of underrepresentation in science-related majors and professions among racial and ethnic minorities, the consensus is that more discussions about diversity are needed in 21st-century science classrooms. Absent among these debates are implications for the role of science in initiating meaningful dialogue about human diversity toward inclusive and transformative ends—inside or outside of the science classroom.

This chapter explores the utility of science as a transdisciplinary, critical method to teach about diversity issues such as race, ethnicity, and culture in teacher education programs (TEPs). It begins with a baseline for the contemporary model of science, followed by the critical postmodern framework through which issues of science and diversity in schools and society will be examined. Next, a brief sociopolitical discussion illustrates how science was often misaligned as a metanarrative that serves dominant class interests. Literature related to science and student diversity is then presented, including contributions, connections, and critiques of science and multicultural education, culturally relevant pedagogy, and critical pedagogy. The chapter concludes with a new direction that employs science as a critical postmodern method to teach about diversity, along with examples and implications. The overall aim is to explore the utility of science to deconstruct flawed narratives of race and human difference that have historically undermined racial parity in schools and society.

What Is This Thing Called Science?

Issues of human diversity carry deep and varied economic, political, and ideological significance for the role of science in society. From medical and technological advances and future job growth to climate change and the biology of human evolution, science has become both a ubiquitous and contested aspect of global discourse. According to the American Association for the Advancement of Science (AAAS), science refers to the "process of trying to figure out how the world works by making careful observations and trying to make sense of those observations" and rests on the premise that the universe is a unified network of consistent patterns of events and phenomena that can be understood through careful, systematic study. While this suggests a stable and coherent basis for science, research has shown a lack of consensus for a singular essence or nature of science. Yet, there are converging areas that allow it to be a substantive mode of inquiry, including a few foundational elements of scientific inquiry to which the scientific community adheres.[1] The National Research Council (NRC) offers that

> scientific research, whether in education, physics, anthropology, molecular biology, or economics, is a continual process of rigorous reasoning supported by a dynamic interplay among methods, theories, and findings. It builds understandings in the form of models or theories that can be tested. Advances in scientific knowledge are achieved by the self-regulating norms of the scientific community over time, not . . . by the mechanistic application of a particular scientific method to a static set of questions.[2]

One fundamental assumption of science implied here is that the systematic processes of inquiry can produce scientific knowledge about the natural world that is both durable and tentative. It also suggests that certain concerns cannot be addressed through science alone, such as personal and cultural beliefs or matters of good and evil. However, the ability to identify and generate a consensus regarding likely causal relationships using science can be helpful in providing context to such issues and in considering practical alternatives.

Using science to conduct critical examinations of diversity can provide valuable insights into sociopolitical issues involving race, culture, and other human differences. In this way, sciences perform a vital task inside or outside of the science classroom, as a critical response to the miseducation of teachers. This perspective asserts that science is neither preexistent nor immutable but one of many narratives or social constructs developed by members of society. While the principles espoused by science cannot encompass all knowledge, they can yield a series of plausible outcomes to help explain the world we all share. This narrative of science also holds empirical truths insofar as the processes through which new scientific knowledge is acquired are replicable, and the results agreed upon through consensus.

This chapter proposes that when used as an instrument for critical appraisals of social constructs such as race, science also helps establish a basis for antiracist teacher education and a means to instill critical awareness about such issues. A critical scientific approach that examines race relations is able to reveal how misguided ideological assumptions about human differences became a stratifying force in society. Using science to teach about diversity not only foregrounds a common humanity, which supports better teaching and racial equality, but addresses the need for a critically thinking and scientifically literate workforce.

Current Issues in Teacher Education

Calls for more equitable and inclusive ways of teaching continue to be heard. Especially in urban schools, where ethnoracial, cultural, and linguistic diversity is often most pronounced and instructional quality and resources most lacking. Investigations of these schools often paint a troubling picture of structural inequalities and minority students who remain overrepresented in the number of dropouts, special education programs, and low education tracks. Much as they have since manufacturing jobs were shipped overseas in the late 1970s and early 1980s, opportunity gaps and restrictions to social mobility resulting from racially motivated social dislocation, the lack of resources and quality instruction in urban schools continue to disproportionately affect students in the most underserved communities in the United States. Given the profound implications of increasing diversity in schools and majority white, monolingual, middle-class teacher workforce whose lived experiences tend to be appreciably different from the students they serve, there is a growing need to prepare teachers to understand and teach about human diversity.

Nearly 83 percent of the 3.85 million school teachers in the United States are white, approximately 76 percent of whom are female, whereas the growing majority of students they teach are from various ethnoracial backgrounds.[3] Demographic trends suggest that many preservice teachers (PSTs) will teach at schools that serve students from a variety of different socioeconomic and cultural backgrounds. However, these teachers often find it difficult to make necessary connections to reach students with backgrounds disparate from their own. As a result, whether by socially or culturally skewed predispositions about race, many PSTs are not prepared to teach in diverse settings. Therefore, despite demographic shifts toward no single racial majority, these neophyte educators will be ill-equipped to meet the needs of an evolving society.

Implicit within these phenomena and the relative silence about issues of race and ethnicity in TEPs is that inadequate preparation of PSTs suggests negative outcomes for nonwhite students. Multicultural classrooms led by teachers who find it difficult to reach students create a costly disconnection, resulting in lackluster instruction and low achievement. This inability to connect with students perpetuates educational inequality through what Joyce King refers to as "dysconscious racism"[4] or inherent sense of privilege and dominance that engenders deficit-based thinking about the intellectual capacity of nonwhite students.

In spite of a diverse social landscape, and behind a veneer of tolerance and pluralism, many TEPs in the United States support a traditionalist model of schooling in which myths of meritocracy and color blindness conceal the reality of limited educational opportunities for minority students. Further, they may require only a single course on diversity that offers but a cursory examination of forces that have and continue to perpetuate racial inequality. Coupled with uncritical assumptions of race and ethnicity, resulting cultural mismatches between students and teachers tend to elicit misconceptions of student ability. This raises an important question of whether using science to understand issues of race and ethnicity from a critical and contextual perspective can assist in preparing PSTs to teach diverse student populations.

Science Miseducation

These cultural disconnections can be historically linked to social, political, and ideological myths and misconceptions used to stratify society on the basis of race and ethnicity, many of which predicated on the notion of scientific validity. Whereas whites were traditionally regarded as the referential group, nonwhites were considered intellectually inferior and morally impoverished. The duplicitous use of science to justify racial discrimination contributed to social stratification through programs such as eugenics and are still evident in education. For instance, the long-debunked notion of race as a "biological imperative"—whereby skin color is haphazardly linked to culture, or considered a determinant of intellectual capacity—remains embedded in schools and society and receives the tacit endorsement of TEPs through the uncritical replication of dominant cultural values. Such pejorative thinking is commonly promoted through the pervasive use of delimiting, implicitly racist achievement gap language. Along with frequently negative portrayals of minority students in the media, PSTs are encouraged to adopt a deficit model of these students wherein success is "viewed as a de-raced phenomenon achieved through meritocracy—if only individuals would try harder to do better."[5]

The pervasive nature of ideology is such that both the flow and the direction of (scientific) knowledge is influenced by social institutions and discourse, as well as the historical context in which they are situated. How and what knowledge is transmitted and received during the learning process necessarily affects the re/production of cultural values and identity in society. In nearly self-regulated fashion, such discursive practices form the parameters and referential measures by which value is ascribed to knowledge. And because education is one of the most effective means to transmit knowledge, racism and discrimination are often socially and culturally situated as well as reproduced through the language and process of schooling. Thus, while traditionally supported by dominant Eurocentric ideologies, deficit-based perceptions of ability inhibit critical learning opportunities for PSTs and ultimately threaten the personal growth and academic performance of their future students. Inasmuch as diversity discourse in TEPs is limited by the absence of critical analyses of racial inequalities, critical postmodern science pedagogy (CPSP) is presented as a move toward an antiracist teacher education.

Critical Theory and Postmodernism

CPSP draws from critical and postmodern theories to link science and diversity to their social and historical contingencies. It aims to assist in the deconstruction and interrogation of scientific knowledge, as well as the critique of discriminatory practices science has helped imbue within the public discourse. Here, critical theory offers an invaluable theoretical perspective from which society can be examined for both hidden and overt oppressions of marginalized groups. Over the years, critical theory has been framed and reframed in many ways to argue against all types of false consciousness, which assumes an inevitable and rational social system at the expense of a critical society. With the goal of human liberation, critical theory questions prevalent assumptions about human diversity born of seemingly benign sociocultural patterns.

Postmodernism helps fill conceptual gaps left by the broad perspective afforded by critical theory. Although the term has been applied in various cultural milieus over the last several decades, the initial aim was to blend and recontextualize modern elements of society into a more heterogeneous view of the world. Jean-François Lyotard describes the postmodern as an "incredulity toward meta-narratives" or skepticism of absolutes. He continues that "postmodern knowledge is not simply a tool of the authorities; it refines our sensitivity to differences and reinforces our ability to tolerate the incommensurable" and is thus a reaction to modernity and its project of self-legitimation.[6] The postmodern is concerned with the historical conditions of postindustrial society, wherein cultural "norms" were replaced by pluralistic worldviews. It reflects cultural, philosophical shift from totalizing discourses of an industrialized culture of efficiency and modernity to one of multiplicity. And with no "grand narrative" guiding this blended style bent on decentering absolutes, all discourses are provided conceptual space for their own truths/reality, which also suggests a lack of clear distinctions or answers.

Critical Postmodern Science Teaching

Even a critical deconstructive framework of science and diversity implies logical critique and analysis. Thus, it is important to delineate the use of empiricism and objectivity in this discussion. In the natural and social sciences this often takes on the form of positivist objectivity, which presumes external influences can somehow be removed from an investigation of an issue or inquiry. Operating under the guise of value-neutrality as traditional science is wont to do, such research is burdened by pursuits of unachievable transcendence and/or abstraction.

The principles underpinning scientific and philosophical traditions are products of their own social and historical contexts; each generation learns from the myopia of the last. Endeavors that involve human interaction are susceptible to external influence by that very fact. Instead of the intractable nature of objectivity as conceived during the Enlightenment, or constitutive essence envisioned in the philosophical tradition of transcendental phenomenology, scientific "knowledge" and "truth" are (and should be) highly contested. Accordingly, science is not exclusively linear but can be applied globally if it remains self-interrogatory. Karl Popper's logic of science is informative in this regard by offering intersubjective testing and criticism for decentering conviction as a mode of establishing stable truth claims:

> A subjective experience, or a feeling of conviction, can never justify a scientific statement, and that within science it can play no part except that of an object of an empirical (a psychological) inquiry. No matter how intense a feeling of conviction it may be, it can never justify a statement.[7]

Therefore, a "scientific statement" is not absolute but intersubjectively testable. It must infinitely undergo testing on the empirical basis of intersubjective testability from which other testable statements can be deduced—one statement testing the next and so on. Consequently, scientific knowledge is stable only until challenged by the next line of empirical questioning. To Popper, this is also the best alternative to inductive reasoning, because it holds no singular statement to be true in the universal sense. If an "essence" of a person or thing did exist, it would likely emerge under such circumstances. It follows that any scientific narrative is (or should be) subjected to its own criticism if it is to contribute to the progress of democracy. This view positions science as an ongoing self-interrogation of scientific knowledge and truth claims.

In his writings on knowledge, truth, and power, Michel Foucault similarly suggests an intersubjective testability of discourse by acknowledging the fragility of objectivity in such statements. He asserts that "Truth" is a contextual scientific discourse conferred upon within social, political, and economic institutions. And further, given that this "political economy or regime of truth" operates circularly within such systems of power, Foucault continues that political problems arising out of the strained condition of scientific discourse and ideology are not matters of truth alone, but rather the confluence of truth *and* power. In this sense, the issue is not merely "changing people's consciousnesses . . . but the political, economic, institutional regime of the production of truth" and subsequent effects of "power" generated "truth" within a society.[8]

The task of intersubjective testability, then, does not involve whimsical attempts to "emancipate" truth from systems of power but in the detachment of the power of truth from the dominant culture, and redirecting it toward transformative ends; to wit: "The political question . . . is not error, illusion, alienated consciousness or ideology; it is truth itself."[9] The organic researcher/teacher intellectual, who seeks neither to hold nor to profess universal "truths," is positioned to confront and dismantle the apparatuses of oppression and related truth claims to power, precisely because of their position within the institution.[10] Thus, it would be a "dangerous error to discount [him/her] politically in [his/her] specific relation to a local form of power."[11] Truth does not exist outside of power, nor does power lack in truth, as such. Rather, it is the effects of power produced by truth claims that are of concern, particularly with respect to (scientific) discourse—truth is what power does.

By this measure, CPSP supports critical awareness and purposeful positioning at institutional levels, which allow truth claims to be tested in teacher education, and the effects of power disrupted in the interest of social transformation. Absent this ability to critique claims of knowledge and truth, the vacuum left will almost certainly be filled with hollow "convictions" rather than constructive criticism, yet to the detriment of society. Therefore, the scientific knowledge referenced throughout this discussion is not regarded as the inflection of an already essentializing force. It is used as a resource for a critical and instructive method to critique the sociopolitical nature of race and ethnicity operating under a "discursive mantle of diversity,"[12] as well as scientific discourse itself, by deconstructing and decentralizing oppressive truth claims.

As suggested, truth claims about the intelligence and cognitive ability of minority students stem from unexamined convictions often made under the aegis of scientific knowledge. While not all subscribe to these truths, their emanation from within institutions has allowed them to manifest in society, perforce, as "Truth." A CPSP framework and method unveils and decenters oppressive discourses by reconstituting science as a means to explore diversity and a transformative activity that reclaims institutional power toward egalitarian ends.

Science, Diversity, and the Sociopolitical

This section offers context for science and diversity and demonstrates traditional misuses of institutionalized truth claims framed as absolute. Particular attention is given to the exclusionary effects of racial discrimination through the duplicitous use of science by traditionally dominant groups to subjugate individuals on the basis of phenotypic variations such as skin color. By documenting historical shifts in understandings about science and human diversity, misguided assumptions of human difference emerge that help explain how racial discrimination developed into such a pervasive, stratifying force in schools and society. Through a CPSP lens, such critiques also provide insights for teaching about diversity.

Omissions and Misappropriations of Science

History provides several examples of attempts to legitimate discriminatory practices by appropriating the narratives of science and culture. Science tends to draw exclusively from a Eurocentric worldview, which forms the basis of Western Modern Science (WMS) and ideology while creating a metanarrative of humanity that bends decisively toward that particular group. In the shadow of WMS, often conspicuously misattributed or omitted from the discourse and tomes of historical and scientific knowledge are contributions of nonwhite cultures, such as the East African descendants of Ancient Egypt (Kemet)[13] to science, medicine, mathematics, philosophy, religion, and aesthetics. While modern medicine is generally traced back to the Grecian, Hippocrates (ca. 460 BCE–ca. 370 BCE), its origins extend much further into the past to his African predecessor and the first known scientist, Imhotep.[14]

Imhotep was a chief official, vizier, physician, and architect of the Step Pyramid at Saqqara under King Netjerykhet (Djoser), ruler of Ancient Egypt/Kemet during the third dynasty (ca. 2980 BCE–ca. 2650 BCE).[15] To the consternation of classical scholars who centralize Europeans as the progenitors of and most significant contributors to civilization,[16] critical applications of scientific inquiry rightly challenge these notions. Not only do critical interrogations of history reveal that Hippocrates is erroneously positioned as the forebear of modern medicine, but a preponderance of evidence suggests that early Ancient Egyptians most closely resemble "black" individuals from sub-Saharan Africa.[17] Such topics are still perceived as a threat to Eurocentric values or, at best, contentious misalignments of history. However, as Cheikh Anta Diop demonstrated in his pioneering, multidisciplinary work that linked Ancient Egypt to sub-Saharan Africans,[18] using scientific inquiry to critique science itself is valuable in revealing commonly overlooked cultural contributions and historical facts and thus in locating "right knowledge" within the human narrative.

Pseudoscience and Scientific Racism

In this age of information, ideas and knowledge are more easily compiled and transmitted but their proliferation has not been without conflict and distortion. Then, as now, many nonwhite cultures suffer in search of human rights and equality, while vestiges of hegemonic ideologies about race seek to sustain a metanarrative in which the values and appearance of a particular group is privileged above all others. One method of distorting information to favor the traditional Eurocentric framework of truth, for example, is through scientific racism and pseudoscience, which privilege WMS over other forms of knowing. "Pseudoscience" refers to methodologically flawed practices or otherwise ineffectual logic that presumes scientific authority. Scientific racism proposes that the human species is naturally divided, and exists as such, on the basis of inherent gradation of human value. Since its late 17th-century emergence, this line of pseudoscientific thinking has been used to maintain racial fallacies, and to justify racial inequality through misguided ideologies presented as scientific knowledge.[19]

Propelled by the burgeoning force of industry and capital in the 18th century, science had become an instrument of authority used to legitimate social stratification on the basis of race. Among the remaining political bastions of this white-hetero-patriarchy is the long-debunked notion of race as a biological imperative.[20] Due to misguided assertions of genetic or phenotypic variability, embodied by pseudoscientific racist practices such as phrenology and eugenics, science has since been instrumental in reinforcing dominant group ideological values and under the auspices of sound empirical research. For instance, using the racially discriminatory practice of phrenology, 19th-century craniologists sought to classify morality and intelligence-based skull features, where nonwhites were regarded as having smaller skulls and thus inferior minds. Science was contorted through the prevailing cultural ideology of white supremacy into a pseudoscience by which the intelligence and "force of mental character" of nonwhites were erroneously held to be deficient, which made them inferior to whites.[21]

Eugenics doctrines of the 19th and 20th centuries sought to bind race and intelligence together to support such claims.[22] Wrongly conflated with the evolutionary theories of species diversity postulated by Darwin as well as Mendel's genetics studies, eugenics became an increasingly popular, "scientifically credible" basis for social and racial stratification.[23] Aimed at "national hygiene," and ostensibly verified by scientific studies and mathematical explanations of intelligence, phrenology and eugenics did more to legitimate racial bias and exclusion.[24] Countless generations have since endured the subjugation, discrimination, and miseducation used to redirect public discourse away from critical dialogue that would challenge the hardline views of ideological fundamentalists which have traditionally been at odds with science and society.

These examples illustrate how science (read: pseudoscience) is embraced by the dominant class when it serves to legitimate and solidify traditional Eurocentric power structures. Accordingly, scientific racism seeks to galvanize ideological power structures in society and deepen false consciousness. Unsurprisingly, when science is used to challenge those same ideological structures, the institution resists; however, each instance of suppressed scientific discovery and critical discourse raises the simple yet complex question: "who benefits?" Who benefits when critical appraisals of institutions are silenced by the clamor of ideology? Who benefits when advancements facilitated by science that offer equitable education and quality of life are suppressed? CPSP suggests that teachers should be prepared to ask such questions in order to uncover racial discrimination in curricula and instructional practice.[25]

Given the sociopolitical context highlighted earlier, it is clear that scientific knowledge is highly implicated in the struggle for racial equality. Indeed, the social and historical contingencies of science illustrate the lack of presumed value-neutrality of science, instead emphasizing that it is one of many narratives with particular truths about the natural world. Further, the suppression and instrumental role of science in shaping social institutions to secure positions of power for a few suggests that scientific knowledge and the language of scientific discourse are contested domains.[26] From a CPSP perspective, the ongoing interrogation of scientific knowledge and discourse in society supports the ability of science to provide context to our shared human experience; in order to transcend itself, it must critique itself.

What follows is a critical analysis of literature associated with the following questions: (1) What is the role of science in teaching about diversity, particularly in TEPs? and (2) how might such an approach impact PSTs across disciplines, in terms of raising greater critical awareness and influencing inclusive classroom practices? As research on using science to teach about diversity in educational settings is limited, the selected literature addresses student diversity and its integration with science. The discussion is organized into three major themes. CPSP is then positioned as a critical method for teaching about diversity issues in the 21st century. This new direction builds on current research regarding science and student diversity.[27]

Science, (Student) Diversity, and (Teacher) Education

During the same historical period as the ascendant role of scientific and technological innovation and diversification of society, social movements and educational reform efforts aimed at mitigating the effects of racial discrimination in schools and society were also emerging. Consistent with the ubiquitous presence of science, rapid demographic shifts, and issues of equity and social justice, this section discusses key research involving science, diversity, and education. These topics are commonly framed within multicultural as well as culturally relevant and responsive methods that employ critical and postcolonial perspectives. This research conceptualizes teaching practices that increase awareness of diversity issues of race, class, gender, language, ability, and cultural epistemologies in the science classroom.[28]

As broad rubrics for diversity and education, this research underscores three major themes. The first two themes address multicultural science education and culturally relevant (science) pedagogy; the more critical varieties of the two are related to the third theme of critical (science) pedagogy. The latter more political forms centralize student and teacher emancipation, agency, and social justice and increasingly include feminist, postcolonial, and postmodern critiques. Although these topics differ in scope and application, their shared commitment to social justice and empowerment of marginalized groups offers significant insights for improving science achievement and making the curriculum more tolerant and inclusive.

Multicultural Education and Science

Following the *Brown Decision* in 1954 and the civil rights movement of the 1960s, the concepts of multiculturalism and cultural pluralism became more prevalent in public and educational discourse and provided a curricular basis for multicultural education (MEd). Though multiply defined, an early vision of MEd was to

> reform the school and other educational institutions so that students from diverse racial, ethnic, and social-class groups ... experience educational equality ... [and] to give both male and female students an equal chance to experience educational success and mobility.[29]

The underlying hope for this new field was providing a means to facilitate increased cultural intersections in society, as well as address issues of achievement disparities among minority students. However, critics of MEd contended that structural effects of racism were understated and the curriculum overemphasized. Supporters of anti-racism argued that multicultural curricula were naively viewed as a panacea for increasing academic achievement and social mobility.[30] Among these debates was the view that MEd was but a neatly framed utopian treatment that was privileged at the expense of deeper analyses of power differentials and race relations and that it lacked sufficient analytical depth and sociopolitical scope to adequately confront issues of racial discrimination that pervaded schools and society.[31] There was also a healthy skepticism about whether the dominant class would allow MEd to develop as proposed. Afrocentric scholars such as Molefi Asante, who being well familiar with the history of suppressed knowledge and cultures of nondominant groups, were concerned with a hidden agenda of white multicultural proponents. Driving this concern was that notion that the multicultural movement would be co-opted and fashioned into another form of Eurocentric hegemony, similar to The Freedman's Bureau's role in the miseducation of blacks in the South after Reconstruction.

From this perspective, MEd could amount to little more than a near-passive addition to the process of schooling, whose covert purpose would be to reinforce Eurocentric values rather than to critically intervene in the political, racialized debates and educational discourse in society. However, as MEd developed and refined its mission, the field continued to gain traction. Subsequently, various academic disciplines began incorporating the tenets of MEd into the curriculum, social studies being among the first domain-specific area to adopt MEd as a curricular disposition and science among the last. The growing diversity in this country suggests that MEd will continue to be as a mainstay of contemporary schooling.

Multicultural Science Education

Owing to recent national attention on underrepresented groups in STEM fields and preparing a scientifically literate workforce, extensive research on science education and diversity has emerged.[32] Since the late 1980s, MEd has been at the forefront of efforts to make science more accessible, under the banner of multicultural science education (MSE). In accordance with the mission of the AAAS that promotes "science for all" students, MSE applies MEd to develop equitable ways of learning and teaching science. Mary Atwater defines MSE as

 a field of inquiry with constructs, methodologies and processes aimed at
 providing equitable opportunities for all students to learn quality science in

schools, colleges, and universities. . . . The basic premises of multicultural science education are (1) all students can learn science, (2) every student is worthwhile to have in the science classrooms, and (3) cultural diversity is appreciated in science classrooms.[33]

MSE has many salient features for increasing minority involvement in science and improving achievement. Among them is decentering science, which as a monolithic specialty is devoid of culture, ethnicity, and gender and is accessible only to certain groups or individuals. For instance, science is still primarily taught from a white, male, Eurocentric perspective. MSE, however, takes a social constructivist stance that seeks to give ownership of science learning to the students, while emphasizing the significance and impact of culture on the learning process. To strengthen this connection, MEd is embedded in "science curriculum, science teacher education, student science learning and instruction, science assessment, and science evaluation."[34]

Critics argued that because of the strong focus on curriculum integration, both MEd and MSE seemed to conveniently elide critical inquiry in general and deeper treatments of race and class in particular.[35] Similar to Asante's suspicions, McLaren and Torres asserted that MEd applications were but repackaged neoliberal market ideologies served as pluralism.[36] Yet despite a heavy curricular focus or supposed capitulation to market-based ideologies, MEd and MSE seek to ensure all students connect to academic content by contextualizing the contributions and perspectives of a multicultural world beyond the borders of Europeanized history and ideology.

Culturally Relevant Pedagogy and Science

MSE is thus informed by culturally relevant and responsive modes of instruction, which aim to connect student culture to school culture. Throughout the 1990s and the 2000s, these pedagogical approaches were infused within the MSE curriculum. Culturally relevant pedagogy (CRP) suggests that how science is taught to students from diverse cultural and linguistic backgrounds is an important aspect of science education. Teachers who use CRP are responsive. They understand the "dynamic or synergistic relationship between home/community culture and school culture," and use "the cultural characteristics, experiences, and perspectives of ethnically diverse students as conduits for teaching them more effectively," and to empower them by facilitating human agency.[37]

Culture is integral in communicating and conceptualizing information and therefore instrumental in human cognition and interactions. Providing equitable access to education requires teachers who are both aware *and* responsive to cultural nuance in the classroom, and who understand the value of inclusion, as well as the importance of culture in how information is transmitted and received. To do so, they must first attend to their own beliefs and (mis)conceptions about different races, ethnicities, and cultures. Responsive, self-aware teachers understand that when situated within students' "cultural and experiential filters" concepts and skills are learned easily and perceived as more interesting and meaningful, and their overall content knowledge more durable. Students who are taught in this way tend to reach high levels of achievement, regardless of academic discipline.

While integrating students' cultures in the classroom can be challenging, teachers with firm scientific knowledge as well as an understanding of language and culture often promote student success in the science classroom as well. Culturally relevant science pedagogy proposes to engage minority youth in ways that increase science achievement, as well as the culturally unaware educator, by drawing their attention to inequities within the communities where they teach and issues of social justice. This perspective also begs questions of "what counts as science, what should be taught, how science is taught, and how student learning can be assessed in valid and fair ways."[38] It further suggests that "the quality of educational experience suffers if Western science is imposed on students who do not share its system of meanings, symbols, and practices."[39] As such, equity of voice in scientific discourse and critiques of scientific knowledge should also be of particular concern.

Together, MSE and CRP point to the critical need to decolonize science curricula and to provide entry points for students of diverse backgrounds to learn and perform science. This includes developing a critical awareness of how dominant cultural groups have traditionally been privileged in the curriculum "through the selective inclusion and exclusion of material" in various textbooks.[40] As Hickling-Hudson argues, the currently embedded discourse of colonialism in education is "culturally problematic" and "does emotional and intellectual violence" to those who do not assimilate to the westernized hegemonic program.[41] Thus, while science and STEM achievement are important, so too are the ramifications of unexamined science practice on local and global societies and its effects on privileging specific forms of knowledge while obscuring issues related to the inequitable distribution of resources in underserved schools. While MSE and CRP offer powerful alternatives to mainstream science teaching and learning, they also suggest the need for critical (scientific) inquiry, particularly one that examines macro-structural obstacles to science teaching and learning in a global political economy, as well as ongoing critical analyses of human diversity. In becoming critical researchers of science, students would also acquire scientific skills.

Critical Pedagogy and Science

Due to a focus on marginalized and underserved populations, critical pedagogy (CP) is often associated with MEd and CRP. Similar to the 20th-century progressive conceptualizations of an authentic, democratic and constructivist education, CP in science education presents knowledge as student-centered and co-constructed (by student and teacher) and poses problems in "real-world" contexts relative to various cultural epistemologies brought into the classroom.[42] The goal is to develop transformative intellectuals instilled with hope, driven by resistance to social oppressions, and grounded in the historical struggle for human agency and radical democracy through critical education and student-centered dialogue.[43] This often takes on a deeply political, emancipatory quality by which students and teachers develop a critical consciousness and awareness to locate inequalities and through informed critiques assist in empowering the human subject as a critical social agent.[44] CPSP therefore suggests profound implications for unearthing latent social oppressions, by confronting dominant narratives of racial stratification through scientific inquiry and investigation.

Given its vast influence on an expanding array of multicultural and culturally relevant modes of teaching and learning science in a knowledge-based economy, the implications of a CP are numerous. The political focus on equity and social justice embodied by CP allows for substantive applications of MSE. It situates MSE within the political economy[45] and by incorporating the responsive nature of CRP and the emancipatory project of CP assists in developing a more transformative agenda for science. Critical multicultural and culturally responsive forms of science offer the ability to politicize macroscopic issues of class, gender, and socioeconomics and to challenge revisionist forms of history that distort or omit the contributions of nonwhite cultures.[46] Thus, rather than *depositing* scientific information to assuage the demands of schooling in this high-stakes era of testing and accountability, CPSP emphasizes ongoing dialogue that challenges hegemonic societal forces by reframing subject content within the social, cultural, and political contexts of a particular historical moment.[47] When empowering the student/subject as such, science is revealed not as a concrete but as a fluid and contestable domain.

Christopher Emdin's 2008 study offers one example of confronting such issues in urban science education from a culturally relevant, critical perspective. His approach consisted of co-generative dialogue through popular culture and autobiographies of learning in which students were able to "read and write the world" through their own voices, using hip-hop and rap music.[48] They became coinvestigators and cocreators of scientific knowledge by rewriting and speaking about scientific information as it applied to their daily lives and cultural backgrounds. Thus able to situate their lived experiences in the world, Emdin demonstrated how urban minority students can be empowered not only to achieve at high levels but to reach higher levels of agency.

This emancipatory potential of science as a political act suggests that problematizing local and global issues while covering science content is one possible approach. Here, students develop scientific knowledge through critically and politically engaging issues beyond the classroom and the high-stakes regime of testing accountability. Such an approach might include critical scientific investigations on the differential effects of the quality, distribution, and consumption of natural resources such as freshwater in poor versus affluent areas. In this sense, science education is not merely a political and contestable arena for challenging distorted power differences but a site of social change. These critical components provide the channel for a less vacuous MEd along with less essentializing forms of anti-racism in (science) education. In practice, the consistent application of such macro-social critiques is often difficult to achieve. Thus, in the ruins of historical power differentials aimed at reproducing the cultural values of the dominant group, CP is often characterized as a combative and divisive tool, or a diluted form of protesting that does little to address issues facing public school systems.

Toward a Critical Postmodern Science Pedagogy of Human Diversity

CPSP has particular implications for teacher education because those who educate PSTs are uniquely positioned to develop critical researchers and stewards of posterity. Critical researchers refer to teachers as change agents, who seek to empower others and to interrupt and transform social and political realities through education.[49] The scientific discourse of CPSP makes use of what is known about the natural world, while rejecting metanarratives and the imposition of pathological hierarchies such as racism and covert discrimination in order to pursue if not achieve the goal of a science of self-interrogation. Moreover, as it attends to the notion that we indeed generate a form of power through the local structures we inhabit, CPSP may be useful in helping PSTs develop more thorough understandings of issues involving race.

One approach involves applying science as a critical method for teaching about diversity, wherein scientific knowledge and discourse illuminate the notion that we share a common humanity comprising irreducible threads of individual existence. By deliberately turning our attention to the premise that we have more in common as humans than we do based on cultural and phenotypic differences, a different picture of diversity may begin to emerge. The following section provides strategies to illustrate what this might look like in a teacher education course about diversity; however, its utility is not limited to teacher education.

Critical Postmodern Science Pedagogical Strategies for Diversity

A CPSP of diversity interrogates, interrupts, and perpetually questions. It is a critical method for deconstructing discourse about diversity and for situating humanity as having a common narrative viewed through a variety of lenses. The goal is not to form yet another metanarrative, or to otherwise escape the complexity of such issues, but through problematizing the very trajectory of humanity become a political tool to develop critical researchers and educators for the 21st century. An added benefit of this approach is that, regardless of discipline, it also speaks to the development of a more critically thinking citizenry, enhancing the potential for a democratic society. Three strategies are presented that incorporate the scientific disciplines of biology, anthropology, genetics, and geography to supplement diversity discussions by problematizing the conflation of skin color with achievement and biologically deterministic misunderstandings of race, ethnicity, and culture. They are based largely on concepts found in K-16 science curricula, though much of this information is either glossed over or forgotten.

DNA ≠ Do Not Ask

One way CPSP can help initiate discussions about diversity involves current scientific knowledge regarding the variation of human DNA. The sum of genetic variation between humans exists within 1/100th of a percent (0.01%), which means that we share 99.9 percent of our DNA sequence. This knowledge is valuable when considering how often phenotypic differences such as skin color are reinforced in society. It also suggests two important points about science and human diversity. The first and perhaps most obvious point is that humans have far more similarities than differences. Much of social life is spent comparing oneself to others with the simple goal of validation within human interactions, which we tend to seek extrinsically rather than intrinsically. By understanding that the genetic variability between individuals is so slim we are encouraged to acknowledge that racial differences are based on social constructions and are thus malleable rather than immutable. This in turn presents an opportunity for changing the way we view ourselves in relation to others, that neither is better or worse than the other, only different. We are entreated to see equal value and meaning in all humans.

The second point is also an indictment. Given that much of global economic sustainability of posterity rests on the knowledge, application, and innovations of science, it would seem prudent to recognize the significance of our similarities. Knowing that humans are 99.9 percent similar presents the glaring implication that social differences between humans are not at all biological but ideological, based on race, and for the purpose of dominance. Reinforcing this scientific discovery in TEPs has the potential of developing students' critical consciousness about racial formation and stratification in the United States. If the reasons and methods for stratifying society by such measures are the result of social and cultural hubris, appealing to one's critical consciousness could reveal a narrative in which each person was valued first on the basis of our common humanity and ancestry.

Pangaea

Another way to begin discussions about diversity using CPSP is through a reteaching of the former supercontinent, Pangaea. This exercise establishes that, approximately 300 million years ago, the continents were connected. And while this information might seem innocuous, the implications of starting a discussion about diversity with such a notion are quite significant. Visualizing continents as they were prior to breaking apart and shifting (as they continue to do) provides a basis for discussing the role of geography in determining the genetic variability in humans. This primordial, postmodern world was without borders. Just as humanity developed through various social and cultural milieus, so too were borders and "ownership" developed. Pangaea demonstrates two important aspects of human diversity. First, it emphasizes the interconnectivity of the world as it exists in nature without human influence. Second, discussing diversity in terms of Pangaea positions difference as a condition of evolutionary survival rather than justification of racial discrimination. Differences in phenotypical features such as skin tone, hair, and the shape and size of body parts depend on geographic location and human development over time. This provides context for human diversity in a contemporary postmodern world.

Media Resources

There are also several media resources that would be informative in such discussions. For example, a video entitled *Race: The Power of an Illusion* produced by PBS demonstrates a DNA lab activity that could be used in conjunction with concepts in the earlier discussion. The lab highlights the notion that there is more genetic variability *within* racial groups than *between* racial groups, which challenges students' misconceptions about human differences based on appearance. Therefore, white students would likely find that their DNA sequence is more comparable to black students than to other white students, because 94 percent of genetic variation exists within racial categories.[50] Another invaluable resource is the award-winning book and documentary by Spencer Wells, a leading population geneticist and director of the Genographic Project from National Geographic, called *The Journey of Man: A Genetic Odyssey*. In it, Wells travels around the world analyzing DNA of hundreds of thousands of participants in a quest to map the history of human migration.[51]

This discussion is in no way exhaustive. These are but a few strategies that could be helpful in discussions about diversity issues with PSTs. Such discussions might focus on the distortions and omissions of (scientific) knowledge that have both contributed to and taken from the human experience to develop critical, contextual 21st-century teachers. There are many other aspects of how and with whom this approach could be used. Despite its scientific disposition, CPSP could be applied in a variety of educational contexts. While it might be particularly useful for science teachers and science teacher educators, the aim is to be transdisciplinary.

Alternate applications of this approach might include using CPSP with in-service teachers in graduate programs and in professional development settings, as well as in K-12 classrooms. In any case, the hope is that current and aspiring educators would be more critically informed and active in the pursuit of social justice, empowerment, and equal representation of all individuals, the anticipated result being teachers who are better prepared to engage diverse classrooms and to support students' self-efficacy and achievement.

Conclusion

The goal of this chapter was to explore the possibility of using science to deconstruct narratives of race and human difference that have historically undermined racial parity in schools and society. Despite increasing discussions about student diversity in (science) education research about critical, multicultural, socially just, culturally relevant strategies and curricula, little has been said about the specific use of science, across disciplines, in TEPs (or otherwise) to show the basis of cultural relevance through our common humanity. To address some of these gaps in teacher education research, and to a growing though still limited understanding of multicultural (science) education, this chapter presented CPSP as a transdisciplinary method of teaching about diversity.

History reminds us that change is constant. And because education is woven so deeply into the fabric of society, critical inquiries of the past using science help to prevent the social construct of race from remaining such a debilitating phenomenon. Moreover, CPSP suggests that learning about and using science should move beyond fetishizing and the false consciousness that follows mindless consumerism, whether in purchasing ideas or in the production of vice and distraction which produce further self-alienation. Highly skilled, but uncritical and historically myopic laborers will ultimately add little value to global society, and even less to themselves. Thus, to avoid becoming another metanarrative, CPSP critiques the domain of science itself through the (self)interrogation of "scientific statements" and their performance in society.

Further, because the social functions of a cultural group are not biologically fixed, but rather external manifestations of that particular group during a specific social and historical period, context is also important to critical discussions about race and ethnicity. In all, CPSP suggests that progress is only as valuable as the level of critique in a society—the extent to which beliefs and actions of individuals or groups are examined from within. Using science as a catalyst for teaching about diversity can unravel misconceptions about race by addressing fundamental aspects of our shared humanity and evoking critical questions about diversity discourse in education.

Notes

1. Abd-El-Khalick and Lederman 2000; Lederman et al. 2002.
2. NRC 2002, p. 2.
3. Milner 2006; National Center for Education Statistics 2013; Swartz 2003.
4. King 1991.
5. Ibid.; Swartz 2003, p. 256.
6. Lyotard 1984, pp. xxiv–xxv.
7. Popper 2002, p. 24.
8. Foucault 1980, p. 133.
9. Ibid.
10. Fischman and McLaren 2005; Giroux 1988; Gramsci 1971.
11. Foucault 1980, p. 131.
12. McLaren, as cited in Nascimento 2007, p. 33.
13. Kemet, var. KMT; kmt, is term derived from Pharaonic language of the Ancient Egyptians and was used to indicate blackness of the earth and the people of Africa (Diop 1981, pp. 41–43).
14. Asante 1990, 2000; Diop 1974, 1981.
15. Asante 2000; Brandt-Rauf and Brandt-Rauf 1987; Diop 1981; Hurry 1926; Osler 1921; The British Medical Journal 1927.
16. See, for example, Lefkowitz 1997.
17. Asante 1990, 2000; Brandt-Rauf and Brandt-Rauf 1987; Diop 1954, 1974, 1981.
18. Diop 1974.
19. Marks 2008.
20. Marks 1996; Omi and Winant 1994; Witzig 1996.
21. Combe 1830; Marks 2008; Wiggan 2007.
22. Herrnstein and Murray 1994; Hilliard 2000; Marks 2008; Wiggan 2007.
23. Bouchard 1988; Marks 1996; Ordover 2003.
24. Collins 1998; Ordover 2003; Proctor 1988.
25. Atwater 2010.
26. Hodson 1993, 1999; Foucault 1980.
27. Here, the term "diversity" is concerned with race, ethnicity and culture. Related issues of discrimination involving class, gender, sexuality, and language are equally important aspects of human diversity. However, they are beyond the scope of the present discussion.

28. Abrams, Taylor, and Guo 2013; Apple 2010; Castro 2010; Freire 2005, p. 200; Giroux 1988; Shizha 2010; Swartz 2003.

29. Banks 1993a, pp. 3–4.

30. Ibid.

31. Ibid.

32. Riegle-Crumb, Moore, and Ramos-Wada 2011; National Academies 2007a, 2007b, 2010.

33. Atwater 1996, pp. 34–35.

34. Atwater 2010, p. 103.

35. May 1999; Nola and Irzık 2005.

36. McLaren and Torres 1999.

37. Gay 2002, p. 106; ibid., p. 467.

38. Lee 2001, p. 499.

39. Ibid.

40. Asante 1991; Kumashiro 2001, p. 4.

41. Hickling-Hudson 2003, p. 3.

42. Dewey 1916; Freire 1970, 2005; Popkewitz 1998; Ültanir 2012.

43. Giroux 1988, 2005; Kanpol and McLaren 1995, p. 5; McLaren 1999.

44. Freire 1970; Kanpol and McLaren 1995.

45. McLaren and Torres 1999.

46. Swartz 2005.

47. Freire 1970; Lipman 2004.

48. Emdin 2008; Freire and Macedo 1987.

49. Creswell 2007.

50. See "AAPA Statement on Biological Aspects of Race" 1996.

51. Maltby 2003; Wells 2003.

Bibliography

Abd-El-Khalick, F., and N. Lederman. 2000. "Improving Science Teachers' Conceptions of Nature of Science: A Critical Review of the Literature." *International Journal of Science Education* 22 (7): 665–701. doi:10.1080/095006900500 44044.

Abrams, E., P. Taylor, and C. Guo. 2013. "Contextualizing Culturally Relevant Science and Mathematics Teaching for Indigenous Learning." *International Journal of Science and Mathematics Education* 11 (1): 1–21. doi:10.1007/s10 763-012-9388-2.

Agger, B. 1991. "Critical Theory, Poststructuralism, Postmodernism: Their Sociological Relevance." *Annual Review of Sociology* 17: 105–131.

Aikenhead, G. 1996. "Science Education: Border Crossing into the Subculture of Science." *Studies in Science Education* 27 (1): 1–52. doi:10.1080/030572696085 60077.

American Association for the Advancement of Science. 1993. *Benchmarks for Science Literacy.* [Online version]. New York: Oxford University Press. http://www.project2061.org/publications/bsl/online.

Anderson, J. 1988. *The Education of Blacks in the South, 1860–1935.* Chapel Hill, NC: University of North Carolina Press.

Apple, M. 1978. "Ideology, Reproduction, and Educational Reform." *Comparative Education Review* 22 (3): 367–387.

Apple, M. 2004. *Ideology and Curriculum.* New York: RoutledgeFalmer.

Apple, M. 2010. "Theory, Research, and the Critical Scholar/Activist." *Educational Researcher* 39 (2): 152–155. doi:10.3102/0013189X10362591.

Apple, M. 2011. "Global Crises, Social Justice, and Teacher Education." *Journal of Teacher Education* 62 (2): 222–234. doi:10.1177/0022487110385428.

Asante, M. 1990. *Kemet, Afrocentricity, and Knowledge.* Trenton, NJ: Africa World Press.

Asante, M. 1991. "The Afrocentric Idea in Education." *The Journal of Negro Education* 60 (2): 170–180. doi:10.2307/2295608.

Asante, M. 2000. *The Egyptian Philosophers: Ancient African Voices from Imhotep to Akhenaten.* Chicago, IL: African American Images.

Asante, M., and D. Ravitch. 1991. "Multiculturalism: An Exchange." *The American Scholar* 60 (2): 267–276.

Atwater, M. 1989. "Including Multicultural Education in Science Education: Definitions, Competencies, and Activities." *Journal of Science Teacher Education* 1 (1): 17–20. doi:10.1007/BF03032129.

Atwater, M. 1996. "Social Constructivism: Infusion into the Multicultural Science Education Research Agenda." *Journal of Research in Science Teaching* 33 (8): 821–837. doi:10.1002/(SICI)1098-2736(199610)33:8<821:AID-TEA1>3.0.CO;2-Y.

Atwater, M. 2010. "Multicultural Science Education and Curriculum Materials." *Science Activities: Classroom Projects and Curriculum Ideas* 47 (4): 103–108. doi:10.1080/00368121003631652.

Atwater, M. 2011. "Significant Science Education Research on Multicultural Science Education, Equity, and Social Justice." *Journal of Research in Science Teaching* 49 (1): O1–O5. doi:10.1002/tea.20453.

Atwater, M., and J. Riley. 1993. "Multicultural Science Education: Perspectives, Definitions, and Research Agenda." *Science Education* 77 (6): 661–668. doi:10.1002/sce.3730770609.

Atwater, M., M. Russell, and M. Butler, eds. 2013. *Multicultural Science Education: Preparing Teachers for Equity and Social Justice.* Dordrecht, Netherlands: Springer.

Banks, J. 1993a. "Multicultural Education: Historical Development, Dimensions, and Practice." *Review of Research in Education* 19: 3–49. doi:10.2307/1167339.

Banks, J. 1993b. "The Canon Debate, Knowledge Construction, and Multicultural Education." *Educational Researcher* 22 (5): 4–14. doi:10.3102/0013189X0220 05004.

Banks, J., and C. Banks, eds. 2010. *Multicultural Education: Issues and Perspectives.* 7th ed. Hoboken, NJ: Wiley.

Barton, A., and C. Berchini. 2013. "Becoming an Insider: Teaching Science in Urban Settings." *Theory into Practice* 52 (1): 21–27. doi:10.1080/07351690. 2013.743765.

Barton, A., and P. McLaren. 2001. "Capitalism, Critical Pedagogy, and Urban Science Education: An Interview with Peter McLaren." *Journal of Research in Science Teaching* 38 (8): 847–859. doi:10.1002/tea.1035.

Bennett, K., and M. LeCompte. 1990. *How Schools Work: Sociological Analysis of Education.* White Plains, NY: Longman.

Blake, N., and J. Masschelein. 2003. "Critical Theory and Critical Pedagogy." In *The Blackwell Guide to the Philosophy of Education,* eds. N. Blake, P. Smeyers, R. Smith, and P. Standish (pp. 38–56). Malden, MA: Blackwell Publishing.

Blumer, H. 1969. *Symbolic Interactionism: Perspective and Method.* Englewood Cliffs, NJ: Prentice Hall.

Bouchard, C. 1988. "Genetic Basis of Racial Differences." *Canadian Journal of Sport Sciences = Journal Canadien Des Sciences Du Sport* 13: 104.

Brandt-Rauf, P., and S. Brandt-Rauf. 1987. "History of Occupational Medicine: Relevance of Imhotep and the Edwin Smith Papyrus." *British Journal of Industrial Medicine* 44 (1): 68–70.

The British Medical Journal. 1927. "Imhotep: The Physician-Architect." *The British Medical Journal* 1 (3458): 734.

Brown, M. 2007. "Educating All Students: Creating Culturally Responsive Teachers, Classrooms, and Schools." *Intervention in School and Clinic* 43 (1): 57–62. doi:10.1177/10534512070430010801.

Buxton, C. 2010. "Social Problem Solving through Science: An Approach to Critical, Place-Based, Science Teaching and Learning." *Equity & Excellence in Education* 43 (1): 120–135. doi:10.1080/10665680903408932.

Carter, N., P. Larke, G. Singleton-Taylor, and E. Santos. 2003. "Multicultural Science Education: Moving beyond Tradition." In *Multicultural Science Education: Theory, Practice, and Promise,* ed. S. Hines. New York: Peter Lang.

Castro, A. 2010. "Themes in the Research on Preservice Teachers' Views of Cultural Diversity Implications for Researching Millennial Preservice Teachers." *Educational Researcher* 39 (3): 198–210. doi:10.3102/0013189X10363819.

Cho, G., and D. DeCastro-Ambrosetti. 2005. "Is Ignorance Bliss? Pre-Service Teachers' Attitudes toward Multicultural Education." *The High School Journal* 89 (2): 24–28. doi:10.1353/hsj.2005.0020.

Choi, J. 2008. "Unlearning Colorblind Ideologies in Education Class." *Educational Foundations* 22 (3–4): 53–71.

Cochran-Smith, M. 2003. "The Multiple Meanings of Multicultural Teacher Education: A Conceptual Framework." *Teacher Education Quarterly* 30 (2): 7–26.

Cochran-Smith, M., and K. Zeichner, eds. 2005. *Studying Teacher Education: The Report of the AERA Panel on Research and Teacher Education.* Mahwah, NJ: Lawrence Erlbaum Associates.

Collins, P. 1998. "It's All in the Family: Intersections of Gender, Race, and Nation." *Hypatia* 13 (3): 62–82. doi:10.2307/3810699.

Collins, P. 2000. "What's Going on? Black Feminist Thought and the Politics of Postmodernism." In *Working the Ruins: Feminist Poststructural Theory and Methods in Education,* eds. E. St. Pierre and W. S. Pillow (pp. 41–73). New York: Routledge.

Combe, G. 1830. *A System of Phrenology.* 3rd ed. Edinburgh, Scotland: J. Anderson.

Corsiglia, J., and G. Snively. 2001. "Rejoinder: Infusing Indigenous Science into Western Modern Science for a Sustainable Future." *Science Education* 85 (1): 82–86. doi:10.1002/1098-237X(200101)85:1<82:AID-SCE11>3.0.CO;2-Q.

Creswell, J. 2007. *Qualitative Inquiry and Research Design: Choosing among Five Traditions.* Thousand Oaks, CA: Sage.

Croizet, J., and M. Dutrévis. 2004. "Socioeconomic Status and Intelligence: Why Test Scores Do Not Equal Merit." *Journal of Poverty* 8 (3): 91–107. doi:10.1300/J134v08n03_05.

Crotty, M. 1998. *The Foundations of Social Research: Meaning and Perspective in the Research Process.* Thousand Oaks, CA: Sage.

Darling-Hammond, L. 2010. *The Flat World and Education: How America's Commitment to Equity Will Determine Our Future.* Columbia, NY: Teachers College Press.

Delpit, L. 2006. *Other People's Children: Cultural Conflict in the Classroom.* New York: New Press.

DeMarrais, K., and M. LeCompte. 1998. *The Way Schools Work: A Sociological Analysis of Education.* 3rd ed. White Plains, NY: Longman/Addison Wesley.

Derrida, J. 1978. *Writing and Difference.* Chicago, IL: University of Chicago.

Derrida, J. 1982. *Positions.* Chicago, IL: University of Chicago.

Derrida, J. 2009. "The Decentering Event in Social Thought." In *Social Theory: The Multicultural and Classic Readings,* ed. C. C. Lemert (pp. 413–417). Boulder, CO: Westview Press.

Dewey, J. 1916. *Democracy and Education: An Introduction to the Philosophy of Education.* New York: Macmillan.

Diop, C. 1954. *Nations Nègres et Culture: De l'Antiquité Nègre égyptienne Aux Problèmes Culturels de l'Afrique Noire D'aujourd'hui.* Paris: Présence Africaine.

Diop, C. 1974. *The African Origin of Civilization: Myth or Reality.* New York: Laurence Hill.

Diop, C. 1981. "Origin of the Ancient Egyptians." In *General History of Africa II: Ancient Civilizations of Africa,* ed. G. Mokhtar. London: Heinemann.

Emdin, C. 2008. "Urban Science Classrooms and New Possibilities: On Intersubjectivity and Grammar in the Third Space." *Cultural Studies of Science Education* 4 (1): 239–254. doi:10.1007/s11422-008-9162-5.

Fischman, G., and P. McLaren. 2005. "Rethinking Critical Pedagogy and the Gramscian and Freirean Legacies: From Organic to Committed Intellectuals or Critical Pedagogy, Commitment, and Praxis." *Cultural Studies <=>Critical Methodologies* 5 (4): 425–446. doi:10.1177/1532708605279701.

Foeman, A. 2009. "Science and Magic: DNA and the Racial Narratives That Shape the Social Construction of Race in the USA." *Intercultural Communication Studies* 18 (2): 14–25.

Foucault, M. 1977. *Discipline and Punish: The Birth of the Prison System.* New York: Vintage Books.

Foucault, M. 1980. *Power/Knowledge: Selected Interviews and Other Writings, 1972–1977.* New York: Pantheon Books.

Foucault, M. 1997. "Technologies of the Self." In *Ethics: Subjectivity and Truth. Essential Works of Foucault, 1954–1984,* ed. P. Rabinow. New York: The New Press.

Foucault, M. 2002. *Archaeology of Knowledge.* Routledge Classics. New York: Routledge.

Foucault, M. 2003. *Birth of the Clinic.* London: Routledge.

Freire, P. 1970. *Pedagogy of the Oppressed.* New York: Continuum.

Freire, P. 2005. *Teachers as Cultural Workers: Letters to Those Who Dare Teach.* Boulder, CO: Westview Press.

Freire, P., and D. Macedo. 1987. *Literacy: Reading the Word and the World.* London: Routledge & Kegan Paul.

Gay, G. 2010. "Acting on Beliefs in Teacher Education for Cultural Diversity." *Journal of Teacher Education* 61 (1–2): 143–152. doi:10.1177/0022487109347320.

Gay, G. 2002. "Preparing for Culturally Responsive Teaching." *Journal of Teacher Education* 53 (2): 106–116. doi:10.1177/0022487102053002003.

Giroux, H. 1980. "Critical Theory and Rationality in Citizenship Education." *Curriculum Inquiry* 10 (4): 329–366.

Giroux, H. 1988. *Teachers as Intellectuals: Toward a Critical Pedagogy of Learning.* Granby, MA: Bergin & Garvey.

Giroux, H. 2005. *Border Crossings: Cultural Workers and the Politics of Education.* 2nd ed. New York: Routledge.

Giroux, H., and P. McLaren. 1986. "Teacher Education and the Politics of Engagement." *Harvard Educational Review* 56 (3): 213–239.

Gramsci, A. 1971. *Selections from the Prison Notebooks of Antonio Gramsci.* New York: International Publishers.

Green, P. 1999. "Separate and Still Unequal: Legal Challenges to School Tracking and Ability Grouping in America's Public Schools." In *Race Is . . . Race*

Isn't: Critical Race Theory and Qualitative Studies in Education, eds. L. Parker, D. Deyhle, and S. Villenas (pp. 231–250). Boulder, CO: Westview Press.

Harry, B., and J. Klingner. 2006. *Why Are so Many Minority Students in Special Education? Understanding Race and Disability in Schools.* New York: Teachers College Press.

Herrnstein, R., and C. Murray. 1994. *The Bell Curve: Intelligence and Class Structure in American Life.* New York: Free Press.

Hickling-Hudson, A. 2003. "Multicultural Education and the Postcolonial Turn." *Policy Futures in Education* 1: 381–401.

Hilliard, A. 2000. "Excellence in Education versus High-Stakes Standardized Testing." *Journal of Teacher Education* 51 (4): 293–304. doi:10.1177/002248 7100051004005.

Hodson, D. 1993. "In Search of a Rationale for Multicultural Science Education." *Science Education* 77 (6): 685–711. doi:10.1002/sce.3730770611.

Hodson, D. 1999. "Critical Multiculturalism in Science and Technology Education." In *Critical Multiculturalism: Rethinking Multicultural and Antiracist Education,* ed. S. May (pp. 236–266). Philadelphia, PA: Falmer Press.

Horkheimer, M. 1982. *Critical Theory: Selected Essays.* New York: Continuum.

Howard, G. 2006. *We Can't Teach What We Don't Know: White Teachers, Multiracial Schools.* 2nd ed. Multicultural Education Series. New York: Teachers College Press.

Hurry, J. 1926. *Imhotep: The Vizier and Physician of King Zoser and afterwards the Egyptian God of Medicine.* Oxford, UK: Oxford University.

Hurtado, S., N. Cabrera, M. H. Lin, L. Arellano, and L. Espinosa. 2008. "Diversifying Science: Underrepresented Student Experiences in Structured Research Programs." *Research in Higher Education* 50 (2): 189–214. doi:10.1007/s11162-008-9114-7.

Hurtado, S., C. Newman, M. Tran, and M. Chang. 2010. "Improving the Rate of Success for Underrepresented Racial Minorities in STEM Fields: Insights from a National Project." *New Directions for Institutional Research* 148: 5–15. doi:10.1002/ir.357.

Irvine, J., and D. York. 1993. "Teacher Perspectives: Why Do African American, Hispanic, and Vietnamese Students Fail?" In *Handbook of Schooling in Urban America,* ed. S. Rothstein (pp. 161–73). Westport, CT: Greenwood Press.

Jameson, F. 1998. *The Cultural Turn: Selected Writings on the Postmodern, 1983–1998.* London and New York: Verso Books.

Kanpol, B., and P. McLaren, eds. 1995. *Critical Multiculturalism: Uncommon Voices in a Common Struggle.* Westport, CT: Bergin & Garvey.

Kellner, D. 2003. "Toward a Critical Theory of Education." *Democracy & Nature* 9 (1): 51–64. doi:10.1080/1085566032000074940.

Kincheloe, J. 2010. "Why a Book on Urban Education?" In *19 Urban Questions: Teaching in the City,* ed. S. Steinberg (2nd ed.) (pp. 1–25). New York: Peter Lang.

King, J. 1991. "Dysconscious Racism: Ideology, Identity, and the Miseducation of Teachers." *The Journal of Negro Education* 60 (2): 133. doi:10.2307/2295605.

Kozol, J. 2005. *The Shame of the Nation: The Restoration of Apartheid Schooling in America.* New York: Crown Publishers.

Kumashiro, K. 2001. "'Posts' Perspectives on Anti-oppressive Education in Social Studies, English, Mathematics, and Science Classrooms." *Educational Researcher* 30 (3): 3–12. doi:10.3102/0013189X030003003.

Ladson-Billings, G. 1995a. "But That's Just Good Teaching! The Case for Culturally Relevant Pedagogy." *Theory into Practice* 34 (3): 159–165. doi:10.1080/00405849509543675.

Ladson-Billings, G. 1995b. "Toward a Theory of Culturally Relevant Pedagogy." *American Educational Research Journal* 32 (3): 465–491. doi:10.3102/00028312032003465.

Ladson-Billings, G. 2000. "Fighting for Our Lives: Preparing Teachers to Teach African American Students." *Journal of Teacher Education* 51 (3): 206–214. doi:10.1177/0022487100051003008.

Ladson-Billings, G. 2006. "From the Achievement Gap to the Education Debt: Understanding Achievement in U.S. Schools." *Educational Researcher* 35 (7): 3–12. doi:10.3102/0013189X035007003.

Ladson-Billings, G. 2009. *The Dreamkeepers: Successful Teachers of African American Children.* San Francisco, CA: Jossey-Bass.

Lederman, N., F. Abd-El-Khalick, R. Bell, and R. Schwartz. 2002. "Views of Nature of Science Questionnaire: Toward Valid and Meaningful Assessment of Learners' Conceptions of Nature of Science." *Journal of Research in Science Teaching* 39 (6): 497–521. doi:10.1002/tea.10034.

Lee, O. 2001. "Culture and Language in Science Education: What Do We Know and What Do We Need to Know?" *Journal of Research in Science Teaching* 38 (5): 499–501. doi:10.1002/tea.1015.

Lee, O. 2011. "Effective STEM Education Strategies for Diverse and Underserved Learners." Washington, DC: National Academies Press.

Lee, O., and S. Fradd. 1998. "Science for All, Including Students from Non-English-Language Backgrounds." *Educational Researcher* 27 (4): 12–21. doi:10.3102/0013189X027004012.

Lefkowitz, M. 1997. *Not Out of Africa: How Afrocentrism Became an Excuse to Teach Myth as History.* New York: Basic Books.

Lipman, P. 2004. *High Stakes Education: Inequality, Globalization, and Urban School Reform.* New York: RoutledgeFalmer.

Lyotard, J. 1984. *The Postmodern Condition: A Report on Knowledge.* Manchester, UK: Manchester University.

Maltby, C. 2003. *Journey of Man: A Genetic Odyssey* (DVD).

Mansour, N., and R. Wegerif. 2013. *Science Education for Diversity: Theory and Practice.* New York: Springer.

Marcuse, H. 2009. *Negations: Essays in Critical Theory.* London: MayFlyBooks.

Marks, J. 1996. "Science and Race." *American Behavioral Scientist* 40 (2): 123–133. doi:10.1177/0002764296040002003.

Marks, J. 2008. "Scientific Racism, History of." In *The Encyclopedia of Race and Racism,* ed. J. Moore (vol. 3) (pp. 1–16). Detroit, MI: Macmillan.

May, S., ed. 1999. *Critical Multiculturalism: Rethinking Multicultural and Antiracist Education.* Philadelphia, PA: Falmer Press.

McLaren, P. 1993. "Multiculturalism and the Postmodern Critique: Towards a Pedagogy of Resistance and Transformation." *Cultural Studies* 7 (1): 118–146. doi:10.1080/09502389300490101.

McLaren, P. 1999. *Schooling as a Ritual Performance: Toward a Political Economy of Educational Symbols and Gestures.* 3rd ed. Lanham, MD: Rowman & Littlefield.

McLaren, P. 2007. *Life in Schools: An Introduction to Critical Pedagogy in the Foundations of Education.* 5th ed. Boston: Pearson/Allyn & Bacon.

McLaren, P., and R. Farahmandpur. 2001. "Teaching against Globalization and the New Imperialism: Toward a Revolutionary Pedagogy." *Journal of Teacher Education* 52 (2): 136–150. doi:10.1177/0022487101052002005.

McLaren, P., and R. Torres. 1999. "Racism and Multicultural Education: Rethinking 'race' and 'whiteness' in Late Capitalism." In *Critical Multiculturalism: Rethinking Multicultural and Antiracist Education,* ed. S. May (pp. 42–76). Philadelphia, PA: Falmer Press.

Milner, H. 2006. "Preservice Teachers' Learning about Cultural and Racial Diversity: Implications for Urban Education." *Urban Education* 41 (4): 343–375. doi:10.1177/0042085906289709.

Milner, H. 2012. "Rethinking Achievement Gap Talk in Urban Education." *Urban Education* 48 (1): 3–8. doi:10.1177/0042085912470417.

Moraes, M., and P. McLaren. 2003. "The Path of Dissent: An Interview with Peter McLaren." *Journal of Transformative Education* 1 (2): 117–134. doi:10.1177/1541344603001002004.

Mukhopadhyay, C., and R. Henze. 2003. "How Real Is Race? Using Anthropology to Make Sense of Human Diversity." *Phi Delta Kappan* 84 (9): 669–678.

Nascimento, E. 2007. *The Sorcery of Color: Identity, Race, and Gender in Brazil.* Philadelphia, PA: Temple University.

National Academies. 2007a. *Beyond Bias and Barriers: Fulfilling the Potential of Women in Academic Science and Engineering.* Washington, DC: National Academies Press.

National Academies. 2007b. *Rising above the Gathering Storm: Energizing and Employing America for a Brighter Economic Future.* Washington, DC: National Academies Press.

National Academies. 2010. *Rising above the Gathering Storm, Revisited: Rapidly Approaching Category 5.* Washington, DC: National Academies Press.

National Center for Education Statistics. 2013. *Schools and Staffing Survey (SASS): Table 1. Total Number of Public School Teachers and Percentage Distribution of School Teachers, by Race/Ethnicity and State: 2011–12.* Washington, DC: U.S. Department of Education. http://nces.ed.gov/surveys/sass/tables/sass1112_2013314_t12n_001.asp.

National Research Council. 2002. *Scientific Research in Education.* Washington, DC: National Academies Press.

1996. "AAPA Statement on Biological Aspects of Race." *American Journal of Physical Anthropology* 101 (4): 569–570. doi:10.1002/ajpa.1331010408.

Nola, R., and G. Irzık. 2005. *Philosophy, Science, Education and Culture.* Dordrecht, Netherlands: Springer.

Oakes, J. 2005. *Keeping Track: How Schools Structure Inequality.* New Haven, CT: Yale University.

Omi, M., and H. Winant. 1994. *Racial Formation in the United States: From the 1960s to the 1990s.* New York: Routledge.

Ordover, N. 2003. *American Eugenics: Race, Queer Anatomy, and the Science of Nationalism.* Minneapolis, MN: University of Minnesota.

Osler, W. 1921. *The Evolution of Modern Medicine.* New Haven, CT: Yale University.

Popkewitz, T. 1998. "Dewey, Vygotsky, and the Social Administration of the Individual: Constructivist Pedagogy as Systems of Ideas in Historical Spaces." *American Educational Research Journal* 35 (4): 535–570. doi:10.3102/0002 8312035004535.

Popper, K. 1966. *The Open Society and Its Enemies: Complete.* 5th ed. Vols. 1 and 2. Princeton, NJ: Princeton University.

Popper, K. 2002. *The Logic of Scientific Discovery.* New York: Routledge.

Proctor, R. 1988. *Racial Hygiene: Medicine under the Nazis.* Cambridge, MA: Harvard University.

Quigley, C. 2009. "Globalization and Science Education: The Implications for Indigenous Knowledge Systems." *International Education Studies* 2 (1). doi:10. 5539/ies.v2n1p76.

Rebell, M., and J. Wolff. 2008. *Moving Every Child Ahead: From NCLB Hype to Meaningful Educational Opportunity.* New York: Teachers College Press.

Riegle-Crumb, C., C. Moore, and A. Ramos-Wada. 2011. "Who Wants to Have a Career in Science or Math? Exploring Adolescents' Future Aspirations by Gender and Race/Ethnicity." *Science Education* 95 (3): 458–476. doi:10.1002/ sce.20431.

Sharpe, J. 2005. "Postcolonial Studies in the House of US Multiculturalism." In *A Companion to Postcolonial Studies*, eds. H. Schwartz and S. Ray (pp. 112–125). Malden, MA: Blackwell Publishing.

Shizha, E. 2010. "The Interface of Neoliberal Globalization, Science Education and Indigenous African Knowledges in Africa." *Journal of Alternative Perspectives in the Social Sciences* 2 (1): 27–58.

Smedley, A., and B. Smedley. 2005. "Race as Biology Is Fiction, Racism as a Social Problem Is Real: Anthropological and Historical Perspectives on the Social Construction of Race." *American Psychologist* 60: 16.

Swartz, E. 2003. "Teaching White Preservice Teachers: Pedagogy for Change." *Urban Education* 38 (3): 255–278. doi:10.1177/0042085903038003001.

Swartz, E. 2005. "Multicultural Education: From a Compensatory to a Scholarly Foundation." In *Research and Multicultural Education: From the Margins to the Mainstream,* ed. C. Grant (pp. 31–42). London: Falmer Press.

Taylor, P. 2006. "Forum: Alternative Perspectives: Cultural Hybridity and Third Space Science Classrooms." *Cultural Studies of Science Education* 1 (1): 189–208. doi:10.1007/s11422-005-9007-4.

Ültanir, E. 2012. "An Epistemological Glance at the Constructivist Approach: Constructivist Learning in Dewey, Piaget, and Montessori." *International Journal of Instruction* 5 (2): 195–212.

Wells, S. 2003. *The Journey of Man: A Genetic Odyssey.* New York: Random House.

Wiggan, G. 2007. "Race, School Achievement, and Educational Inequality: Toward a Student-Based Inquiry Perspective." *Review of Educational Research* 77: 310–333.

Winant, H. 2000. "Race and Race Theory." *Annual Review of Sociology* 26: 169–185.

Witzig, R. 1996. "The Medicalization of Race: Scientific Legitimization of a Flawed Social Construct." *Annals of Internal Medicine* 125 (8): 675. doi:10.7326/0003-4819-125-8-199610150-00008.

Woodson, C. 1933. *The Mis-education of the Negro.* New York: AMS Press.

Chapter 7

Increasing Achievement by Strengthening Resilience: An Ecologically Based Intervention for African American Students

Cheryl P. Talley, John E. Fife, Toni S. Harris, and Oliver W. Hill Jr.

Introduction

The year 2014, marked the 60th anniversary of *Brown v. Board of Education of Topeka*, the landmark case that struck down America's version of apartheid in public education. Yet, according to a recent report by the Civil Rights Project, segregation is still alive and growing.[1] The report described contemporary educational segregation as a "double segregation" of both race and poverty. While European American and Asian American students are more likely to live in middle-class and upper middle-class neighborhoods and attend well-resourced schools, a majority of African American and Hispanic American students live in low socioeconomic neighborhoods with poorly resourced schools.

According to Garcia-Coll and colleagues, the social position variables of race, gender, and socioeconomic status (SES) combine to enhance or interfere with the developmental outcomes of children due to the cumulative impact of racism, discrimination, prejudice, and bias that plagues their developmental environments.[2] Thus, the educational experience of racial minorities with a history of oppression and who live in low-income neighborhoods will be vastly different from other students attending schools in higher-income districts. Moreover, the differences will reach beyond external factors such as facilities and course offerings. One important difference may be evidenced in common and covert biases and prejudice, which contribute to low academic expectations and, as we argue here, can lead to low academic achievement. Research findings from social psychology and sociology provide evidence that the implicit meaning given to race and class differences is deeply entrenched in American culture and can have effects that pervade the entire educational system. Teachers, administrators, and policy makers are not immune, nor are the students.

In this chapter we review some relevant findings from the fields of psychology, sociology, and neuroscience that can help to inform views on the impact of long-term, pervasive, and intransigent racial distinctions. We hope to show that while the meanings given to racial and class differences can impact the entire educational context for low-income students, the students, themselves, can also be provided tools that will help them build the resilience needed to succeed in school.

Preliminary findings from a study conducted at Virginia State University and funded by the National Science Foundation are also presented in this chapter. We believe that the results of our study point to the prevalence of two types of internalized messages that influence African American student achievement. We refer to these impactful messages that students may internalize as "I don't belong" and "I don't care." Specifically, we propose that the message "I don't belong" is a response to culturally disseminated stereotypes about people of color and the economically disadvantaged, while "I don't care" is an attitude cultivated early in the educational experience as protection from a sense of failure and to bolster self-esteem.

Recent studies from cognitive and social psychology reveal that police profiling or discriminatory banking practices represent just one small part of modern racism. More subtle racist views are much more common and are likely to be implicit, operating below conscious awareness. In addition, there is evidence from educational psychology that for most African American students, it is not racial segregation *per se* that is responsible for race-related achievement gaps. Rather it is the presence of poverty and resource disparity that are associated with differences in academic achievement. Admittedly, class distinctions are due to much larger political, economic, and social forces. However, we believe that the subtle effects of segregated schools combined with economic disparity are, in part, responsible for strengthening and perpetuating stereotypical views by the culture at large. Furthermore, the perpetuation of stereotypes from one group creates a reciprocal need for protection against the negative views by the other.

Finally, we further define the internalized messages of "I don't belong" and "I don't care" as they have been examined by our research. We present evidence of a promising intervention strategy that has been employed at Virginia State University, a primarily minority-serving institution. Our work is showing that students can be provided cognitive and emotional tools that encourage resilience thereby enhancing their sense of belonging and decreasing self-handicapping behaviors. We also explain how the intervention may be adapted for secondary school students.

The Ethos of Not Belonging: The Wide Reach of Stereotype Threat

On May 17, 1954, a unanimous Supreme Court declared that the separate but equal doctrine, codified in 1895 by the case *Plessy v. Ferguson,* was unconstitutional when applied to public schools. Part of the evidence used in the 1954 case *Brown v. Board of Education of Topeka* was testimony by social psychologists Kenneth and Mamie Phipps Clark. The Clarks had conducted studies with over 200 black children who were given two identical dolls that differed only by skin color. The children were then asked which doll was "nice" and which doll was "bad." The majority of the children labeled the white doll "nice" and the black doll "bad."[3]

A facsimile of the Doll study was conducted again in 2006. Seventeen-year-old filmmaker, Kiri Davis, presented black and white dolls to New York City preschoolers. When given a forced choice, 16 of the 21 children surveyed characterized the white doll as "nice" and the black doll as "bad." In the film, one child received a follow-up question. She was asked, "Which doll looks like you?" The child hesitates for a moment and then pushes forward the black "bad" doll.[4]

The original Clark study was conducted in the 1950s before the modern era of civil rights. To have similar results over half a century later speaks to the power and persistence of cultural messages that are at the foundation of perceived racism. Sociologists consider the demeaning of one's own race as a form of "internalized" racism. Of course, the effects of such internalized messages are not limited to preschoolers or to those in the stigmatized group. Bigler and Liben demonstrated that Euro-American children in rural Ohio, who had little or no interaction with African American children, were more likely to remember stories that were consistent with cultural (racial) stereotypes and had poorer recall of stories that were inconsistent.[5] Dr. Birgitte Vittrup Simpson of the University of Texas found that even the most liberal parents were unwilling to openly discuss race with their children.[6] This is very different behavior from "nonwhite" parents, 75 percent of whom openly discuss race with young children. The study went on to show that when white parents did discuss race, their children were more likely to have more positive racial attitudes.

The absence of a parental conversation leaves children to form opinions about race from peers and popular culture. However, despite the election of President Obama and the popularity of rap music, racist attitudes in American culture have proven difficult to eradicate. One reason for this is that, for the most part, contemporary cultural attitudes and mores favor the concealment of racist sentiments according to a study by cognitive psychologists, Cunningham, Preacher, and Banaji.[7] The research revealed that it was much easier for participants to associate "white" and "good" and "black" and "bad" than to make the association "white" and "bad" and "black" and "good." In addition, the study showed dissociation between implicit and explicit measures of racist attitude. The participants, Ohio State University students, simultaneously self-reported non-prejudiced attitudes toward black Americans while showing a difficulty in associating African Americans with positive attributes. This dissociation is referred to as "implicit racism."

Furthermore, numerous studies outlined in a review by social psychologist Derald Weng Sue reveal that the greatest damage to the life experiences of people of color is from racial "microaggression," brief and commonplace daily verbal, behavioral, and environmental indignities whether intentional or unintentional that communicate hostile or derogatory racial slights and insults. People of color find overt and obvious racist acts less offensive than microaggressions. Yet white Americans find it difficult to believe that they engage in microaggressive acts.[8]

"I don't belong" is an internalized message that we believe is related to both class and racial segregation and the forces that continue to sustain them, such as implicit racism, internalized racism, and microaggression. In addition, the message that "I don't belong" may be present when African American students are confronted with racial stereotypes or when girls are in educational contexts in which there are traditionally few female role models. The tendency to perform worse in a stereotyped setting is known as stereotype threat.

Much of the stereotype threat literature focuses on finding that awareness of a competence-related stereotype can lead to poorer task performance. In their landmark study, Steele and Aronson found that African American students who were told that their performance on the test would be a good indicator of their underlying intellectual abilities (stereotype threat condition) performed significantly worse than their white counterparts, but African Americans who were told that the test was simply a problem-solving exercise and was not diagnostic of ability (non-threat condition) performed equally with their white counterparts.[9]

The need to address a broader range of outcomes than those directly associated with the stereotype threat condition comes from evidence of stereotype threat "spillover" or behaviors and decisions in domains affected by but unrelated to the threatening stereotype. For instance, research has suggested that stereotype threat can lead to self-uncertainty about one's abilities and one's belonging in a particular setting. Another result of stereotype spillover is the reduction in aspirations in stereotyped domains. Schmader, Johns, and Forbes have elucidated three possible ways in which stereotype threat (and by implication, stereotype spillover) impairs performance on cognitive and social tasks.[10] They purport that stereotype threat causes (1) physiological stress responses that directly impair brain activity in the prefrontal cortex; (2) a tendency by the student to actively monitor performance; and (3) attempts to suppress negative thoughts and emotional responses while simultaneously attending to the task. All of these factors combine to impair performance on social and cognitive tasks.

Learning Not to Care: An Ego-Protective Strategy against Failure

We believe that the coping strategies related to stereotype threat and stereotype spillover can lead to a detrimental belief about a student's own academic abilities. Statements like "I'm just not a good student" or "school is not me" exemplify this type of belief. This type of internalized message is known as disidentification or academic disengagement. Schmader and colleagues found that in African American students, the perception of racial injustice predicted academic devaluing rather than the students' own academic performance.[11] In that study the opposite was true for white students. From these and similar findings, Steele concluded that disidentification is "a reaction to the ability-stigmatizing stereotypes in society." One result of disidentification is the dissociation of school achievement with self-esteem.[12]

Indeed, the coping response of disidentification, as it relates to stereotype threat, could help to explain why African Americans have lower achievement outcomes (e.g., grades and test scores) than European Americans. As reported by Osborne, "African Americans show a pattern of weakening correlations between academic outcomes and self-esteem from the 8th to 12th grades."[13] Ogbu further argued that some individuals may even foster an identity "oppositional" to success in academics.[14]

Examination of affective factors in student learning is not new. Researchers in education and developmental psychology have long explored the question, "What motivates students to learn?" For instance, according to achievement goal theory, students engage in the learning process for one of two purposes. One purpose is the goal of enhancing their knowledge or mastering an area of study. This is a Mastery learning style. The other purpose is to communicate their ability to others in an effort to be respected or admired. This is called a Performance learning style. These two styles differ in one important aspect: the relationship with failing. An adaptive approach to failing is necessary in attaining mastery. Students with a Mastery learning style will regard failing as a teaching opportunity or even a challenge. These students are receptive to critique of subpar work in order to improve over time. Performance learning style is a response to learning in which students require external validation in order to feel good about succeeding. Consequently, students with a Performance learning style are likely to avoid failure and the negative feelings associated with it. One response to the fear of failure may be to take less challenging courses. Another response is to totally disengage from academic pursuits. We have titled this response of full or partial disengagement as "I don't care."

Students who lack a sense of belonging or who no longer care about academic success may be motivated to induce their own failure. There is research from developmental psychology suggesting that academic self-handicapping is favored among some students because it allows them to avoid attributing failure to their own ability and instead to a created obstacle. "Academic self-handicapping" refers to the act of acquiring or claiming self-defined obstacles or strategies that often impede academic achievement. Recent studies from our institution have shown that African American students are far more likely than white students to practice a Performance learning style and to exhibit self-handicapping. Furthermore, unlike Caucasian students, even African American students who utilize a Mastery learning style will also still engage in self-handicapping.

The pervasive intransigence and covert nature of racism in America makes for interesting and stimulating research. However, the most heinous effects of modern racism may be the contribution to student perceptions that fuel an "I don't belong" or "I don't care" attitude. Within a racial or even a gender-conscious context some students will not only perceive themselves to be different from other students but will also form opinions about their own abilities based on that perceived difference. Be it a minority student in a predominantly white institution, a poor student getting a "free" ride, or a female student in a field of study that is predominantly male, it is possible to succumb to stereotype threat. Then, in an attempt to protect their self-esteem, students learn to place less importance on academic performance.

In this chapter we posit that the perception that the majority group considers certain students academically inferior produces stereotype threat. As stated earlier, when stereotype threat is present, individuals tend to self-handicap by rationalizing a possible failure. For example, in the study by Steele and Aronnson, African American students were more likely to blame a subpar performance on external factors, such as less sleep or an inability to focus, when the test was presented as diagnostic of their intellectual ability.[15] This effect is not limited to academic environments. In a Belgium study conducted by Klein and colleagues, participants originally from sub-Sahara Africa completed an intelligence test as part of a simulated job application process. Prior to testing, the participants were told that Africans' average performance on this test was generally better (positive comparison), worse (negative comparison), or equal to Belgians' performance. The control group received no such information. The results showed that test performance was lower in the group in which intergroup comparisons were negative, as compared to the equal and control conditions. Like the Steele and Aaronson study, the participants in the Belgian study were more likely to attribute lowered performance to external factors.[16] While these studies show how self-handicapping may be useful as a coping strategy, we posit that self-handicapping, as an ego-protective device, is maladaptive in educational setting.

Classism and Racism: The Benefit of Cultural Capital and Cost of Race-Related Stress

There is long-standing evidence from neuroscience associating negative emotions like fear and anxiety with changes in cognition. Additional evidence has revealed that even nonphysical threat, such as stereotype threat, can create a specific stress-related brain state in which cognitive functioning is altered. Also, recent studies in affective neuroscience suggest that cultural differences may contribute to variations in the manner of neural processing or "modes of thought" among individuals within distinctive social groups.

Culturally specific modes of thought have been documented. Using a cross-cultural perspective to compare Japanese Americans and native Japanese students, the research by Ishii suggests that views of self, social norms, communication practices, and modes of thought are all interconnected. For instance, Kitayama and Uskul showed that the independent view of self, dominant in Western cultures, promotes low-contextual communication and is related to a logical and analytic mode of thought.[17] Conversely, the interdependent view of self, that is more common in East Asian cultures, promotes high-contextual communication and corresponds to a more holistic and dialectical mode of thought.

The differences between Western and East Asian cultures represents one example of how cultural norms give rise to different social behaviors. Traditionally, social and behavioral scientists viewed cultural norms to be regulated by explicit societal rules and the related consequences for nonconformity. However, more recent studies in neuroscience reveal that over time socialization breeds psychological tendencies that are linked to certain brain regions. These psychological tendencies are therefore rooted in neural structures whose activities are autonomous, spontaneous, and, most of the time, operating below conscious awareness. Just as implicit racism operates below conscious awareness, it is also possible that the perceptions associated around stereotype threat are not obvious to African American or poor children.

Cross-cultural studies that have examined class differences within the United States share striking similarities to the work examining "modes of thought." Some of that research focuses on "cultural capital." "Cultural capital" is defined as "forms of knowledge, skills, education, and advantages through which a person gains higher status in society." Parents provide their children with cultural capital by transmitting the attitudes and knowledge needed to succeed in certain social contexts such as an educational system.

The idea of cultural capital is used by social science researches in diverse fields to analyze culture and cultural processes within various areas of stratification. For instance, the conceptualization used by Lareau and Weininger stresses the micro-interactional processes through which individuals comply (or fail to comply) with the evaluative standard of dominant institutions.[18] According to many researchers schools play a crucial role in the transmission of advantage across generations as the evaluative standards used in schools are biased toward the middle class.

In an insightful paper detailing the effects of cultural capital, Lareau and Weininger provide a case study of two African American mothers as they interact with school personnel on their daughters' behalf.[19] The girls attend different schools. One family lives in the suburbs and the other in public housing. The paper points out that on entering the school building, both mothers are confronted with a set of standards and expectations. The standards stress how parents should be. The expectation is that parents are "active, involved, assertive, informed and educated advocates" for their children. In the scenarios presented, the suburban mother clearly has the advantage.

The suburban mother has successfully shepherded her daughter Stacy into gifted and talented programs despite the fact that Stacy initially did not receive high enough test scores to be admitted. Her mother, who has a master's degree, had Stacy retested by a private testing service. The testing service was identified through the mother's informal network of acquaintances. Even after Stacy just barely failed to make the cutoff the second time, her mother was still able to convince the school administrator to grant Stacy admission to the program.

The case study goes on to chronicle the success that Stacy has had in a private, gymnastics program, in large part due to her mother's intervention. Also noted was that with each encounter, 12-year-old Stacy was learning the practices associated with advocacy that were being demonstrated on her behalf.

In the other scenario we meet Tara (pronounced Ti-ray) who lives in public housing. Unlike Stacy, Tara does not reside with her nuclear family but with her maternal grandmother who receives public assistance for her support. Tara's mother lives nearby and has daily contact with Tara. Both Tara's mother and grandmother stress the importance of doing well in school and Tara's mother regularly attends Parent–Teacher Association meetings. However, there is a difference in the type of advocacy employed by Tara's mother. The researchers describe a parent–teacher conference where the teacher refers to Tara as "Tah-rah" and is not corrected by her mother. Tara's mother mostly listens and does not ask detailed substantive questions about her daughter's educational experience. In fact, the responsibility is turned over to the teacher. The authors note that Tara's mother is quite vocal and assertive in social settings so the demeanor displayed at the school appeared atypical.

The presentation of Tara's and Stacy's story is not intended to provide evidence for a "deficit" view of the poor but rather to highlight, as does the full paper, the built-in advantage that middle-class parents have when encountering

the American educational system. The system of advantage makes it more difficult for low-income parents of any race to navigate successfully as the expectation of what advocacy looks like has been previously defined.

Yet there are social scientists and nonscientists, including media personalities and politicians, who do take a deficit view of the urban poor, views
that can be simplistic at best or racist at worst. We would venture to guess
that like most of white America, they lack actual experiences with poor
people or people of color. A recent report by the Economic Policy Institute showed that while only 5 percent of white kindergartners attend high-
poverty schools, over half, 57 percent, of black kindergarten students are in
high-poverty classrooms.[20] Furthermore, the racial segregation is not likely
to abate as students move to higher grades. This racial and economic disparity is no accident. Cultural capital writ large becomes social, economic,
and political structures that provide barriers to success in schools for poor
children. Examples of such barriers are the $1:3 average differential in fund-
ing between poor and middle-class schools; systems of advantage within
schools that tend to place poor children into lower academic tracks and the
wealthier children into higher tracts; and the greater proportion of teachers in wealthier schools with degrees in the subject area in which they teach.
This careful and deliberate management of policies, personnel, and practices works to cement educational disparity in place. Therefore, culture capital is "institutionalized" with cultural signals of white middle-class attitudes,
preferences, formal knowledge, behaviors, and credentials as the standard.
Because the signals have achieved wide social consensus among the dominant group, they can then be used for the purpose of inclusion and exclusion.

Public education is not the only institution that demonstrates a systematic difference in terms of outcome measures between both racial and income groups. Such factors as race, ethnicity, and SES have also been shown
to be associated with increased morbidity and mortality among ethnic minorities in the United States. Commonly termed "race-related health disparity" this tendency for those wealthy and white to have better health
outcomes than the poor or people of color was highlighted in an entire
volume of the Annals of the New York Academy of Sciences. The volume
titled "The Biology of Disadvantage" contained a leading article describing
how health disparity persists across the lifespan.[21] There is much evidence
to suggest that racism contributes to the disparate effects of physical and
mental health outcomes by providing a source of stress and stressors that
members of the dominant group do not experience.

There are numerous studies suggesting that ethnic minorities in the
United States experience race-related health disparity; higher levels of

mortality; and the experience of more negative health outcomes than white Americans, even when income and education are taken into account.[22] There is also a mounting body of evidence indicating that the mere *perception* of discrimination or racism actually contributes to race-related health disparity. A recent meta-analytic review examined 134 studies and revealed that perceived discrimination had a significant negative effect on both mental and physical health.[23]

There are a variety of factors that have long been identified to account for the negative health effects that are commonly seen in groups with low SES, including exposure to environmental toxins; employment in jobs with a high risk of injury; lack of access to high-quality health care; and non-participation in health-promoting behaviors, (i.e., good nutrition, physical exercise) and participation in adverse health behaviors, such as smoking, excessive alcohol, or drug use.[24] However, the mental and emotional mechanisms involved in linking perceived racial discrimination to ill health are increasingly becoming a focus of research interest.

Since 2002, more than 100 studies have been published documenting the harmful effects of perceived racial discrimination. These studies attempt to distinguish and isolate the effects on health due to an individual's perception of out-group status separate from the effects of SES. The results are compelling. For instance, data derived from the Black Women's Health Study has shown that African American women who reported discrimination on the job had a higher risk of breast cancer than others who did not report job discrimination.[25] When the sources of reported discrimination spread to housing and included encounters with police, the rate increased to a 48 percent greater likelihood of breast cancer. Another study of African American women found that chronic emotional stress due to experiences of racism was associated with a higher incidence of more severely blocked carotid arteries.[26] In addition, a 2007 study reported that perceived racism was associated with a significantly increased risk of uterine fibroids in black women regardless of differences in health care utilization.[27]

In their review, Pascoe and Richman showed that perceived discrimination produced significantly heightened stress responses.[28] There is research suggesting that psychological stress is associated with a number of additional factors, such as the interaction of race with low SES. For children in poverty the 35 percent higher reported incidences of daily hassles and stressors are attributed to various sources. Poor children have 50 percent more busy streets to cross and with that comes six times the risk of being in a pedestrian accident. Children in poverty are less likely to be seen by a doctor, and such things as unexamined head injuries or undiagnosed depression or behavioral disorders can impede academic performance. In addition, children in poverty see more violence. They are twice as likely to report seeing weapons or fights at school and are more often the victims of violence themselves.

Findings such as these suggest the clear possibility that the effects of perceived racism are not limited to health outcomes but could also impact student learning. In addition, the effects of poverty provide additional sources of stress. Therefore, effective interventions for enhancing academic achievement cannot ignore these factors. Until the time that a good public education becomes available for all children, we suggest building resilience in students in order to ameliorate the effects to racism and classism.

Targeting Affective Factors to Improve Academic Performance

A social psychology study with African American freshmen at Stanford University showed that a one-hour intervention addressing stereotype threat was able to improve their academic performance for the remaining six semesters.[29] The intervention did not address any specific academic subject matter. Instead, the intervention provided the freshmen cognitive strategies for reexamining difficult but common experiences and removing any racialized interpretation. Therefore, the students were taught how to enhance their "sense of belonging." Interestingly, the results of the study also indicated that the participants were healthier. Students who participated reported fewer symptoms of illness and documented fewer trips to the infirmary than nonparticipants. Apparently, the intervention was effective in shifting some psychological core belief the students had about themselves within the social setting of Stanford University. The shift in belief had the additional effect of a physiologically strengthened immune system. These findings speak to the social-psycho-biological connections that are an intrinsic part of the human experience and for the most part are ignored in educational research. The way that sociological distinctions become psychological tendencies and biological reactions is through emotions.

Studies with stereotype threat show that emotional or affective factors play an important role in academic achievement in terms of student beliefs, initiative, and motivation in school. As stated earlier, stereotype threat is the realization that one's performance on a particular task might confirm a negative stereotype about one's group. Since the majority of primary and secondary schools are racially segregated in the United States, the number of young African American primary and secondary students who will find themselves as a racial minority in a classroom is relatively small. However, this is not the case for African American college students, the majority of whom attend predominantly white institutions.

It can be argued that the combined effects of stress, performance monitoring, and emotional suppression are processes associated with emotional regulation and have negative impact on students' learning. Therefore, the successful interventions for stereotype threat have not focused on cognitive ability, as in remediation or enhanced instruction, but have instead targeted modes of thought and the related emotional content that foster an academic sense of belonging.

Among the first of studies that utilized a "sense of belonging" intervention to address stereotype threat was the Stanford University study. In that study African American freshmen were invited to participate in what they believed was a marketing program for future freshmen. In reality the students were given a one-hour intervention in which their own feelings of (not) belonging were targeted. The freshmen first saw a video of minority upper-class men recalling events from their freshmen year. The depictions were specifically chosen to demonstrate how an event that could be interpreted as stereotypical could be reframed. The upper-class men spoke of how they reinterpreted a professor's reluctance to call on them, or being excluded from a study group, for instance. After viewing the film, the freshmen were asked to write a reflection on how they might reinterpret a similar event that they had experienced. Finally the freshmen were asked to read their written statement (with feeling) in front of camera in which they were told future freshmen would view.

The study by Walton and Cohen effectively combined aspects from social psychology, such as group identification and helpfulness.[30] However, strategies from cognitive psychology, namely metacognition, reflection, and cognitive reframe were also employed. Cognitive psychologists have shown that the ability to critically evaluate one's own thinking is important in regulating emotional content.[31] Other studies have shown that student beliefs about themselves or about the nature of intelligence can also be targeted in efforts to improve student performance.[32]

The Stanford study focused on addressing negating internalized messaging regarding racial differences. However, more research is needed on how the combined effects of stereotype threat, microaggression, self-handicapping, implicit and institutional racism, and cultural capital affect students who don't attend schools like Stanford University. We feel that it is imperative that interventions be designed for students who attend minority-serving institutions and who have, for the most part, attended de facto segregated public schools.

One line of research that has reported academic improvement at an historically black college and university (HBCU) was work conducted by Pamela Hall.[33] Hall examined the use of meditation as a means of teaching emotional self-regulation to students in her classes. The study revealed an increase in grade point average (GPA) following meditation training, which included guidance in simple attention focusing and relaxation. The training was provided for 10 minutes at the beginning and end of a one-hour weekly study session. A control group was given no instructions on meditation but merely attended a separate study group. Students in the meditation group were asked to practice the meditation technique daily and before exams. Although the groups did not differ in GPA prior to the study, by the end of the semester following the intervention, students who had been trained in the meditation practice had a significantly higher GPA than those students in the control group. Hall postulated that the students were more relaxed following the meditation training and noted that based on her findings training in meditation may have a useful place in academic settings. "The rigid, tense, anxiety-filled semesters that students have come to dread may be replaced with calm, relaxed sessions dedicated to optimal learning and cognitive development for those who choose to participate."[34]

A more recent study conducted in California examined the use of meditation in a public middle school. The study demonstrated improvement in math and English proficiency by students following training in Transcendental Meditation.[35] The school was located in a large, urban school district that was further described as being primarily of low SES, populated with racial and ethnic minority students, and currently performing in the lower half of all the district middle schools. Participants in the study included 189 students (125 meditating and 64 non-meditating) and a matched control subgroup used to establish baseline of 100 students (50 meditating and 50 non-meditating). Following the instruction period that included introductory and preparatory lectures, individual interviews, and personal instruction, the students were led in the meditation for 12 minutes at the beginning and at the end of the school day. Students were also asked to continue the practice on weekends. The entire period of the study was three months. Results showed a significant improvement in both English and math proficiency as assessed by the California Standards Test, a standardized academic achievement measure. Of particular interest was the improvement seen in students who began the study at below grade level. It is also note-worthy that the largest increase was seen in math proficiency. Like the Hall study, Nidich and colleagues reported that not only did the students demonstrate improvement in academic performance, but according to teachers' reports, students were "calmer, happier, less hyperactive, friendlier and had an increased ability to focus on schoolwork."[36] In addition, the teachers reported less student fights, less abusive language, and an overall more relaxed and calm atmosphere.

These studies show that providing students tools needed to build their emotional resilience may alter the negative social/cultural influences on academic outcomes.

Building Resilience: The PVEST Theoretical Framework

After examining hundreds of research studies, the American Psychological Association's Task Force on African American Resilience determined that a broad comprehensive theory was needed to encapsulate academic achievement and well-being for African American students (American Psychological Association Task Force).[37] The task force based its recommendation on the Phenomenological Variant of Ecological Systems Theory or PVEST.[38] PVEST provides a cultural-ecological perspective that acknowledges differences in protective factors, stressors, coping strategies, and identities of students of color in the United States. Within this context the report also sought to define "resilience."

PVEST links an individual's perceptions of his or her experiences and self-appraisals throughout development. The framework is particularly relevant for adolescents, as identity formation (awareness of self and context) becomes heightened as a function of development. Optimal resilience will enable students to demonstrate skills and abilities that are conducive to high academic achievement. Such skills include the ability to objectively evaluate new stressors, establish new coping strategies, and redefine the students' view of themselves appropriately within different contexts.

According to the American Psychological Association Task Force report, enhancing resilience in African American students must take into a consideration a broad range of common and also unique characteristics that are loosely defined as resilience. The report defines resilience as follows:

(1) Resilience is a fluid process that is not easily encompassed by a list of protective factors, rather it is the interaction of strength, resources, and risk factors within a context and across space and time.

(2) Resilience is also a dynamic, multidimensional construct that incorporates the bidirectional interaction between individuals and their environments within contexts (family, peer, school community and society).

(3) Resilience occurs in the presence of real or perceived risk or adversity and includes more than merely surviving but also encompasses the ability to be empowered to live life fully.[39]

The task force also noted how difficult resilience is to assess as the preceding definitions are resistant to qualitative study and measurement. It concluded that this difficulty in assessment might be one reason that most research on resilience does not benefit from systematic theory development and testing. In addition, few educational studies and fewer school policies acknowledge how cultural or race-related factors influence adaptive behaviors in school. In other words, PVEST provides a theoretical basis for the study of academic achievement with a consideration of the potential reach of stereotype threat and institutional racism. However, the task force did acknowledge the difficulty in applying traditional methods of analysis, which tend to be myopic in nature.

The task force identified the following areas, which should be the focus for future study. The areas combine the domains identified by the PVEST theory with the themes identified from hundreds of research studies that examined African American youth. The areas are interconnected and are represented here by a grid with columns of the PVEST developmental domains (depicted by numerals 1–4) and rows of the relevant themes compiled by the APA task force (depicted by letters A–D). The grid allows for the conceptualization of the multidimensional and interactive nature of the PVEST/APA Task Force framework.

PVEST Developmental Domains

The APA task force identified key developmental domains of the PVEST theory as follows:

Identity Development (A)—Positive gendered and racial identities are anchored in social relationships within and across groups—including academic groups. Formation of an academic identity occurs within the context of other identities, such as family member, church member, club member etc.

Emotional Development (B)—The need to cope with destructive emotions like envy and anger due to oppressive conditions and marginalization. Emotional regulation (2a) requires skill in fostering the emotional forces necessary to motivate beneficial behavioral outcomes across different contexts. Such emotional skills call for Emotional competence; (2b) which is developed from previous successful encounters and Emotional knowledge; (2c) which is based on introspection and self-knowledge.

Social Development (C)—Effective management of negative social interaction is necessary but not sufficient for optimal functioning. What is also needed is sense of collective agency/efficacy that provides for lifelong civic engagement and service: the perception of self as a positive change agent.

Cognitive Domains (D)—High academic achievement is not enough. Also needed are self-motivated learning and higher order thinking-analysis, synthesis and innovation and creativity.[40]

APA Task Force Themes

In addition to the PVEST domains, the APA task force identified four themes that are consistent with "six Cs" previously associated with positive youth development—competence, confidence, connection, character, caring, and contribution.[41] According to the report, when presented along with the developmental domains these four themes, allow for a more systematic and focused scholarship. The report presents the four themes as follows:

Critical mindedness (1)—Helps protect against experiences of discrimination and facilitates a critique of existing social conditions.

Active engagement (2)—Includes agentic behavior in school, at home and with peers allowing for students to be proactive and make a positive and effective impact on their environment.

Flexibility (3)—Promotes adaptation to cognitive, emotional, social and physical situational demands. Includes bicultural competence or fluency across multiple cultural contexts (including the academic context).

Communalism (4)—Includes the importance of social bonds and social duties, reflects a fundamental sense of interdependence and primacy of collective well-being.[42]

Table 7.1 provides a visual representation of PVEST and the interactive nature of the domains and themes. While investigating the background literature for our research study, we noted that many interventions provide program elements that focus on social and cognitive development. These interventions include remediation and/or social activities and support. However, the results from studies on stereotype threat reported in this chapter indicate that emotional regulation and cognitive reframing were used to

TABLE 7.1   This grid designating the domains and themes allows for the conceptualization of the multidimensional and interactive nature of the PVEST/APA Task Force framework.

	1. Critical Mindedness	2. Active Engagement	3. Flexibility	4. Communalism
A. Identity Development	A.1.	A.2	A.3	A.4
B. Emotional Development	B.1	B.2	B.3	B.4
C. Social Development	C.1	C.2.	C.3	C.4
D. Cognitive Domain	D.1	D.2	D.3	D.4

Source: Palmer, K., S. Scherer, C. Talley, J. Fife, and O. Hill. "Learning to Be a Straight 'A' Student: Targeting Affective Factors to Increase Freshmen STEM Retention." Submitted to *the Journal of College Student Retention.*

reinterpret negative or non-affirming situations as racial slights. In fact the ability to reframe and reinterpret can apparently be taught to college freshmen in a one-time, one-hour session and result in significant increase in GPA that lasts for the remaining three years of their college career.

Project Knowledge: An Intervention Aimed at Building Resilience

The study reported here was conducted at Virginia State University and utilized the PVEST theoretical framework. We attempted to design an effective intervention for African American college students attending a historically black university. Our goal was to incorporate program elements that specifically addressed Identity and Emotional Development. We expanded Emotional Development to include emotional regulation as distinct from emotional knowledge and competence and used as our goals aspects of the APA task force report in which the themes and developmental domains were more fully described (Table 7.2). Our fundamental goal was to create an intervention that would increase self-regulation while decreasing self-handicapping. We believed that this would ultimately lead to an increase in student grades.

Nearly sixty rising freshmen were recruited from the pool of incoming students. Their parents received invitation letters that described the project

TABLE 7.2 An expanded grid enabled certain interactions such as emotional development and identity formation to be more carefully scrutinized.

From APA Task Force, 2007	Critical Mindedness (1)	Active Engagement (2)	Flexibility (3)	Communalism (4)
Identity Development (A)	Positive gendered and racial identities. Positive sense of self. Formation of academic identity	Agentic behavior that produces positive impact on environment	Promotes adaptation to situational demands; including bicultural (academic) competence and fluency	Freedom to express different identities across contexts
Emotional Development: Knowledge (B-i)	Cultivation of introspection and self-knowledge	Ability to recognize and to take action against maladaptive forces	Freedom to adapt. Motivation to change if necessary to meet meaningful goal	Self-knowledge is affirmed by the community
Emotional Development: Competence (B-ii)	Ability to trust behaviors that are emotionally generated based on previous successful outcomes	Strong sense of self-efficacy. Ability to mobilize appropriate resources and acquire new insights		Social relationships can support student goals and values
Emotional Development: Regulation (B-iii)	Ability to marshal most effective emotion-generated behaviors or to shift emotions depending on the context	Ability to re-frame toxic situations and *act in the manner that is not maladaptive or self-defeating*	*Ability to "re-frame toxic situations* and act in the manner that is not maladaptive or self-defeating	Close familial relationships are positively related to mature social development

(Continued)

TABLE 7.2 (Continued)

From APA Task Force, 2007	Critical Mindedness (1)	Active Engagement (2)	Flexibility (3)	Communalism (4)
Social Development (C)	Perception of self as positive change agent	Ability to act as active change agent	Ability to recognize mal-adaptive group behavior and act accordingly	Positive Peer Norms
Cognitive Development (D)	Confident engagement of academic material	*Recognition of own gaps in knowledge or limitations and ability and willingness to address them*	Recognition of own gaps in knowledge or limitations and *ability and willingness to address them*	Preference for learning contexts that support expression of communal orientation. Teachers who are "warm demanders"
Physical Health (5)	Optimal self-care in terms of eating and exercise	Takes responsibility for health	Adoption of healthy behaviors	Positive peer norms

Source: Palmer, K., S. Scherer, C. Talley, J. Fife, and O. Hill. "Learning to Be a Straight 'A' Student: Targeting Affective Factors to Increase Freshmen STEM Retention." Submitted to *the Journal of College Student Retention.*

as an academic enhancement program. The students arrived on campus one week before the semester started and participated in academic skill-building and social activities. The freshmen were assigned to mentor groups with upper-class mentors who attended all activities. During the school year, the freshmen met once per week for one hour and in addition were contacted throughout the week by their mentors.

The participants were administered over 25 psychological and behavioral assessments during their freshman year. A preliminary analysis of the data revealed, among other things, clear positive correlations between GPA and Grit, time perspective, and self-regulation. Consistent with the literature, GPA and self-handicapping were negatively correlated. The study continues with an emphasis on examining and strengthening mediating factors associated with the factors associated with a higher GPA.[43]

Building Resilience before College: Suggestions for Secondary Schools

Successful academic achievement occurs as a result of numerous influences combining to accomplish one major goal: to inspire children to be curious and want to learn. Students who attend under-resourced schools can be taught to overcome challenges and maintain a positive academic identity and a sense of self-efficacy. However, the type of training necessary, in our view, does not stop at what students know but includes how they feel about learning.

The following suggestions for secondary educational settings are designed to encourage educators to closely examine their personal and institutional experiences with African American students. We understand that the issues and problems affecting urban schools were not created by educators nor is it in their power to completely ameliorate them. However, we do believe that acknowledging negative perceptions can lessen the effect of microaggression in educational environments. We also believe that understanding the effects of stereotype threat can also help educators to focus on the affective components of the learning situation.

Suggestions for Secondary Schools Informed by Project Knowledge and PVEST

- Determine the number of teachers who actually desire to teach in that school. This will provide information to administrators that the students already know about the emotional climate. You must be willing to have institutional "soul-searching."

- Develop ongoing dialogues that address potential biases and concerns that relate to lowered expectations of student performance and behavior. You must be willing to talk about race and power.
- Be open to culturally relevant (and personally significant) learning materials that can assist students in understanding, not only the importance of obtaining an education but also the crucial role the student plays in his or her own community. You must be willing to engage community leaders.
- Don't assume that students know why they should do well in school or have the skill set or support structure to do so. You may have to engage in innovative teaching and learning strategies in light of their realities.
- Institute time for meditation or other meta-cognitive training and also academic skill building for students. The research suggests that emotional regulation, included as part of an academic skill set, can improve learning.
- Institute time for meditation, focused relaxation, or other meta-cognitive training for teachers. The research suggests that focused relaxation can decrease stress and improve teaching.

Conclusion

The literature cited in this chapter suggests that successful academic interventions must address the unique social and psychological needs of minority students, particularly those who attend under-resourced schools. There will always be a need for the traditional tutorial and other content-based remediation efforts. However, we can no longer ignore the effects of race and class distinction on how students think of themselves. The Sathya Sai Education in Human Values is one intervention that has been successfully utilized in the United Kingdom that embeds the core human values of love, peace, truth, right action, and nonviolence as a regular instructional component. In the United States, Carol Dweck has also developed a comprehensive curriculum supplement for K-12 teachers to help them engender a "growth mind set" in students—that intelligence is not fixed and that through sustained effort, all students can learn.

Budgetary limitations often cause K-12 and college administrators to hesitate to invest the time and capital that these programs require; however, the research literature is clear in its general effectiveness. It represents an investment that pays dividends in increased academic performance and higher retention rates.

Sixty years after the Brown decision, we still do not have equality of educational opportunity in the United States. The kind of interventions outlined in this chapter, if widely implemented, could have a major impact on minority educational achievement. The United States cannot afford to lose the human capital represented by underperforming minority students. Such innovations as described here could represent the best hope for fulfilling the promise of quality education as a civil right for all.

Notes

1. Orfield et al. 2014.
2. Garcia-Coll et al. 1996, p. 1891.
3. Clark and Clark 1947, p. 169.
4. Davis 2007.
5. Bigler and Liben 1993, p. 1507.
6. Simpson 2007.
7. Cunningham, Preacher, and Banaji 2001, p. 163.
8. Sue et al. 2007, p. 271.
9. Steele and Aronson 1995, p. 797.
10. Schmader, Johns, and Forbes 2008, p. 336.
11. Schmader, Major, and Gramzow 2001, p. 93.
12. Crocker and Major 1989, p. 606; Major et al. 1998, p. 34; Tesser and Campbell 1980, p. 341.
13. Osborne 1995, p. 449; Osborne 1997, p. 728.
14. Ogbu 1987, p. 312.
15. Steele and Aaronson 1995, p. 797.
16. Klein, Pohl, and Ndagijimana 2007, p. 453.
17. Kitayama and Uskul 2011, p. 419.
18. Lareau and Weininger 2003, p. 567.
19. Ibid.
20. Weiss and Garcia 2014.
21. Adler and Stewart 2010, p. 5.
22. Ibid.; Djuric et al. 2008, p. 7; Pascoe and Richman 2009, p. 531; Williams and Mohammed 2009, p. 20; Williams et al. 2010, p. 69.
23. Pascoe and Richman 2009, p. 531.
24. Matthews, Gallo, and Taylor 2010, p. 146.
25. Taylor et al. 2007, p. 46.
26. Troxel et al. 2003, p. 300.
27. Wise et al. 2007, p. 747.
28. Pascoe and Richman 2009, p. 531.
29. Walton and Cohen 2007, p. 82; Walton and Cohen 2011, p. 1447.
30. Walton and Cohen 2011.
31. Goldin et al. 2008.
32. Blackwell, Trzesniewski, and Dweck 2007, p. 246; Walton and Cohen 2011.

33. Hall 1997.
34. Ibid., p. 408.
35. Nidich et al. 2011, p. 556.
36. Hall 1997; Nidich et al. 2011, p. 556.
37. American Psychological Association 2008.
38. Spencer, Dupree, and Hartman 1997.
39. American Psychological Association 2008.
40. American Psychological Association 2008.
41. King et al. 2005.
42. American Psychological Association 2008.
43. Talley et al.

Bibliography

Adler, N., and K. Newman. 2002. "Socioeconomic Disparities in Health: Pathways and Policies." *Health Affairs* 21 (2): 60–76.

Adler, N., and J. Stewart. 2010. "Health Disparities across the Lifespan: Meaning, Methods, and Mechanisms." *Annals of New York Academy of Sciences* 1186: 5–23.

American Psychological Association. 2008. "Task Force on Resilience and Strength in Black Children and Adolescents." Accessed March 16, 2015. http://www.apa.org/pi/families/resources/resiliencerpt.pdf.

Aronson, J., and M. Inzlicht. 2004. "The Ups and Downs of Attributional Ambiguity: Stereotype Vulnerability and the Academic Self-Knowledge of African American College Students." *Psychological Science* 15: 829–836.

Attar, B.K., N.G. Guerra, and P.T. Tolan. 1994. "Neighborhood Disadvantage, Stressful Life Events and Adjustments in Urban Elementary-School Children." *Journal of Clinical Child Psychology* 23 (4): 391–400.

Beilock, S.L., R.J. Rydell, and A.R. McConnell. 2007. "Stereotype Threat and Working Memory: Mechanisms, Alleviation, and Spillover." *Journal of Experimental Psychology: General* 136: 256–276.

Bertrams, A., C. Englert, O. Dickhäuser, and R. Baumeister. 2013. "Role of Self-Control Strength in the Relation between Anxiety and Cognitive Performance." *Emotion* 13 (4): 668–680. doi:10.1037/a0031921.

Bigler, R.S., and L.S. Liben. 1993. "A Cognitive Developmental Approach to Racial Stereotyping and Reconstructive Memory in Euro-American Children." *Child Development* 64: 1507–1518.

Blackwell, L.S., K.H. Trzesniewski, and C.S. Dweck. 2007. "Implicit Theories of Intelligence Predict Achievement across an Adolescent Transition: A Longitudinal Study and an Intervention." *Child Development* 78 (1): 246–263.

Braveman, P.A., C. Cubbin, S. Egerter, D.R. Williams, and E. Pamuk. 2010. "Socioeconomic Disparities in Health in the United States: What the Patterns Tell Us." *American Journal of Public Health,* Supplement 100: S186–S196.

Clark, K.B., and M.P. Clark. 1947. "Racial Identification and Preference in Negro Children." In *Readings in Social Psychology*, ed. T. Newcomb and E. Hartley (pp. 169–178). New York: Holt.

Covington, M.V. 2000. "Goal Theory, Motivation and School Achievement: An Integrative Review." *Annual Review of Psychology* 51: 171–200.

Crocker, J., and B. Major. 1989. "Social Stigma and Self-Esteem: The Self-Protective Properties of Stigma." *Psychological Review* 96: 606–630.

Crocker, J., B. Major, and C. Steele. 1998. "Social Stigma." In *The Handbook of Social Psychology*, eds. D.T. Gilbert, S.T. Fiske, and G. Lindzey (4th ed.) (pp. 504–553). Boston: McGraw-Hill.

Cunningham, W.A., K.J. Preacher, M.R. Banaji. 2001. "Implicit Attitude Measures: Consistency, Stability, and Convergent Validity." *Psychological Science* 12 (2): 163–170.

Davies, P.G., S.J. Spencer, and C.M. Steele. 2005. "Clearing the Air: Identity Safety Moderates the Effects of Stereotype Threat on Women's Leadership Aspirations." *Journal of Personality and Social Psychology* 88: 276–287.

Davis, K. (Producer). 2007, May 28. A Girl Like Me. Accessed July 19, 2014. http://www.mediathatmattersfest.org/films/a_girl_like_me/.

Djuric, Z., C.E. Bird, A. Furumoto-Dawson, G.H. Rauscher, M.T. Ruffin, R.P. Stowe, et al. 2008. "Biomarkers of Psychological Stress in Health Disparities Research." *The Open Biomarkers Journal* 1: 7–19.

Dweck, C. 1986. "Motivational Process Affecting Learning." *American Psychologists* 41: 1040–1048.

Elliot, A.J., M.M. Shell, K.B. Henry, and M.A. Mair. 2005. "Achievement Goals, Performance Contingencies and Performance Attainment: An Experimental Test." *Journal of Educational Psychology* 97(4): 630–640.

Garcia-Coll, C., G. Lamberty, R. Jenkins, H.P. McAdoo, K. Crnik, B.H. Wasik, et al. 1996. "An Integrative Model for the Study of Developmental Competencies in Minority Children." *Child Development* 67: 1891–1914.

Goldin, P.R., K. McRae, W. Ramel, and J.J. Gross. 2008. "The Neural Bases of Emotion Regulation: Reappraisal and Suppression of Negative Emotion." *Biological Psychiatry* 63: 577–586.

Hall, P. 1997. "The Effect of Meditation on the Academic Performance of African American College Students." *Journal of Black Studies* 29 (3): 408–415.

Ishii, K. 2013. "Culture and the Mode of Thought: A Review." *Asian Journal of Social Psychology* 16: 123–132.

Jones, E.E., and S. Berglas. 1978. "Control of Attributions about the Self through Self-Handicapping Strategies: The Appeal of Alcohol and the Role of Underachievement." *Personality and Social Psychology Bulletin* 4: 200–206.

King, P. E., E. M. Dowling, R. A. Mueller, K. White, W. Schultz, et al. 2005. "Thriving in Adolescence: The Voices of Youth-Serving Practitioners, Parents, and Early and Late Adolescents." *Journal of Early Adolescence* 25: 94–112.

Kitayama, S., and A.K. Uskul. 2011. "Culture, Mind, and the Brain: Current Evidence and Future Directions." *Annual Review of Psychology* 62: 419–449.

Klein, O., S. Pohl, and C. Ndagijimana. 2007. "The Influence of Intergroup Comparisons on Africans' Intelligence Test Performance in a Job Selection Context." *The Journal of Psychology: Interdisciplinary and Applied* 141 (5): 453–468.

Koenen, K.C., T.E. Moffitt, A. Casipi, A. Taylor, and S. Purcell. 2003. "Domestic Violence Is Associated with Environmental Suppression of IQ in Young Children." *Development and Psychopathology* 15: 297–311.

Lamont, M., and A. Lareu. 1988. "Cultural Capital: Allusions, Gaps and Glissandos in Recent Theoretical Developments." *Sociological Theory* 6: 153–168.

Lareau, A., and E.B. Weininger. 2003. "Cultural Capital in Educational Research: A Critical Assessment." *Theory and Society* 32 (5): 567–606.

Link, B.G., and J.C. Phelan. 1996. "Understanding Sociodemographic Differences in Health: The Role of Fundamental Social Causes." *American Journal of Public Health* 86 (4): 471–473.

Major, B., S. Spencer, T. Schmader, C. Wolfe, and J. Crocker. 1998. "Coping with Negative Stereotypes about Intellectual Performance: The Role of Psychological Disengagement." *Personality and Social Psychology Bulletin* 24: 34–50.

Matthews, K.A., L.C. Gallo, and S.E. Taylor. 2010. "Are Psychosocial Factors Mediators of Socioeconomic Status and Health Connections?" *Annals of New York Academy of Sciences* 1186: 146–173.

McPherson M., P. Arango, H. Fox, C. Lauver, M. McManuz, P.W. Newacheck, J.M. Perrin, J.P. Shonkoff, and B. Strickland. 1998. "A New Definition of Children with Special Health Care Needs." *Pediatrics* 102 (1): 137–140.

Nidich, Sanford, S. Mjasiri, R. Nidich, M. Rainforth, J. Grant, L. Valosek, W. Chang, and R.L. Zigler. 2011. "Academic Achievement and Transcendental Meditation: A Study with At-Risk Urban Middle School Students." *Education* 131 (3): 556–565.

Ogbu, J.U. 1987. "Variability in Minority School Performance: A Problem in Search of an Explanation." *Anthropology & Education Quarterly* 18: 312–334.

Orfield, G., F. Frakenberg, E. Jongyeon, and J. Kuscera. May 2014. "Brown at 60: Great Progress, Long Retreat, Uncertain Future." Accessed August 27, 2014. www.civilrightsproject.ucla.edu.

Osborne, J.W. 1995. "Academics, Self-esteem, and Race: A look at the Underlying Assumptions of the Disidentification Hypothesis." *Personality and Social Psychology Bulletin* 21: 449–455.

Osborne, J.W. 1997. "Race and Academic Disidentification." *Journal of Educational Psychology* 89: 728–735.

Osofsky, J.D., S. Wewers, D.M. Hann, and C. Fick. 1993. "Chronic Community Violence; What Is Happening to Our Children?" *Psychiatry* 56: 36–45.

Palmer, K., S. Scherer, C. Talley, J. Fife, and O. Hill. 2015. Submitted "Learning to be a Straight 'A' Student: Targeting Affective Factors to Increase Freshmen STEM Retention."

Pascoe, E., and L. S. Richman. 2009. "Perceived Discrimination and Health: A Meta-analytic Review." *Psychological Bulletin* 135 (4): 531–534.

Rosenberg, M., and R. Simmons. 1971. "Black and White Self-esteem: The Urban Schoolchild." In *The Arnold and Caroline Rose Monograph Series in Sociology,* ed. A. J. Reiss, Jr. (pp. 135–145). Washington, DC: American Sociological Association.

Schmader, T., C. E. Forbes, S. Zhang, and W. B. Mendes. 2009. "A Meta-cognitive Perspective on Cognitive Deficits Experienced in Intellectually Threatening Environments." *Personality and Social Psychology Bulletin* 35: 584–596.

Schmader, T., M. Johns, and C. Forbes. 2008. "An Integrated Process Model of Stereotype Threat Effects on Performance." *Psychological Review* 115: 336–356.

Schmader, T., B. Major, and R. H. Gramzow. 2001. "Coping with Ethnic Stereotypes in the Academic Domain: Perceived Injustice and Psychological Disengagement." *Journal of Social Issues* 57: 93–111.

Serpell, Z., O. Hill, O. B. Pearson, and M. Faison. In preparation. "Self-Handicapping Mediates the Relationship between Achievement Goals and Math Performance for African American Adolescents."

Serpell, Z., O. Hill, B. Pearson, and M. Faison. 2015. The Mediating Role of Self-Handicapping in the Relationship between Goal Orientations and Math Achievement in High Schoolers. Poster presented at the biennial meeting of the Society for Research on Child Development. Philadelphia, PA.

Simpson, B. 2007. "Exploring the Influences of Educational Television and Parent-Child Discussions on Improving Children's Racial Attitudes." Unpublished dissertation, University of Texas at Austin.

Spencer, M. B., D. Dupree, and T. Hartman. 1997. "A Phenomenological Variant of Ecological Systems Theory (PVEST): A Self-organization Perspective in Context." *Development and Psychopathology* 9 (4): 817–833. doi:10.1017/S0954579497001454.

Spencer, S. J., C. M. Steele, and D. M. Quinn. 1999. "Stereotype Threat and Women's Math Performance." *Journal of Experimental Social Psychology* 35: 4–28.

Steele, C. M. 1997. "A Threat in the Air: How Stereotypes Shape Intellectual Identity and Performance." *American Psychologist* 52: 613–629.

Steele, C. M., and J. Aronson. 1995. "Stereotype Threat and the Intellectual Test Performance of African Americans." *Journal of Personality and Social Psychology* 69: 797–811.

Sue, D. W. 2010. *Microaggressions and Marginality: Manifestation, Dynamics, and Impact.* Hoboken, NJ: John Wiley & Sons.

Sue, D.W., C.M. Capodilupo, G.C. Torino, J.M. Bucceri, A.M. Holder, K.L. Nadal, et al. 2007. "Racial Microaggressions in Everyday Life: Implications for Clinical Practice." *American Psychologist* 62 (4): 271–286.

Taylor, T.R., C.D. Williams, K.H. Makambi, C. Moulton, J.P. Harrel, Y.C. Coxier, J.R. Palmer, et al. 2007. "Racial Discrimination and Breast Cancer Incidence in US Black Women: The Black Woman's Health Study." *American Journal of Epidemiology* 166 (1): 46–54.

Tesser, A., and J. Campbell. 1980. "Self-Definition: The Impact of the Relative Performance and Similarity of Others." *Social Psychology Quarterly* 43 (3): 341–347.

Troxel, W.M., K.A. Matthews, J.T. Bromberger, and K. Sutton-Tyrell. 2003. "Chronic Stress Burden, Discrimination and Subclinical Carotid Artery Disease in African American and Caucasian Women." *Health Psychology* 22: 300–309.

Walton, G.M., and G.L. Cohen. 2007. "A Question of Belonging: Race, Social Fit, and Achievement." *Journal of Personality and Social Psychology* 92: 82–96.

Walton, G.M., and G.L. Cohen. 2011. "A Brief Social-Belonging Intervention Improves Academic and Health Outcomes of Minority Students." *Science* 331 (6023): 1447–1451.

Weiss, E., and E. Garcia. June 2014. "Black and Hispanic Kindergartners Are Disproportionately in High-Poverty Schools." Economic Snapshot: Education. Economic Policy Institute. Accessed July 27, 2014. http://www.epi.org/publication/black-hispanic-kindergartners-disproportionately.

Williams, D.R., and S.A. Mohammed. 2009. "Discrimination and Racial Disparities in Health; Evidence and Needed Research." *Journal of Behavioral Medicine* 32 (1): 20–47.

Williams, D.R., S.A. Mohammed, J. Leavell, and C. Collins. 2010. "Race, Socioeconomic Status and Health: Complexities Ongoing Challenges and Research Opportunities." *Annals of New York Academy of Sciences* 1186: 69–101.

Wise, L.A., J.R. Palmer, Y.C. Cozier, M.O. Hunt, E.A. Stewart, and L. Rosenberg. 2007. "Perceived Racial Discrimination and Risk of Uterine Leiomyomata." *Epidemiology* 18 (6): 747–757.

Chapter 8

Critical Management Studies' Role in Productive Conversations about Racism

Laura M. Harrison

In 2013, Minnesota Community and Technical College censured Shannon Gibney for offending students by discussing racism in class. What makes teaching about racism so challenging? It is unlikely that Dr. Gibney would have faced criticism for celebrating Martin Luther King Day or mentioning the evils of slavery in a lecture. Why are certain conversations about race threatening to some students? Part of the answer lies in whether racism is framed as a personal character flaw or a systemic problem. Students socialized in a Western, individualistic cultural frame have an easier time grasping issues rooted in personal shortcomings. As a result, many students genuinely believe they are not racist because they do not have negative feelings toward people of color on a personal level. Like the students in the Shannon Gibney case, they "don't want to hear about race all the time" because they do not see what they need to learn about the issue. In order for students to begin to understand racism or any other issue on the systemic level, they first need an education in the fact that the power structures they often understand as neutral are continually shaped in ways that promote the status quo. Fortunately, critical management studies (CMS) provides a framework for interrogating the hierarchies we have come to accept as the natural order of societal structures. In this chapter, I present the basic tenets of CMS and provide concrete strategies for using these constructs to help students engage in productive conversations about racism.

Introduction to Critical Management Studies

Discussing racism requires the ability to examine systemic power. Unfortunately, mainstream secondary schools rarely provide the kind of critical education necessary for such analysis. Unlike their European counterparts that mandate courses in media literacy, for example, U.S. educational institutions increasingly promote pedagogies that drill students to prepare for standardized tests. Lacking habits of the mind geared toward critical thinking, students understandably gravitate toward face-value explanations for phenomena. Consequently, they enter conversations about complex phenomena like race without the foundational knowledge necessary to examine thoughtfully the myriad power dimensions involved. Hence, the first step in approaching conversations about racism in the classroom frequently necessitates teaching about how power works.

Many intellectual traditions theorize power well, but they often prove inaccessible to students. This seems particularly true of students in applied fields like mine (counseling and higher education), where complicated lectures about epistemology tend to fall flat. My students grow impatient with material that they perceive to be esoteric or impractical. As a result, I find CMS to be a palatable frame for this audience because it originated in business schools and retains the straightforward language typical of the discipline. At its most basic level, CMS is an intellectual project designed to interrogate mainstream notions of hierarchy as natural, desirable, and the only way to organize. Where most business education aims to teach students how to gain power, CMS critiques the many misuses of power in organizations. As importantly, CMS offers an alternative to the taken-for-granted assumption that hierarchical structures create the best organizational outcomes.

A key feature of CMS is its focus on systemic power. This characteristic makes CMS useful in helping students understand racism beyond the level of individuals. Often, students don't know how to talk about racism because they don't know how to talk about power. Without an intellectual framework for understanding racism in the bigger picture, students tend to focus on individual examples like the fact that we have a black president. President Obama achieved extraordinary heights and is therefore probably a great choice for studying personal leadership qualities. This is also true of many successful individuals of all races, genders, and other demographic characteristics. But racism extends far beyond the individuals and students need a more sophisticated lens for interrogating systemic oppression. By shifting the focus from individual attitudes to the systems we engage every day, CMS exposes how inequality is built into the very fabric of the structures that shape our experiences. CMS can be used as a tool for helping students understand why racial disparities persist despite greater levels of societal acceptance of diversity. The Native American Reject and Protect group protesting the Keystone XL oil pipeline in the western United States illustrates this difference between understanding racism as personal prejudice and systemic oppression. The oil companies advocating the pipeline do not explicitly aim to discriminate against Native Americans; their goal is simply more profit for their companies. A CMS perspective allows students to see the systemic racism that occurs when one set of organizational practices becomes the basis for decision making while another group's are silenced. The oil companies' organizational structures assume short-term profit as the driving force, an assumption that society reifies as natural law rather than simply one way of doing business among many possibilities. Alvesson, Bridgeman, and Willmott explain both this phenomenon as well as how CMS serves as a corrective to it:

> Markets are also widely seen as self-evidently efficiency-producing givens which only ignorant people would seek to prevent governing economic life, and perhaps life in general. Greed and competitiveness are also widely assumed to be natural and so on. CMS challenges these kinds of assertions, identifying them as manifestations of a particular, capitalist, and possessive individualist ideology, and thereby endeavors to de-naturalize them by recalling their context-dependence.[1]

The Keystone XL Pipeline case offers a particularly relevant example because the Native American activists' opposition stems from their own organizational structures which require them to consider how decisions impact people seven generations from their own. Mainstream news coverage very rarely discusses how oil companies' organizational practices fail to prioritize their effect on future generations. A non-CMS approach renders the Native American Seventh Generation ethos invisible, allowing the Keystone XL Pipeline issue to be framed solely in environmental terms while missing the race angle. This subtle, but important distinction demonstrates the inconsistent and confusing nuances in the ways contemporary racism manifests. The oil companies involved in advocating for the pipeline likely recruit multicultural employees, including those of Native American descent. These diversity initiatives are likely sincere; employees of color are welcome to participate in the system as it is. What they are not welcome to do is to try to change, challenge, or disrupt its terms or structures in any substantive way.

The Keystone XL Pipeline issue illustrates the difference between understanding racism as a personal prejudice and a systemic problem.

CMS provides a framework for studying racism on the systemic level by surfacing the "business as usual" organizational assumptions we take for granted. Ultimately, teaching about racism necessitates teaching students how structural power works. Because it is in the best interest of those in power not to be transparent about how they gain and maintain power, these are generally hidden processes. As a result, educating students about how racism works requires accomplishing specific tasks related to the overarching job of helping them understand how power works more generally. In the sections that follow, I present four tasks in teaching about racism and demonstrate how CMS approaches them. These four tasks are (1) unpacking neutrality, (2) understanding reality as co-constructed, (3) revealing dominant narratives, and (4) getting past the personal prejudice paradigm.

Unpacking Neutrality

CMS reveals the racist underpinnings in the Keystone XL Pipeline issue by refusing to allow the oil companies' organizational structures to be framed as neutral. By questioning what is normally concealed, a CMS framework creates space for alternative organizational principles, in this case, the Native Americans' seventh-generation ethos. While it is challenging to teach students to critique what they typically understand as simply neutral reality, this knowledge is foundational in unpacking less overt forms of racism. One way to begin is to simply ask students what they knew they were supposed to do on the first day of class. With some prompting, they will offer examples such as knowing they should sit at a desk rather than standing at the podium and that they should raise their hands and wait to be called on before speaking. When I ask students how they knew these things, they almost never remember being taught, yet they know they were not born with this knowledge. Most important, they easily distinguish these learned practices from natural processes like breathing or eating. We spend some time talking about how habits become default settings of sorts, functioning and feeling like natural order when they are in fact learned behaviors. This is an important point for students to understand deeply because it serves as a building block for learning how to interrogate more significant defaults they bring to learning generally and to learning about race specifically.

Once students understand that they have defaults, the next step is to help them begin to examine the source of these settings. Sticking with the first day of class example, I begin to introduce the idea that students sitting while teachers stand and students raising hands to speak while teachers talk freely are not benignly neutral practices. I enter this terrain gently in order to avoid students jumping too quickly to comments like "Well, you'd have chaos otherwise!" or "You need some way to organize the class!" I make it a point to state that there is not necessarily anything wrong with the way we start class; in fact, it does have some advantages in terms of efficiency. What is more significant here is for students to see how what appears to be natural is actually a learned, ideological construction. We may decide the teacher standing while the students sits makes perfect sense, but it matters that students see the difference between this being an active choice rather than a natural law. Some students start to make the connection here that the first step in changing a phenomenon is conceptualizing that thing as something that can in fact be changed. Other students resist this notion, correctly identifying it as inherently threatening. For these students, a different metaphor sometimes helps. I ask them to think about a fish in water and engage them in a conversation about how the fish doesn't know it's in water because water is its reality. The only way it can know there is another reality is to be yanked out of the water, which will cause it to flop around, desperately trying to return to the water. Water is the safer normalcy for a fish, so its reaction makes sense. Yet the desire for a world of water does not negate the existence of land.

Students are often surprised to learn that neither nature nor neutrality accounts for their default understandings about how to conduct themselves in a classroom. The intellectual task now is for them to see the ways in which specific ideologies serve as the actual underpinnings for what they experience as normal. Here is where I introduce Freire's banking concept of education to demonstrate how conventional notions of who is capable of knowing have influenced the development of classroom practices and procedures:

> Education thus becomes an act of depositing, in which the students are the depositories and the teacher is the depositor. Instead of communicating, the teacher issues communiqués and makes deposits which the students patiently receive, memorize, and repeat. This is the "banking concept" of education, in which the scope of the action allowed to the students extends only as far as receiving, filing, and storing the deposits. They do, it is true, have the opportunity to become collectors or cataloguers of the things they store. But in the last analysis, it is the people themselves who are filed away through the lack of creativity, transformation, and knowledge in this (at best) misguided system.[2]

I have frequently observed Freire's words resonating strongly with students. While my own K-12 education contained its share of "banking" elements, my generation just missed the hyper-testing era that defined most of my students' educational experiences. I am becoming increasingly cognizant of this difference as the age gap between my students and me grows. I sometimes find it challenging to teach outside of the banking model because the students are so accustomed to it that they are often perplexed by the contrasting "problem posing" approach Freire advocated. In the problem posing method, teachers and students discuss critically questions and issues to which there are not pat answers waiting to be memorized and regurgitated on standardized tests. Students often need some guidance in adjusting to the problem posing context because it requires skills they failed to learn in banking-oriented schools. Some classroom manifestations of students' confusion include demanding to know the answers and what will be on the test. I used to find these questions frustrating, judging students as disinterested in learning because their words reflected a "jump through the hoop" attitude about education as a means to an end. This may be the case for some students, but I'm finding that most students respond very positively to the problem posing approach once they understand it as a contrast to what often frustrates them about school.

Students' experiences of school provide a common foundation from which to introduce the concept of ideology. For my purposes, it is enough for students to understand ideology simply as a point of view contrasting with the notion of neutrality. Banking versus "problem posing" represents ideological differences about what we tend to think of as neutral educational practices. We can then start to analyze the stories we tell about education and see how the banking approach forms the dominant narrative in our society as test scores and vocationalism eclipse other functions like critical thinking and citizenship. Problem posing educational practices provide a counternarrative by naming the ideological impulses underlying the seemingly neutral mainstream education discourse. As importantly, the counternarrative provides an alternative ideology based on equality and education as a public good rather than hierarchy and education as a private commodity. By applying the concepts of ideology, narrative, and counternarrative to the common experience of the first day of school, students begin to practice interrogating what they think they know, a habit of the mind that proves useful when discussing race.

Understanding Reality as Co-constructed

The first day of class continues to serve as a useful metaphor as I shift the conversation to how we understand classroom behavior as something we socially construct by participating in it together. This provides the critical foundation from which students can make the leap to race as constructed social reality, a crucial starting point for productive conversations about race. Students can see that part of how they knew to sit down and raise their hands in class came from observing other students' acceptance of these practices as part of what constitutes educational reality. I drive home the point that there is nothing natural, normal, or neutral about students sitting while teachers stand; we do these things simply because they are part of the fabric of the world that is presented to us.

In much the same way, we "do" race. Markus and Moya present this point in their introductory essay to *Doing Race,* arguing compellingly that it is critical to understand race as something we do as opposed to something we are. If students cannot understand race as a cocreated phenomenon, they will think racism is about personal feelings about groups of people rather than structural inequality. The sweet, but simplistic memes of multicultural children holding hands with captions like "No one is born a racist" offer a good example of this point. Contemporary racism rarely takes the form of surface-level repugnance and casting the issue this way confuses the point. More often, contemporary racism begins with blindness about one's own position, mistakenly seeing it as neutral rather than a part of the equation of racism. Markus and Moya present the stereotype of Asians being difficult to read as an example of how "doing race" works.

> Understanding that "inscrutability" is not an essential characteristic of a group of people but rather a judgment that rests on the particular perspective of the person making the observation requires an acknowledgement that there are other viable ways of being in the world. It also requires the recognition of multiple legitimate perspectives on what is considered culturally "normal" or "neutral."[3]

Because racism is so often framed as an issue about minority populations, the role of the dominant group is easy to overlook. Yet the dominant group provides the most appropriate site for interrogation since its assumptions, operating principles, and practices are frequent locations for racism. Again, the racism discussed here is not of the personal feeling variety; most people espouse beliefs in diversity and fairness. Markus and Moya's example illustrates the more complex racism that results from having one's own reality so thoroughly reinforced through societal structures like education and media that others' realities are rendered invisible. In this process, one's own ability to see the assumptions and frameworks shaping one's own understanding of reality is also rendered invisible as it starts to feel more and more like objective reality. Analyzing the philosophical possibilities of objective reality in the physical world is beyond the scope of this piece, but it is important to examine the process by which *my* way becomes *the* way. My way might actually be pretty good, as in the example of the first day of class. There might be a logic behind my way that works in a particular context. But if I impose that way without acknowledging that there are other valid ways, I engage in a legacy of disregarding and silencing other peoples' lived experiences. Regardless of philosophical leanings, it would be difficult to argue that a person's reality is not deeply shaped by his or her lived experiences. When one set of lived experiences is continually reinforced while others are left out, misinformation and incomplete understanding of important social phenomena result.

Conversely, deeper and richer explanations become possible when truly diverse voices contribute to our collective understanding of a complex issue. Claude Steele's work on stereotype threat illustrates this point. Confused by the consistently lower scores of high-achieving black, Latino, and female students on some tests, Steele conducted a series of experiments to look more closely at the psychological elements of how students from various backgrounds experienced measures of academic performance.[4] When negative stereotypes about a group were prompted in the testing environment, students consistently performed lower than those in control groups. Steele and Aronson's famous golf test experiment demonstrates the idea.[5] Black and white students were assigned to two integrated groups; one group received instructions describing the test as an assessment of natural athletic ability, and the other was told the test measured strategic thinking. Black students consistently scored lower when examiners highlighted the intellectual nature of the test and white students consistently scored lower when physical aspects were emphasized. Another experiment compared female students' math scores in all female versus mixed gender testing environments, finding significantly higher performance in the first group. This research provides important insight into how powerfully environmental factors impact seemingly fair, neutral, and objective performance measures. As Steele explains, "We emphasize the things we can see. We emphasize things about the actor—characteristics, traits, and so on—that seem like plausible explanations for her behavior. And we deemphasize, as causes of her behavior, the things we can't see very well, namely, the circumstances to which she is adapting." Without the research on stereotype threat, educators may misdiagnose the root causes of academic underperformance in some situations. Worse, they might exacerbate the problem by assuming lack of motivation and increase students' stress levels in the very ways that led to the problem in the first place.

Steele's research has the potential to interrupt the vicious circle that results when solutions embody the same underlying assumptions that created the problem. Senge wrote of the "virtuous circles" that can result when people apply systems thinking rather than linear thinking to problems.[6] Systems thinking can be viewed as a precursor to CMS in that it moves past reductive analysis focused on parts of a problem to a holistic approach that encourages an examination of underlying causes. In the case of high-achieving black and Latino students' lower test scores, a linear analysis might conclude these students simply were not quite as smart or motivated as their white and Asian counterparts. Steele's work exemplifies an effective application of systems thinking by examining the tests themselves as well as offering a more comprehensive look at how messages in these students' environment might connect to performance. Steele's work also typifies CMS by not assuming neutrality in either the tests or students' environments, making it possible to apply new thinking to old problems. Rather than being stuck with the assumption that there is something inherent to black and Latino students that causes lower test scores, students and teachers gain an expanded array of possibilities for designing more positive and effective interventions. In this way, teachers and students are able to co-construct a more positive social reality based on a more nuanced interpretation of an issue.

Revealing Dominant Narratives

While the notion of a co-constructed social reality might not be a concept that is frequently taught in schools, it is not a new idea for those in the political realm. Politicians and the think tanks that drive them know the person who controls the story wins the election. The first two tenets of CMS, the rarity of neutrality and co-construction of social reality, prove important in understanding how some narratives that drive our politics perpetuate racism. Until this point, we focused largely on how race is hidden, but here it's both hidden and signaled. This creates confusion in our political discourse as some politicians woo racist constituents while simultaneously denying any racial element to the policy or practice they advocate. Lopez coined the term "dog whistle politics," to describe how this process works and offers the following example:

> Stressing illegality provides a way to seed racial fears without directly referencing race. Scapegoating unauthorized immigrants carries a façade of neutrality insofar as it purports to refer to all persons present in the United States

without proper authorization. Ostensibly, this would include the German cit-izen here on a tourist visa who takes a job . . . yet these are not the faces that come to mind when the term is bandied about. Rather the usual suspects—the unavoidable suspects when Tea Party patriots spit out the phrase at ral-lies on the southern border—are undocumented immigrants from Latin America, especially Mexico . . . by constantly drumming on the crises posed by "illegals," the right fuels a racial frenzy but can deny its intention to do any such thing.[7]

This description demonstrates how some political leaders manage to gain votes by making racist appeals while escaping reproach by hiding behind legality as a neutral concept. In order to comprehend this process fully, one must also be able to understand legality as socially constructed. While stu-dents would probably be able to articulate the difference between natural laws and people-made laws, our discourse can be misleading. The law ap-pears both neutral and natural, which gives the illusion of fairness on the surface. Dig deeper and its complicity as both a mask and an engine for structural inequality becomes visible.

Lisa Dodson's scholarship epitomizes a CMS approach by offering a counternarrative to the "law as neutral and natural" idea.[8] Dodson con-ducted a series of studies of people who broke the law to help other people in economic hardship. For example, one participant was a physician who prescribed medicine for an insured relative when the actual patient lacked the insurance coverage necessary to pay for the medicine. Another par-ticipant was a fast-food manager who sometimes added extra hours to a worker's timecard when that person would otherwise not be able to pay rent. When I've taught Dodson's work in class, students often react strongly with a law and order narrative about how we might feel badly for poor people but can't have lawlessness. I do not deny this tension, but I do point out how they are speaking from a law and order narrative rather than some objective stance. Laws reflect constructed social realities, in this case, one that allows a fast-food company executive to be paid 1,200 times what the front line employees take home.[9] Students will push back that the answer is to change the law, a fair argument in one sense, but one that also requires some solutions about how people are to pay their bills in the meantime. Some students will turn the law and order narrative around, pointing out the unevenness in how the law is enforced with examples like tax loop-holes, racial disparities in drug sentencing, and phenomena like "driving while black." Some students will also argue that we now admire people like Martin Luther King Jr. and Rosa Parks for breaking laws we view as unjust in hindsight. This discussion also presents a good opportunity to point out how the now revered Nelson Mandela was once a terrorist under U.S. law. This is not something students can write off as ancient history since he was removed from the terror watch list only in 2008, well within their lifetimes. CMS provides the foundational framework for students to be able to critique the unequal ways in which societal practices and procedures are applied, thus deepening their understanding of racism as a structural rather than emotional phenomenon.

While some issues seem ripe for racial coding, others seem to evade any discussion of race despite its relevance to the issue under discussion. Alcohol abuse on college campuses provides one example of this. Research on the subject shows African Americans are underrepresented in the binge drinking behavior that permeates many college campuses.[10] Yet the issue is almost never framed as a white student problem. We are so accustomed to viewing students of color through a deficit lens that issues like this prove difficult to appreciate fully. Even well-intentioned scholars often frame research questions from deficit perspectives, focusing on where a given marginalized group struggles rather than where it thrives. Consequently, we fail to ask the questions that might get us to new knowledge on long-standing issues like alcohol abuse on college campuses. If we took an assets-based approach to students of color, we might ask questions like, how do African American students find opportunities to socialize without the need for heavy alcohol consumption? Or how do the parents of African American students talk to them about the consequences of alcohol abuse on campus? Rather than constantly seeking ways to "help" marginalized groups acquire the practices of mainstream students, perhaps we could gain more traction by looking at what assets the marginalized groups might bring to the table and see if they are replicable with mainstream students' deficit in a particular area.

The issue of white students' disproportionately high rates of alcohol abuse also provides a rare opportunity to expose the underlying racism in how questions are frequently framed. For example, I ask students to think critically about why we typically don't ask questions like, is there something about white culture that causes white students to binge drink at higher rates that other student groups? We generally understand that it would be difficult to define "white culture" due to the diversity within it, yet rarely acknowledge this kind of complexity in other groups. A more provocative question I sometimes ask rhetorically is, "If white students disproportionately fail to meet the behavioral standards of a university, should we consider this in the admissions process?" I know if I started the conversation with this question, students would very likely react defensively and miss the point entirely. CMS allows students to grasp organizational context generally first and then apply this tool to issues of race more specifically. By wrestling with concepts like neutrality, constructed social reality, and narrative, students develop the critical thinking necessary to understand the complexities of contemporary racism more thoughtfully. They move past the overly simplistic "no one is born racist" emotional explanation into more clarity about racism as structural inequality.

Getting Past the Personal Prejudice Paradigm

In 2013, three white students at Minnesota Community and Technical College filed a complaint against a black communications professor because they perceived her portrayal of "white men as always the villains."[11] The vice principal for academic affairs censured Dr. Shannon Gibney for "creating a hostile learning environment" despite her explanation to both the students and administration that she was referring to institutional racism, not specific white students. Is it possible neither the students nor the administration could understand the distinction Dr. Gibney was making? Based on my experience teaching diversity-related content in counseling and higher education courses, I suspect it is possible.

While we do not know all the specifics of Dr. Gibney's case, the situation described plays out in many classrooms. Certain conversations about race seem acceptable, though often benign. I have yet to hear a student complain about a Martin Luther King Day celebration or a critique of early colleges' exclusion of students of color. Yet discussions about contemporary, systemic racism often stimulate both defensiveness and genuine confusion. While some of these reactions may result from actual prejudice, I find a good deal of them are actually more attributable to a lack of intellectual tools for really understanding structural inequality. We are too used to thinking of racism as a personality problem rather than a systemic phenomenon. Part of the reason may be that it's simply easier to "teach tolerance" instead of digging deeper into the ways in which contemporary racism manifests.

Students often need help in conceptualizing racism as something beyond how they feel about a group of people. As long as they think racism is about not being nice, students will fail to grasp how and why racism proliferates in a society where the vast majority of white people do not express hateful views toward people of color *personally*. They will ask misguided questions about racial phenomena they observe and draw shallow conclusions as a result. Darling-Hammond offers a powerful example of this problem in her scholarship on the racial disparities in academic success, pointing out how the issue is nearly always framed in terms of a question about black and Latino underachievement.[12] Darling-Hammond unpacks the assumptions underlying that question: "The presumption that undergirds much of the usual conversation is that equal opportunity now exists; therefore, continued low levels of achievement on the part of students of color must be intrinsic to them, their families, or their communities." This distinction can seem subtle to students, but it has significant impact on how people understand racial disparities in academic achievement and how these understandings inform the way they vote, teach, and develop policies. The real-world implications cannot be overstated. If policy makers attribute black and Latino students' lower test scores to the fact that they are overrepresented in impoverished school systems, they are likely to support a different intervention than if they believe there is something *intrinsic* to these groups that causes lower academic performance. In the absence of an education about how to think systemically about race and racism, people tend to default to stereotypes, even if they do not think they are racist.

The example regarding black and Latino students' test scores demonstrates the importance of teaching students to frame questions that move beyond the individual into the systemic. This idea assumes students will ask the questions in the first place, which is not always the case. It has been my experience that white people actually have a lot of questions about race. Many white people suspect some of their questions are offensive, though, so they fail to ask them. From my perspective, this is a mistake because failing to address these questions does not make them go away. Jared Diamond's bestseller *Guns, Germs, and Steel* owes much of its popularity to the fact that it addresses head-on the question of why some parts of the world developed advanced tools and economic systems more quickly than others.[13] Not naturally inclined toward detailed science texts, I nonetheless bought the book because I was curious about its central question. It had been a guilty curiosity I had experienced in the back of my mind for several years while watching news coverage of Africa and wondering why the continent's problems seemed so intractable. Lacking another frame, my default assumption had been the one Diamond described in the first pages of the book, namely, that there was something about groups of people either psychologically or culturally that influenced their proclivity toward what is generally considered development (e.g., tools and animal domestication).

Diamond cites refuting that very claim as his purpose in writing the book: "Authors are regularly asked by journalists to summarize a long book in one sentence. For this book, here is such a sentence: 'History followed different courses for different peoples because of differences among those peoples' environments, not because of biological differences among the peoples themselves.'"

Diamond's words seem so simple and obvious to me now, but it's important to stay in touch with that time when they did not. Painful as it is to admit, I don't pretend that there wasn't a time when my thinking about development could be categorized as racist. For one thing, being honest about it helps me avoid what Wiggins and McTighe call the *expert blindspot*.[14] The *expert blindspot* refers to the challenge of explaining what is so obvious to the teacher that it is difficult to think of all the necessary background a student might need to complete a task. Group work provides a great example of this. Teachers frequently assign a group project without offering the necessary foundational information for how to work together as a team. One member trying to dominate while another member underperforms are phenomena we can anticipate given how often they happen, yet we don't always help students troubleshoot how they might address these problems if they occur. Offering ideas like establishing ground rules or letting team members state how they prefer to receive feedback might assist students in engaging in group work more effectively. Yet we tend to simply give the assignment and let the students sink or swim. I find that teaching about racism contains some similar expert blindspot challenges. If students lack the background knowledge necessary to express an informed opinion about development, how can I expect them not to operate out of faulty assumptions? This mistake becomes easier to avoid when I realize I made it myself not too long ago.

The expert blindspot offers an intellectual reason for remembering one's own ignorance on a topic. The second reason is more emotional and personal. I work to remember the experience of being changed by *Guns, Germs, and Steel* because this kind of revelation provides an opportunity to role model the value of humility in studying an experience outside of one's own. *Guns, Germs, and Steel* came out in when I was in my mid-twenties. I think of this as an age when I should have "known better," an attitude shared by many of my 20-something students. Maybe ironically, the opinion that they *should* know better sometimes makes students think they actually *do* know better, which can stimulate defensiveness. Admitting my own ignorance sometimes opens the door for students to take risks and voice the gaps in their own knowledge. I make a point to state explicitly that it's okay to have questions—even misguided ones—about other groups of people, but one has to listen deeply to the answer and accept challenges to one's own thinking in order for real growth to occur. I also talk intentionally about feeling both guilty and stupid for having fallen into the kind of trap I associate with the racist rhetoric of texts like Herrnstein and Murray's *The Bell Curve*.[15] Sometimes the desire to avoid feeling guilty and/or stupid impedes students' academic and personal growth in ways that leave them stuck in the same place with regard to their attitudes about racism. I try to challenge this approach by sharing that while feeling embarrassed isn't fun, one doesn't die from it despite the feelings of fight or flight it can initiate. I also argue a moment of embarrassment is well worth the satisfaction that comes from understanding something important in a new and deeper way.

Diamond's work has the added benefit of providing an opportunity to introduce the concept of narrative as an intellectual tool necessary for examining systemic oppression. Diamond's work is on development, a concept used positively or at least neutrally in the mainstream media. The dominant narrative is generally that developed nations are ahead and developing nations are behind in some never-quite-explained contest. A counternarrative sometimes discussed in alternative media sources is that some nations are actually overdeveloped if we consider a factor like environmental sustainability as a metric for success. CMS provides some intellectual tools for helping students begin to critique seemingly neutral concepts like "development," a vital step in beginning to understand how contemporary, structural racism works.

Conclusion

Uncomfortable though it might be, maybe the most useful end point for this chapter is a confession: until the last class in the last year of the last degree I would earn, I secretly took the attitude that many of my students take when it comes to discussing race. The following points characterize the attitude:

(1) I am liberal, so education about racism doesn't apply to me.
(2) I am white, so education about race doesn't apply to me.
(3) I am a member of other marginalized groups (women, lesbian, gay, bisexual, and transgender) so I already understand prejudice and discrimination.

I did not feel hostile toward diversity courses or programs I was required to attend. I just thought they didn't apply to me. I don't think I was even aware that I thought they didn't apply. I just found myself checking out during these classes and felt a little curious about that. After all, I've always identified as politically progressive. Now I realize my boredom was not due to my great knowledge about racism but rather to my overly simplified perspective on the topic. I genuinely thought racism was wrong and that those who commit hate crimes should be sent to jail but did not realize there was more to racism than hate crimes. Worse, I didn't realize I thought racism was just about hate crimes. I lacked the tools to examine the issue in a more nuanced way until the last class of my entire educational career. Neither the words "race" nor "diversity" appeared in the title or course description, which I hate to admit was probably helpful in not cuing my "I already know this" attitude.

The words that did appear were "critical pedagogy" and "participatory research," both of which provided frameworks for examining structural power relationships in ways my mind had not been trained to think. Once I had some practice in unpacking neutrality and understanding social construction, I could make connections between the rest of my doctoral coursework in organizational leadership and the social justice issues I cared about, but struggled to understand and articulate. Studying CMS specifically helped me understand how underlying structures replicate racism and other social injustices despite the positive intentions political and educational leaders often espouse.

Shannon Gibney's case is now in the back of my mind when I teach about racism, but I think I would be abdicating my responsibility as an educator not to do everything I can to give students the intellectual tools they need to navigate this important issue. I also know my white skin lowers the risk I take when challenging students about racism, so I feel even more responsible to try. Framing education about racism in terms of the "four tasks" and explaining it to students this way has helped us move past some of the traps that get us stuck in either defensive or benign conversations. When students start to apply some of the CMS approaches, they engage in more meaningful and humble discussions about racism. To be sure, they still disagree and feel exposed sometimes, but they have some tools for navigating this complexity more effectively. They also start to make sense of their worlds in new ways. Ta-Nehisi Coates expresses this experience eloquently: "When I was young man, I studied history at Howard University. Much of my studies were focused on the Black diaspora, and thus white racism.

I wish I had understood that I was not, in fact, simply studying white racism, but the nature of power itself."[16] We will continue to replicate the same system without thoughtful, critical analysis about the assumptions that drive the current power structures. Progress on racism demands getting to the heart of how power has worked in the past and deciding proactively how we want it to work in the future.

Notes

1. Alvesson, Bridgeman, and Willmott 2009.
2. Freire 2000.
3. Markus and Moya 2010.
4. Steele 2010.
5. Steele and Aronson 1995.
6. Senge 1990.
7. Lopez 2014.
8. Dodson 2009.
9. Berfield 2014.
10. Skidmore et al. 2012.
11. McDonough 2013.
12. Darling-Hammond 2010.
13. Diamond 1998.
14. Wiggins and McTighe 2005.
15. Herrnstein and Murray 1994.
16. Coates 2014.

Bibliography

Alvesson, Mats, Todd Bridgman, and Hugh Willmott, eds. 2009. *The Oxford Handbook of Critical Management Studies.* New York: Oxford University Press.

Au, Wayne. 2011. "Teaching under the New Taylorism: High-Stakes Testing and the Standardization of the 21st Century Curriculum." *Journal of Curriculum Studies* 43 (1): 25–45.

Berfield, Susan. 2014. "Fast-Food CEOS Make 1000 Times the Pay of the Average Fast-Food Worker." *BloombergBusinessweek* (April 22). http://www.business week.com/articles/2014-04-22/fast-food-ceos-make-1-000-times-the-average-fast-food-worker.

Coates, Ta-Nehisi. 2014. "Germans Are the Masters and Poles Are the Slaves." *The Atlantic* (January 13). http://www.theatlantic.com/international/archive/2014/01/germans-are-the-masters-and-poles-are-the-slaves/283017/.

Cottom, Tressie. 2013. "Want to Teach Your Students about Racism? Prepare for a Formal Reprimand." *Slate Magazine* (December 3): 3. http://www.slate.com/articles/life/counter_narrative/2013/12/minneapolis_professor_shannon_gibney_reprimanded_for_talking_about_racism.html.

Darling-Hammond, Linda. 2010. *The Flat World and Education: How America's Commitment to Equity Will Determine Our Future.* New York: Teachers College Press.

Diamond, Jared M. 1998. *Guns, Germs and Steel: A Short History of Everybody for the Last 13,000 Years.* New York: Random House.

Dodson, Lisa. 2009. *The Moral Underground: How Ordinary Americans Subvert an Unfair Economy.* New York: The New Press.

Freire, Paulo. 2000. *Pedagogy of the Oppressed.* New York: Continuum.

Goodman, Amy. "Native Groups, Ranchers Launch D.C. Protest against Keystone XL Pipeline." Democracy Now, April 23, 2014. http://www.democracynow.org/2014/4/23/headlines/native_groups_ranchers_launch_dc_protest_against_keystone_xl.

Haney-López, Ian. 2014. *Dog Whistle Politics: How Coded Racial Appeals Have Wrecked the Middle Class.* New York: Oxford University Press.

Herrnstein, Richard J., and Charles Murray. 1994. *Bell Curve: Intelligence and Class Structure in American Life.* New York: Simon & Schuster.

Markus, Hazel, and Paula M.L. Moya. "Doing Race: 21 Essays for the 21st Century." 2010.

McDonough, Katie. "Three White College Students File Racial Discrimination Complaint against Professor over Lesson on Structural Racism." Salon, December 2, 2013. http://www.salon.com/2013/12/02/three_white_college_students_file_racial_discrimination_complaint_against_professor_over_lesson_on_structural_racism/.

Senge, Peter. 1990. *The Fifth Discipline: The Art and Practice of Learning.* New York: Doubleday.

Skidmore, Jessica R., James G. Murphy, Matthew Martens, and Ashley A. Dennhardt. 2012. "Alcohol-Related Consequences in African American and European American College Students." *Journal of Ethnicity in Substance Abuse* 174. *Academic OneFile,* EBSCO*host.* Accessed June 2, 2014.

Steele, Claude M. 2010. *Whistling Vivaldi: And Other Clues to How Stereotypes Affect Us* (Issues of Our Time). New York: W.W. Norton, p. 242.

Steele, Claude M., and Joshua Aronson. 1995. "Stereotype Threat and the Intellectual Test Performance of African Americans." *Journal of Personality and Social Psychology* 69 (5): 797.

Wiggins, Grant P., and Jay McTighe. *Understanding by Design.* Ascd, 2005.

Chapter 9

Moving beyond the Urban Initiative: Programmatic Efforts to Foster Critical Counternarratives

Anthony Collatos

UPTEC keeps us from blaming the kids or the schools. In other classes when I express my concerns, I am often advised to find another school or another district because working in urban schools is too difficult. UPTEC never gives me that out.
—Melissa, UPTEC High School Social
Studies Teacher

The more I thought about it, the more I realized that people thought that just because we are from a low-income community—regardless of the color of our skin—that we would not be able to manage our dreams.
—Maria, YEARS High School Senior

This chapter documents the efforts of a university-led strategic effort, the Urban Initiative (UI), to create university–community partnerships that disrupt traditional patterns of racial inequality and educational inequity within our American public schools. Grounded in social theory and critical research, two UI programs empowered urban youth, families, and teachers with the theoretical and analytical tools necessary to increase student success and teacher retention. The first program, the Urban Parent Teacher Education Collaborative (UPTEC), is a community-based model of teacher education that includes urban parents in the education and mentoring of teacher educators. The second program, the Youth Empowerment and Research Seminar (YEARS), offers urban high school students opportunities to investigate critical issues such as inequity, civic engagement, and race and racism. Engaging participants as critical researchers and creating spaces for self-reflexive racial dialogue impacted their ability to enact social change for their school communities and their own educational pathways. From these programs, it is clear that effective teacher education and intervention programs must involve a critical examination of race, privilege, and access across and within schools. Ultimately, this work calls for university–community partnerships that empower urban youth, parents, and educators to challenge existing policies and practices of racial inequality within schools.

Reframing how we value knowledge is critical to the future of educational reform. In earlier work I have urged interested educators, researchers, and activists to consider the benefits of working with students and teachers on educational research and reform efforts that included authentic and meaningful dialogue and a commitment to social action. I have advocated for the use of critical and counterhegemonic spaces that facilitate students' movement from the periphery to core participation as youth researchers working for social justice. This work calls for further examples of programmatic efforts that forefront the knowledge and voices of urban students and parents at the center of school reform. UPTEC and YEARS represent two efforts to implement university–community partnerships designed to empower students, parents, and teachers toward urban educational reform.

What Is the Role of the University in Educational Reform?

Educational researchers recognize that university–community partnerships are necessary to establish programs and spaces to counterexisting educational inequities. Scholars have advocated for the establishment of university-led "educational field stations" and research centers to reframe the role of higher education in our attempts to reform urban education.[1] Hugh Mehan et al. (2010) support the creation of educational field stations on University of California (UC) campuses as an effort to increase the number of underrepresented students prepared for admission to UC schools. They cite the creation of the Center for Research in Educational Equity, Access, and Teaching Excellence and the Preuss School on the UC San Diego campus in 1997 as effective examples. Scholars also recognize a "bottom-up" approach to community empowerment is essential to sustainable university–community partnerships. For example, Jeannie Oakes, John Rogers, and Martin Lipton (2006) documented how UCLA's Institute for Democracy, Education, and Access led to increased partnership with community-based organizations and critical research that served urban communities and influenced educational policy. University–community partnerships can also play a crucial role in the disruption of traditional patterns of racial inequality and educational inequity within our American public schools and communities. Pepperdine's Graduate School of Education and Psychology (GSEP)—situated in one of the most diverse communities in the United States—developed a "UI" that also sought to serve the most under-resourced urban students and families in Los Angeles. In 2009, influenced by similar UC efforts, Pepperdine University launched a UI committed to establishing stronger university–community partnerships that tackled issues of educational inequity, mental health, and the marginalization of urban neighborhoods.[2]

The Urban Initiative Answers a Call to Serve

Similar to Mehan's call for *educational field stations,* Pepperdine's Urban Initiative (2008) sought to develop a national model for preparing professionals to work in underserved communities. The UI calls for sustainability models that build partnerships between universities and urban communities, develop community networks, and design participatory action research that responds to community needs. The initiative strives to redefine the relationship between the university and the community. In so doing, it hopes to better prepare the next generation of mental health and educational professionals with the particular tools needed to serve in urban, multicultural communities. The UI White Paper (2008) grounds this work in social action, "A moral imperative drives this response to call for social justice. GSEP accepts its responsibility as a graduate school of education and psychology on the edge of one of the most challenged urban areas in the country and answers that call with its Urban Initiative." Through participation in these projects, the UI hopes to serve as a national resource for universities seeking to engage in urban community development in the areas of education and mental health programs. Essentially, the UI aspires to create multiple educational and mental health field stations.

The UI led to multiple programs developed to serve the educational and mental health needs of urban students and families in Southern California. I had the opportunity to initiate two programs—the UPTEC and the YEARS—that served urban school communities. More important, these two programs provided spaces for preservice teachers and urban high school students to challenge their preconceived notions of the role of race, class, and gender within educational inequality. Within the UPTEC program, graduate students working toward a teaching credential (i.e., student teachers, preservice teachers, or teacher candidates) were provided a space to challenge cultural deficit models and examine their own privilege as successful students.[3] Similarly, YEARS created opportunities for urban high school students to explore how race and privilege mediated civic leadership and college access pathways.

Programs Create Spaces for Counternarratives to Emerge

Critical research and participatory action research offer a learning environment that encourages students to use their biographies, identities, and experiences as intellectual resources.[4] The UPTEC and YEARS participants continually examined their own past and present stories, imagined their possible futures, and then reflected on relations of power and marginalization within schools and communities.[5] Chapman (2003) refers to these stories as *critical personal narratives,* created to question power relations and to work toward change. Similarly, *counternarratives* serve as stories to dispel myths, stereotypes, and dominant narratives about low-performing, minority students.[6] The UPTEC and YEARS participant experiences—as critical personal narratives or counternarratives—proved essential for students, parents, and teachers to develop new identities as scholars and activists within their school and community.[7]

Teacher education and college access literature indicate that existing intervention models lack a critical approach and these models fail to challenge systemic racism in school structures, policies, and practices. Critical theorists believe educational reform must empower students, parents, and teachers to change the systems of domination.[8] Although content knowledge and academic skills are essential to successful teacher education and intervention programs, participants must be engaged critically. Kumashiro (2002) calls on educators to utilize anti-oppressive education and appeals to researchers to explore "more implications of traditionally marginalized or yet unexplored perspectives."[9] Similarly, critical pedagogy must involve an active and political position that works toward "affirming the voices of marginalized students" and simultaneously transforms "their communities into sites of struggle and resistance."[10] Enabling students to challenge the social order is part of engaging students in the learning process. A teacher education and intervention program engaged in critical research must create spaces for participants to acknowledge the systemic flaws of schooling and to examine the education system.

Both the UPTEC and YEARS represent programmatic efforts to create spaces for counternarratives that challenge deficit model explanations about race, educational opportunity, and equity.

What Is the Urban Parent Teacher Education Collaborative?

In fall 2006, Pepperdine's Master of Arts in Education with Teaching Credentialing (MAETC) program initiated a two-year plan to revise the teacher education curriculum to better prepare teachers to educate the most underserved student populations. Breaking from a tradition of serving more suburban and high performing schools, the revised teacher education program produced a commitment to work in urban schools and their surrounding communities. Framed by the UI and an MAETC commitment to work in urban schools, the UPTEC emerged.

UPTEC was a six-year longitudinal study designed to develop and test a community-based model of teacher education that fully included urban parents and community leaders in the education of preservice teachers. UPTEC sought to understand how a community-based approach—courses co-taught by a university faculty member and a grassroots organizer/advocate—shaped preservice teachers' ability to teach and their retention within low-performing urban schools communities. UPTEC (2006–2012) worked with a total of 60 teacher candidates over 6 cohorts.

UPTEC included community leaders as teacher educators within a series of year-long teacher education courses offered at a small private university in the metropolitan Los Angeles area. I co-taught UPTEC with Mary Johnson—a well-known community organizer and the president of Parent U-turn—a multicultural grassroots student and parent advocacy organization. The course curriculum combined the historical, philosophical, social, cultural foundations of education and action research. In turn, the course content provided a foundation for preservice teachers to examine theory, practice, and research around issues of social theory, multicultural education, and culturally relevant teaching. Upon successful completion of the UPTEC program, graduates receive a master's degree in education and are eligible to apply for their teacher credential through the California Commission on Teacher Credentialing.

UPTEC is grounded in a philosophy that all PreK-12 students deserve the right to a quality education that prepares them for a four-year university education and to participate in a democracy as critically minded individuals. To successfully achieve these goals, especially for urban students, teachers need to be prepared to work within the constraints of low-performing urban schools and with the students' families and communities. Informed by teacher education literature, UPTEC included parent and community leaders during the preservice education experience as an attempt to better prepare future urban teachers and, consequently, to increase the quality of education that urban students deserve.

UPTEC Moves beyond Limited Teacher Education Models

Teacher education programs rarely educate future teachers how to work with urban families, in particular, and within urban communities. In his call for a new framework for effective urban teaching, Murrell (2001) explains, "This country has yet to produce a system of teacher education that successfully, and in sufficient numbers, prepares teachers for effective work in diverse urban school settings."[11] Programs seldom prepare teachers to work within the context of a school community and with students' families and, at best, parents or local leaders may be included in the teacher education process as guest speakers or in isolated moments of the preservice experience. While numerous educational researchers have called for the inclusion of parents in the educational process, seldom have they provided a culturally relevant model that recognizes different parent groups—especially first-generation, low-income, language-minority, and immigrant families. Few, if any, of the existing models call for full participation by urban parents and urban community leaders in the teacher preparation process.

Teacher education programs also struggle to recruit diverse and culturally competent teacher candidates. Over 15 years ago the National Center for Education Statistics (1998) predicted that public schools in the United States needed to recruit, train, hire, and mentor nearly 3 million teachers. We have yet to successfully attract and prepare enough teachers to replace a generation of educators retiring from the field. The huge task of ushering in a new generation of teachers was, and is, exacerbated by the fact that public schools are increasingly diverse with respect to culture, ethnicity, primary language, and socioeconomic status. In California, during the 2004–2005 academic school year, 69 percent of public school students were students of color (African American, Latino, Asian, and American Indian), but only 26 percent of the teachers shared similar racial/ethnic backgrounds as their students.[12] Almost 10 years later teachers of color are still disproportionately underrepresented when compared to students of color, 34 percent to 74 percent, respectively.

Similarly, the UPTEC preservice teachers seldom represent the racial/ethnic demographics of their public school students. During the 2006–2012 academic school years, the UPTEC preservice teachers, on average, were 30 percent Caucasian, 20 percent Asian, 33 percent Latino, and 17 percent African American. Yet, in the Los Angeles Unified School District, where most of our preservice teachers are placed, African American and Latino students made up more than 83 percent of the total PreK-12 district enrollment. Certainly, a major challenge is to recruit a teaching force that reflects the ethnic and cultural diversity of a rapidly changing student body.

A related challenge for teacher educators is to create preservice programs wherein teacher candidates can develop knowledge and teaching practices that are effective across multiple lines of diversity—race/ethnicity, culture, socioeconomic status. In urban teacher education programs our task is to devise strategies that help teacher candidates forge meaningful relationships with students who often come from different cultural and socioeconomic backgrounds than the teachers. We must help preservice teachers value these differences as assets and see this knowledge as critical to successful practice. This presents a tremendous opportunity for progressive teacher educators who wish to develop teacher-training programs that value and affirm the contributions of urban students, urban families, and members of urban communities.

Becoming Community-Based Teacher Educators

The UPTEC program was heavily influenced by Peter Murrell's (2001) call for community-based models of teacher education that are "community-dedicated, research-focused, collaboration-oriented programs of urban education."[13] UPTEC aimed to go beyond the partnership model of the Professional Development Schools by creating a triad of teacher education, schools, and community programs with a better chance of producing *communities of learning* from which a new generation of community teachers might emerge with the knowledge, the skills, and the dispositions to serve urban schools and communities. These teacher education programs would become "community-responsive and urban focused."[14]

Creating Spaces for Deconstruction and Counternarratives

Part of becoming a community teacher involves deconstructing preconceived notions of urban schools and communities. In order to foster counternarratives, preservice teachers need space to explore existing deficit model explanations. UPTEC has provided such a space. UPTEC's critical personal narratives illustrate how a community-based approach led to reflections of race, privilege, and identity. These critical personal narratives describe how UPTEC's community teacher-based approach helped participants challenge a fear of the unknown and deficit model explanations to create counternarratives that empowered teachers and parent leaders.

"Why Aren't We Prepared to Work with the Families of Our Students?"

As a strategy to better prepare teacher education students for urban schools, members of Parent U-Turn, a grassroots parent advocacy group from Southeast Los Angeles, were often invited to class to share their experiences. Moreover, our graduate classes were often held within parent centers on local high school and elementary school campuses. Teacher candidates quickly found that the parents' experiences brought the course content, data, and community teacher framework to life.

Murrell (2001) suggests there is a "crisis of knowledge" in teacher education and claims the first essential quality of a community teacher is a "conception of quality education formed from the perspective of the communities, students, and families being served."[15] In short, teachers need to understand how their students and the students' families perceive and define quality education. Melissa, a social studies teacher from the inaugural UPTEC cohort, described the impact of including parents as educational experts, "Mary [Johnson] very much makes it real. We do not only going to talk about breaking down these perceptions, we are going to go out and physically do it." Charise—an African American, elementary school teacher—shared, "The UPTEC program gave us the skills and desire to become active members of the communities and lives of the students in our classrooms; in spite of our ethnic and socio-economic differences." Similarly, Veronica, a Latina elementary school teacher highlighted the importance of self-reflection across boundaries:

> Most teacher preparation programs do not provide space for pre-service teachers to explore self-perceptions of saving students of color nor their lack of knowledge of cultures outside of their own are not explored in . . . UPTEC allowed us to explore our biases early, which helped once we stepped into classrooms during our first year of teaching.

UPTEC preservice teachers recognized the need for a more community-based model of teacher education and the importance of critical reflection. It is important that teacher candidates have multiple opportunities to develop critical relationships with the students and parents they will serve.

The presence of Mary Johnson as a co-teacher bridged the distance between the teacher candidates' preconceived notions of urban schools and their own educational experience. Melissa identified as "half Latino, and half white" but clearly identified more as a white female and shared her apprehension to being placed in an urban school. She explained, "Initially, I was nervous about traveling outside my own community. But knowing Mary was going to be there to meet me at the school and show me around made it a lot easier. It didn't take long for my perceptions to change." Veronica agreed, "Through example, Mary showed us how important community is for the students to succeed. She demonstrated the importance in creating healthy relationships with the families that we serviced." The UPTEC community-teacher approach shifted the dialogue from a crisis of knowledge to recognition of multiple forms of community-based knowledge. Yosso (2005) describes this community-based knowledge, or multiple forms of capital, as *community cultural wealth*. UPTEC students utilized the community cultural wealth to become better teachers and community participants.

Challenging Deficit Models–Overcoming the Fear of the Unknown

Too often, preservice teachers decide not to work in urban schools because of preconceived notions of urban schools and a fear of the unknown. *Nayana* graduated from the UPTEC program in 2009 and recently began her fifth year as an elementary teacher at a public charter school serving low-income and predominantly Latino students. The youngest daughter of Sri Lankan immigrants, Nayana attended a highly resourced, private school from 1st to 12th grade. Nayana describes her sheltered upbringing:

> I was taught that public schools were filled with crime and were a place where all the "inner-city" children were bussed in. My parents worked hard to ensure that I had the best possible education, but more importantly that I was shielded from the realities of the world. Even my college education was within 10 miles of my home. I have always remained in a bubble that my parents created for me.

UPTEC provided Nayana with a new experience outside her community. Nayana's clinical placement occurred at an inner-city, Title I school serving 99 percent Latino students. She would now commute 90 minutes a day from her own suburban neighborhood to a working-class community in Southeast Los Angeles.

Upon her acceptance to the UPTEC program, Nayana received numerous phone calls from family members discouraging her from joining the UPTEC program. She was told, "A *girl* [her emphasis] like you cannot make a difference in an urban school." Nayana shared, "On my first day of school I cried the entire commute as my mind ran wild with self-doubt and fear of the unknown." Nayana questioned whether she would be able to relate with students and if the students and their families would accept her. Upon arrival, she found the staff and students welcoming and "felt at home." Upon reflection, Nayana recognized how her privilege impacted her preconceived notions of an inner-city school and community; however, Nayana struggled to convey her newfound comfort level with her concerned close-knit family.

At the suggestion of Mary Johnson, Nayana invited her family—father, mother, and sister—to attend Back to School Night. Ironically, as Nayana met her elementary students' parents, her students and their families were able to meet their teacher's family. Following a positive evening, Nayana's dad would go on to volunteer in the class on several occasions throughout the year. By the end of her student teaching experience, Nayana proudly proclaimed that "the school and community had become a second home." This narrative is powerful for multiple reasons. Becoming a community teacher means learning from local leaders, parents, and students. It also involves a dialogic process whereby the teacher and the student continually shift roles as both the teacher and the learner. Beyond race, socioeconomic status, or privilege, both Nayana's and the students' families recognized a mutual respect for the family. Without realizing it, Nayana increased the familial capital of all involved. Overcoming a fear of the unknown must involve a willingness to challenge our deficit models and create counternarratives.

Nayana's and Melissa's initial reservation to working in urban schools—and the cautious reactions of family members—is not uncommon when preservice teachers are placed within urban communities different from their own K-12 schooling experience. Melissa shared both internal and external reservations initially.

When I expressed my concerns about working in urban schools, which mostly revolved around safety. I was told not to. I think this fear factor gets back to a fear of the unknown and what is it really about and what are the perceptions that we have about working in an urban environment. UPTEC really helped me to face my fears about working in unfamiliar communities.

Beyond family concerns, Melissa explained how university faculty also suggested she "might want to work for a few years in a 'regular' school before you sign up to work in an urban school." Each summer, new incoming teacher education students are invited to consider joining the UPTEC program. Every year a large number of preservice teachers choose not to work with urban schools because of the fear of the unknown or unfamiliar.

Nayana has continued to work with families at her current school and recently led professional development about community engagement for her fellow faculty. Nayana credits Mary Johnson for her commitment to families and overcoming deficit models, "If I had not worked with Mary, I would have never known the most valuable resource I have to educate children are their parents and care-givers. I would have continued to subscribe to my belief that the parents of urban youth simply, do not care, a sentiment that I still hear teachers sharing in the lunchroom."

The inclusion of Mary Johnson and community leaders helps to minimize a fear of the unknown and lead to teacher retention and sustainability. Despite massive teacher layoffs and budget cuts between 2008 and 2013, over 80 percent of UPTEC alums continue to teach full-time in PreK-12 schools and/or are pursuing advanced degrees in education. Of those teaching, over 82 percent work in urban schools or with marginalized student populations. Moreover, many of the 2006–2012 UPTEC graduates are already leaders on their school campuses (e.g., assistant principals, department chairs, coaches, school site council members, and community representatives) and several are currently enrolled in, or graduates of, education-related graduate (e.g., administrative credential, speech pathology, special education) and doctoral programs (e.g., educational leadership and urban education).

Challenging Deficit Models with Counternarratives

I work hard not to save my students or community but to empower them. I share data with my students all the time and the negative perceptions of our families and communities brought upon by deficit models. And that is our job, one by one, to change that perception. We are not "illegal;" we are not "thugs and gangsters;" or "drug users." We do not get shot at, nor do we shoot people. We are

a community of diverse people trying to fight for what is fair. We fight, but not with each other. We fight for a better education, the opportunity to go to college, and the right to better our community.
—Beto, UPTEC High School Social Studies Teacher.

A graduate of the 2007–2008 UPTEC cohort, Beto is currently a high school social studies teacher, mentor teacher, and baseball coach. In contrast to Nayana and Melissa, Beto "grew up in the local community" where he student taught and he described the opportunity to teach locally "like a homecoming." Although Beto was not challenged by a fear of the unknown, he did struggle with his own deficit explanations of educational inequity:

> Through UPTEC I learned what I already knew from my own experience, but I had no way to convey those experiences. I needed to empower others. As a Latino male from an urban community, attending local schools, I faced many obstacles throughout my educational career. I saw myself in my students and realize it was not their fault.

It is necessary to provide all teachers and students with the spaces and tools to deconstruct cultural deficit explanations of educational inequities. Nayana described how UPTEC helped bridge the cultural distance from her own upbringing and schooling experience to her eventual professional school community. In contrast to Nayana and Melissa, Beto was raised in the local community and shared a similar cultural background and neighborhood experience with his students. Yet, Beto also credited the UPTEC program with helping him to challenge his own notions of parent involvement and to dispel cultural deficit explanations.

Like Nayana, Beto expressed concern to Mary about potential low attendance for his first Back to School Night. Mary suggested he call his students' homes and invite each family to attend. After calling home to every caregiver, Beto realized most parents could not attend because they held multiple jobs and struggled with childcare issues. Through his effort to reach out, Beto realized that the parents' inability to attend was not a reflection of how deeply they cared about their child's education.

We must continue to challenge assumptions that shared racial and cultural backgrounds equate to shared understandings of the educational challenges that different students and families face—especially across intragroup differences such as socioeconomic, immigrant/generational, language, and educational attainment status. Regardless of a teacher's personal background, it is important to provide all teachers with the opportunities to recognize and challenge how privilege mediates our understanding of educational inequity and the challenges that students face.

Beto currently teaches in the same working-class community where his family has lived for 19 years. His commitment to becoming a community teacher manifests in his desire to empower urban students with a counternarrative that fosters multicultural college-going students and community, "As a teacher I have found my calling. I still work long hours and now I fight against the perceived notion that urban students cannot succeed and that urban families do not care about their children. And I love it." Beyond merely challenging deficit model explanations, UPTEC teachers developed counternarratives to guide their teaching and careers.

Reflections of a Parent Teacher Educator

UPTEC creates transformative experiences for parent teacher educators as well. One unintended impact of the UPTEC community model involved parent empowerment. Mary Johnson believes the opportunity to co-teach within the UPTEC program validated her knowledge and the inclusion of community leaders reframes how we prepare preservice teachers for urban schools. UPTEC consciously privileged the experiences of urban parents and leaders; however, the positive impact on Johnson and parent participant speaks to the multidimensional benefit of creating spaces to shift power relations and create counternarratives. Johnson described UPTEC's approach, "In this new model, the roles are reversed. Parents are now valued as experts with valuable information to share with new teachers . . . UPTEC ultimately valued my cultural knowledge, embraced my life struggles, and considered me an expert." An unintended consequence of this dialogic approach led to a greater understanding on behalf of the community teachers and the parents. Johnson explains further, "As their co-teacher, the cohort students have taken my advice and put it into practice. And I have learned from them. I have learned that parents and teachers have the same fears of out-reaching to one another. I have truly learned to see both perspectives— as a parent and what kinds of resource/support teachers need to be effective in the classroom." In recognition of the program, the Los Angeles County Office of Education recognized UPTEC as one of the 2008 Best Practices for Parent Involvement in Los Angeles County. The county found that the qualitative and longitudinal data indicates this comprehensive and interactive approach builds a professional community that best prepares teacher candidates for public education in California K-12 schools.

The UPTEC preservice teachers, like the YEARS participants, continually examined their own past and present stories, imagined their possible futures, and then reflected on relations of power and marginalization within schools and communities.

The Youth Empowerment and Research Seminar

Like the UPTEC program, the UI led to the development of the YEARS. Between summer 2008 and spring 2009, 13 urban high school students participated in the YEARS, a program designed to provide urban students with an opportunity to investigate critical issues that influence democratic participation and the educational achievement of youth. At the heart of the program, students engaged in complex discussions regarding educational inequity, college access, civic leadership, and race and racism. YEARS was based on the principle that when urban youth are provided the opportunity, the space, and the tools necessary to critically examine the education system and democracy, they engage in transformative experiences that lead them to become critically minded leaders in their school and community. During this seminar, YEARS participants interviewed over 250 civic leaders at the 2008 Democratic National Convention and the 2009 California Republican Party Convention to better understand what motivates elected officials to serve their community. YEARS students shared their findings with local community leaders and engaged in numerous advocacy efforts in their local school and city.

Critical Sociology and Critical Race Theory Guide YEARS

Just as the community teacher model guided UPTEC, critical sociology and critical race theory (CRT) informed the YEARS' program design and research. *Critical sociology* seeks to develop citizens who are able to use the language and tools of sociology not just to describe but to transform the social order.[16] Critical sociologist Pierre Bourdieu's later work provides insight into the content of such a program. Bourdieu (1998) proposes critical sociology as a tool for promoting social change and, in particular, for disrupting social reproduction. He argues that the same forces of capital that legitimize inequality can be used for systemic transformations in the social world. These transformations can empower marginalized individuals and groups.

Similarly, CRT seeks to understand race, class, and gender within educational and critical research settings and commits to empower marginalized groups.[17] CRT forefronts the intersection of race, class, and gender to empower marginalized and oppressed groups in the United States. Rooted in legal studies, CRT seeks to expose the myriad of ways apparently race-neutral social policies and educational practices marginalize students of color.[18] Traditional analyses of social and educational inequalities were framed by class;[19] however, CRT situates the racialized experiences of people of color in conjunction with class and gender to gain a greater understanding of how race, class, and gender influence the urban youth's experiences and how schools structure those experiences.[20] CRT emphasizes the legitimacy of student narratives often marginalized within traditional explanations of student failure.

YEARS as an Evolution of the Futures Project

The YEARS program was greatly influenced by the Futures Project, a longitudinal ethnographic study (1998–2005) of 30 Latino and African American high school students who attended one of the most economically and racially diverse public schools in California. Like many college access programs, Futures aimed to minimize the disparity of educational opportunities between working-class students from underrepresented minority groups (African American and Latino) and more affluent white and Asian students at their school. Futures sought to examine, and to intervene in, the pathways of students of color as they navigate toward college. Unlike most college access programs, Futures engaged high school students as critical researchers in the sociology of education and situated the students' research and lives at the center of the curriculum. During the 1998–2001 summers, the Futures students participated in a series of academically rigorous, research seminars that introduced them to the sociology of education. The Futures students participated in a learning enterprise where they appropriated new roles as critical researchers and as scholars.[21] As a precursor to YEARS, in summer of 2000, the Futures students joined with other local high school students in a summer seminar to engage urban youth as researchers during the Democratic National Convention in Los Angeles.

The success of Futures as a critical research program is well documented.[22] For example, Futures students navigated the academic pathway through high school to college more successfully than similar non-Futures classmates and statewide peers.[23] Beyond the classroom, engaging urban youth as critical researchers led to a commitment to social justice, created multiple spaces for urban youth to take on new identities,[24] fostered the development of a multicultural college-going identity,[25] increased literacy development,[26] and promoted parents' knowledge and navigational capital[27] and students' college retention.[28] All of these Futures-related findings greatly informed the structure and delivery of the YEARS program.

Critical Research Influences Youth Counternarratives

YEARS students, like the UPTEC preservice teachers, developed counternarratives based on their opportunities to examine their own past and present stories and their critical research experience. Through multiple examinations of their educational pathways and reflections on power and marginalization, YEARS students reimagined possible futures and appropriated new identities as school and community leaders. Their daily activities within the context of the YEARS project served to stereotypes and dominant narratives about low-income students of color. This work illustrates how engaging youth in critical research within a CRT framework creates critical spaces for urban students to explore the intersections of race, class, and gender. Most important, this research provides a framework for helping urban youth to examine their multiple identities, to increase agency, and to become civically engaged at the local, state, and national levels.

Maria is the youngest of five children raised by her Nicaraguan dad and mom from Jalisco, Mexico. Growing up in the same working-class neighborhood her whole life, she credits her parents for her strong work ethic. Fully bilingual in Spanish, Maria self-identifies as "Mexican American" but acknowledges that she often faces unintended racism and discrimination because she "can pass for white." She explains, "It is unbelievable what some people will say to you when they don't know your background."

Throughout the YEARS program, Maria's confidence and ability to read situational context led to highly effective interviews with political and community leaders. Even when among professional reporters, Maria often landed the interview because her insightful questions emerged from understanding her role as a youth researcher. This skill assisted Maria in her role as DNC correspondent while writing an educational blog for her hometown newspaper. Along with her colleagues, Maria did not limit her research to elected officials but also included other leaders at the convention. She wrote in her convention blog:

> Monday, August 26, 2008—YEARS students are witness to a historic Latino delegate meeting where Senator Hillary Clinton announces her endorsement

of Barack Obama. Soon after, Lori Montenegro, a national anchorwoman for a Spanish language news affiliate, interviews several YEARS students. Within minutes, her microphone is laid on the chair and multiple digital recorders appear in front of her as the youth researchers turn the table; they now deliver their questions to her. With a growing momentum of emotion, Montenegro answers every question. She states emphatically, "Don't allow people's words to knock you down. Let it be your catalyst to work harder." Sitting in a now-empty ballroom, we are listening to an impassioned professional tell her struggles to overcome discrimination and prejudice within the Latino and professional broadcast community.

Maria was inspired by Lori Montenegro's determination to become an anchorwoman in Washington, D.C. Several months later, in fall 2008, Maria spoke at the launch event of Pepperdine's UI. Sitting atop the roof of the Union Rescue Mission in Downtown Los Angeles, Maria shared the impact of her interview with Lori Montenegro, "She [Montenegro] was an anchor woman from Washington D.C. and she is Cuban. She told us how she basically had been looked down upon because the color of her skin. She had been discouraged from her job and they did not think that she would be able to make it." This powerful YEARS experience caused Maria to reflect on her own pathway as a Latina from a working-class community. She continued further:

This impacted me so much because the more I thought about it, the more I realized that people thought that just because we are from a low-income community—regardless of the color of our skin—that we would not be able to manage our dreams. The fact is that, after this [YEARS] program, I realized that what they think doesn't matter. Their words will *not* impact us because we are so much more powerful than that. We have so much to offer. And as you can see this beautiful city behind me and people like us [YEARS students], we will impact cities like this all over the world, not just in this country—because we can, because we have something to offer.

A CRT framework allowed Maria to identify the racial microaggression experienced by Lori Montenegro as a Woman of Color discouraged from chasing her dream of becoming a reporter because of her skin color. Moreover, Maria credits her critical research experience for helping her to find her voice and YEARS for creating a space for transformation to occur.

Raised in Southeast Los Angeles, *Carolina* lived in the same neighborhood her whole life and hoped to "one day to change the reality and stereotypes our community faces." Like Maria, Carolina reflected on her YEARS experience at the UI event, "I realized that my opinion is not insignificant but, in fact, [it] can take me into becoming active in civic engagements where I can represent my community and myself in local and national concerns." Carolina's reflections highlight a sense of agency that rises from understanding the intersectionality of race, class, and gender. She posits, "While most students read about history in their classes, we were living it. The YEARS program opened the door for me to learn what it takes to become an immigration lawyer someday. And after I become a lawyer I want to be a congresswoman." Grounded in social theory, her counternarrative contrasts deficit model explanations of students and communities of color and centralizes her positionality as a critically minded, female, urban youth researcher. Youth researchers from both Futures and YEARS are now university student representatives, community advocates and school liaisons, psychologists, social workers, university professors, and leaders in their communities.

Ultimately, engaging youth as critical researchers is a transformative experience that leads to participants becoming leaders on their campuses and in their communities.[29] The inclusion of CRT allows for students to better understand how multiple factors, most centrally race, influence how they navigate a K-16 educational pipeline and into a world of work and civically engaged adults. I envision the YEARS program as a model that can be replicated across the state and nation whereby elected official and local area leaders can establish youth advisory councils to better inform leaders and to empower youth as democratic participants.

What Have We Learned from UPTEC and YEARS?

UPTEC and YEARS illustrate how institutions of higher education can facilitate spaces and opportunities for university and school community stakeholders to deconstruct traditional master narratives that blame low academic achievement on urban students and their families. In fact, this work shows that strategic university–school community partnerships and a foundation in social theory can provide teachers, students, and their families with spaces to develop counternarratives that empower community members and educators alike. It is within these critical spaces that partnerships foster socially just educators and critically minded youth toward academic access and longevity within the field of public education.

The 2008–2009 YEARS provided the opportunity for urban youth researchers to develop the skills necessary to collect and analyze data about civic engagement and educational equity. Furthermore, their immersion into the sociology of education literature and educational research created space for the YEARS students to appropriate sociological tools and theoretical foundations—tools they could use to demand a quality education from their schools and to empower civic participation in their communities.

Both UPTEC and YEARS were not limited to the traditional classroom sites; rather, they included spaces beyond the university and school campuses and took place outside of the traditional school day. For example, graduate classes were often held in parent centers and/or in the community and the youth researchers interviewed civic leaders at political conventions. Weis and Fine (2000) describe such sites "both within and outside schools as critical spaces of educational practices." Within these "critical" or "in-between" spaces," Weis and Fine (2000) believe "youth form and reform identities, develop and reframe social relations, and, in some cases, spawn the seeds of youth organizing."[30] I would argue that adult participants, as witnessed by the UPTEC critical personal narratives, also form and reform identities within these critical spaces. It is within these spaces that critical examinations of race, culture, and educational inequality occur.

Recommended Strategies for Improved Transformative Spaces

Institutions of higher education have a responsibility to serve and to partner with marginalized schools and communities. A discussion of how we partner has never been more urgent. Underserved communities need their higher education neighbors to work in collaboration on the educational and mental health problems in under-resourced communities. In turn, the university community must continue to learn from our community partners how to design effective programs to serve their needs.

It is important that we create spaces and opportunities for students, teachers, and leaders to challenge current explanations of educational and racial inequality. Without such spaces, educators and leaders may reinforce existing deficit models that blame students and their families for inequities within educational attainment. Equally important, we must provide teachers with a space to examine social constructs of race and the role of race in educational inequity. Teachers need spaces for deconstruction, spaces to make sense of their everyday realities within classrooms and their school communities. Similarly, urban youth require opportunities and the theoretical tools to critically investigate their community.

Moreover, we need to document best practices for creating safe spaces and providing critical activities that allow *all* teachers (and students) to identify privilege and how it manifests within their pedagogy, practices, and the policies of the school or district. A series of scholars such as Peggy Macintosh (1989), Christine Sleeter (1996), and Tim Wise (2011) have documented how white privilege manifests throughout their educational and daily experience. However, I have found that many of my teacher candidates— particularly teachers of color—also identify multiple ways that their socioeconomic, gender, generational, and linguistic privilege mediates their schooling experience. For example, several teacher candidates have taught at the same schools they attended in middle or high school. Even though they shared similar cultural backgrounds as their PreK-12 students, they found difficulty relating to students because of socioeconomic, generational, or ethnic differences. As we prepare teachers to work across racial and cultural differences, we must not exclude the variety of ways teachers of color may also experience challenges of nonracial privilege and how it may impact their students. We need to continue to document this phenomenon and support all teachers for all students.

We must continue to acknowledge the impact of race. Like the social construction of privilege and power, we cannot shy away from discussing the implications of race in American schools. In our efforts to find more appropriate ways to describe the conditions faced by urban schools and community members, we often neutralize the dialogue by denying the central role of race in educational and structural inequity. For example, in the UI White Paper (2008) the term "race" is excluded. This was not an accidental omission, rather a reflection of a collectively authored, 3,000-word document that purposely avoided using the word. The term "urban" is used 76 times throughout the paper and other euphemisms such as "students of color," "those of color," and "persons of colors" are present several times. As a sociologist of education, I often struggle with descriptive language that best describes the location and context of my work in urban schools and communities. Within my own work I find myself using descriptors such as *underserved, students of color, urban students, underrepresented students, working class,* and *inner city.* However, we cannot retreat from naming the social construct of race and identifying how it manifests in our educational experiences.

As a professor who teaches social and cultural foundations, I understand how and why we often retreat from naming race and racial inequality at the forefront of our dialogues. Most students and adults have not had the space or opportunities to safely explore the role of race in their lives and how it has afforded privilege and/or marginalization. While I believe all of us have, consciously or unconsciously, experienced the impact of race personally, few have had the opportunity to collectively deconstruct how these racialized experiences impact our ability to navigate school or influence our perceptions of students and the local school community.

As we have seen in Ferguson, Missouri, this summer and in St. Louis this fall, we must not forget that race in America has real implications both inside and outside of school. We must continue to dialogue about race, privilege, and power and develop theories and provide spaces for us to make sense of our roles in education. This is especially important for urban youth and the teachers who serve them. We must be vigilant in our efforts to create educational field stations that challenge the educational inequities that race, privilege, and power deny students in our country. Programs like UPTEC and YEARS and the UI are examples of effective efforts to provide empowering and transformative spaces on university campuses and in our local schools and communities. Through authentic partnerships between institutions of higher education and local community, educational field stations can foster counternarratives that highlight racial inequalities and educational inequity.

Notes

1. Mehan et al. 2010.
2. Urban Initiative n.d.
3. Valencia 1991.
4. Bruner 1996.
5. Collatos 2005.
6. Solorzano and Delgado-Bernal 2001.
7. Johnson 2012.
8. Freire 1970.
9. Kumashiro 2002, p. 48.
10. McLaren and Hammer 1989, p. 41.
11. Murrell 2001, p. 1.
12. CDE, accessed August 15, 2014.
13. Murrell 2001, pp. 3–4.
14. Ibid., p. 4.
15. Ibid., p. 34.
16. Bourdieu and Wacquant 1992.
17. Crenshaw 1995.
18. Tate 1997.
19. Apple 1996.

20. Tate 1997.
21. Rogers 2001.
22. Morrell 2004.
23. Collatos 2005.
24. Oakes, Rogers, and Lipton 2006.
25. Collatos et al. 2004.
26. Morrell 2004.
27. Auerbach 2004.
28. Saunders and Serna 2004.
29. Ginwright, Noguera, and Cammarota 2006.
30. Weis and Fine 2000, pp. xi–xii.

Bibliography

Apple, Michael. 1996. *Cultural Politics and Education*. New York: Teachers College Press.

Auerbach, Susan. 2004. "Engaging Latino Parents in Supporting College Pathways: Lessons from a College Access Program." *Journal of Hispanic Higher Education* 3 (2): 123–145.

Bourdieu, Pierre. 1998. *Acts of Resistance: Against Tyranny of the Market*. New York: The New Press.

Bourdieu, Pierre, and Loic Waquant. 1992. *An Invitation to Reflexive Sociology*. Chicago, IL: University of Chicago Press.

Bruner, Jerome. 1996. *The Culture of Education*. Cambridge, MA: Harvard University Press.

California Department of Education (CDE). 1999. "California Basic Educational Data." Accessed May 4, 2004. www.cde.ca.gov/demographics/reports/state wide/sums98.htm.

California Department of Education (CDE). 2014. "Educational Demographics Office Teacher Race Ethnicity 2012–13." Accessed August 15, 2014. http://dq .cde.ca.gov/dataquest/Staff/StaffByEth.aspx?cYear=2012–13&cChoice=State Num1&cType=T&cGender=&Submit=1.

Chapman, V. 2003. "On Knowing One's Self, Writing, Power and Ethical Practice: Reflections from an Adult Educator." *Studies in the Education of Adults* 35 (1): 35–44.

Collatos, Anthony. 2005. "Critical College Access: Reframing How We Empower Urban Youth toward Higher Education and Social Change." Unpublished dissertation, University of California Los Angeles.

Collatos, Anthony, and Ernest Morrell. 2003. "Apprenticing Urban Youth as Critical Researchers: Implications for School Reform." In *Critical Voices in School Reform: Students Living through Change*, eds. Beth Rubin and Elena Silva (pp. 113–131). New York: Routledge/Falmer.

Collatos, Anthony, Ernest Morrell, Alejandro Nuno, and Roger Lara. 2004. "Critical Sociology in K-16 Early Intervention: Constructing Latino Pathways to Higher Education." *Journal of Hispanic Higher Education* 3 (2): 164–179.

Crenshaw, Kimberle. 1995. "Mapping the Margins: Intersectionality, Identity Politics, and Violence against Women of Color." In *Critical Race Theory,* eds. Kimberle Crenshaw et al. New York: New Press.

Darder, Antonia. 1993. "How Does the Culture of the Teacher Shape the Classroom Experience of the Latino Students?: The Unexamined Question in Critical Pedagogy." In *The Handbook of Schooling in Urban America,* ed. Stanley W. Rothstein (pp. 195–221). Westport, CT: Greenwood Press.

Delpit, Lisa. 1995. *Other People's Children: Cultural Conflict in the Classroom.* New York: The New Press.

Epstein, Joyce. 1995. "School/Family/Community Partnerships: Caring for the Children We Share." *Phi Delta Kappan* 76 (9): 701–712.

Freire, Paulo.1970. *Pedagogy of the Oppressed.* New York: Continuum.

Ginwright, Shawn, Pedro Noguera, and Julio Cammarota. 2006. *Beyond Resistance! Youth Activism and Community Change: New Democratic Possibilities for Practice and Policy for America's Youth.* New York: Routledge Press.

Giroux, Henry. 1983. *Theory and Resistance in Education: A Pedagogy for the Opposition.* South Hadley, MA: Bergin and Garvey.

Johnson, Mary. 2012. *The 21st Century Parent: Multicultural Parent Engagement Leadership Strategies Handbook.* Scottsdale: IAP.

Kumashiro, Kevin. 2002. "Toward a Theory of Anti-oppressive Education." *Review of Educational Research* 70 (1): 25–53.

Ladson-Billings, Gloria. 1995. "Toward a Theory of Culturally Relevant Pedagogy." *American Educational Research Journal* 32 (3): 465–491.

Ladson-Billings, Gloria. 2001. *Crossing over to Canaan: The Journey of New Teachers in Diverse Classrooms.* San Francisco: Jossey Bass.

Lynn, Leon. 1997. "Teaching Teachers to Work with Families." Harvard Education Letter (September/October). http://hepg.org/hel-home/issues/13_5/hel article/family-involvement-in-schools_357.

Macintosh, Peggy. 1990. "White Privilege: Unpacking the Invisible Knapsack." *Peace and Freedom* (July/August 1989): 9–10; repr. in *Independent School* 49: 31–35.

Mclaren, Peter, and Rhonda Hammer. 1989. "Critical Pedagogy and the Postmodern Challenge." *Educational Foundations* 3 (3): 29–69.

Mehan, Hugh, Gail Kaufman, Cecil Lytle, Karen Hunter Quartz, and Rhona Weinstein. 2010. "Educational Field Stations: A Model for Increasing Diversity and Access in Higher Education." In *Equal Opportunity in Higher Education: The Past and Future of Proposition 209,* eds. Eric Grodsky and Michael Kurlaender (pp. 173–194). Cambridge, MA: Harvard Education Press.

Morrell, Ernest. 2004. *Becoming Critical Researchers: Literacy and Empowerment for Urban Youth.* New York: Peter Lang Publishing.

Morrell, Ernest, and Anthony Collatos. 2002. "Toward a Critical Teacher Education: High School Student Sociologists as Teacher Educators." *Social Justice* 29 (4): 60–70.

Murrell, Peter. 2001. *The Community Teacher: A New Framework for Effective Urban Teaching.* New York: Teachers College Press.

National Center for Education Statistics. 1998. *Projection of Education Statistics to 2008.* Washington, DC: U.S. Department of Education.

Noguera, Pedro. 2001. "Transforming Urban Schools through Investments in Social Capital of Parents." In *Social Capital in Poor Communities,* eds. Susan Saegart, J. Phillip Thompson, and Mark R. Warren (pp. 189–212). New York: Russell Sage Foundation Press.

Oakes, Jeannie, John Rogers, and Martin Lipton. 2006. *Learning Power.* New York: Teachers College Press.

Rogers, John. 2001. "Navigating Futures: An Introduction to Emergent Understandings." Paper Presented at the Annual Meeting of the American Educational Research Association, New Orleans.

Saunders, Marisa, and Irene Serna. 2004. "Making College Happen: The College Experiences of First-Generation Latino Students." *Journal of Hispanic Higher Education* 3 (2): 146–163.

Sleeter, Christine. 1996. *Multicultural Education as Social Activism.* New York: State University of New York Press.

Solorzano, Daniel, and Dolores Delgado-Bernal. 2001. "Examining Transformational Resistance through a Critical Race and LatCrit Theory Framework: Chicana and Chicano Students in an Urban Context." *Urban Education* 36: 308–342.

Stanley, William, B. 1992. *Curriculum for Utopia: Social Reconstructionism and Critical Pedagogy in the Postmodern Era.* Albany: State University of New York Press.

Tate, William. 1997. "Critical Race Theory and Education: History, Theory, and Implications." In *Review of Research in Education,* ed. Michael Apple (pp. 95–247). Washington, DC: AERA.

The Urban Initiative White Paper. 2008. "Answering the Call to Serve: The Urban Initiative." Accessed August 15, 2014. http://gsep.pepperdine.edu/urban-initiative/white-paper/.

Valencia, Richard. 1991. *Chicano School Failure and Success.* London: Falmer Press.

Weis, Lois, and Michelle Fine. 2000. *Construction Sites: Excavating Race, Class, and Gender among Urban Youth.* New York: Teachers College Press.

Wise, Tim. 2011. *White Like Me: Reflections on Race from a Privileged Son.* Berkeley, CA: Soft Skull Press.

Yosso, Tara. 2005. "Whose Culture Has Capital? A Critical Race Theory Discussion of Community Cultural Wealth." *Race, Ethnicity and Education* 8 (1): 69–91.

Chapter 10

Addressing Inequity in Education: Transformative Leadership

Carolyn M. Shields

The byline of a March 2014 press release by the U.S. Department of Education screamed, "Expansive Survey of America's Public Schools Reveals Troubling Racial Disparities."[1] In the same year in which America celebrated the 50th anniversary of the still controversial 1964 Civil Rights legislation that prohibited discrimination on the basis of race, color, religion, sex, or national origin and that witnessed the powerful Freedom Summer movement in Mississippi, one could hope that the sacrifice of those who advocated these changes might already have been justified. One might dare to anticipate that the promise of education, seen by advocates of the Freedom Schools as the way of addressing racial inequities, the promise of the subsequent 1965 Voting Rights Act, and the end of miscegenation laws in 1967, might have been realized.

However, Giroux cites Omi's observation that this is far from the truth. He states that

> despite legal guarantees of formal equality and access, race continues to be a fundamental organizing principle of individual identity and collective action. I would argue that, far from declining in significance . . . the racial dimensions of politics and culture have proliferated.[2]

This reality is borne out by the comprehensive civil rights report on the state of education in the United States, released by the Department of Education that revealed racial inequities in school outcomes at every age and grade from kindergarten to high school completion and throughout the country. The researchers found well-known disparities related to retention and high school graduation but reported lesser-known data about access to higher-level courses in high school and suspension and discipline rates in preschool. Further, at a time when there are few countries in which income inequality is rising faster than in the United States, compelling data demonstrates clear correlations between education and poverty as well as poverty and race. Coley and Baker found, for example, that

> more than one in five U.S. children live in "official" poverty today, with an even higher rate for Black and Hispanic children and for those in families headed by a single parent. Among the world's 35 richest countries, the United States holds the distinction of ranking second highest in child poverty [and] the achievement gap between the poor and the non-poor is twice as large as the achievement gap between Black and White students.[3]

Although in raw numbers, more white children than others live in poverty, the *rate* of poverty is considerably higher among African Americans and Hispanics. Those who are born into poverty complete less schooling, experience poorer general health, and earn considerably less over a lifetime than those who are more advantaged at birth. Males born into poverty are more likely to be arrested or to spend time in jail; their female counterparts are more likely to have children out of wedlock. These strong correlations among education, race, and poverty must be addressed.

The foregoing data all suggests that significant changes are needed in the ways in which race is treated in schools in order for all children to have an equal opportunity for success. At present, Horace Mann's hope that education would be the "great equalizer of the conditions of men, the balance-wheel of the social machinery" is far from being fulfilled.[4]

Yet some actually dismiss the foregoing data, arguing that America is a post-racial land of opportunity in which everyone with the appropriate motivation and effort can achieve success. Others simply argue that "there is no such thing as race" and hence, that disparities must be explained in other ways, usually through explanations that "blame the victim."

Whether we are examining race as a stand-alone issue or as confounded by poverty, there are few issues of greater importance than this current examination of race and American education. At the same time, the very contested nature of the concept of race must be acknowledged and addressed here. At one time, researchers attempted to explain disparate outcomes through pseudoscientific data that purported to find differences in skull or brain size or other physical differences. However, for at least half a century, researchers have known that, in a purely genetic sense, "human DNA does not differ significantly across populations." In fact, numerous scientists concur with Dr. Venter, head of the Celera Genomics Corporation in Rockville, Maryland, who asserts that "race is a social concept, not a scientific one." He continues, "We all evolved in the last 100,000 years from the same small number of tribes that migrated out of Africa and colonized the world."[5]

This does not however, in any way, diminish the presence of prejudice and discrimination based on the social construct of race; another scientist, Dr. Wallace, posits that "the criteria that people use for race are based entirely on external features that we are programmed to recognize."[6] Thus, the distinction between the genetic findings and the impact of race as a social construct is critically important in that we have historically developed assumptions and shaped laws, policies, practices, and beliefs based on *phenotypical* traits of both individuals and groups. Whereas "genotype" refers to the genetic make-up of an individual, the "phenotype" includes observable characteristics and how they are constructed in a specific environment. Hence, the ongoing debates related to the integration and segregation of public schools, race-based admissions or scholarship policies, or the academic achievement gap are firmly grounded in irrefutable data that point to explanations related to social constructs.

In this chapter, I propose transformative leadership as a way of addressing inequality and inequity in schools. Here, following a brief discussion of how transformative leadership both differs from other concepts and theories and how it upholds academic excellence, inclusion, equity, and social justice, I will elaborate the role of *transformative leadership*, using examples from the practice of two school leaders, to demonstrate how each of its eight tenets can help to promote "racial" equity in today's schools.

Transformative Leadership: A Theory of Justice

In November 1950, a group of 50 professors from 20 leading universities traveled by car, train, and plane to Chicago to attend a seminar called *Administrative Theory in Education*.[7] From that meeting, an influential group of professors and school-based administrators, subsequently called the "Chicago School," focused on making educational administration a respected scientific discipline and hence one in which interpretation, emotions, and values were, at minimum, pushed to the background and largely ignored and theories of administration and leadership have proliferated. Following a quarter century of "scientific approaches," Greenfield's paper, presented at the 1974 International Intervisitation Program in Bristol, England, questioned the "prevailing belief that a general science of organizations has provided the needed theoretical underpinnings for understanding schools and for training the administrators."[8] He went on to posit that "organizations are cultural artifacts which man shapes within limits given only by his perception and the boundaries of his life as a human animal."[9] These arguments launched a theoretical debate often known as "the paradigm wars" and also and perhaps more importantly began a movement that soon (in Griffith's words) understood that organizations "are dependent on meanings and purposes that individuals bring to them from the wider society."[10] By the 1990s these meanings and purposes had begun to include the notion of equity and social justice.

Initially this emphasis was as controversial as Greenfield's notion of organizations as cultural artifacts and was denounced as fringe and even as irrelevant to leadership studies. However, the term "social justice" soon permeated educational discourse to the point where the now ubiquitous term was being used to describe competing policies and practices. Some would argue it was "just," for example, to treat everyone exactly the same way and to institute straight "three strikes" discipline policies in schools; others would argue that justice required treating students with different home situations differently. Increased clarity was necessary to distinguish between equality and equity and various notions of justice.

As a result, rather than adopting the increasingly empty term of social justice, I sought a more robust and already developed approach to leadership and thus settled on the concept of *transformative leadership*. Transformative leadership traces its roots to the work of James MacGregor Burns (1978) although Burns used the terms "transformational," "transforming," and "transactional," but never "transformative" per se. Nevertheless, Burns's notion of leadership that results in significant, even "revolutionary" change provides the basis for what many authors have developed into the theory of transformative leadership. Blackmore distinguishes between transformative and transformational leadership in this way:

> According to its advocates, *transformational* leadership addresses key issues in education, redressing past neglect, for example, about teacher emotions, inequality of student learning outcomes, cultural diversity and pedagogy. . . . I argue that while seductive, this transformational leadership discourse appropriates critical perspectives while depoliticising their social justice intent because the notion of transformational leadership has been framed narrowly

within the school effectiveness/improvement paradigms. In contrast, *trans-formative* leadership discourses derive from a critical tradition promoting emancipatory pedagogies arising from political and social movements, feminist perspectives and critical pedagogy.[11] (italics mine)

Starratt also distinguished *transformational* and *transformative* leadership, saying, "The distinction between transformational leadership and transformative leadership is an important one, not only for the field of education, but also for leadership theory and research in other fields." He went on to assert that "transformative leadership starts out with a focus on the most obviously disadvantaged students who arrive at the schoolhouse door on the first day of school."[12]

Transformative leadership in education is therefore a theory that embraces critical and emancipatory perspectives that focus on equity, inclusion, deep democracy, and social justice. It addresses issues of injustice and recognizes that material realities outside of school, such as poverty, discrimination, and racism, impinge on the ability of students to succeed and on the ability of schools to help them succeed. Hence, transformative leaders adopt an approach to social justice that not only addresses what happens within schools and educational institutions but also helps students understand the social constructions and practices of inequity and to identify their own roles and responsibilities within the wider society.

It is not adequate to ensure that every student passes required standardized tests or that subgroups within a school all meet the expected standards, although this is certainly a requisite task for educators; instead, students and teachers alike must learn about the socioeconomic, political, and cultural conditions that create and perpetuate inequities and how to rectify them. Transformative leadership, practiced not only by formal but also by informal educational leaders throughout a school, is not a soft and fuzzy approach to social justice but assumes goals of high expectations and outstanding academic performance by all students in addition to greater understanding of issues of equity, justice, interdependence, and deep democracy. In this context, deep democracy expresses what Green identifies as the "experience-based possibility of more equal, respectful, and mutually beneficial ways of community life."[13]

For this reason, the eight tenets of transformative leadership articulated by Shields can help educators to provide a socially just education for all students as well as a social justice education that addresses the wider context of racial, sexual, religious, and other discriminatory constructs that perpetuate inequity in this country. The distinction is important, for a *socially just education* is the fundamental right of every student—the right to equally good teachers, adequate resources, an opportunity to achieve in ways that permit access to one's chosen career path, and so on. A *social justice education* takes this right one step further and prepares students for life in a just, inclusive, and democratic society.

The rest of this chapter clarifies, through the use of data and anecdote, the following eight tenets as they address discriminatory educational policies and practices:

- Engage in deep and equitable change
- Deconstruct and reconstruct knowledge frameworks
- Focus on democracy, equity, and justice
- Address the inequitable distribution of power
- Private and public good
- Interdependence, interconnectedness, and global awareness
- Balance critique with promise
- Exhibit moral courage[14]

To illustrate, I focus primarily on the practice of an elementary principal, Catherine Lake, and some of the changes she instituted in a school in which demographics had changed rapidly from being 70 percent Caucasian to 40 percent Caucasian in two years.

Deep and Equitable Change

The need for deep and equitable change in American education is almost irrefutable and, as the 2014 U.S. Department of Education study found, begins in preschool and permeates every aspect of American education. Disproportionate representation of African American students in disciplinary incidents, suspension, and special education classes has long been known. In the recent study, the authors found, that "black students represent [only] 18% of preschool enrollment but 42% of students suspended once, and 48% of the students suspended more than once."[15] They further found that schools serving large percentages of poor and minoritized students often have fewer resources, fewer advanced-level courses, and lower graduation rates. Specifically, they found that "less than half of American Indian and Native-Alaskan high school students have access to the full range of math and science courses in their high school" and that the graduation rate in 2005 in urban areas (where there are higher concentrations of poor and minoritized students) was 53 percent "compared with 71 percent in the suburbs."

Doing more of the same, seeking replicable data-based programs, developing school improvement plans, and restructuring schools by hiring a new cadre of educators who perpetuate current practices under the guise of reform, has not worked and will not work. As Oakes and Rogers have clearly stated, there is no reason to believe that reforms whose explicit goals are not equity and social justice will result in increased equity. They state:

> Technical changes by themselves, even in the hands of committed and skillful professional "change agents" or backed by court orders, are too weak to interrupt the intergenerational transmission of racial inequality.[16]

Hence, educators who are concerned about the racial disparities identified earlier (and throughout this volume) must adopt educational practices focused on the desired equity outcomes. Tinkering around the edges will not result in social justice. Indeed, addressing the deeply seated and institutional beliefs and assumptions that perpetuate racism and inequity is the only way forward.

Thus, if an educator finds, on taking up his or her work in a given school, that there is a wide achievement gap between rich and poor, racialized and dominant ethnic groups, language learners and those who already speak the language of instruction, and between those who for one reason or another may be marginalized and those who are typically included in the mainstream of school life, then my argument is that one should consider adopting a form of transformative leadership. This was the approach of Catherine Lake, one elementary school principal of my acquaintance, who found that the academic performance of Caucasian and Latino students in her school exceeded that of the African American students by a considerable margin. She explains:

> Even more critical is an examination of who is exceeding and at what rate. Looking more closely at the same 5th grade data, 44% of white 5th graders exceeded on ISAT reading while only 5% of black 5th graders did. This information must be shared among all school staff and questions must be asked. Sharing this information publicly is risky, especially in an era of high-stakes accountability, because presenting the information publicly is not enough. Dialogue in response to data is critical and, all too often, lacking.

When Catherine recognized the problem and asked her staff to explain why the African American students whose home language was English might be performing worse than the Latino English-language learners, she quickly identified the need to deconstruct attitudes and beliefs that perpetuated these inequitable outcomes.

Deconstruct and Reconstruct Knowledge Frameworks

Oakes and Rogers address the inequitable outcomes in our schools in this way:

> Rather than blaming racially skewed schooling outcomes on norms and politics that lead to disparate resources and opportunities, our society often blames those who do not fit the prevailing ideologies of intelligence and merit. Social science itself has played an unsavory role in underlying concepts that soon serve as conceptual and linguistic proxies for race, such as "culture of poverty," "at risk," "non verbal learning style," and "oppositional behavior," to justify the persistence of inequality. All contribute to the fear and loathing of the racialized other, and allow subtler but powerful forms of inequality to fill the gap left by the end of *de jure* segregation and "in-your-face" racism.[17]

This was the situation that principal Catherine Lake needed to address. Teachers in her school argued that unsuccessful African American students came from families in which education was not a priority, with parents who had not progressed beyond high school and were often unemployed, and in which fathers were often absent. Catherine quickly countered by identifying Caucasian and Latino students whose home situations were similar but who were succeeding at school.

What Catherine had uncovered was a form of deficit thinking that needed to be replaced by an awareness that all children bring to school capacities and competencies from their home lives but that not all conform to the too often generally accepted middle-class norms of schooling. She needed to convince her teachers of the validity of the findings from a study by Wagstaff and Fusarelli (1999) that the single most important factor in the academic achievement of minoritized children is educators' explicit rejection of deficit thinking. Deficit thinking is a way of thinking about those who are in some ways different that constructs difference as deficit, that places the need for change (as well as the blame and shame) on children and their families, and that suggests that if only they changed, the problem would be fixed.[18] This kind of thinking ignores the ways in which educational institutions marginalize and exclude nondominant values, cultures, and practices and privileges the lived experiences of dominant groups. Hence, the problem, as delineated by the teachers, belonged to the families and did not require radical pedagogical change either on their part or that of the school.

In short, Catherine needed to deconstruct the thinking of her teachers about the African American students in their classes and help them to reconstruct it in more accurate and appropriate ways. She needed the teachers to acknowledge the difference between a child's prior opportunity to learn and his or her intrinsic ability to learn. She also needed teachers to recognize that institutional racism was alive and well and that their beliefs about the lack of support for education in the African American community were misplaced and inaccurate. She introduced her staff to freewriting activities that required them to make their assumptions explicit and to identify alternative explanations. She helped them understand that by pretending to be "color-blind" they were ignoring the underachievement of African American students whose prior lived experience differed from that of the Caucasian students in the school. They discussed items in the news addressing continued housing and employment discrimination in their community. And she initiated numerous discussions about how teachers could take responsibility for the learning and success of all students.

Ultimately teachers identified ways to regularly group and regroup students for each new skill in ways that would ensure that each one would be taught whatever he or she needed to succeed. Teachers determined that instructional materials are needed to reflect the lived experiences and interests of all students and pooled their resources to purchase culturally relevant materials. They instituted new practices that placed the students who were most in need of assistance in the smallest groups so they could progress more quickly, held them to high expectations, and placed parent assistants with students who most needed their support (and not necessarily with their own children's groups). Not surprisingly, as educators changed the ways in which they thought about all students, the overall achievement of the school improved for all children.

Focus on Democracy, Equity, and Justice

In this way, Catherine deconstructed knowledge frameworks that perpetuated injustice and replaced them with ways of thinking that had the potential to promote democracy, equity, and social justice. But changing thinking must be followed by changed practices and new ways of operating within the school. To ensure that everyone was more fully included in the activities of the school, Catherine initiated what she called "community meetings"—weekly gatherings in which all staff and students participated and that were often attended by parents and community members as well. The school music teacher wrote an original school song that opened each assembly and students themselves created a school dance to accompany it. Individual students auditioned with the principal to demonstrate a skill or to teach it to the gathering, classes performed readers' theater or a song or dance for the group, and awards were given to deserving students, and by students to staff or community members. Speakers addressed current events and community leaders talked about opportunities in the community. At first teachers complained about the lost teaching time but quickly came to acknowledge that the emphasis on the whole community, the celebration of its achievements and talents, had brought all students together in mutually beneficial ways.

During staff meetings, freewriting was a regular feature as Catherine asked teachers to address challenges and issues that arose. For example, teachers wrote about how to help children understand what they had never experienced, such as a trip to the beach; they shared their ideas both at whole staff meetings and in team meetings. They discussed how to deal with bullying, with racial slurs, or with negative comments using inappropriate language like "terrorist" or "gay." At first teachers resisted writing and complained when asked to address issues in this way. But soon, teachers encountering a problematic situation in their classroom or teaching approached the principal, asking her if their issue could be the subject of freewriting at the next meeting. Now that their negative and deficit-oriented thinking had been overcome, the power of reflective and creative thinking became evident.

Every decision, from dealing with fighting on the bus or inappropriate classroom behavior, purchasing supplies, or planning holiday celebrations, was seen as an opportunity for enhancing equity and social justice and for eliminating practices that marginalized or excluded some students. Teachers were amazed at how many inequitable practices needed to be addressed. For example, it had become common practice in the school for individual classrooms to hold celebrations and parties to mark occasions such as Halloween, birthdays, or Valentine's Day. As staff discussed their celebrations, it became apparent that for children in the classes identified as "gifted"—largely children from middle-class, Caucasian families—classroom celebrations were quite elaborate with parents contributing games, party favors, and home baking. They also acknowledged that children in other classes, especially the special education classes in which they found disproportionate representation of African American and Latino children, rarely enjoyed parties or celebrations that comprised more than cookies or a pizza purchased by the teacher. Individual class celebrations were soon ended and replaced by schoolwide celebrations whenever they were warranted.

These attempts at creating more equitable and more just practices were simply a beginning but certainly reflected Green's concept of deep democracy in which she advocates a form of democracy "that expresses the experience-based possibility of more equal, respectful, and mutually beneficial ways of community life."[19] Indeed, moving toward practices that resulted in mutual benefit was but one step forward as educators in this school worked to ensure the inclusion of all children in high-level and engaging activities. Moreover, they took seriously DuBois's challenge that the future of democracy in the United States is inextricably linked "to the outcomes of racial politics and policies, as they develop both in various national societies and the world at large."[20]

Addressing the Inequitable Distribution of Power

Catherine soon found deeper and more complex issues that needed to be addressed. Throughout this discussion, I have used the term "minoritized" instead of minority to reflect the reality that a numerical majority may still be excluded and marginalized if members of that group are not represented in decision-making bodies. In other words, those with the power to define curriculum, to determine school policies, and, in general, to make the rules governing a particular institution, regardless of whether they represent a small power elite or a numerical majority, are in control. This is consistent with Delpit's notion that in every organization there are largely unrecognized rules of power that operate to the benefit or some and the disadvantage of others. Moreover, Delpit asserts that those who have the power are generally the least aware of it and of the implicit rules of the organization, and hence, those without power need to be taught its rules to be able to fully participate in the life of the school. Delpit writes:

> I further believe that to act as if power does not exist is to ensure that the power status quo remains the same. . . . if we are truly to effect societal change, we cannot do so from the bottom up, but we must push and agitate from the top down. And in the meantime, we must take the responsibility to teach, to provide for students who do not already possess them, the additional codes of power.[21]

To address unequal power relations, Catherine needed to ensure that the rules of her school were explicit and that everyone knew how to access power. She needed, for example, to ensure that her Parent–Teacher Committee was diverse and included members of many community groups rather than simply those who had always held power. Enlisting members of minoritized groups to participate in decision-making bodies is not always easy in that they often feel insecure and inexperienced. Many are afraid to volunteer. Hence, it is often necessary to recruit through individual contact and to provide training and mentoring as Catherine did.

But inequitable power relations go beyond what can be seen on the surface. Because public school in America was, in large part, developed to ensure appropriate socialization of newcomers, it was created based on Caucasian and middle-class norms, values, and expectations. Freedom schools were intended to develop literacy among blacks but were staffed by well-meaning whites whose cultures were very different from that of their students. In the years since the Civil Rights Act and school integration, many excellent black teachers lost their jobs, as African American children were integrated into white schools, with white norms, and white curricula. The situation is similar for students of Native American, Latino, and many immigrant cultures: they fail to see themselves and their cultures reflected in the curriculum and, for that reason, are largely disenfranchised and marginalized.

Oakes and Rogers argue that if "the distribution of power is never explicitly addressed, technical change strategies tend toward consensus rather than conflict."[22] Hence, transformative educators like Catherine must work to open the curriculum, to develop spaces in which each child may bring his or her lived experience, without shame, and without needing to hide his or her perspective, into the curricular conversations and activities of the school.

Addressing Both Private and Public Good

Often, as stated earlier, a socially just education implies leveling the playing field through offering remedial instruction so that all students, regardless of home culture, may demonstrate equal outcomes on standardized tests. Indeed, Catherine was determined to ensure excellent achievement on the part of every student but rejected the common approaches requiring remedial classes, noon hour instruction, after-school or Saturday tutoring, and test preparation, saying that if teachers had not done everything in their power to equalize educational opportunities by changing their assumptions and their pedagogical approaches, it was inappropriate to deprive children of their free play time to focus on testing. She was convinced that educating all children was her responsibility and that of her teachers.

At the same time, Catherine recognized that to ensure future opportunities for higher education and career, achieving good test results is a necessary focus but one that cannot and should not be the only or even the primary focus of the school. Hence, she ensured that in every class, whether art or music or math, children were developing skills that would help them succeed on the standardized tests—skills that provide personal advantages sometimes referred to as "private (or individual) good."

But, too often, we hold out to minoritized students the carrot of higher lifetime earnings, better housing, and even better health, if they go on to college or university, without, at the same time, acknowledging the public good of having everyone achieve to appropriate high levels. It is not only unjust for individuals but detrimental to a country as a whole to have subgroups based on racial phenotypes who have less education, who are incarcerated (inappropriately) at higher rates, and who are less involved in public policy and less represented in legislative bodies. Indeed, some would argue that the most important factor in the development of a strong democracy is a well-educated middle class. Barber, for example, asserts that "for true democracy to exist, there must be citizens." And, citizens, he states, "are women and men educated for excellence [. . .] the knowledge and competence to govern in common their own lives."[23] The increasing political polarization and gridlock of American society, the widening gap between rich and poor, the increasing number of legal decisions that exacerbate the difficulties of voting for members of poor or minority groups, and the elimination of affirmative action and desegregation policies—all point to a society in which democracy is threatened by racism and by an education system that fails to acknowledge its critical role in the education of citizens.

Acknowledging Interdependence, Interconnectedness, and Global Awareness

It is, in part, for these reasons that transformative leaders must help educators and students alike to understand how we are all interconnected and interdependent. We cannot survive as a democratic society if we continue to marginalize so many citizens. We cannot survive as a strong and influential nation if we do not acknowledge the ways in which we are also connected to the rest of the world and to those who lack safety, security, clean water, adequate food, and so forth.

It is not enough to ensure that each student succeeds on standardized tests; rather, every student must be taught to understand how and why prejudice and disparities emerge and are perpetuated. No student can be allowed to believe there is something wrong with his or her family because they live in poverty. No child should wish for a different-colored skin tone or a different kind of hair, because he or she believes it would make him or her more loveable and more accepted.

Transformative leaders must therefore advocate social justice education—approaches that help students understand the social construction of discrimination or poverty. They must understand how inequities have emerged, how they are perpetuated, and how they may be overcome. Children need to understand notions of privilege as well as of disadvantage in order to be able to subsequently and equitably take their places as participating members of civil society. Elsewhere, I have recounted the anecdote of one of my former students who objected to the premise of an article by Bigelow. In it, he was suggesting a pedagogical activity that focused on understanding the nature of child labor and its implications by examining and writing about a soccer ball. As our class discussed the activity my student blurted out, "But if we do this, our students won't even enjoy shopping anymore!" Destroying students' enjoyment of everyday activities is not the goal of transformative leadership, but it is nevertheless critically important to increase their awareness of disparities and their impact on the lives of others.

In studies in which I have asked school principals to share their definition of social justice, the common response has been "for all students to pass the tests." When, on occasion, I have asked principals what social justice might look like in affluent or more advantaged, middle-class schools, they have often seemed stymied and stammer something about all children having problems that need to be addressed. How unfortunate that these educational leaders see social justice as the need to address individual differences, described as "problems," rather than to understand and address socially constructed barriers to equitable participation in democratic society. Hence, although it sometimes seems easier and more appropriate to focus on social justice in a school which is socially and culturally highly diverse, others also have a role to play.

Here I think of the efforts of another transformative elementary school principal, John Law, whose school was located in a very affluent and more homogeneous neighborhood. His school was always near the top but did not always "top" the district in test scores, parents were highly satisfied and heavily involved in their children's education, and yet, he was disturbed by the sense of entitlement and privilege often spontaneously expressed by the students. He recounts, for example, his "surprising" interaction with a third-grade child who, one morning, asked if he wanted to see a picture of his birthday gift—a new pony. Assuming the pony would be a toy, John recounted his own discomfort when the child went on to display a real pony, "housed with his sister's horses at a nearby stable." Of course, the child was unaware of his privilege and the extravagance of the gift.

Thus, to begin to help his students understand their privilege and how privilege and its accompanying power help to create and perpetuate injustice in the world, John initiated schoolwide book studies of other countries, twinned classrooms with classes overseas, and held "who is your neighbor days." In short, he developed a curriculum that helped students understand their advantages and their social responsibility in the global community. Other educators have introduced the notion of "sundown towns"[24] to their students and helped them discuss the extent to which their communities have historically marginalized and excluded those who are different.

Whether we are helping students understand historic discrimination at home, or the impacts of economic development in the global community, or simply helping a classmate struggling with a particular task or activity, it is important to overcome the sense of competition that implies we are only in this "for ourselves" and to teach about interconnectedness and interdependence.

Balance Critique with Promise

One of the key components of transformative leadership is to balance critique with promise. Most educators are well aware of the history of oppression in this country—of African Americans, of Native Americans, of Chinese railway workers, of Japanese immigrants during the world wars, and so on. Many are aware of the ongoing controversies related to "illegal" immigrants or undocumented workers. Many of our students have formed opinions of these issues by listening to adults who rarely stop to provide a balanced or complete explanation of the evolution of these issues. Hence, once again, it is up to thoughtful educators to ensure that students access primary documents, multiple accounts, and data that can help to provide a more complete picture of our history. At the same time, being able to identify and describe an inequitable situation is only a beginning.

American students should know some facts.

- African Americans make up roughly half of the United States' massive population of prisoners (2 million) and only 13 percent of the population.
- Blacks are much less likely to own their own homes than whites.
- The poverty rate for blacks is more than twice the rate for whites.
- African Americans are twice as likely to be unemployed as whites.
- The median black household income ($27,000) is less than two-thirds of median white household income ($42,000).
- Blacks suffer disproportionately from irregularities in the American electoral process, from problems with voter registration to the functioning of voting machinery.
- One in 6 students attend a school that some call a "dropout factory"; 1 in 3 minority students (32%) attend a dropout factory, compared to 8 percent of white students.
- In the United States, high school dropouts commit about 75 percent of crimes; 9.6 percent of African Americans drop out of school, 17.6 percent of Hispanics, and only 5.2 percent of Caucasians.
- People of color are more likely to be uninsured compared to whites.
- Minorities experience higher rates of diseases, disability, and death than the overall U.S. population.[25]

The list could extend for several pages. But the point is that inequities must become part of the daily conversations in schools. At the same time, knowing the facts and addressing inequities are very different. Oakes and Rogers argue that "merely documenting inequality will not, in and of itself, lead to more adequate and equitable schooling. Straightforward and obvious claims of injustice can be transformed . . . into highly technical disputes about statistical methods or esoteric debates about motivational theories."[26] In fact, in describing a contentious change initiative in one school they had studied, they concluded simply that "when reason met power, power won."[27] For transformative educators, this must not be an acceptable outcome.

Transformative educators will need to act deliberately and consistently to effect change. They will need to address issues such as color-blind racism, institutionalized racism and discrimination, inequitable power elites, and unjust resource allocation. Teachers will need, as Weiner advocates, to begin the process in the classroom by "taking a position on a socially relevant subject. . . . [and recognizing] the classroom as a site of struggle."[28] They will need

to insert an ethical as well as a political discourse back into the language of education, confront the discourse of reactionary ideologues, and make visible to students and others alternative viewpoints as well as the mechanisms of power and domination that structure the corporate government complex and the dismantling of democratic institutions.[29]

Indeed, whenever decisions are being made, educators will need to acquire the habit of asking themselves about the possible unintended outcomes and determining who is advantaged and who is disadvantaged by the proposed action.

Exhibit Moral Courage

These changes are not easy. They challenge the very roots of what people believe and how they have always acted. They require careful reflection and deep change on the part of many educators. Hence, there will be backlash and resistance. There may be rumors, innuendos, and politically motivated complaints. Despite the success of the changes initiated by Catherine Lake and considerably improved test scores and school climate, she faced opposition that resulted in hearings by her school board. Parents who preferred the status quo, in which they could advocate on behalf of their own children instead of all children ironically complained that she was prejudiced. Despite the fact that Catherine was absolved for each charge, the opposition took considerable time and energy. Thinking back to a conflict related to a lottery for places in an all-day kindergarten class which, because of its timing, tended to exclude many poor and minoritized children, she reflects:

> Ten years later, I still remember the animosity and tension of that time. I still remember the difficulty of going to work every day and trying to balance my responsibilities while a group of parents and teachers impugned my reputation and attacked my integrity. I still remember the anxiety-ridden nights and that feeling of standing alone. What I remember even more poignantly, though, are the voices of the families whose children were moved to full-day kindergarten over the winter break. I remember the mother who kept saying, "Muchas gracias" again and again and again. I remember the 58 families who thanked me for helping their children.

Thus, educators wanting to effect equitable change must be clear about what guides and what grounds them. In Catherine's words, they must know their "non-negotiables," or in the words of the popular cliché, we must know what hill we are willing to die on. This is particularly true because, as Weiner states, school principals are in a peculiar situation in which they are appointed because of their support for and cooperation within the system. This creates a challenging situation for those focused on equity, one in which

> as actors inside dominant structures, transformative leadership must always make problematic the institutional power it wields. Of course, part of their power comes from the institution itself, but [. . .] this does not automatically necessitate the seduction and co-option of critical perspectives.[30]

To effect change, transformative educators must walk a careful tightrope, supporting the policies of the state and district and simultaneously critiquing them to promote and support deep and equitable change.

Conclusion

If a school is running effectively and efficiently and is providing an optimal learning environment for all students, then educational leaders may be content with tinkering around the edges of the status quo, making small but technical changes. But this is generally not the case in American schools. Too often, our educational institutions are riddled with injustice based on racial phenotypes, religious beliefs, sexual orientation, socioeconomic status, and other ways of constructing difference. Thus, new approaches to leadership, pedagogy, and educational policy and practice are called for. I have argued here that, unlike other leadership approaches, *transformative leadership* may advance notions of social justice and equity. It begins with Freire's contention "that education is not the ultimate lever for social transformation, but without it transformation cannot occur."[31] It takes into account the material-lived realities of all students and argues for changes in assumptions and beliefs, policies and curriculum, pedagogies and practices—to ensure that schools are inclusive and welcoming and hold similar high expectations for all students. Weiner summarizes it in this way:

> This is the responsibility of transformative leadership; it implies the necessity to link not only the private and public, but also the empirical and theoretical, the everyday and the future, the imaginative and the real, the past and the forgotten, history and tradition, power and knowledge, and learning and life.[32]

Linking the private and the public, the educative and the political in this decade, 50 years after the introduction of the Civil Rights Act, requires that transformative educators confront what Giroux describes as "the conundrums of a limited identity politics and begin to include in its analysis what it would mean to imagine the state as a vehicle for democratic values and a strong proponent for social and racial justice."[33] In other words, given that public schools function as an instrument of the state, it is critically important for transformative educators to safeguard the interests of not only the privileged but those who have been marginalized and excluded.

In 1986, Foster[34] argued that educational leadership "must be critically educative; it can not only look at the conditions in which we live, but it must also decide how to change them." Transformative leadership therefore offers an approach for doing so. By examining our deep-seated beliefs, values, and assumptions, deconstructing knowledge frameworks that perpetuate inequity, and focusing on deep democracy, inclusion, and justice for all, acknowledging and challenging unequal power relations, we can move forward. As we introduce concepts related to the public good, to our interconnectedness with the global community, we can effectively offer promise and hope to those for whom education has not always opened new doors of opportunity. Only as educators take a courageous stand and act audaciously on behalf of those who have for so long been marginalized and excluded will it be possible for Mann's (1848) hope for education to be the "great equalizer of the conditions of men, the balance-wheel of the social machinery" to be realized.

Notes

1. United States Department of Education 2014.
2. Giroux 2003.
3. Coley and Baker 2013, p. 3.
4. Mann 1848.
5. Angier 2000.
6. Ibid.
7. Culbertson 1995, p. 34.
8. Greenfield 1978, p. 1.
9. Ibid., p. 2.
10. Ibid., p. 3.
11. Blackmore 2011, p. 21.
12. Starratt 2011, pp. 131–132.
13. Green 1999, p. vi.
14. Shields 2013, 2014.
15. USDE 2014.

16. Oakes and Rogers 2006, pp. 21–22.

17. Ibid., p. 33.

18. For additional reading on deficit thinking, see Shields, Bishop, and Mazawi (2004) and Valencia (1997, 2010).

19. Green 1999, p. vi.

20. Cited in Winant 2002, p. 33.

21. Delpit 1990, pp. 98–97.

22. Oakes and Rogers 2006, p. 32.

23. Barber 2001, p. 12.

24. Loewen 2005.

25. These data come from various sources: Street (2002) and websites such as Kaiser Family foundation, National Institutes of Health, and Dosomething.org.

26. Oakes and Rogers 2006, p. 13.

27. Ibid., p. 28.

28. Weiner 2003, p. 100.

29. Ibid., pp. 101–102.

30. Ibid., p. 93.

31. Freire 1998, p. 37.

32. Weiner 2003, p. 98.

33. Giroux 2003, pp. 207–208.

34. Foster 1986, p. 35.

Bibliography

Angier, N. 2000. "Do Races Differ? Not Really, DNA Shows." *The New York Times* (August 22). Accessed June 2014. http://www.nytimes.com/library/national/science/082200sci-genetics-race.html.

Barber, B.R. 2001. "An Aristocracy of Everyone." In *The Last Best Hope: A Democracy Reader,* ed. S.J. Goodlad (pp. 11–22). San Francisco, CA: Jossey-Bass.

Bigelow, B. 1998. "The Human Lives behind the Labels—The Global Sweatshop, Nike, and the Race to the Bottom." In *Teaching for Social Justice,* eds. W. Ayers, J.A. Hunt, and T. Quinn (pp. 21–38). New York: Teachers College Press.

Blackmore, J. 2011. "Leadership in Pursuit of Purpose: Social, Economic, and Political Transformation." In *Transformative Leadership: A Reader,* ed. C.M. Shields (pp. 21–36). New York: Peter Lang.

Burns, J.M. 1978. *Leadership.* New York: Harper & Row.

Coley, R.J., and B. Baker. 2013. *Poverty and Education: Finding the Way Forward.* Princeton, NJ: Educational Testing Service. Accessed June 2014. http://www.ets.org/s/research/pdf/poverty_and_education_report.pdf.

Culbertson, J. A. 1988. "A Century's Quest for a Knowledge Base." In *Handbook of Research on Educational Administration,* ed. N. J. Boyan (pp. 3–26). New York: Longman.

Delpit, L.D. 1990. "The Silenced Dialogue: Power and Pedagogy in Educating Other People's Children." In *Facing Racism in Education,* eds. N.M. Hidalgo, C.L. McDowell, and E.V. Siddle (pp. 84–182). Reprint Series No. 21 ed. Cambridge, MA: Harvard Educational Review.

Foster, W. 1986. *Paradigms and Promises.* Amherst, NY: Prometheus.

Freire, P. 1998. *Pedagogy of Freedom: Ethics, Democracy, and Civic Courage.* Lanham, MD: Rowan and Littlefield.

Giroux, H.A. 2003. "Spectacles of Race and Pedagogies of Denial: Anti-Black Racist Pedagogy under the Reign of Neoliberalism." *Communication Education* 52 (3/4): 191–211.

Green, J.M. 1999. *Deep Democracy: Diversity, Community, and Transformation.* Lanham, MD: Rowman & Littlefield.

Greenfield, T.B. 1978. "Reflections on Organization Theory and the Truths of Irreconcilable Realities." *Educational Administration Quarterly* 14 (2): 1–23.

Loewen, J.W. 2005. *Sundown Towns: A Hidden Dimension of American Racism.* New York: Simon & Shuster/Touchstone.

Oakes, J., and Rogers, J. 2006. *Learning Power: Organizing for Education and Justice.* New York: Teachers College Press.

Shields, C.M. 2008. *Courageous Leadership for Transforming Schools: Democratizing Practice.* Norwood, MA: Christopher-Gordon.

Shields, C.M. 2011. "Transformative Leadership: An Introduction." In *Transformative Leadership: A Reader,* ed. C.M. Shields (pp. 1–17). New York: Peter Lang.

Shields, C.M. 2013. *Transformative Leadership in Education: Equitable Change in an Uncertain and Complex World.* New York: Routledge.

Shields, C.M. 2014. "Leadership for Social Justice Education: A Transformative Approach." In *International Handbook of Educational Leadership and Social (In)Justice,* eds. I. Bogotch and C.M. Shields. Dordrecht, Holland: Springer (Business Division), ch. 19.

Shields, C.M., R. Bishop, and A.E. Mazawi, 2004. *Pathologizing Practices: The Impact of Deficit Thinking in Education.* New York: Peter Lang.

Starratt, R.J. 2011. "Preparing Transformative Educators for the Work of Leading Schools in a Multicultural, Diverse, and Democratic Society." In *Transformative Leadership: A Reader,* ed. C.M. Shields (pp. 131–136). New York: Peter Lang.

USDE. 2014. "Expansive Survey of America's Public Schools Reveals Troubling Racial Disparities." Accessed June 2014. http://www.ed.gov/news/press-releases/expansive-survey-americas-public-schools-reveals-troubling-racial-disparities.

Valencia, R.R. ed. 1997. *The Evolution of Deficit Thinking: Educational Thought and Practice.* New York: RoutledgeFalmer.

Valencia, R.R. 2010. *Dismantling Contemporary Deficit Thinking: Educational Thought and Practice.* New York: Routledge.

Wagstaff, L., and L. Fusarelli. 1995. "Establishing, Collaborative Governance and Leadership." In *Lessons from High-Performing Hispanic Schools: Creating Learning Communities,* eds. P. Reyes, J. Scribner, and A. Scribner (pp. 19–35). New York: Teachers College Press.

Weiner, E. J. 2003. "Secretary Paulo Freire and the Democratization of Power: Toward a Theory of Transformative Leadership." *Educational Philosophy and Theory* 35 (1): 89–106.

Winant, H. 2002. "Race in the Twenty-First Century." *Tikkun* 17 (1): 33–40.

Chapter 11

Afrikan American Identity Reconstruction: A Case for Independent Schools

Duane L. Davis

The psychology of a culture is to a great extent a symbolic precipitant of the kinds of experiences forced upon a group of people by their history. We must recognize the intimate relationship between culture, history, and personality. If we do not know our history then we do not know our personality. And if the only history we know is other people's history then our personality has been created by that history.

—Amos Wilson

One ever feels his twoness,—an American, a Negro; two souls, two thoughts, two unreconciled strivings; two warring ideals in one dark body, whose strength alone keeps it from being torn asunder.

—W.E.B. DuBois

If you understand the design of the United States it's still intact no matter what kind of words they use this country was designed for free White Protestant males. Middle class and up those who agreed with the prevailing status quo and who owned property. When they said liberty and justice for all that was the all they were talking about. So if you are clear about that then you will know educationally what you must do.

—John Henrik Clarke

Introduction

In this chapter the argument will be made for the development of independent schools in the United States dedicated to the education and uplift of our children who are of Afrikan ascent in America. It will examine how the Afrikan identity was deconstructed through the process of chattel slavery and then reconstructed through the system of education. The development of the education system, as a tool of cultural imperialism, will be reviewed as will also the history of education for Afrikans in the United States. Finally, suggestions will be offered as to how Afrikan ascendants can establish control of the educational process of their children by developing independent schools within the Afrikan American community.

It should also be understood that the use of the spelling of the term "Afrika" with a "k" is a personal choice of the author so as to remain consistent with the way it has been spelled before the European invasions of the continent and subsequent slave trade. Using this spelling establishes the distinct difference between the Afrikan and European consciousness. The Portuguese and English replaced the "k" with a "c," which was more in line with their own languages, as cited by Dr. Kwame Nantambu, professor emeritus of Pan-Afrikan Studies at Kent State University.[1]

At this point in history many Afrikan Americans, hereafter referred to as "Afrikan ascendants," in the United States were educated by religious and state-sponsored education systems. The term "ascendant" used throughout this chapter refers metaphorically to the family tree, with the roots being the ancestors. The roots grow downward as the rest of the tree "ascends" toward the sun. The impact of this change in terminology also parallels the rise in the Afrikan consciousness throughout the world diaspora.

As a result, the assimilation or civilizing process started beginning with slavery and has continued until this day. This process, designed to separate the enslaved Afrikan from his or her original identity, succeeded in creating a group of people who are confused, scattered, and highly susceptible to adopting any identity projected onto them by the dominant white culture through the media and other sources. Assimilation has as its objective the complete separation of the Afrikan from his or her true nature and identity and as a result the destruction of any remnant of his or her true culture, history, spirituality, and knowledge of self. There are many mechanisms by which this assimilation process is promulgated, one of them being the mechanism of "education." In order for Afrikan ascendants in America to reconstruct a true Afrikan consciousness, it is proposed here that through development of *independent* schools Afrikan ascendants can regain control of their collective identity.

Several key terms are used to support the framework of this discussion. They are defined here:

(1) Collective identity—"the shared definition of a group that derives from members' common interest, experiences and solidarity."[2] Ascendants of

enslaved Afrikans in the United States have been assigned many different labels throughout the history of this country. These names evolved in response to external social circumstances within the white supremacist power structure. Afrikan ascendants accepted these labels in an effort to define themselves.

(2) Hegemony—"the social, cultural, and ideological or economic influence exerted by a dominant group."[3] In this chapter hegemony will be used to describe the exertion and acceptance of Eurocentric ideals and philosophy by Afrikan ascendants.

(3) Collective consciousness—the "totality of beliefs and sentiments common to the average members of a society."[4] Collective consciousness is developed in much the same way as collective identity. Both are established through shared experiences and common interests within a group, and it is through this consciousness that people find their meaning and locate their existence. The collective identity and consciousness of enslaved Afrikans and their ascendants has been deconstructed and reconstructed to serve the interest of the white supremacist power structure within the United States.

Afrikan Identity in Slave America

As an ascendant Afrikan male born in the United States during the civil rights era, I have grown up with an acute awareness of, and interest in, cultivating a strong Afrikan identity. The history of Afrikan identity during slavery (or lack thereof) explains a great deal about how Afrikan ascendants view themselves today. Since the beginning of the Atlantic slave trade, the identity of the Afrikan in the United States has been under attack. Efforts by the European and European American power structure to deconstruct Afrikan identity and reconstruct it in a manner that would support white supremacy and privilege have been ongoing and continue to this day. The dehumanizing process began with the capture of Afrikans and proceeded through the middle passage travel to the new world. It was continued through the sale, possession, and abuse of Afrikan slaves. The idea was to "break" the slaves and strip them of their former identities, thereby forcing them to occupy a subhuman status exacerbated by the imposition of a new language. Hence forward, American "society has developed and hierarchical structure that reflects striations from top to bottom. With the dominant (white) group controlling the accepted values, positive and negative stereotypes and consequences for behavior within the structure, the subordinate groups struggle to survive."[5] The quest for Afrikan identity in

America has been a process of dehumanization and objectification controlled by the dominant white population.

From its inception the United States was a design in social engineering. It started as an expansion of European cultural imperialism and evolved into an experiment on Americanism. The autochthonous people the Europeans found on this continent were viewed as impediments to this design; consequently, through the process of cultural imperialism and genocide, they were removed as obstacles. The original hegemonic influence was largely British as many of the colonies were under the rule of the British Crown. However, as the New World became more prosperous and embroiled in the Trans-Atlantic slave trade, the desire for independence began to grow and take root within the colonies. The economics of free labor provided by virtue of enslaved Afrikans fueled the prosperity experienced by the elite class of Europeans within the new colonies. "The economic advantages afforded the dominant group via the institution of chattel slavery spurred the creation of laws and policies reinforcing the subaltern position occupied by the Africans and their descendants of this country."[6] As a result, the economy became dependent on the slave trade and relegation of Afrikans to a permanent underclass. In order for this permanent underclass to stay in place, Afrikans were exposed to a process of indoctrination that separated them from their indigenous Afrikan identity, replacing it with an identity that was neither Afrikan nor European but one that reinforced the underclass status of a slave. The brutal conditions imposed on the Afrikans through chattel slavery did not require a formal education and one was not afforded them. This conditioning process supplanted the culture, history, and traditional practice of Afrikan society with whatever the slave owner deemed necessary for the maintenance of his property.

The conditioning process presents an enduring problem for Afrikan ascendants residing in the United States today. As a result there has always been a monumental struggle both within the group and externally to define just what it means to be "Afrikan American" in the United States. Ascendants of Afrikans in the United States were defined by the European language and culture. Names used to describe Afrikans were many; "niggers," "jigaboo," "tar baby," and "pickaninny," to name a few, were monikers given to the slaves and incorporated into the English language. This circumstance is instrumental with our struggle for identity definition to this day and is perpetuated through our educational system.

The educational process in America continues to reward and promote those who most portray the ideals and values of the dominant white culture.

A method of selection that has at its root a mechanism that was honed and perfected during the period which found the Afrikan enslaved by European captors, treated as less than human and bartered on the "free" market as a commodity. The dehumanization process was started then, but continues today as we try and demonstrate to others that we are "like" them. The question of identity remains a center of controversy in the United States for Afrikan ascendants. It has been a question in the minds of "Americans" of Afrikan ascent in this country since the United States was founded. From Denmark Vesey, Gabriel Prosser, Nat Turner, Richard Allen, Henry McNeal Turner, Marcus Garvey, Huey P. Newton, Malcolm X, and Martin Luther King, the struggle for identity recognition and equality has persisted. There is no reason to think that since we have come into the 21st century anything has changed.

The struggle is perpetuated by the current education system. Twentieth-century educator Carter G. Woodson wrote extensively about the condition of Afrikan ascendants in America, and particularly about what he called the "mis-educated Negro." In one of his most well-known works "The Miseducation of the Negro," he articulated how this system conditioned Negroes to think of themselves as inferior. Woodson elaborated, "As another has well said, to handicap a student by teaching him that his blackface is a curse and that his struggle to change his condition is hopeless is the worst sort of lynching. It kills one's aspirations and dooms him to vagabondage and crime."[7] Woodson argued further that the historical act of lynching evolved from an outright murderous act to a more subtle act in the classroom. Young Negroes were taught to believe they were inferior. Many accepted and internalized the assumption that they were less than their white counterparts in every way that mattered. Hence, Woodson posited, the larger white population has continued to devalue the Negro because the Negro does not respect himself.

Woodson distinctly underscores his argument by explaining how the method by which ascendants of Afrikans was educated within the United States. Mainstream curricula, Woodson contends, ignores the history and psychology of Afrikan ascendants and does little to equip them with the skills they need to identify and address the plight of their community. "Educated Negroes" are indoctrinated to service the white power structure. An indoctrination of this type places the educated Negro in a precarious position relative to his peer group. Woodson states that this education, which has estranged him from his people, only serves to reinforce what his real place in this society is. The education he receives makes him palatable to the whites in society but creates an incompatibility between him and the people in his community. Woodson elucidates:

> If after leaving school they have the opportunity to give out to Negroes what the traducers of the race would like to have it learn such persons may thereby earn a living at teaching or preaching what they have been taught, but they never become a constructive force in the development of the race.[8]

The education received teaches him that the values and traditions of his people are of no consequence. It also reinforces the notion that he should aspire to the greater ideals of the dominant population even though once released from the halls of academia the reality quickly sets in that the ideals are not attainable. Woodson explains, "When a Negro has finished his education in our schools, then he has been equipped to begin a life of an Americanized or Europeanized white man, but before he steps from the threshold of his alma mater he is told by his teachers that he must go back to his own people from whom he has been estranged by a vision of ideals which in his disillusionment he will realize that he cannot attain; he goes forth to play his part in life, but must be both social and biosocial at the same time."[9] The education which enslaved Afrikans have become a part of is a "sanitizing indoctrination" that is designed to erase any vestige of a previous ethnic identity and replace it with an imposed identity fabricated in the minds of the oppressors and used when necessary to control the unmotivated Negro and create the illusion of acceptance within the American "culture." As Mr. Woodson indicates, our nature is to create a "duality," to be both social and biosocial in order to survive this process. This dichotomy allows Afrikan ascendants to navigate between what they perceive to be their true ethnic identity and the imposed identity projected on them from the Caucasian ego.

W.E.B. DuBois (1994) elaborated on the unique position of the Negro in his landmark work *The Souls of Black Folks*:

> After the Egyptian and Indian, the Greek and Roman, the Teuton and Mongolian, the Negro is a sort of seventh son, born with a veil, and gifted with second-sight in this American world,—a world which yields him no true self-consciousness, but only lets him see himself through the revelation of the other world. It is a peculiar sensation, this double-consciousness, this sense of always looking at one's self through the eyes of others, of measuring one's soul by the tape of a world that looks on in amused contempt and pity. One ever feels his two-ness,—an American, a Negro; two souls,

two thoughts, two unreconciled strivings; two warring ideals in one dark body, whose dogged strength alone keeps it from being torn asunder.[10]

The image created by the reflection that "sanitized" or assimilated slaves projected is easily digested by the oppressor. The reciprocal act of subordinate and dominant identity projection has the effect of making the oppressor recipient feel more comfortable with the oppressed in many social as well as professional situations, because the behavior of the oppressed can be predicted. "The problem of holding the Negro down, therefore, is easily solved. When you control a man's thinking you do not have to worry about his actions."[11] As the subordinate identity recipient, there are many signals given off in order to underscore their subservient position in the society. One of them is the ability to regurgitate and reproduce the behaviors taught to them through the educational system.

Educational Mechanism of Cultural Imperialism

"Cultural imperialism" is defined as the "creation and maintenance of unequal relationships between civilizations favoring the more powerful civilization." As such within the structure of white supremacy, the formal education system is the method by which the oppressor class asserts, maintains, and perpetuates its power. Through it the "state" indoctrinates its students as to how those who are taught by it are to be subordinate as well as how to view history, citizenship, economics, religion, and other areas vital to its structure and philosophy. The European belief of a "superior" white way of life or civilization is considered dominant over the Ancient Afrikan civilization and through a framing of history is taught to each student in the educational system. Within the system, students are "instructed" on how to become good Americans, and since any knowledge of the Ancient Afrikan way of life has long since been discarded and deemed unnecessary, the ascendants of Afrikans in the United States are subject to accept the European way of thought in order to gain acceptance. In and of itself this process appears to be noble in its purpose. But for ascendant Afrikans in America the assimilation process has devastating consequences, particularly where identity is concerned. As reflected in many curricular programs around the country, for example, "the philosophy and ethics resulting from our educational system has justified slavery, peonage, segregation and lynching."[12] This view held by Carter G. Woodson was true in 1933 when his book was written and it holds true even today as some of us imagine the illusion of a "post-racial" America. "The system has also perpetuated the positioning of people of color as the other and the white, European American culture as the mainstream and the norm."[13] This view of the dominant white culture as "the norm" places its philosophies, behaviors, and attitudes as the standards to which all others who wish to be accepted should aspire forsaking their own cultures in the process.

For most groups who came to the United States this process was and is voluntary with the exception of the American of Afrikan ascent. Afrikans were forced to separate from the culture of their birth and were compelled to conform to stereotypes and disparaging linguistic norms imposed on them by Europeans. This was the first form of education experienced by Afrikans in the Americas.

The effects of this form of hegemony, as perpetrated through the educational system, are manifested in many different aspects in the lives of Americans of Afrikan ascent. Control is maintained in most cases through the structural power imparted to the superior culture over the culture considered inferior; in this case, the Afrikans and their ascendants in the United States.

One pronounced effect is the achievement gap in the educational performance levels of many black students. In the area of language performance, this gap may be the result of one residual aspect of slavery. Initially the enslaved Afrikans in America were separated from their common tribal relations and denied the opportunity to communicate in their native language. The captives were also denied the opportunity to learn the new language. This forced depraved positon which has had lasting effects on subsequent generations experiencing the hegemonic effects of this treatment through the system of education. Chancellor Williams asserted in his work "Destruction of Black Civilization" that "Blacks at home and in Africa and Blacks scattered over the world bore the names of their enslavers and oppressors, the ultimate self-effacement that promoted a self-hatred which make pride in the race difficult."[14] Williams's observation frames the current situation Afrikan ascendants face today, one that makes it difficult to take pride in the Afrikan race as a group. Not only does it make pride in the group difficult but it also makes it nearly impossible for the group to act in concert with one another to achieve a common goal. Woodson supports Williams's assertion that our education fosters self-hatred in that "the educated Negroes have an attitude of contempt toward their own people because in their own as well as in their mixed schools Negroes are taught to admire the Hebrew, the Greek, the Latin and the Teuton and to despise the African."[15] The lack of self-expression in the Afrikan native tongues left them vulnerable to the created stereotypes by the language leading to the teaching and acceptance of self-denigrating ideals. Language has been identified as the "strongest link to one's culture."[16] Once Afrikans were separated from their language, the subsequent abandonment and rejection of Afrikan culture was inevitable. Osalbo notes concerning Filipino Americans, that "Filipino American elders who are discouraging their youth from learning their heritage language is the cause for Filipino youth to abandon their culture."[17] Loss of heritage language produces an abandonment of a person's source culture in an attempt to assimilate into the dominant culture. The resultant contrived identity has been constructed, propagated, and reinforced through the educational system, which has as its goal the imposition of the dominant cultural ideology. This form of imperialist philosophy is deeply integrated within the curriculum constructs of the American education system. It is chiefly through the teaching of a history curriculum that the oppressor class creates, revises, and imposes the hegemonic influence of its perceived superiority on those who are considered inferior.

Dr. Amos Wilson articulated the intimate relationship between culture, history, and the expression of behaviors of Afrikan ascendants in this society. The current form of education does not teach Afrikans their real history or cultural identity, thus forcing them to accept the Europeans view of them. Amos Wilson, a noted psychologist, explains this phenomenon:

> The psychology of a culture is to a great extent a symbolic precipitant of the kinds of experiences forced upon a group of people by their history. We must recognize the intimate relationship between culture, history, and personality. If we do not know our history then we do not know our personality. And if the only history we know is other people's history then our personality has been created by that history.[18]

The idea here is that a people who do not know their own history are vulnerable to having a historical identity created for them through the history of others and can be considered "identity replacement." This leaves them vulnerable to being "typecast" in a way that maintains an inferior status within the society because their true identity or personality is not known to them. Under the guise of civilizing allegedly inferior peoples, whites have employed identity replacement for many years as evidenced in an educational system designed to predict and control the behavior of marginalized groups.

Religious Education and Imperialism

Religious education has most often been used as the handmaiden of European and American cultural imperialistic expansion intentions. The culturally dominant ideology of the whites is that "civilization is an expression of the mind of a people, the capacity to acquire an alien form is dependent upon the preliminary acquisition of certain definite mental characteristics: in other words, the Afrikan must first be endowed with a European mind if he is to be civilized in the European manner."[19] Edwin W. Smith wrote about the notion of replacing the Afrikan mind in the 1920s. Assigned as a Methodist missionary, Smith assisted the British Crown in its conquest of Ghana and the subjugation of the Ashanti people. Smith's statement reveals the intent of the British hegemonic agenda.

The American government adopted a similar approach earlier in its desire to expand the influence of the United States in the Hawaiian territory. As Hawaii was increasingly becoming more influenced by American imperialistic schemes, this paternalistic methodology was employed to replace the Hawaiian culture and expand economic interests. "After 1820, the Hawaiian monarchy and American missionaries established a cooperative relationship that enabled American hegemony to be expanded by the consent of the Hawaiians."[20] The cooperative formed was an example of the Hawaiians consenting to the destruction of their own culture through the acceptance of the American religious education. Kalani Beyer underscores cultural encroachment "when missionaries sought to Christianize and "civilize" Hawaiians. Working with Hawaiian leaders, the educators strove to use education in the formation of consciousness by getting native students to accept the superiority of the *haole* culture and the inferiority of their own culture." "Haole" is a pejorative term used to describe the white culture. Beyer notes here that the reason for the education was to form the American consciousness of the Hawaiian in a manner that would be acceptable to American philosophy and customs. It becomes apparent that "in North America culture was imposed, with the schools as the vehicle of 'Americanization.'"[21]

Formal Education and the Slave

Enslaved Afrikans were forced through brutality and the withholding of necessary resources, that is, food and water, in order to convince them to cooperate as property in the creation of a permanent underclass in this new "civilized" culture. For example "Sarah Benjamin who was born on a Louisiana plantation recalled the fate of fellow slaves whose masters discovered that their "property" had secretly learned to read and write": "If yer learned to write dey would cut yer thumb er finger off."[22] The barbarous treatment the Afrikans and their ascendants experienced at the hands of their enslavers taught Afrikans certain lessons, the primary lesson being survival was dependent on acceptance of the subordinate status projected on them by the dominant culture. Initially, being denied any formal education with which to navigate the new civil society, Afrikans learned through situations and circumstances in the slave culture.

Considering that the first slaves arrived in Jamestown, Virginia, in 1619, the initial indoctrination to slave culture in the British colonies began. "In 1695 Maryland imposed a fine of one thousand pounds of tobacco on teachers who instructed blacks."[23] Several generations would pass before formalized legislation was implemented in 1740, specifically prohibiting the education of the enslaved Afrikans in the areas of writing. The penalties for disregarding these laws for whites ranged from heavy monetary fines to imprisonment. The penalties for Negroes teaching Negroes also included whippings.

Fear of creating an edified Negro through formal education evoked anxiety among whites "that slaves could not be enlightened without developing within them a longing for liberty, not a few masters maintained that the more brutish bondmen the more pliant they become for purposes of exploitation."[24] There were even those slave owners who ascribed to the notion that it was cheaper to work slaves to death and purchase another than educate them to improve the efficiency of work on the plantation. There were, however, advocates for the uplift and edification of the Negro slave. A few of the slave masters understood the benefit in having an educated slave and how it impacted the economic efficiency of the labor supply. These slaveholders often educated their slaves in defiance of any civil law because it improved the work environment on their plantations and brought in more profit for them. Although resistance to the wholesale education of Afrikan slaves persisted among Southern plantation, religious organizations took up the cause.

"The first real educators to take up the work of enlightening American Negroes were clergymen interested in the propagation of the gospel among the heathen of the world."[25] It was through the efforts of these religious organizations namely the Quaker, Methodist, and Catholic churches that many ascendants of enslaved Afrikans learned to read and write. However, the concern was raised among those who advocated for the education of the slaves that religion was overwhelmingly the dominant means used to educate these slaves. The process was clearly not used to restore the Afrikan's identity but was used as a device to increase the numbers within their own particular denominations. Many whites questioned the motives of these clergy.

Some objected to the Christian education of slaves and then allowing them to "share" the same worship spaces as whites. Other religious groups objected to the enslavement of Afrikans but used the Bible to justify the process if it had the intent of ushering them to Christ. Efforts to educate the slaves did provide some degree of satisfaction to those who sought to ease the plight of the slave in assimilating to the dominant culture. It nonetheless still had the deleterious effect of moving the enslaved Afrikans further away from their original cultural identity, thereby diminishing the knowledge of themselves. The result was that successfully educated Negroes were now actively engaged in reconstructing a new identity framed by the dominant culture, the "new" identity dominant culture as endowed with the European mind so that they may be civilized in the European manner as stated by Smith. This is the ultimate objective of the education system.

The First Negro Schools

The progress of the Afrikan ascendant in the United States has come at a great cost. Although many obstacles have been overcome through the education and training processes, it has not taught the necessary components for Afrikan ascendants, as a people, to become independent and self-reliant. Instead, religious education has promoted the cultural imperialism of the European. Many of these religious efforts were developed despite vehement opposition from colonial and state legislatures as well as intransigent slave owners. This resistance occurred not only in the South but also in the North as most notably the Quakers established schools where freed and escaped Negro slaves could be taught to read and write.

During Reconstruction Negroes gained greater access to education. The residual effects of slavery however began to surface in the performance of the children of slaves during this time. Although the students exhibited the zeal to learn and performed well in the primary grades, subjects beyond these grades posed a difficulty for children whose parents were not literate. Other difficulties they experienced had little to do with their cognitive abilities but more to do with the economic situations their families endured.

Share cropping was one of the major modes of employment for the families in the South; therefore, the planting and harvesting seasons posed one of the biggest obstacles for consistent attendance in school. Other impediments were in the form of violence from the same whites who refused to pay taxes to support the education of the Negro. "Hostile whites sometimes ran teachers out of town or burned schools, even when the children arrived at school, it was not always staffed or even standing."[26] Economic obstacles as well as the violent response of whites who virulently disagreed with the education of the former slaves and their children presented monumental obstacles to their progress. But nonetheless courageous people endeavored to persevere through the opposition. The first black secondary school for Negroes was established in Washington, D.C., in 1870, first as an educational mission by the Presbyterian Church and the later named M Street High School Paul Laurence Dunbar. Also freed slaves along with the assistance of the American Missionary Association began to create "normal" schools to help develop teachers to go into the rural communities and teach. Many of these schools were the precursors for today's historically black colleges and universities.

The modest gains Negroes realized during Reconstruction were short-lived. For a period of 12 years the system provided an avenue through education for the children of the Negro slaves. The era ended with the return to power of the same bigoted whites who lost their power as a result of the civil war. Their return to power signaled not quite a complete reversal of government policy toward Negroes and education, but many of the gains realized were drastically scaled back. The institution of slavery was replaced with the institution of Jim Crow. Southern legislatures, now controlled by segregationist whites, passed laws preventing Negroes and whites from sharing facilities. "The heart of the Jim Crow system, and the institution most central to its functioning, was the segregated school system. Consignment of black children to separate schools kept them 'in their place' and safely away from white children."[27] The system of "separate but equal" was a façade and became the basis for the educational challenge of *Brown v. The Board of Education* in 1954. The decision proffered by the court heralded a significant defeat for those supporting segregation and gave energy to those who were beginning to frame the civil rights movement. Although the decision affected some of the physical barriers that hindered an equal opportunity for the descendants of Afrikan slaves, it did little to change the attitudes of those who had always feared the "rising" up of the Negro to a status of that equal to whites.

This pervasive attitude of white supremacy and privilege maintained throughout the history of the United States made the gains achieved by Americans of Afrikan ascent bittersweet. The *Brown* decision led to the desegregation of many school districts and other court decisions that allowed for the busing of black children into unreceptive white districts, but not white children into all black districts. This clear fact is also a tacit admission that not only do whites have the superior resources within their school districts, but it also underscores the image of black districts of having inferior resources as well as providing a subpar educational experience relative to whites. It is the persistent projections of inferiority and noncitizenship projected upon Afrikan ascendants by whites that should be the lesson learned. The education system controlled by the power structure will not significantly promote the achievements and gains of the Afrikan community.

A Return to Jim Crow

As America enters into the 21st century, it appears that it has reentered into another era of separate but equal relative to the educational experiences the ascendants of slaves receive. White populations in large cities namely Chicago, Boston, and Detroit violently responded to the integration and busing efforts ordered by the courts. Their overall reaction was to relocate to the suburbs and create school systems where they felt comfortable not interacting with diverse populations. The resultant demographic shift, labeled "white flight," effectively reproduced segregated schools districts.

One court case that helped to solidify resegregation as a practice in the consciousness of the American people was *Milliken v. Bradley* (1973). Milliken argued concerning the busing and integration practices in the Detroit area. Argued in 1970 the case outlined the problem many urban areas faced with their school boards. During this time, cities were divided up along segregated census tracts. The problem was exacerbated by the fact that area school boards manipulated attendance areas to reflect the racial make-up of the neighborhoods. The result was that the city school district created racially isolated schools where there were more than 90 percent black or white, depending on the neighborhood. The suit filed on behalf of students and parents in the city of Detroit by the National Association for the Advancement of Colored People (NAACP) demonstrated that even though desegregation orders had been in place for some time, local school boards still found loopholes that accommodated the prejudices of the white population. The judge ruled in favor of the NAACP and its clients and stated "that Detroit officials had intentionally segregated the city's schools by building new schools well inside neighborhood boundaries, to keep black and white students in separate schools rather than placing new schools in areas that would draw students from both races."[28] The ruling forced two-way busing of students from black neighborhoods to white neighborhoods and white to black neighborhoods, including not only the Detroit school district but the surrounding adjacent suburbs as well. Needless to say, the ruling was not accepted by the whites and the state legislators who opposed the new integration plan. The decision was challenged all the way to the Supreme Court where it was reversed. The reversal returned segregated school districts to both northern cities and the South.

The intransigence of the white community concerning the integration and education of the black in America suggests that it is not a desired effect to have the Negro educated to the point of independence in the United States. This obfuscation throughout the history of America with respect to developing a system that highly educates as many Negroes as possible should be a signal that it is time Afrikan ascendants become responsible for educating their own children.

Lessons Learned

George Santayana once wrote, "Those who do not learn from history are doomed to repeat it."[29] This quote encapsulates what Afrikan ascendants in the United States are experiencing today. Afrikan ascendants are once again being forced politically into another post-Reconstruction period. All of the advancements that have been garnered through the sacrifices of many people are being scaled back. From voting rights, education, and women's reproductive rights, all are being abolished. It appears that as a people Afrikan ascendants have not yet learned from history the implications of their plight, having reaped the benefits of their parents' struggle through the civil rights era only to squander them on individual material pursuits. Currently, the far right elements of American society have nearly regained control of the political system. Although many ascendant Afrikans have enjoyed successes through most every avenue opened to them, they have failed to control the institutions that impact most of the other less fortunate people of the race. Most have lost sight of who they are as a people and have become enamored with a national identity that has never really afforded acceptance, having draped themselves in the false identity afforded them by their European captors and enjoyed the false security it provides at the expense of their dignity as a people. Ascendant Afrikans have become too attached to the "good Negro" identity which has thus far facilitated their survival in this country because a good Negro knows his place. It is time to realize that as they trek further into the future with a fragmented identity they will soon lose any concept of who they are and what their true nature is as Afrikans.

There are three major lessons Afrikan ascendants should take from their sojourn in the United States, thus far. The first lesson is as follows:

(1) "Hegemony is power achieved through a combination of coercion and consent."[30]

Afrikan ascendants must first understand that their current plight is a direct result of fear of reprisal from the dominant culture and it continues because they agree to its conditions. "The limits of tyrants are prescribed by those they oppress."[31] Frederick Douglass indicates in his 1857 speech that the oppressors can go only as far as the oppressed allows them. Today Afrikan ascendants have been seduced through various tactics which affords them the illusion of power and status within the current power structure. It has created a complacency that does not challenge the predominant hegemonic influence. "They must understand that the ruling classes achieve domination not by force or coercion alone, but also by creating subjects who willingly submit to rule."[32] Afrikan ascendants must accept the fact that we have been willing accomplices in the compromise of their dignity and in the condition they presently find themselves. This has been done through an educational conditioning that removes their identity as Afrikans and replaces it with a European mind-set. They should also be aware of the fact that this happens only because we agree to it. Once this fact has been admitted, then strategies must be developed to counter the strong hegemonic influences they have been exposed to for hundreds of years in the United States.

(2) Any degree of change in our condition will be directly proportional to the degree of struggle they experience.

As Afrikan ascendants become more aware that complacency is the enemy of progress they will begin to realize what Frederick Douglass said in the same 1857 speech: "If there is no struggle there is no progress."[33] They must prepare themselves for strenuous resistance if they are to ever extricate themselves from this slave mentality and the conditions associated with it. It has been demonstrated from historical experience that once whites understand that Afrikan ascendants are asserting their right to be who they are, and begin to seriously reconstruct their collective Afrikan consciousness, it may precipitate strong violent reactions from them. Their ancestors endured lynching, castrations, mutilations, and other forms of barbarity when they stood up to be recognized and treated equally as human. If the struggle and sacrifices are great, then the benefits derived from them will be great; however, if they remain stagnant in pursuing and reconstructing their true Afrikan history and identity, then they must not expect much change in their present condition. The relationship between how much work is done toward rebuilding the Afrikan collective identity is directly related to how much progress will be realized in its formation and its consequent expression in the things the group endeavors to accomplish.

(3) Afrikan ascendants in the United States must gain control over the institutions in their community that directly impact the groups' well-being.

As the first two lessons are more conceptual in nature, this third lesson must involve an active engagement of the community. As a people, Afrikan ascendants have little control over any of the organizations that impact the daily lives of their people. They do not control hospitals, grocery stores, or any businesses that produce or manufacture needed items.

Afrikan ascendants are not in control of any social agencies that are charged with the social welfare of our elderly, women, or children. Their most vulnerable assets, the children, are left exposed to the despicable devices of the dominant culture through the education institutions. As long as Afrikans ascendants leave these institutions in control of the white culture and are "dependent on them for our jobs, our housing, the cleaning of our streets, the education of our children, . . . we can cut it any way we want to, we are still enslaved."[34] Since they have little or no control over any of these institutions, particularly education, they are still subject to behaving in ways that are predictable and expected. Afrikan ascendants will still occupy the inferior stereotypes and engage in the predictable behaviors that have characterized them since the beginnings of slavery. One way for them to begin to deconstruct these negative stereotypes is through gaining control of the education of their children. Although they are all susceptible to the hegemonic influences that are interwoven into this American society, it is the children with their impressionable pliant personalities that are most susceptible to the images that are projected on them by the dominant culture and popular modalities and in formal educational settings. Until Afrikan ascendants can truly control the educational institutions in their communities *independent* of government and religious control, they will not truly know how much of a difference can be made in the lives of future generations.

Gaining Control through Independent Schools

It is essential that, as ascendants of Afrikans begin to understand who they are, they must gain control over significant sectors of their communities. Within the areas of business, health care, and education, there must be a resurgence of spirit of self-reliance among ascendant Afrikan people. Although not advocating segregation per se, there are behaviors that were demonstrated during that era which forced their dependency on one another. These behaviors such as cooperative business practices where blacks created and traded within their own communities whenever possible or the development of black health clinics and hospitals, staffed and run by blacks, will help to begin to reconstruct the atmosphere in which an emergent Afrikan identity and consciousness can be reconstructed. Ascendants of Afrikans must be clear as to the nature of the ideals on which the United States was founded.

The precepts of this country were not penned with the enslaved Afrikan in mind. Afrikan ascendants must "understand the design of the United States is still intact no matter what kind of words they use, the United States was designed for free White Protestant males. Middle class and up those who agreed with the prevailing status quo and who owned property. When they said liberty and justice for all that was the *all* they were talking about. So if you are clear about that then you will know educationally what you must do."[35] Educationally they must begin to understand the true nature of the United States and how Afrikan ascendants are trained to serve the power structure and how their true identity has been compromised. Ascendant Afrikans must begin to strategize and develop institutions that reconstruct the Afrikan identity and teach the children the concepts of nation building and in the process reconstruct the Afrikan collective consciousness. This goal can be achieved through the development of independent schools which will place the control of the children who are the ascendants of slaves' education in the hands of their own community. There must be a resurgence within the black community. Pivotal in this resurgence must be the development of Independent Black Institutions (IBI). The educational institutions must be developed in order for the ascendants of Afrikans to convey their story and ensure that future generations can build self-reliant communities for themselves.

Although there are in America schools and school systems that have Afrikan ascendants as superintendents, principals, and members on school boards, true control still rests with the state governments or religious organizations that create and dictate the policies and practices these leaders are to follow. The creation of IBIs can provide autonomous control over the activities of the school, including providing a culturally responsive curriculum to children of Afrikan ascent who will be the principal stakeholders in the learning environment. "Through the development of IBI's in the community "a proactive stance, defining within a community context the possibilities and gifts that Black children offer the world, and creating community institutions to manifest its ideals." Institutions validate knowledge, help to shape visions, inculcate values, and provide the foundation for community stability."[36] Through providing a curriculum that addresses the cultural developmental needs of children of Afrikan ascent, IBIs will lay the foundation for future community plans and visions. This approach allows the teachers, parents, and the community to begin to restore the collective Afrikan identity which has been deconstructed through specific hegemonic influences and images imposed on them in the current educational paradigm.

An Afrikan-centered curriculum is the best vehicle to address the reconstruction of the Afrikan identity in their children. An Afrikan-centered curriculum should have specific aims that reflect the values and goals of the Afrikan community. "An Afrikan-centered pedagogy should fulfill the following aims:

(1) Legitimatize African stores of knowledge;
(2) Positively exploit and scaffold productive community and cultural practices;
(3) Extend and build upon the indigenous language;
(4) Reinforce community ties and idealize [the concept of] service to one's family, community, nation, race, and world;
(5) Promote positive social relationships;
(6) Impart a worldview that idealizes a positive, self-sufficient future for one's people without denying the self-worth and right to self-determination of others;

(7) Support cultural continuity while promoting critical consciousness; and
(8) Promote the vision of individuals and communities as producers rather than simply as consumers."[37]

The mission and focus of the Afrikan-centered IBIs should tie each lesson, activity, and field trip, and community activity should be linked to one or more of the aims mentioned earlier on every grade level so that the reconstruction of a unified collective identity can be realized.

These goals create a framework for the development of a nurturing environment that teaches children of Afrikan ascendants to think critically and learn how to problem solve. The institution should prepare its young men and women with the skills that will allow them to function as autonomous entities. In other words, if America were destroyed today they would have the ability to create another society and all that entails. The current system prepares them to serve only it and no one else. When ascendant Afrikans become producers and not just merely consumers, they will begin to gain respect both in America and in the world. As Marcus M. Garvey stated from the Tombs Prison in 1923, "The Negro will have to build his own government, industry, art, science, literature and culture, before the world will stop and consider him."[38] Garvey demonstrates an understanding of the need to develop within people of Afrikan ascent nation-building skills. IBIs can help Afrikan ascendants function productively as a nation unto themselves.

IBIs will also address the three lessons Afrikan ascendants should have learned from their history in America. First, through their development our community will learn to take a proactive stance to white supremacy and counter the negative hegemonic influences of the dominant culture. It will represent a resistance to the coercion of the negative stereotypes and create a tangible dissent to it. IBIs will represent their collective dissent to the power of hegemony in this American society.

Second, the movement to regain control of our educational institutions will not be an easy one. It will represent the struggle Frederick Douglass referred to in his advice to the ascendant Afrikan people. The struggle will result in progress for Afrikan ascendants as a group. There will also be other challenges to the building of IBIs. Funding is currently a monumental problem, and it will be for any organization deciding to develop an IBI school. Developing streams of funding for community IBIs will demonstrate a positive use of our collective economic resources. It will be a tangible demonstration of our collective power in action. Establishing economic goals for the IBI's and achieving them will significantly lend energy to the reconstructive efforts in rebuilding our collective Afrikan identity. Another challenge will be overcoming our community's lack of confidence in its ability to accomplish collective goals independent of the established power structure. Our community must overcome the feelings of self-hatred, inferiority, and lack of confidence in its ability to produce a quality educational program.

The third lesson the IBIs address is that Afrikan ascendants would no longer look to other people to educate their children. One fine example of such a school is the New Concept Development Center (NCDC) of Chicago, Illinois, founded in 1972. NCDC serviced students from preschool age to sixth grade. The school has had a significant impact on the neighborhood. "They are decidedly not among the gang members, dope dealers, and high school dropouts that plague our communities. NCDC alumni have graduated from or are currently enrolled in some of the most prestigious public schools and gifted programs in the Chicago school system. Public school principals enthusiastically welcome NCDC graduates because they have come to expect these students to enjoy reading, patiently engage in mathematical and scientific problem solving, think critically about social issues, be well rounded in their creative interests and talents, and behave well."[39] NCDC in recent years has been forced to reduce its grade-level capacity due to some of the funding and support problems experienced by independent institutions. Its plight underscores the difficulty ascendant Afrikan communities have in developing self-reliant attitudes. IBIs will have to persevere through what appears to be hard times as they endeavor to positively impact their communities. They represent a commitment to reconstruction of a positive image for the Afrikan collective identity. Their existence demonstrates the effort to develop an independent ideology concerning the education of the children of Afrikan ascendants. These schools are critical in the understanding of how a community can build, nurture, and sustain an institution that has the potential to redefine its image. IBIs can be a glimmer of light and hope in the otherwise dim landscape of urban public education.

Notes

1. www.trinicenter.com/kwame/2002/Feb/172002.htm.
2. Ritzer 2007.
3. www.merriam-webster.com/dictionary/hegemony.
4. Durkheim 2013, p. 7.

5. Tatum 1997.
6. Davis 2004, p. 42.
7. Woodson 1933, p. 3.
8. Ibid.
9. Ibid., pp. 5–6.
10. Du Bois 1994, p. 2.
11. Woodson 1933, p. xix.
12. Woodson 1933, p. xviii.
13. Lei 2003, pp. 158–181.
14. Williams 1987.
15. Woodson 1933, p. 1.
16. Zentella 1997.
17. Osalbo 2001, p. v.
18. Wilson 1993, p. 23.
19. Smith 1927, p. 174.
20. Beyer 2012, pp. 515–535.
21. Epstein 1987, pp. 1–23.
22. Irons 2002, p. 1.
23. Ibid., p. 3.
24. Woodson 1919a.
25. Ibid., p. 5.
26. Irons 2002, p. 3.
27. Ibid., p. 12.
28. Ibid., pp. xii–xiii.
29. Santayana, 1998, p. 284, Vol. 1.
30. Gramsci 1971.
31. Foner 1999, p. 367.
32. Gramsci 1971.
33. Foner 1999, p. 367.
34. Clarke 1994.
35. Ibid.; Lee 1992, pp. 160–177.
36. Ibid.
37. Lee, Lotomey, and Shujaa 1990.
38. Garvey and Blaisdell 2004.
39. Lee 1992, pp. 160–177.

Bibliography

Beyer, Kalani. 2012. "A Century of Using Secondary Education to Extend an American Hegemony over Hawai'i." *American Educational History Journal* 39: 515–535.

Clarke, John Henrik. 1994. *Who Betrayed the African World Revolution? and Other Speeches*. Chicago, IL: Third World Press.

Davis, Duane L. 2004. *A Correlative Study of Africa-American Adolescent Identity Development and the Levels of Cultural Mistrust: Implications for Ethical Educational Leadership* (*Dissertation*). Bowling, Green, OH: Bowling Green State University.

DuBois, W.E.B. 1994. *The Souls of Black Folks*. New York: Dover Publications Inc.

Durkheim, Emile. Trans. George Simpson. 2013. *The Division of Labor in Society*. New York: Simon & Schuster.

Epstein, Erwin H. 1987. "The Peril of Paternalism: Imposition of Education on Cuba by the United States." *American Journal of Education* 96: 1–23.

Foner, Philip S., ed., Yuval Taylor ad. 1999. *Frederick Douglass Selected Speeches and Writings*. Chicago: Lawrence Hill Books.

Garvey, Marcus Mosiah, and Bob Blaisdell, eds. 2004. *Selected Writings and Speeches of Marcus Garvey*. Mineola, NY: Dover Publications Inc.

Gramsci, A. 1971. *Selections from the Prison Notebooks*. London: Lawrence and Wishart.

Irons, Peter. 2002. *Jim Crow's Children: The Broken Promise of the Brown Decision*. New York: The Penguin Group.

Lee, Carol D. 1992. "Profile of an Independent Black Institution: African-Centered Education at Work." *Journal of Negro Education* Spring: 160–177.

Lee, C.D., K. Lomotey, and M.J. Shujaa. 1990. "How Do We Sing Our Sacred Song in a Strange Land?" *Journal of Education* 61: 436–454.

Lei, Joy L. 2003. "(Un)Necessary Toughness?: Those 'Loud Black Girls' and Those 'Quiet Asian Boys.'" *Anthropology & Education Quarterly* 34 (2): 158–181.

Osalbo, Jennifer Guiang. 2001. *Filipino American Identity development and Its Relation to Heritage Language Loss*. Sacramento, CA: California State University.

Ritzer, George, ed. 2007. *Blackwell's Encyclopedia of Sociology*. Malden, MA: Blackwell Publishing Inc.

Santayana, George. 1998. *Life of Reason* (Vol. 1–5). New York: Prometheus Books, p. 284.

Smith, Edwin W. 1927. *The Golden Stool: Some Aspects of the Conflict of Cultures in Africa*. London: Holborn Publishing House.

Stewart, Alison. 2013. *First Class: The Legacy of Dunbar, America's First Black Public High School*. Chicago, IL: Lawrence Hill Books.

Tatum, Beverly Daniel. 1997. *Why Are All the Black Kids Siting together in the Cafeteria? and Other Conversations about Race*. New York: Basic Books.

Williams, Chancellor. 1987. *The Destruction of Black Civilization: Great Issues of a Race from 4500 B.C. to 2000 A.D.* Chicago, IL: Third World Press.

Wilson, Amo. 1993. *The Falsification of Afrikan Consciousness*. New York: Afrikan World Infosystems.

Woodson, Carter G. 1919a. *The Education of the Negro*. Washington, DC: Associated Publishers.

Woodson, Carter G. 1919b. *The Education of the Negro Prior to 1861: A History of the Education of the Colored People of the United States from the Beginning of Slavery to the Civil War.* Lexington, KY: Traffic Output Publications.

Woodson, Carter G. 1933. *The Mis-education of the Negro.* Chicago, IL: The Associated Publishers.

Zentella, A.C. 1997. *Growing Up Bilingual: Puerto Rican Children in New York.* Malden, MA: Blackwell Publishing.

Chapter 12

African American Racial Solidarity as a Solution to Educational Inequality

Candice Jimerson-Johnson

What the Negro in America is to be, and what the Negro in Africa is to be, and in short, what the Negro in the world is to be, we are called to be instrumental in deciding.

—Rev. G.M. Elliott, Alabama State
Teachers Association, 1888.[1]

Overview

Few would argue against the fact that institutionalized racism has contributed to the educational inequities we see today. However, this chapter argues that in some ways African Americans of the post–civil rights era have unwittingly contributed to the continuation of these inequities. The author maintains that a return to African American racial solidarity, shared common values, and a revival of the partnerships among African American leaders in politics, religion, education, and communities will yield the greatest gains for African American children. Though not dismissing the need for African Americans to work with allies of other ethnic backgrounds to ameliorate this dire situation, the work focuses on drawing lessons from those who fought for equal opportunity and access under segregation to break through today's stagnation and move toward a prosperous future. The current expectations of African American educators and community members toward public schools and toward African American children must change if we are to see positive change. The fight must be twofold: to improve poor-quality schools forged in racist beliefs that currently serve African American children and to root out the complacency in the African

American community born of the selfishness and materialism that capitalism engenders. The author of this piece, an African American educator, argues for a Call to Action that defies the assumption that desegregation has brought numerous benefits and challenges African American educators to indeed be their "brother's keepers."

Researchers have documented the persistent underperformance of African American students in multiple areas: standardized test scores, graduation rates, and college matriculation rate. Often institutionalized racism, capitalism, or the cultural deficit model is blamed for this group's seemingly inability to demonstrate lasting educational achievement gains. The question that nags is, "What can be done to improve African American student academic performance?" If *Plessey v. Ferguson* and Jim Crow laws were iron shackles hindering African Americans' ability to obtain educational access and achievement, desegregation and the loss of ethnic solidarity has been a set of golden handcuffs that continue to hinder African Americans from lasting and pervasive educational progress. This piece addresses these major questions: What community mores and ethnic group characteristics were evident before desegregation that allowed African American students to survive and, in some cases, thrive under systematic and unrelenting de jure and de facto segregation? To what extent can these same characteristics enable African American students to thrive in the 21st century? What responsibility should African Americans have in the academic success of African American students?

Limited Effects of *Brown v. Board*

Prior to 1954, it was well known that thanks to institutionalized racism, school buildings for African American children were poorly built and maintained, that school resources were not well supplied, and that teachers were scarce and often not given quality teacher preparation. In the pursuit of equality, the NAACP argued in *Brown v. Board of Education* (1954) that racial segregation of schools resulted in inferior facilities and teaching. Moreover, testimony of social scientists in the case argued that "Black children in segregated schools could not learn effectively as White children due to compounding psychological and emotional exigencies brought about by segregated facilities."[2] Although the many years of court battles finally yielded some instances of small successes in the integration of public schools, the prevailing thought following the trial served to undermine ethnic solidarity; to challenge the idea that education was essential to economic, political, and social success; and to erode the belief that African Americans' leadership in education was necessary—a belief that the community had constructed during decades of segregation. This focus on the negative effects of segregation on African American children implied an inherent inferiority of African American teachers and predominantly African American schools. Jacqueline and Russell Irvine wrote, "The Brown decision considerably altered the nature of the African-American community, diluting its collective whole, collective struggle, and collective will."[3] Unfortunately, the expected benefits of *Brown v. Board* have never truly been realized; public schools remain largely segregated on racial lines, and African American children still struggle to achieve academically. Instead of fostering more African American leadership in public education, school desegregation placated and anesthetized the African American community into believing that integration in and of itself was the ultimate goal. The prevailing assumption was that just sitting next to white students would improve the education of African American children.[4] Once integration was achieved, many thought that African American children would receive better instruction and thus perform at higher levels. However, little consideration was made that "the power to control desegregation was placed in the hands of those who fought so hard to retain segregation."[5] Ironically, many of the hopes of *Brown* were dashed when in *Miliken v. Bradley* (1974) "the Supreme Court reversed the court of appeals, ruling that school district lines could not be crossed to desegregate schools absent proof of an interdistrict violation. In short, poor, minority students would stay in the cities, and the suburbs would be spared from busing."[6] Thus, today the majority of African American and Hispanic students attend schools in urban areas while white students attend suburban schools. The fact that African Americans legally have the ability to attend predominantly white schools seems to have been enough to squelch the outrage so many once felt regarding the inferiority of segregated schools. The reality is that the inferiority still exists, not always in the quality of the school facilities but in the discrepancies in per pupil expenditures, teacher qualifications, curriculum resources, and quality of the education itself. "Schools with significant numbers of ethnically diverse students are often segregated schools where students of color and low-tracked classes and where White students are overrepresented in honors, Advanced Placement, and college preparatory classes."[7] Most parents in urban schools do not see these discrepancies because they have neither visited suburban schools nor seen their district budgets. Greater awareness of this gross inadequacy must be realized if we are to garner the level of support needed to transform our schools. The goal must be equity in resources, staff, facilities, curriculum, not just the legal right to sit next to a white student in a classroom. Yes, the *Brown* decision was historic and necessary to further the cause for civil rights in the United States. Subsequent segregationist practices were reversed and struck down thanks to the decision, and it was essential in shaping the United States we know today, opening the door for many other groups of people to obtain legal rights they did not have previously. Still, Wiley (1994) states,

> Today, 40 years later, the euphoria of Brown, has been supplanted by a sense of resignation, a feeling that the ruling was extremely helpful at that time but did not anticipate or do anything to correct modern problems, such as the disproportionate number of disciplinary actions taken against Blacks, tracking African-Americans into special low-achievement classes, disparity in standardized test results and the academic gap between Black males and females.[8]

Decline in African American Teacher Status

The decline in the role of African American teachers serves as an example of the negative effects of desegregation. From emancipation until desegregation, African American teachers have documented that they were dedicated to their students and that a sense of moral obligation to racial uplift permeated their work. In spite of the lack of books, pencils, school buildings, or training, they felt supported by the African American community to continue to do the best they could with very little because they held fast to the conviction that education would be the only way to the advancement of future generations.

> As described in teachers' memoirs and oral history interviews, black schools were places where order prevailed, where teachers commanded respect, and where parents supported the teachers. Teachers, pupils and parents formed an organic community that treated schooling as a collective responsibility. . . . Integration destroyed that relationship by undermining the position of the teacher as a mentor, role model and disciplinarian. It caused a loss of interest in learning on the part of black pupils.[9]

Several factors brought about the disenfranchisement of African American teachers. Civil rights legislation opened many more career paths to African Americans, drawing many would-be educated professionals away from teaching—a traditional career field for the ethnic group. In addition,

African American teachers and principals were fired, reassigned, made to feel inferior, and pushed out of schools.[10] Most important, predominantly African American schools were dismantled through busing and redistricting to accomplish racial integration. Thus, African American teachers no longer taught majority African American students. In Table 12.1, the decline in the numbers of African American teachers is shown. Note the disproportionality between the racial background of teachers and students in the 21st century. Some would argue that in the United States where racial diversity should be valued, this change should be desired. We should all learn to appreciate one another's differences, and teachers of any background should want what is best for their students and should challenge those students to achieve their best. However, the training of white teachers did not change quickly in the post-Brown era; white teachers were still taught that African

TABLE 12.1   The Loss of African American Teachers Following *Brown v. Board of Education*

Period	Status of African American Teacher Employment
Pre-1954	Approximately 82,000 African American teachers were responsible for the education of 2 million African American children
1954	The *Brown v. Board* decision was handed down
1954–1965	More than 38,000 African American teachers and administrators in 17 Southern and border states lost their jobs
1975–1985	The numbers of African American students majoring in education declined by 66%.
1984–1989	An estimated 37,717 minority candidates and teachers—including 21,515 African Americans—were eliminated as a result of newly installed teacher certification and teacher education program admissions requirements.
2000	Less than 5% of the teaching force will be of minority background, while 35% of the student population will be people of color.

Source: Adapted from Hudson, M.J., and B.J. Holmes. 1994. "Missing Teachers, Impaired Communities: The Unanticipated Consequences of *Brown v. Board of Education* on the African-American Teaching Force at the Precollegiate Level." *The Journal of Negro Education* 63: 389.

Americans were inferior and less capable than white students. White teachers taught African American children believing these fundamental racist concepts. One may be able to change the law, but the law cannot change the heart. The fact that it took 44 years and 3 months after the historic *Topeka v. Board of Education* (1955) case for the district court to declare compliance with *Brown I* shows that segregationists were obstinately noncompliant.[11] The residual psychological effects of decades of discrimination still lingered. Even today, studies have concluded that white teachers expect less of their African American students, thus decreasing the rigor of the assignments and negatively influencing African American students' test performance.[12] In addition, Irvine and Irvine (2007) cited a quantitative study by Meier, Stewart, and England (1989) that concluded, "In school districts with large proportions of African American teachers, the researchers found that fewer African American students were suspended, expelled, or placed in special education classes. In addition, more African American students were placed in gifted and talented programs and graduated from high school. The investigators emphatically concluded that 'Black teachers are without doubt the key' to (Black) students' academic success."[13] Furthermore, white students need to see teachers of color as strong role models in order to combat racist ideas, to demonstrate the diversity of abilities people have, and to prepare white students to work in the world with people of many different backgrounds. Regrettably, the changes in African American schools caused deterioration in the African American community's sense of ownership of the schools. No longer is it believed that "in the hands of the Negro teachers rests the destiny of the race" as the U.S. Office of Education stated in the 1930s.[14]

In the early 20th century, African American churches and social organizations partnered with teachers to support the schools. Countless stories of African Americans fundraising for school buildings, supplies, teacher salaries, and so on have been documented.[15] African American people saw that the white establishment would not provide the education their African American children needed, so they led the efforts to meet the needs. This partnership constructed a shared determination and accountability for the children of the community, a determination that has been lost. Fairclough describes the connection this way:

> Moreover, black schools and black churches were often closely linked, the church served as the schoolhouse, and the preacher was also the teacher. For most African-Americans, integration was an irrelevant abstraction. Like

churches, the public schools acted as agencies of race sentiment and community identity. "I suppose all southern people know the effect the churches and school houses have upon the colored people in keeping and bringing them together." Testified one Louisiana Republican in 1877.[16]

Regrettably, the refrain that African American schools were inferior due to segregation created a public perception that African Americans, even given adequate training and materials, would be unable to lead successful schools. Government policy, which had to force many school districts to comply with the *Brown* decision, unconsciously decentralized the power of homogeneity that the African American community relied on to meet its children's needs. With the children being bused to schools far from their neighborhoods, or school district lines being redrawn to meet integration requirements, African American communities could not focus their efforts on a few neighborhood schools. With African American children being sent to supposedly better schools and stronger teachers, African Americans' once constant drive to improve the schools dissipated. Community leaders focused their attention on other pressing civil rights issues. The emphasis on integrating with white students eroded the status of African American educators and the partnerships within the African American community. Sadly, African American children needed the combined efforts of African American teachers and community agencies even more than they had prior to *Brown*. Although facilities and teacher training were subpar under segregation, at least the schools and community members affirmed the students' work while helping them construct dreams for a brighter future, even in a racist world. Oates's (2009) review of five explanations of the black–white achievement gap found that "from racial (and socioeconomic) privilege ensures access to better quality schools and receipt of more stimulating interpersonal 'signals' from gatekeepers. From these resources ensues enhanced performance."[17] The negative psychological effects of institutionalized racism within previously all-white schools eroded African American students' self-concept and performance in spite of the students learning in better maintained facilities.

The Weakening of Racial Identity and Solidarity

African American neighborhood leadership base deteriorated as African Americans increased their personal wealth and were able to move into integrated neighborhoods. Middle- and upper-class African Americans seemed to no longer have the same racial concept that once bound them geographically, economically, and legally to their poor and working-class brothers and sisters. This detachment weakened the strength of the previous efforts to improve the community's schools. The African Americans who remained did not have the cultural, social, political, or economic capital to maintain the fight for equality. Therefore, as one African American noted, "We turned our kids over to someone else for their education because we thought that was the answer."[18] The once strong ethnic cohesion among African Americans waxed and waned around particularly abhorrent racist statements or actions, never able to sustain the momentum of the civil rights movement of the 1950s and 1960s. The opening of more job opportunities through integration legislation in the 1970s and the economic prosperity of the 1980s brought further deterioration of community cohesion since many in American society ascribed to the belief that they were living in a "post-racial" society where race no longer served such a defining role in American life. Many African Americans did not participate in ethnic civic organizations or were no longer living in predominantly African American communities. This contradicted how Fairclough (2004) described the feelings of African Americans toward the end of the 19th century. "As racial proscription reinforced race consciousness, a strong sense of providential mission promoted the belief that God had given educated blacks the duty of redeeming their race from ignorance and degradation." No longer did African Americans feel this same pressure to uplift the race through education. Individualism pervaded the community. African Americans who denounced their ethnic backgrounds and acted more like the white ruling class in speech, activities, and values were rewarded with promotions and higher salaries. Unfortunately, African American teachers adopted the stereotypical beliefs of whites toward African American students which led to lower expectations and apathy toward student achievement. Teachers' respect and position in American society in general had declined, which only exacerbated the already precipitous demise of the position of African American teachers. The power base from which an effective movement could draw had disappeared. The legacy of the fight for educational equity which had sustained the African American community for over a century had not continued into the 1980s. This unfortunate reality continues to hinder any significant reform in the educational system.

One major obstacle to reestablishing leadership focused on improving schooling for African American children is that African Americans continue to struggle with the modern definition of "The African American community." Although not entirely in agreement with Irvine and Irvine's (2007) argument that "given the ascendancy of a post-modernist world-view, the African-American community is complexly fractionalized and no over-riding single variable, such as color, is sufficient to unify it," this author is increasingly concerned that without the willingness to forge alliances, sacrifice time, expend energy, and spend money within their own neighborhoods for the betterment of the schools, African American children's academic performance will continue to decline. Despite the fact that African Americans are still more heavily concentrated in urban areas, the political, religious, and social mores of the group have become much more diverse. African Americans who can afford to do so move out of poor districts for better schools. Others enroll their children in private or charter schools to avoid the problems that urban schools present. For that reason, the ability to garner solid support and establish a movement around improving urban, public schools has proven a great challenge. Parents in urban schools who seem to understand the subpar education that their children's schools are providing fight hard to ensure the best experience for their children, but do not work with school staff to better the entire school for the good of all students. Certainly, there are few recent instances where parents have banded together to demand that an entire school district improve its service to children. The sentiment from the early 20th century that Fairclough articulates as "the sense that black communities 'owned' their public schools"[19] has not endured into the 21st century. Once government oversight and the accountability movement pervaded public schools, parents felt confused and helpless to lead the necessary changes. Fairclough (2000) also argues that in the 19th century, "The people in the forefront of the struggle for education played a critical role in defining, articulating and advancing the aspirations of the race."[20] This is no longer the case. Presently, lobbyists, legislators, unions, state education, and district staff direct the schooling of children, regardless of race or class and the effects either might have on children's needs. Although parents have the ability to elect board members, speak at public forums at board meetings, and serve on Parent–Teacher Associations, a small percentage of parents do so. Irvine and Irvine (2007) says this about the effects of increased federal government involvement in education, "Its (government's) focus on testing rather than the more significant issue of structural inequalities deludes the public in believing that poverty is solely related to low school performance. The unfortunate message to African-American students is that their poor performance on tests is the reason for their inability to gain access to higher education and jobs."[21]

This circular rhetoric only reinforces the hopelessness poor students of color already feel when considering post–high school options. More often than not, the small percentage of active parents are those from the more affluent neighborhoods in the district, who have the education, confidence, and time to be more involved in local education matters. Unfortunately, African American parents who are actively engaged in school decision making are not proportionate to the number of African American students in urban, public schools. However, as Jordan-Taylor (2010) reminds us, "Power and prosperity are not prerequisites for educational agency."[22] Civil rights movement workers often had neither power nor prosperity individually, but collectively, with unwavering determination and dedication to the cause won many battles for equality. The lack of what Irvine and Irvine (2007) call the "collective will" of African Americans has stymied many efforts at school or district reform. Without a clear and unified focus and strong leadership, ideas and potential protests to improve African Americans' educational experiences have withered on the vine.

Self-Empowerment through Racial Solidarity

African Americans must regain interest and realize the power they have in their children's educations. The African American community as a whole must take the lead in rectifying the problems that have developed in predominantly African American public schools. Urban civic and community leaders must help its members see that racial solidarity does not necessitate discrimination against other groups, but does require a passion for the betterment of the race. They must also reach out to African Americans in the suburban areas to build connections across class lines and re-create a sense of obligation for the welfare of all African American children. African American leaders should more aggressively partner with community activists from other ethnic groups positioned in cities to lobby legislators, educate parents, and volunteer in the daily operations of schools so that the neediest children in cities will be served effectively. Although each ethnic group's needs may vary in some areas, the combined power of various groups' resources and numbers will facilitate success. The realization that education truly is the best means to end poverty must be achieved if we are to see the reversal of decades of neglect from which our urban schools suffer. Education must be a specific committee in the structure of civic organizations with a line item budget to connect parents to schools. Civic and community leaders must meet with local school personnel to understand the school's needs and partner to meet those needs. We cannot wait for the generosity of others to transform our schools and communities. In a capitalist society, such generosity rarely comes before people's materialist desires. If as Rucker and Jubilee (2007) state "in 1867, Black Georgians donated in excess of $3,500 per month towards educational expenses,"[23] how much more can we do today when so many more African Americans earn substantially more than blacks did then? African Americans today cannot feel any more disenfranchised than those of the 1860s who had not won the right to vote, who were restricted from most educational decisions, and who, on the whole, were prevented from earning the money necessary to feed their families, let alone to fund schools. Poverty and lack of education cannot be parents' excuse for not demanding better schools. We had much less in 1914 than we have in 2014, yet the zeal for equity raged in the African American community 100 years ago. Lynchings were frequent, yet African Americans spoke out. No longer victims to other people's decisions, our power must come from within, from the recognition that we have more opportunities, resources, rights, and possibilities than any other generation of African Americans before us. Equity is not in the interest of those in power in a capitalist economy. Therefore, the demand for change must originate from within our own community, build momentum through partnerships with other underrepresented groups, and establish relationships with allies who currently hold decision-making power until more people who understand the issues of African American children are the decision makers. We must regain a sense of urgency that without drastic measures, our children and our communities will deteriorate precipitously to the point that more government intervention in schools will occur and more inadequate and inappropriate curriculum and pedagogy will be instituted in the name of "saving schools."

A segment of this "power in community" has to come from a traditional base among African Americans, the church. African Americans still attend church in high numbers; thus, the opportunity for local churches to assist parents in meeting children's needs remains high. After discussing the school's needs with the staff, churches and other religious institutions can provide supplies, large equipment items, and volunteers to schools. They can establish after-school mentoring programs that will bolster students' social and emotional needs. At the church itself, members who are educators can lead informational sessions for families, tutor students, and fundraise for local schools. Just as in the case of the civic groups, education needs to be a structured element in the church's organizational plan and discussed at church meetings wherein a committee is charged with monitoring, reporting, assessing, and, hopefully, meeting, school needs. Clearly, the practices listed here are not new ideas; African Americans had done them in the segregationist era out of desperation for their children. These efforts are present in pockets throughout the United States. However, a widespread, multifaceted, relentless work by African Americans for African Americans to no longer accept low student achievement is essential. Parents have to understand specifically what their role in the education of their children should be in order to reverse chronic underachievement.

Schools must see parents as a key element in the success of their schools and encourage and educate parents as to how this complex system works from educational legislation all the way to the classroom desks. Schools should be accountable to the parents of the schools' students, not board members or district offices. A major goal needs to be determining the root cause of the lack of parent involvement in schools. Parent surveys do not provide a complete understanding—canvassing the community door to door, setting up informational tables at local grocery stores, meeting parents where they go most frequently will enable schools to deepen their understanding of how parents are thinking about their children's education. African Americans must regain the feeling of ownership of schools to which Fairclough (2004) refers. Only then will parents develop the necessary resolve to fight for the best that schools can offer. Facilities will be better maintained. Outdated curriculum resources will be replaced. Ineffective teachers will be forced to improve or resign. Administrators will be challenged to believe in children's abilities and create a culture of excellence. School boards will be pressured to make appropriate decisions on behalf of students, not based on their political leanings. State legislators will be forced to hear parent concerns. This happens in private and charter schools because parents are highly engaged in the educational process. However, these actions do not have to be limited to those schools. With effort and strategic thinking, large public schools can also experience high parental engagement, not just in extracurricular activities such as athletics or clubs but in the academic life of a school. Although speaking about schools in the South, perhaps Rucker and Kaleen (2007) may have stated best what all predominantly African American schools need when they argued,

> Perhaps, then, the most effective model for education in the Black South would be one which combines the best elements of the education paradigms articulated by Washington, DuBois, Cooper and Reconstruction-era Black

Georgians, in this regard, an effective synthesis of these approaches would include: a) the development of educational institutions that are owned and controlled by the communities in which they are situated; b) the creation of effective high school and college curricula combing vocational training and liberal arts; c) the development of a curricular emphasis on the cultural traditions, history and literature of Africans and their diasporic (sic) descendants; and d) the establishment of organic links between schools, at various levels, and their surrounding communities.[24]

Conclusion

Some might view this chapter as supporting a more conservative agenda, one that releases whites from any responsibility for the creation and perpetuation of racist beliefs, while placing all of the responsibility on African Americans to rectify the present situation. However, that is not the case. This was written as a Call to Action, a reminder of what we, as African American people, were able to accomplish in the face of unbelievable circumstances and a charge to no longer settle for less than the best for our children. As a public school administrator, I have seen the complacency in parents that has led to children not having the maximum opportunities possible for their education. From not keeping updated records so that schools can contact them to not arranging parent–teacher conferences when their child is not doing well, many parents contribute to their children's underachievement through negligence alone. The parents who are connected and active focus on their children in particular and do not necessarily work to transform the educational system for the betterment of all children. Parent–Teacher Association (PTA) membership in underperforming schools is quite low. Often this agency can both pressure schools to improve and support schools that are trying to improve. Without members, however, it is impotent. Parents cannot assume schools are always doing what is best for students, even if school administrators and teachers are African American. They must monitor and question school goals, policies, and procedures. Previous generations of African Americans did not trust their children's futures to anyone—they took responsibility for leading the change they wanted to see, in the face of nearly insurmountable circumstances.

Moreover, we cannot continue to allow government agencies to determine what our children need. Obviously schools cannot run without the billions of dollars allocated to them each year by local, state, and federal governments; we need government funding. Yet we can impact the ways in which and to whom those dollars are allocated. Although the courts determined in *San Antonio v. Rodriguez* (1973) that education is not a fundamental right, it is certainly a fundamental expectation of American citizens that government provide some form of public schooling for its children. The government's role should be to provide the resources and oversight of the use of the resources for an educational agenda that is set by the combined efforts of educators and parents. We cannot rely entirely on the government, nor can we release the government from any responsibility toward our children. Victimization cannot be a part of our ethnic community's psyche. However, the truth of the inequalities in the current educational system cannot be overlooked. We must speak truth to power and continue the struggle begun so very long ago. Cann (2004) interprets recent court decisions in this way:

> "By Scalia's reasoning, if the result is resegregation, there is not much government can or should do about it. Thus, what justice Henry Billings Brown argued for the majority in Plessy is what Justice Scalia argues today: the authority of government stops when it has provided for political and legal equality of the races and is has no responsibility to ameliorate the racial cleavage." Considering the Court's view of the government's role in remedying current patterns of resegregation, African-Americans have no choice but to actively engage in this fight for school equity.[25]

African American civic, religious, community, parental, and educational groups must press those local school boards to determine appropriate policy. Different ethnic and socioeconomic groups have distinct needs; therefore, local school boards must recognize this and set policy accordingly. We should all continue to work to diversify schools. Nevertheless, given the current demographic homogeneity of cities and suburbs and the reluctance of people to live in integrated communities, the focus must be on the current reality. Without ignoring the need for alliances with other ethnic groups, African Americans must identify our specific needs and collaborate with those allies to achieve the goals that serve all students. We cannot expect people outside of the ethnic group to fully understand those needs without a process of informing them. Oates (2009) summarized it this way, "Those who have the best interests of Black communities in mind should be the ones who make the decisions regarding the role and place of educational institutions in the Black South."[26] Oates spoke of the Black South, but the statement applies to all regions of the United States where African American communities exist. A diversity of people may have the best interests of black communities in mind; however, we, as African Americans, should have the primary interest in the schools that serve our children. These are our children and no one should care for them more than we do. African Americans who lived in the segregation era understood this. We must reclaim that sentiment and act.

Notes

1. Fairclough2000, p. 77.
2. Green 2004, pp. 268–284.
3. Irvine and Irvine 2007, pp. 297–305, 524–525.
4. Green 2004, p. 267.
5. Fairclough 2004, p. 49.
6. Ryan 2014, p. 23.
7. Irvine and Irvine 2007, p. 299.
8. Wiley 1994.
9. Ibid., pp. 43–44.
10. Wiley 1994, p. 30. Wiley notes that Southern and border states saw a loss of more than half of the black principals and the dismissal of more than 6,000 black teachers the year after Brown I was issued.
11. Cann 2004, p. 77.
12. St. C. Oates 2009, pp. 416–441.
13. Irvine and Irvine 2007, p. 299.
14. Fairclough 2004, p. 47.
15. Fairclough 2000, p. 65.
16. Fairclough 2004, p. 46.
17. Oates 2009, p. 438.
18. Wiley 1994, p. 30.
19. Fairclough 2004, p. 47.
20. Fairclough 2000, p. 65.
21. Irvine and Irvine 2007, p. 301.
22. Jordan-Taylor 2010, pp. 92–100.
23. Rucker and Jubilee 2007, p. 157.
24. Ibid., p. 164.
25. Cann 2004, p. 78.
26. Rucker and Jubilee 2007, p. 166.

Bibliography

Cann, Steven. 2004. "Politics in Brown and White: Resegregation in America." *Judicature* 88 (2): 74–78.

Fairclough, Adam. 2000. "'Being in the Field of Education and Also Being a Negro . . . Seems . . . Tragic:' Black Teachers in the Jim Crow South." *The Journal of American History* 87 (1): 65–91.

Fairclough, Adam. 2004. "The Costs of Brown: Black Teachers and School Integration." *The Journal of American History* 91 (1): 43–55.

Green, Paul. 2004. "The Paradox of the Promise Unfulfilled: Brown v. Board of Education and the Continued Pursuit of Excellence in Education." *The Journal of Negro Education* 73 (3): 268–284.

Irvine, Jacqueline, and Russell Irvine. 2007. "The Impact of the Desegregation Process on the Education of Black Students: A Retrospective Analysis." *The Journal of Negro Education* 76 (3): 297–305, 524–525.

Jordan-Taylor, Donna. 2010. "African-American Educators Misconstrued." *The Journal of African-American History* 95 (1): 92–100.

Meier, Kenneth, Joseph Stewart, Jr., and Robert England. 1989. *Race, Class, and Education: The Politics of Second-Generation Discrimination.* Madison, WI: University of Wisconsin Press.

Rucker, Walter C., and Sabriya Kaleen Jubilee. 2007. "From Black Nadir to Brown v. Board: Education and Empowerment in Black Georgian Communities— 1865-1954." *Negro Educational Review* 58 (¾): 164–168.

Ryan, James. 2014. Brown at 60 and Miliken at 40. *Ed. The Magazine of Harvard Graduate School of Education,* Summer, 23.

Sitkof, Harvard. 2001. "Segregation, Desegregation, Resegregation: African-American Education, A Guide to the Literature." *OAH Magazine of History* 15 (2): 6–13.

St. C. Oates, Gary. 2009. *An Empirical Test of Five Prominent Explanations for the Black-White Academic Performance Gap.* New York: Springer Science+Business Media, May 2009, pp. 416–441.

Wiley III, Ed. 1994. "Black America's Quest for Education: The Euphoria of the 'Brown' Decision Has Fade to Reveal Recurring Problems of Access and Inequality." *Emerge* VIII: 30.

Chapter 13

The Case for a Social Justice Context

Tema Okun

Teaching our students in a culture still reeling from the legacy of centuries of structural, cultural, and personal racism without grounding them in a social justice context is like

    (a) calling for "diversity and inclusion" without asking who's being included into what and on whose terms;

    (b) using "multiculturalism" as code for "celebrating" differences without talking about oppression;

    (c) defining student "success" primarily as the ability to go to college, get a job, and make money;

    (d) all of the above.

As educators, we are living, teaching, and leading in a time where on the one hand we acknowledge the serious achievement and opportunity gaps between students of color and their white peers while on the other we are unwilling to address the historic legacy of racism responsible for this gap. In most education settings, we talk about how to "help" students of color be more "successful." Diversity and inclusion are invoked to suggest that the goal is to celebrate or acknowledge diversity in order to include students of color into a white world.

My purpose with this chapter is to make the case for an acknowledgment of our racist legacy, a legacy that calls us to place ourselves as educators squarely in a social justice context. Celebrating diversity without helping students understand that every institution in this country participated in (and continues to perpetuate) a construction of race as a hierarchy designed to validate whiteness at the expense of other racialized categories does not serve any of our students well. Defining "success" as the ability to go to college in order to get a "good" job without regard to how that job may perpetuate inequity does not serve any of our students well.

I am not suggesting that we should be unconcerned about the ability of people to earn enough money to house, feed, and take care of themselves. I am aware that African Americans in college now have to earn higher levels of degrees than their white peers to achieve the same probability of procuring a job. I am also aware that each degree achieved increases the potential wages of the job seeker, in some cases proportionately higher when the job seeker is a person of color.

I am, nonetheless, suggesting that education, like race, is a construct. We have a responsibility to those we teach, to ourselves for that matter, to make sure we are providing an education that provides more than a job. Specifically, I point to educator Sonia Nieto's four aspects of a social justice education. She argues that we have a responsibility to educate in ways that encourage our students to challenge misinformation that perpetuates structural inequity, support students to live into their full potential through access to resources and skill-building, recognize and pull from the cultural capital that each student brings (regardless of dominant culture beliefs about the value or lack of it), and build learners with critical (and compassionate) thinking and practice.

The Current Context

I invite you into any one of my classrooms—undergraduates preparing for a teaching career, experienced teachers seeking a master's degree credential, or a doctoral cohort of administrators. In every case I ask students to create a list of the most pressing challenges that we as a local, regional, national, or global community face in our current historical moment. Undergraduates might name poverty and doctoral students point to structural economic disparities; regardless of the varying sophistication of their analysis, the list they create inevitably incorporates issues related to the inequitable distribution of resources, the environment, health care, gender and violence, war, dwindling access to and quality of water, housing, globalization, and access to education. Sometimes the list includes racism, sexism, homophobia, ableism, and other oppression issues tied to the ways in which some identities are validated while others are disparaged. When I follow up by asking what our K-12 schools—public, private, charter—are currently doing to help us prepare for these challenges, to bring a social justice lens to these issues, my students become restless and then silent, a silence that deepens as they come to the collective realization that at best, we are helping a particular individual acquire the necessary skills to be successful enough to make a contribution as yet unknown or named. Certainly we are not providing the kind of education that Nieto outlines earlier; we are not preparing ourselves for a collective dive into the long-term problem solving that will help us create a critical and compassionate community where we know how to care for each other and our world.

For the most part, our schools are stuck in the task of fulfilling a vague promise of a job whose unstated yet powerfully assumed purpose is to support an unsustainable standard of living that encourages us to consume at ever higher levels.

Our schools operate (and always have) as one part of an economic construct that designs every economic transaction to insure that "higher profits trump all else," regardless of the cost to the larger community.[1] As a result, our cultural definition of "success" is a narrow focus on individual ability to profit economically while ignoring the people and communities who pay the cost, which is a major reason we end up with the list that students create in my classrooms.

We are living and teaching and working in the midst of an economic system posited by those in power as irrefutable. This economic system depends on a series of constructs—race, gender, class, among others—that work together to weave a complex web of structural and cultural justification for serving a few at the expense of most of us.

Education has played, and continues to play, a key role in these intricate and interdependent constructions.

Writer and social critic James Baldwin, in his 1963 letter to teachers, describes how the "crucial paradox" of education "occurs within a social framework . . . designed to perpetuate the aims of society," which is essentially "a citizenry which will simply obey the rules."[2] Baldwin is speaking about how schools teach us how and what to think about ourselves and our role in society. Joel Spring, author of over 20 books investigating the history and role of U.S. education, wants us to understand that public schools were established to teach a common set of values, including unquestioning patriotism, the "Americanization" of newly arriving European immigrants into the Protestant ethic, and compliance in order to create a workforce prepared to serve the profit engines of business.[3]

Schools "play a central role in the distribution of particular knowledge."[4] This knowledge is not "neutral" and is most often constructed to serve those in power. As critical historian James Loewen notes, we may think that "education's main function is to promote inquiry,"[5] but in its role as the great socializer, schools tell us what to think, how to act, and, most important, how to conform. This construction of schools as "managers of ideas and cultural values"[6] is supported by a dominant narrative, an education "speak" that concentrates on defining successful students as those who contribute uncritically to an inequitable economic system.

Public schooling has always played a "sorting" role, where students are essentially "assigned" or socialized into their futures; the education a child receives indicates at a glance the role that student is assumed (and assigned) to play in this system. Children of the poor, particularly black and brown children, are pushed out of school or into the prison system; the children of the working class are taught to obey,[7] the children of the vanishing middle class are squeezed between anxiety about what kind of job will actually pay a living wage and whether they can find or hold onto one in an increasingly competitive economy, while the children of the educated upper class are trained to either lead (to rule) or live into their creative desires (a highly privileged choice).

One of the many ways I know this is true is because whenever I teach about intersections of race and class to undergraduate students, whether in a public university where students are often the first in their families to go to college or in an elite private university, I have to undo the damage of deeply racist and classist cultural conditioning that has students believing poverty is caused by a lack of willingness to work hard that is in its turn a reflection of low morals housed mostly in the bodies of black and brown people. Counteracting these internalized messages can be challenging, particularly when the rhetoric has been deeply absorbed, even by those who are the subject of the message.

Another way to see the role that education plays in conditioning us into unquestioning obeisance is to look at what our culture assumes as "normal" in our system of education. We can identify "normal" in two ways—through either how a behavior and attitude is accepted without question or protest (normal) or how a behavior and attitude is consistently punished (not normal, therefore defining normal). So, for example, our culture accepts as normal the reality that African American, Latino, and Native American students are disproportionately suspended or expelled.[8] Our culture accepts as normal the reality that our "gifted and talented" classrooms are filled with white students[9] while our black and brown students "are far more likely to be subjected to harsh punishments in school than whites"[10] including attending schools with greater levels of surveillance.[11]

Our culture accepts as normal that the young white women who are the majority demographic of those going into classrooms to teach young black and brown children do not understand how their race and/or the race of their students is relevant to their teaching and the students' learning. Most young white women come into their preservice classrooms believing they are inherently qualified to help the black and brown children they will teach. At best, they understand their "helping" role as smoothing the way for black and brown children to assimilate into their world. They almost always lack any understanding of the complexities of racism, either structurally or in its daily manifestations. Instead, they assume (like most white Americans do) that their lack of racist intent and their desire to be one of the *good* and "color-blind" white people is enough and thereby perpetuate the very racism they are so sure is a thing of the past.

Our culture accepts as normal how most schools of education either do not offer courses that support teachers to better understand the complexities that race, class, gender, sexuality, ability, and disability play in our lives and our classrooms or, as was true in my doctoral program, turn the one required class focused on these topics into an elective in order to find more room in students' schedules for classes focused on how to teach to the test.

Our culture accepts as normal the ability of our schools to operate without any explicit talk about race and racism and instead to position success to mean students who get good grades (as opposed to students who are curious and engaged, critical and compassionate), go to college (as opposed to identifying the longings and interests that will drive their lives), and enter the workforce (as opposed to finding meaningful work that balances individual skills and desires with responsibility to their community). Most of our schools teach an assimilation curriculum, aimed at helping students of color "succeed" in the same ways that success is defined for white children—going to college so they can engage more fully in an economic system set by and designed for the country's economic and political power brokers.

When dominant cultural rhetoric does address race or race equity, one of many unspoken assumptions is that the focus and benefit of equity efforts are on and for students of color; in other words, the goal of race equity is to help students of color become more successful, a kind of success determined by a school system and culture that both supports a very narrow view of what success means and refuses to acknowledge the social/political needs of those on the receiving end of system oppression. The accompanying assumption is that white students, particularly those who are middle

and upper middle class and get good grades, are better prepared to participate in the world, get good jobs, make good money, and consume without
acknowledgment or concern about their inherited privilege.

All we have to do is look at the school systems—public, private, and
charter—responsible for teaching our children. When we look at schools
serving predominantly white students, we rarely find curriculum that supports these students to understand what it means to be white in a racist society.[12] When we look at "integrated" schools or schools serving black and
brown children, almost without exception, they, too, are failing to teach a
curriculum that embraces frank race talk, speaks to the potential for a liberatory approach to teaching and learning, or offers even a version of culturally relevant curriculum.

Operating in this environment without a social justice lens means even
the most well-meaning teachers participate in an assimilationist approach
that fails to serve any student. Our role, our responsibility as teachers, is to
disrupt the dominant narrative and give our students a chance to remember what it means to engage critically and compassionately with the world.
Baldwin, in his letter to teachers, points to what the society actually needs,
which is a citizenry able to "examine society and try to change it and to
fight it."[13]

The Case for a Social Justice Lens

The late historian Howard Zinn proposed an alternative "master narrative,"
one that would highlight "the continual struggle of people for justice, the
continual struggle of people for equal rights," noting how this theme of
struggle "runs all through history."[14] Educator and writer Charles Payne
frames the possibility of an education "intended to help people think more
critically about the social forces shaping their lives and think more confi-
dently about their ability to react against those forces"[15] and, I would add, to
shape them. What might be possible in our classrooms if we looked at the
history of the United States "as one long struggle for justice by the majority
of the American people against a small elite of slave owners, of bondhold-
ers, of rich people who have so far dominated our political system and who
so far have monopolized the wealth of this country?"[16]

In my teaching, I encourage white students to think about how often we,
in our role as teachers, holding no racist intent or lacking structural analysis of how racism operates, perpetuate racism precisely because we are unaware of how it manifests institutionally (structurally), culturally, and in

our own socialized conditioning. Our dominant culture supports the notion that if we wake up in the morning without the intent to be racist or to perpetuate racism, if we declare our intent to be one of the good "nonracist" white people, then many if not most of us assume racism is not happening. People of color are not immune to participating in the perpetuation of racism; more and more students come into classrooms assuming a level playing field, largely because the dominant cultural rhetoric of individual responsibility and blame has robbed them both of language to talk about their own experiences of racism and of knowledge about their ancestors' brave struggles to provide education and opportunity against overwhelming odds.[17]

Teaching about race and racism requires separating intent from impact and helping us all to see what we are well trained to ignore—that we perpetuate the very oppressions we claim to abhor through our ignorance of how they actually manifest. One reason I argue for the importance of a social justice context is because that context requires us, in our role as teachers, to place ourselves in that context and understand how oppression operates.

One of the most critically important concepts I teach to help students develop agency toward their own potential for social justice practice is something I learned from Viktor Frankl's seminal work on freedom. In this work, he defines freedom as the space between what happens to us and how we choose to respond.[18] A World War II Holocaust survivor, Frankl was a psychotherapist when he was shipped to the first of several concentration camps; as he lived through his own suffering, he observed those imprisoned with him, noticing how some were more free than their guards because of how they used that space, small as it was in that time and place.

As teachers committed to social justice working in systems that are not, we need to consider how to recognize and use the space between what's happening to us in our schools and how we choose to respond. And we need to help our students do the same.

Our first responsibility as educators is to educate ourselves, to make sure we are grounded in an understanding of what it means to teach or lead in a system that assumes assimilation rather than justice is the goal. We need to make sure we have a strong understanding of how our personal identities and experience frame and inform our worldview; we need to be clear about our own relationship to our racial identities and to the role racism has played in forming them. Instead of reproducing an ideology and practice where to be white in American is not to have to think about it, those of us who are white can take responsibility for understanding structural and cultural racism and the role that white privilege and internalized white superiority has played in shaping us. Instead of adhering to the dominant culture practice of focusing on acts of racism performed by individuals (e.g., the recent brouhaha over NBA team owner Donald Sterling's extremely racist comments), we need to develop our ability to identify and understand the pervasive systemic racism embedded in our institutional practices (look at any of the statistics related to income, wealth, education, housing, employment, health care). We can also take responsibility for helping our students get acquainted with their own conditioning, teaching them to see education as constructed, as anything but neutral, so that they can begin to think critically and compassionately for themselves.

We can look to the many examples offered by those who have walked this path before us. We can turn to teachers like Mary Ann Cowhey, who offers a social justice curriculum to her first and second graders.[19] She describes how she "critically teaches" young first and second graders based on questions they pose for themselves and learn to answer in ways that challenge the dominant culture narrative of assimilation. We can learn from Brian Schultz who organized his fifth-grade classroom in an urban Chicago school to develop the year's curriculum based on replacing their dilapidated school building,[20] a problem the students themselves identified as the pressing issue that they wanted to address.

We can pursue resources created by educators and teachers who are deeply committed to a social justice approach to education. Rethinking Schools[21] provides culturally relevant, social justice curriculum guides on a whole host of topics. The Algebra Project,[22] founded by former Student Nonviolent Coordinating Committee leader Bob Moses, builds on the lessons of the Freedom Schools, using everyday issues to engage students in a rigorous math curriculum. The Algebra Project birthed in its turn the Young People's Project, which promotes math literacy as a tool for social justice activism. Teaching for Change[23] hosts the Zinn Education Project website, among others, offering a range of materials to support teachers and students to explore an alternative master narrative grounded in a social justice agenda.

I am not suggesting this is easy, only that it is necessary. Brian Schultz notes that "in justice-oriented classrooms, the risks for teachers and students potentially multiply" as teachers put themselves in the "line of fire" of teachers and administrators and even parents discomfited by such approaches.[24] Howard Zinn talks about how we have to "play a kind of guerrilla warfare with the establishment in which [we] try not to be fired."[25] Given the risks, this is not a solitary activity.

Because of our cultural emphasis on individualism, both we and our students are well conditioned into the compelling myth of the solitary "hero" story, where we think of activism as a solo activity; many of us have little experience of the collective as a vehicle for social change.[26] In addition, most of our new teachers and their students have no living memory of organized resistance, having been born years, even decades, after the peak of the powerful civil rights, labor, farmworker, and women's rights movements. Some may have experience with organizing for the environment or for gay/lesbian/bisexual/transgender/queer rights, although these experiences tend to be isolated from the larger social context of resistance so present in the 1960s and early 1970s.

This means that when we, or our students, do act, we often make it easy for those in power to marginalize or target us. To counter this, we must learn to develop what I call "organizing mind" and educator Parker Palmer calls "a movement approach."[27] These approaches encourage us to find others who think like we do, who share our values and desires and longings for meaningful learning in the service of justice. Then we work together to collaborate and consolidate and console and act. As our energy builds, we draw in and reach out to others who are excited by the possibilities that we are creating.

So, for example, I look to a whole host of educator activists and organizations using organizing approaches to build communities, networks, and coalitions. We can draw from the example of the early Freedom Schools of the 1960s, which trained teachers to use popular education strategies to teach reading, writing, and arithmetic skills while also incorporating history and civics lessons aimed at preparing whole communities of people to fight for their civil and human rights. We can look to Arizona's Education for Liberation Network and its Teacher Activist Groups, who along with brave students, stood up to challenge a local school district's ban of their successful Mexican American Studies program. We can look to the courageous DREAMers, who risk deportation to stand up for their rights to an education. I can look out my backdoor to the inspiring and courageous work of Organize 2020 here in North Carolina, a growing group of educators fighting for public education, teachers', and students' rights in my home state.

Educating with a social justice lens requires rigor, from both the teacher and the student. To support ourselves and our students to be both critical and compassionate and to understand our responsibility to ourselves and each other require that we collaboratively develop multicultural and anti-racist curriculum and practice that is grounded in the lives of students, is visionary and joyful, is action oriented and culturally relevant.

Teacher and activist bell hooks talks about educating as "the practice of freedom" a practice that she exhorts any teacher can learn.[28] Our schools, our classrooms, and our individual bodies "should be laboratories for a more just society than the one we now live in."[29] Our world is in serious trouble and we need to anchor our students, and ourselves, in the sense of possibility that we can together live into a shared vision grounded in our shared commitment to social justice.

Notes

1. Barsamian 2014.
2. Baldwin 1985, p. 326.
3. Spring 2005, p. 4.
4. Ibid.
5. Loewen 2007, p. 350.
6. Spring 2005, p. 5.
7. Lubrano 2004.
8. National Center for Education Statistics 2010.
9. Barlow and Dunbar 2010.
10. Justice Policy Institute 2011.
11. Ibid., p. 22.
12. Bartoli and Bartoli 2014.
13. Baldwin 1985, p. 331.
14. Bigelow 2010.
15. Payne 2008, pp. 1–2.
16. Bigelow 2010, p. 23.
17. Perry 2003.
18. Frankl 1959.
19. Cowhey 2006.
20. Schultz 2008.
21. Rethinking Schools, http://www.rethinkingschools.org/index.shtml.
22. The Algebra Project, http://www.algebra.org.
23. Teaching for Change, http://www.teachingforchange.org.
24. Schultz 2008, p. 127.
25. Bigelow 2010, p. 23.
26. Okun 2010.
27. Palmer 1992.
28. hooks 1994, p. 13.
29. Lee 2007, p. x.

Bibliography

Baldwin, James. 1985. "A Talk to Teachers." In *The Price of the Ticket, Collected Non-fiction 1948–1985* (pp. 325–332). New York: St. Martins Press.

Barlow, Kathleen, and Elaine Dunbar. 2010. "Race, Class, and Whiteness in Gifted and Talented Identification: A Case Study." *Berkeley Review of Education* 1 (1): 63–85. Accessed June 30, 2014. http://escholarship.org/uc/item/247908gb.

Barsamian, David. 2014. "Noam Chomsky: On How the U.S. Breeds Inequality at Home and Instability Abroad." *The Sun Magazine* 462: 4–14.

Bartoli, Ali, and Eleonora Bartoli. 2014. "What White Children Need to Know about Race." *Independent School Magazine* (Summer). Accessed June 25, 2014. http://www.nais.org/Magazines-Newsletters/ISMagazine/Pages/What-White-Children-Need-to-Know-About-Race.aspx.

Bigelow, Bill. 2010. "One Long Struggle for Justice: An Interview with Historian Howard Zinn." *Rethinking Schools* 24 (3): 17–23.

Cowhey, Mary Ann. 2006. *Black Ants and Buddhists: Thinking Critically and Teaching Differently in the Primary Grades.* Portland, ME: Stenhouse Publishers.

Frankl, Viktor. 1959. *Man's Search for Meaning: An Introduction to Logotherapy.* Boston, MA: Beacon Press.

hooks, bell. 1994. *Teaching to Transgress.* New York: Routledge.

Lee, Enid. 2007. "Creating Classrooms for Equity and Social Justice." In *Rethinking Our Classrooms,* eds. Wayne Au, Bill Bigelow, and Stan Karp (pp. x–xi). Milwaukee, WI: Rethinking Schools, Ltd.

Loewen, James W. 2007. *Lies My Teacher Told Me: Everything Your American History Textbook Got Wrong.* New York: Touchstone.

Lubrano, Alfred. 2004. "Blue-Collar Roots, White-Collar Dreams: The Divided Soul of a Brooklyn Boy Who Straddles the Class Line." *Utne Reader* (March/April), pp. 76–80.

National Center for Education Statistics. 2010. "Status and Trends in the Education of Racial and Ethnic Minorities." Washington, DC: U.S. Department of Education. http://nces.ed.gov/pubs2010/2010015/indicator4_17.asp.

Nieto, Sonia. 2006. *Teaching as Political Work: Learning from Courageous and Caring Teachers.* Bronxville, NY: Sarah Lawrence College, Child Development Institute.

Okun, Tema. 2010. *The Emperor Has No Clothes: Teaching about Race and Racism to People Who Don't Want to Know.* Charlotte, NC: Information Age Publishing.

O'Sullivan, Rory, Konrad Mugglestone, and Tom Allison. 2014. *Closing the Race Gap: Alleviating Young African American Unemployment through Education, A Policy Brief.* Washington, DC: Young Invincibles.

Palmer, Parker. 1992. "Divided No More: A Movement Approach to Educational Reform." *Change Magazine* 24: 10–17. Washington, DC: Heldref Publications.

Payne, Charles. 2008. "Introduction." In *Teach Freedom: Education for Liberation in the African-American Tradition,* eds. Charles M. Payne and Carol Sills Strickland (pp. 1–11). New York: Teachers College Press.

Perry, Theresa. 2003. "Up from the Parched Earth: Toward a Theory of African-American Achievement." In *Young, Gifted, and Black: Promoting High Achievement among African-American Students,* eds. Theresa Perry, Claude Steele, and Asa Hilliard III (pp. 1–10). Boston, MA: Beacon Press.

Rothberg, Peter. 2012. "Challenging Arizona's Ban on Ethnic Studies." *The Nation* (February). http://www.thenation.com/blog/165989/challenging-ariz onas-ban-ethnic-studies.

Schultz, Brian. 2008. *Spectacular Things Happen Along the Way: Lessons from an Urban Classroom.* New York: Columbia University, Teachers College Press.

Spring, Joel. 2005. *The American School: 1642–2004.* New York: McGraw-Hill.

Spring, Joel. 2013. *American Education.* New York: McGraw-Hill.

Chapter 14

Critical Ethnic Studies and Women and Gender Studies: Education for Justice, Transformation, and Progressive Social Change

Margo Okazawa-Rey

Introduction

Current trends toward corporatizing the higher education system in this country, alongside spurious characterizations of U.S. society being "post-racial," "post-feminist," and replete with instances of "reverse discrimination," pose real threats to the existence of Ethnic Studies and Women and Gender Studies (ES/WGS), demanding an organized and systematic response. The purpose of this chapter is to discuss the origins and purposes of ES/WGS, to argue for their continuation, indeed their elevation, in the education of all undergraduate students in U.S. academies, in a nation that purports to be a multicultural democracy. Using an analytical framework that incorporates the intersections of race and gender and an understanding of capitalist processes, I seek to answer the following questions:

- What has been and is the role of ES/WGS in developing the consciousness of all students, supporting especially marginalized and underrepresented students, and advancing social justice as an educational goal in higher education?
- How have the original promise and purpose of liberation and social transformation in ES/WGS been affected by institutional politics and wider

neoliberal trends and agendas, including the co-optation of multicultural-ism, in higher education?

- Going forward, how must the institutional position of ES/WGS, alongside their theoretical frameworks and curricula, be changed to meet the challenges of the changing educational landscape and the deteriorating material conditions and rising inequalities that face people in the United States and around the world?

Although I will be employing the general term ES/WGS, it is important to acknowledge the variations existing in ES/WGS schools, departments, and programs across the United States. These variations include differences of structure, purpose, mission, political orientation, and faculty and student composition. Therefore, my argument should be considered in that light.

At the outset, I clarify three terms used throughout the paper: oppression, social change, and liberation.

Oppression

I draw on the work of feminist philosopher Iris Young who, in "Five Faces of Oppression," asserts that oppression is first and foremost a structural construct that affects *groups* of people *systematically*. Groups are oppressed because of

> unquestioned norms, habits, and symbols, in the assumptions underlying in-stitutional rules and the collective consequences of following those rules. . . . In this extended structural sense, oppression refers to the vast and deep in-justices some groups suffer as a consequence of unconscious assumptions and reactions of well-meaning people in ordinary interactions, media, and cultural stereotypes, and the structural features of bureaucratic hierarchies and market mechanisms—in short, normal processes of everyday life.[1]

Hussein Abdilahi Bulhan further argues:

> All situations of oppression violate one's space, time, energy, mobility, bonding, and identity. The oppressed finds his or her physical and psychological space unacknowledged, intruded into, and curtailed. The oppressed is not allowed any claim to territoriality nor is his or her privacy respected. Of the twenty-four hours of each day, there is less time the oppressed can call his or her own, to be used at will for self-development and/or leisure. . . . The movements of the oppressed are controlled and curbed. Equally crucial, his or her personal, as well as collective, identity is also challenged, undermined and confused.[2]

In short oppressed people face the loss and appropriation of identity, voice, and agency.

Progressive Social Change

Social change can be either progressive or retrogressive. Progressive social change is the struggle against oppression. It can take many forms, can vary with respect to the speed with which it happens and the degree to which the society is altered. One obvious kind of change occurs when regime change replaces one form of government with another, whether as a result of nonviolent or violent revolution. It was through this kind of change that dictatorship of President Hosni Mubarak in Egypt was replaced by another government in the "Arab Spring" of 2011. Revolution is only one kind of social change. Reform is also a process of change, albeit adaptive and more incremental, hence more acceptable to people in the main.

Reconstruction and *transformation* are other possible ways to create changes in a society. For both reconstructive and transformative processes, education and schooling are useful and necessary. Reconstructive and transformative processes change a society by changing individuals, groups, and communities in ways that develop their agency to become active participants in the struggle against oppressive structures and ideologies and, most important, to envisage alternatives and possibilities of a just society.

Liberation

According to Brazilian social activist and radical educator Paulo Freire, "Liberation is . . . the action and reflection of men [*sic*] upon their world in order to transform it."[3] Liberation through schooling and education rests on the assumptions that "the virtue of humanity is diminished when (an individual's) judgment is overruled by authority" and that one can be free only where "citizens are successfully trusted with the responsibility of judgment."[4] This particular kind of judgment is the ability critically to analyze definitions, explanations, and solutions to problems that one may have taken for granted or whose manifestations may have been accepted as inevitable, during the course of what Young refers to as "everyday life."[5] More generally, this critical judgment is the ability "to unveil reality."[6] To unveil reality, one must be able to generate and understand alternative possibilities. What C. Wright Mills calls "sociological imagination"[7]—the ability to see oneself and society from the perspectives of other times and places—makes the comprehension of alternatives possible. Liberation, however, takes more than judgment and imagination. It requires action. Persons, therefore, are liberated to the extent that they have the will as well as capacity to act, what Henry Giroux terms "civic courage,"[8] and to act in concert with others. Thus, an education that fosters judgment, imagination, and the capacity to act is an education that can liberate individuals and groups—a necessary precondition for progressive social change.

There are two basic premises underlying this paper:

(1) Education for liberation and for social change is an integral part of the overall actions for social change.
(2) Institutions of higher education can and must assume a share of the responsibility for creating justice, equity, and democracy in society because they remain foundational social institutions, define what counts as valid knowledge, and are the training grounds for future leaders/generations.

These premises then raise the following important questions:

(1) Is social change an appropriate purpose and role for schools?
(2) If schools ought to act as social change agents, how can and should they do so?

In the following section, I briefly trace the development of using schools and education as a vehicle for creating progressive social change in the United States. The focus is on analyzing and critiquing the institution of education from several perspectives, with particular attention to the work of critical theorists who maintain that schooling and education are possible sites for transformation despite the fact they are often accepted as institutions charged with maintaining the existing social order and, at times, a vehicle for reactionary interests.

Historical Perspectives on Education for Social Change

What are the purpose and role of schools? Since ancient times, Plato's *Republic* is evidence of his firm conviction that the state must take an active interest in the upbringing of children who were perceived, first and foremost, as future citizens and leaders of the nation. In his view, education is meant to develop character and moral and aesthetic judgment as they are conceived by the state. However, Plato was describing the ideal state, yet to be created, and its elite members.

In the 20th century, educators and the state have asserted various perspectives regarding the aims of education.[9] They have described the purpose of schooling and education, for example, as acculturating immigrants to the ways of the "new world";[10] as a means of preparing youth to enter the labor force; and as a mechanism for social control adapting youth to the existing social order. These views suggest, if not explicitly then implicitly, a conservative educational agenda that will maintain the existing order.

Alternative views, however, boldly hailed schooling and education as potential vehicles for social change during the Progressive Era in education in the United States, most notably in the 1920s and 1930s, and again in the era of student movements of the 1960s.[11] For example, they were seen as the great equalizer for enhancing individuals' and communities' opportunities for advancement and creating conditions for social equality.[12]

The Marxist school critics of the 1960s used the educational system's role in social reproduction as a basis for critique, rather than an accolade for schooling. They asserted that educational institutions merely reproduce the existing socioeconomic order characterized by structural inequalities based on class, race, gender, and other social ascriptions and that relations within schools replicate those in the wider society.[13] Accordingly, through shaping behaviors, values, and attitudes, students are being prepared to support the hierarchal, capitalist order. Consequently, students' self-image and social identity can thrive only when they match those presented from the dominant societal perspective. These critics of the 1960s argue that schools have no place in changing society and that only a revolution—large systemic changes—can adequately rectify the situation because, without systemic change, schools merely reinforce and reproduce dominant/subordinate social relations, unequal distribution of goods and power, and social stratification of the labor force and in the wider society. Despite the structurally deterministic view of some, educational institutions have been the sites of ongoing struggle for justice and equality, starting with challenges to the Slave Codes that outlawed teaching enslaved African people to read and write, to university education for women, to racial desegregation of public schools, and to the current battles regarding university Affirmative Action policies and the banning of teaching of ethnic studies in certain states in the United States.

The Rise of Ethnic Studies and Women and Gender Studies

In the United States, teaching about oppression, liberation, and social change in schools and universities and the development of critical and feminist pedagogies emerged out of the radical student movements of the 1960s. In this context, they are based on the premise that "educational institutions are the purveyors of American tradition and culture" and, therefore, that injustices and inequalities "should be addressed through educational systems."[14] The first to feel the initial impacts were the colleges and universities; the identified injustices of the times were racism and sexism.

Student protests against racist practices and structures began off campus, with civil rights groups such as the National Association for the Advancement of Colored People (NAACP), Southern Christian Leadership Conference, and Congress of Racial Equality, for example, and then moved to campuses when students began "to see the university as a key institution within the larger system of coercive institutions created by the established order to maintain control and perpetuate its role."[15] The first meeting of the Student Non-violent Coordinating Committee, led by Ella Baker, grassroots activist with NAACP and Southern Christian Leadership Conference and called "Fundi"—teacher, was held at Shaw University, an historically black university (HBCU).[16] Alongside involvement in political actions off campus, students demanded the inclusion of "relevant" courses in the traditional liberal arts curriculum as a way to challenge accepted ideas, values, beliefs, and assumptions about the lives of African American people in the United States specifically and about the social, political, and economic order in the wider world more generally. According to Maurana Karenga, many of the activists, in fact, saw Black Studies courses as "the most trenchant criticism and most definitive mirror of American society."[17]

Initially, changes in curricula were confined to the addition of single courses most notably black history and literature. By the end of the school year in 1968, after an intense and confrontational five-month strike, the radical multiracial coalition of students, faculty, and staff—the radical Third World Liberation Front (TWLF) based at San Francisco State College—succeeded in establishing the first Black Studies department in the country. In addition to curricular changes, the TWLF demanded changes in university policies, such as those governing student admissions and faculty hires, and in the "town and gown" relationships between the college and the surrounding communities, alongside curricular innovations.

The creation of the Black Studies Department at San Francisco State College (now San Francisco State University) forged the way for radical campus activists of color in other institutions. As R.H. Brisbane states, "By fall of 1968, the experiences of San Francisco State were being duplicated on dozens of campuses through the country"[18] and, one year later in the fall of 1969, leading HBCUs like Howard and Fiske and prestigious white institutions like Harvard, Yale, and the University of California in Berkeley and Santa Barbara had all established Black Studies. It is noteworthy that scholars such as W.E.B. DuBois and Carter G. Woodson identified the need for and conceptualized Black Studies decades before the rise of the movement in the 1960s. DuBois's work to include African American history began in 1896[19] and Woodson created Negro History Week in 1926.[20]

Martha Biondi has demonstrated the powerful impact of black student activists on colleges and universities across the United States. Following the trajectory of the multiracial coalition at San Francisco State College, black students challenged existing curricula and, more fundamentally, redefined the very purpose of higher education by demanding equity in student admissions and enrollment services and in faculty hiring, agitating to secure autonomous spaces for themselves, and establishing links with marginalized communities as part of their activism and scholarship and to overcome the separation of the university from the community.[21]

Victory in the black students' fight for recognition led to recognition of and similar demands by other students of color. The subsequent movements to include studies of other ethnic groups in the university curriculum challenged altogether the very nature of the liberal arts tradition. In *Black Studies: Pedagogy and Revolution,* Johnnella Butler captures the spirit of the movement:

> It is general knowledge that in the wake of the Afro-American struggle for Black Studies/Afro-American Studies programs and departments, other culturally and ethnically different groups followed suit; courses, programs, specialties began to appear throughout higher education. Simply by virtue of the recognition of information about the diverse cultural realities and ethnic variations in America, the definition of the Western heritage upon which the liberal arts tradition was found and which it was historically structured to convey became subject to change.[22]

As the struggles for racial justice and equality intensified through the 1960s and into the 1970s, the internal contradictions within the movements, namely around the "woman question," generated the women's liberation movement.[23]

Feminist student, faculty, and staff activists in the academy demanded the creation of women's studies as activists in the black, Chicano, Asian American, and Native American nationalist movements were doing. In 1970,

San Diego State University established the first Women's Studies department in the country. According to Mariam K. Chamberlain, in the beginning, women's studies course offerings were introduced as experiments in the forms of seminars and colloquia and no outside funding was available for curriculum development; hence, "the new courses were the result solely of volunteer efforts by pioneering feminist scholars on the faculty."[24] By 1974, over 4,000 courses were being taught by more than 2,000 faculty in nearly 1,000 institutions across the United States.[25] According to Chamberlain, the radical edge of the emerging field was "the willingness to share new teaching information in a new field (that) was unique to academe. . . . We read this willingness as an indication as the strength of the feminist ideology that had had spawned women's studies in the first place."[26] Equally far-reaching, these feminist scholars' focused attention on the development of liberatory pedagogies laid the groundwork for what has become a hallmark of WGS: feminist pedagogy that engages "the head, heart, and hands."[27] A decade or so later, lesbian and gay studies emerged in the 1980s, disability studies began to flourish in the mid-1990s, and, currently, queer studies (gay, lesbian, bisexual, transgender, and gender nonconforming people) is slowly gaining acceptance as recognizable academic fields of study.

Similarly, starting in the late 1970s, anti-imperialist scholars in independent postcolonial states in Africa, the Caribbean, Latin America, and India, alongside others in the respective Diasporas (including those in one or other form of exile from their own contexts), began building what would later become known as postcolonial studies. Their social theories and literary works, by definition, expanded and reframed the often-parochial conceptualizations of U.S. ES/WGS also to address the systemic forces of imperialism and colonization, and included seething critiques of less-than-democratic, and increasingly authoritarian independent states deemed to have fallen short of their original purpose. According to the Frankfurt Research Centre for Postcolonial Studies:

> Postcolonial Studies aims to explore the legacies and consequences of European colonialism in its various aspects—literal, figurative, spatial, historical, political and economic. . . . That which is often referred to as "modern Europe" is read as an outcome of colonial interaction, even as (former) colonies are understood as "laboratories of modernity." As an influential body of theory, Postcolonial Studies includes analyses of the political, economic and cultural developments in the global South as well the examination of the above-mentioned entanglements with the global North.[28]

In the new areas of study mentioned here, it can be inferred that the levels of excitement and curiosity must have been palpable, that faculty were compelled to read outside their own disciplines for more information and deeper understandings, and that, for the first time in the history of the academy, faculty and students institutionally could and had to focus on matters directly relevant to their own lives. Thus, the rallying cry of the women's movement, "the personal is political," was taught as central construct of not only women and gender studies but also ethnic studies.

Institutionalization of Ethnic Studies and Women and Gender Studies

During the 45 years that have lapsed since the creation of Ethnic Studies and Women's Studies courses and programs, activist scholars in U.S. academies have cut such a swath in the landscape of higher education that it has been possible for ES/WGS faculty to hold out the promise of liberatory education, particularly for undergraduate students. ES/WGS constitute ever-expanding and varying discourses and theoretical perspectives, interdisciplinary scholarship, research, and hundreds of programs and departments for undergraduate students and increasing numbers of masters and doctoral programs for graduate students.[29] Both have become institutionalized, that is, "become background . . . creat[ing] a sense of ease and familiarity, an ease that can also take the form of incredulity at the naiveté or ignorance of the newly arrived or outsider" who may not know of their existence.[30]

In the 1980s and 1990s, scholars in ES/WGS, along with feminist and critical theorists of education, published a plethora of articles, books, and research reports regarding theories, curricula, and ideas about pedagogy related to education and schooling for liberation and for social change and about the transformation of existing liberal arts curricula to align with those aims.[31] Faculty affiliated with these fields also formed professional organizations such as the National Association of Ethnic Studies and National Women's Studies Association and specific identity-based groups like the Asian American Studies Association, the National Association for Chicana and Chicano Studies, and the Society for Disability Studies, along with numerous identity caucuses within them, such as LGBTQ caucuses.

More recently, in 2000, a consortium of academics and institutions launched the historic Future of Minority Studies (FMS) Research Project based at Cornell University composed of an interdisciplinary and multigenerational group of scholars across the disciplines, administrators, and students at higher-education levels, from community colleges to liberal arts colleges and from HBCUs to elite universities such as Cornell and Stanford. According to the website, "FMS is organized as a mobile 'think tank' designed to facilitate focused and productive discussions across disciplines. These discussions focus on carefully defined questions about the role of higher education in a multicultural democracy and the need for an adequate conception of minority identities as the basis for progressive social change."[32]

The power and influence of ES/WGS on institutions and students are exerted in partnership with the identity-based, student-led clubs and organizations and the academic centers and institutes they generated. On many college and university campuses, academic programs and departments work closely with these entities to ensure student success and their quality of campus life, to support faculty and staff, to help provide an additional forum for the discussion of relevant issues, to organize for change, and to hold institutions accountable for their espoused commitment to diversity and inclusion. ES/WGS departments and programs and research centers that have dedicated themselves to these ideals affirm, inspire, and support the creation of new knowledges and methodologies, such as the loosely framed decolonizing knowledge and methodologies and, more recently, "research justice," for example, by knowledge-producers outside the established canons and beyond the academy. In short, as a result of prolonged and ongoing struggles about their legitimacy, value, and places in the academy, ES/WGS have been institutionalized on many campuses across the United States, to varying degrees.

Ongoing challenges remain to keep ES/WGS intact and maintain their integrity and legitimacy, however, particularly where they are not institutionally placed as autonomous departments, but rather left to rely on the beneficence of dedicated faculty and liberal administrators. They are rather precariously, sometimes problematically, ensconced within academic institutions and face three major threats: "culture wars," liberal multiculturalism, and internal controversies. The first, which has existed from the early days, is ES/WGS sitting as one of the most visible targets of the culture wars, where they have battled opponents to secure rights and entitlements for students marginalized by race and class including Affirmative Action, begun in the 1980s. The successes of ES/WGS have led to an outcry by reactionary forces that colleges and universities have been "taken over" by liberals, queers, people of color, and others heretofore considered "outsiders" despite the demographic statistics and experiences documented by women of color in the academy say otherwise.[33] Conservative and Right Wing opponents have succeeded in slowly dismantling many of the educational gains made in previous decades. The rollback of Affirmative Action policy at the University of Michigan[34] in one instance and the outlawing of teaching ethnic studies in Arizona are recent dramatic examples.[35]

Second, supporters of ES/WGS as autonomous formations argue that the trend toward multiculturalism and diversity on campuses also poses a threat to ES/WGS in several ways, although often well intentioned. Curricular integration projects seeking to "mainstream" ES/WGS perspectives and scholarship into traditional disciplines only add on and dilute content. Metaphorically, these efforts assume a "heroes and holidays" approach that includes simplistic content and relegates the content to a token position in the syllabus and highlights developments and achievements often most obviously during the months designated for "special interests" like ethnic and women's months.[36] Such critics argue that a shift to multiculturalism will co-opt ES/WGS and blur the boundaries between them and traditional disciplines by erasing their distinct curricular features such as concepts like structural inequalities, oppression, and colonization in favor of more acceptable ones like discrimination, prejudice, and immigration, thus "trivialize(s) the political claims of the discipline, reducing the analysis of power relations and their interventions to cultural celebrations and lessons in cultural competence."[37] Also, there is concern that specific interests of particular groups of marginalized people will be further erased under the rubric of "multiculturalism."

ES/WGS are, like the traditional disciplines, mired in internal controversies as well. The critiques are shaped by two, intertwined, strands: respective limitations and possibilities around boundaries of inclusion and exclusion that undergird identity politics.

The demarcation and definition of ES/WGS on the basis of ethnoracial and gender identifications as one of their central features is because of their genealogy of political activism that challenged the stratification and various forms of oppression and rooted in dominant classification systems established for the very purposes of stratifying and oppressing. Identity politics is the organization of political activism around particular identities and has its roots in successful social movements where activists asserted its epistemological and organizational necessity, as articulated cogently by the Combahee River Collective: "[F]ocusing upon our own oppression is embodied in the concept of identity politics. We believe that the most profound and potentially most radical politics come directly out of our own identity, as opposed to working to end somebody else's oppression."[38] Activists invoked identity as an important basis of knowledge and for knowing, and called for movements to be led by members of oppressed groups presumed to have firsthand knowledge and experience of the oppression that the movement seeks to eradicate. In the academic arena as well, identify politics has been "a grounding assumption" and has led to asking different kinds of questions across the disciplines than typically associated with them.[39] Such questions relate, for instance, to contemporary social issues that negatively affect many communities across the United States, such as economic inequalities, neoliberal economic policies, and immigration policies, as well as violence committed by the state and social actors.

The earlier theorizations of identity in the context of identity politics assumed essentialist racial and gender identities, thereby leading to essentializing effects and political splits within social movements and academia. Moreover, essentialist conceptualizations of identities ironically contributed to their maintenance, while proponents simultaneously critiqued the socially constructed social ascriptions on which they are based in the dominant sociopolitical order. Since then, identity politics has generated disfavor "from left, right, and center" of the political spectrum, according to Linda Alcoff and Satya Mohanty.[40] Gary Y. Okihiro argues that ethnic studies "lost its bearings in the thicket of identity politics and nationalism" and further argues that, in so doing, has essentially reproduced and fortified the dominant social relations:

> Black power and its permutations, an effective antidote to the poison of a colonized mentality and a radical declaration for self-determination, also bore the stain of white identity politics and programs of national and manly reconstitution. Patterned on nationalisms abroad and identity politics at home that promoted homogeneity and punished difference for the sake of solidarity, U.S. cultural nationalism among peoples of color pursued that same policing of the borders it struggled against, along with the nation-state's patriarchy and heterosexuality. As feminists of color have pointed out, cultural nationalism was saturated with patriarchy and homophobia, and in that way mimicked and formed alliances with the dominant order.[41]

Essentialist identity politics has similarly intervened into WGS programs:

> The dangers of identity politics and the threatening allegation of essentialism have fractured women's studies departments and programs. But disciplinary

identities can be as dangerous, such that the feminist literary critic or the feminist sociologist hearkens back to her disciplinary language and methodology, even as she is opposed to those disciplines' contents. What often happens now in women's studies programs is that the senior faculty continue their disciplinary identity, leaving the junior faculty to be the "identity reps" of racial and ethnic groups and fall prey to the charge of essentialism.[42]

The loosely illustrative essence of the often-repeated phrase, "all the women are white, all the blacks are men,"[43] captures the fact that, even now, white women dominate women and gender studies as men of color dominate ethnic studies. Moreover, both areas of study are limited by the parochialism intrinsic to U.S. academic disciplines in general, as transnational thinkers have rightly charged: "There is often a conflict between those faculty who 'privilege gender or gender and sexuality, as analytical frameworks, and those who also incorporate race, colonialism, and class.' . . . And often in the United States, globalization is little more than 'a Cold War production of knowledge,' which compares other areas to the United States to their detriment, continuing a dangerous U.S.-centrism."[44]

Although the authors mentioned earlier are criticizing women and gender studies, the charge of single focus and U.S. centrism applies to ethnic studies as well. In an April 2014 panel at the National Ethnic Studies Association Annual Conference in Oakland, California, Professor Angela Davis reminded the audience of the history of "problematic moments" that surfaced internal contradictions within ethnic studies, for example, resistance to including courses about gender and sexuality. She also recalled that those who "struggled for the institution" conceptualized it as "Third World Studies," reflecting internationalist perspectives and political commitments.[45]

The conditions of the formation of ES/WGS were conditions of social upheaval and hope for social change on a grand scale. The radical activists of the 1960s and 1970s—based on pursuing nationalist, internationalist, feminist, and socialist/revolutionary ideals—aspired to challenge the divisive patriarchal, capitalist system by mobilizing and organizing communities for significant change, albeit often in times parallel spheres. Educational institutions were one of the major sites of this struggle.

Neoliberal educational "reform" has divested higher education, working in synch with political conservatism, and changed the terrain to reactive instead of assertive, thereby undercutting the transformative potential of fields with radical births as described earlier. Concomitant political conservatism has ushered in academic conservatism. In this regard, for example, evaluations for tenure and promotion, that is, judging the value of the work and merit of faculty, are quickly reverting to conventional definitions and expectations of scholarship, even though the movement away from them was never radical. Gwyn Kirk and Margo Okazawa-Rey (2013) argue, for instance, that

> women's studies scholars are under pressure from the university system to undertake research and writing that meets "scholarly standards." This has meant that much published work is overly abstract and inaccessible to many readers. As women's studies has become more established and professionalized, it has tended to grow away from its movement roots. At the same time, women's studies remains marginalized and still under attack, as universities move closer to corporate goals, organizational styles, and funding priorities.

Incorporation and Absorption

Reemerging political conservatism in the academy, hence the blunting of the sharp political edges of ES/WGS, can be understood through the lenses of what Michael Omi and Howard Winant have described as the incorporation and absorption processes within institutions to end conflicts between it and their challengers and to co-opt potentially transformative social movements while simultaneously, in fact, changes are actualized.[46]

One of the notable contributions of ES/WGS is their role in the development of interdisciplinarity, one facet among several of what Roderick Ferguson refers to as "interdisciplines." Interdisciplinarity aims to challenge canonical definitions and structures of knowledge and episteme, and knower and known. Ferguson contends that the period of the 1960s and 1970s "occasion[ed] a change in power/knowledge" and "new disciplines arose to study previously excluded subjects."[47] The rise of interdisciplinary areas of study created unprecedented new opportunities and capacities to explore the lives, cultures, material conditions, histories, and politics of previously excluded peoples.

An unintended consequence of their institutionalization was the reshaping of ES/WGS into faux disciplines that "mimic" traditional academic disciplines, as the founders and later supporters "bargained" their way into the institutional structures that pre-dated them and were rooted in the separation of academic disciplines. This reshaping may have been unintended on the part of the founders of ES/WGS, but it could be argued that the universities allowed access only on these terms, even if that was not apparent in the beginning. As a result, the very regulation and management of knowledge and knower in traditional disciplines have been reproduced. Lisa Lowe considers this point:

> Institutionalizing such fields as Ethnic Studies still contains an inevitable paradox: institutionalization provides a material base within the university for a transformative critique of traditional disciplines and their traditional separations, and yet the institutionalization of any field or curriculum that establishes orthodox objects and methods submits in part to the demands of the university and its educative function of socializing subjects into the state.[48]

"Back to the Future": Threat of Advanced Corporatization

Today the most serious and insidious challenge to ES/WGS and, indeed, to the founding principles of the higher education system overall, is corporatization. As Steck argues, corporatization, "the entanglement of the business sector with the university," is not a recent trend but began in the 19th century during a time of great industrial expansion in the United States, when corporate interests influenced the governance of the university through seemingly benign ways such as the presence of corporate officials on boards of trustees, funding for buildings and programs, endowed chairs provided by wealthy donors, and the establishment of entire new institutions.[49] For example, Leland Stanford Junior University was birthed by a $24 million donation (at a time when a donation of thousands of dollars was considered significant) in memory of his deceased son, from the estate of Stanford Leland, California governor, U.S. senator, and wealthy railroad magnate.[50] During this period, Thorsten Veblen presaged the dilemma that higher education faces today: "The intrusion of business principles in the universities goes to weaken and retard the pursuit of learning, and therefore to defeat the ends for which a university is maintained."[51] In short, "the universities were obliged to meet the social and ideological needs as the captains of industry defined them."[52] Just as Western philosophers and natural scientists who challenged earlier worldviews and ideologies faced interference by religious leaders and institutions, political and social scientists who criticized capitalism and its related processes have faced threats to their expertise and academic freedom from the owners of capital and the governments that support them.

In the current era of neoliberalism, described by proponents of corporate investment in education as "an exciting and important time in our nation's history—one where private capital can earn attractive returns while facilitating the transformation of an outmoded educational system,"[53] curricula in the humanities, social sciences, and the liberal arts have been judged "unprofitable" and "irrelevant." Consequently, ES/WGS, heavily located both in two of these increasingly vulnerable disciplinary areas and in undergraduate-serving institutions, are under threat as the neoliberal educational agenda takes shape. Although the founders of ES/WGS were not naive to the power of capitalist and institutional processes, the dramatic shifts and the pace at which they have taken place could not have been foreseen, particularly in light of the economic expansion and the existence of radical political movements of those times.

Ethnic Studies, Women and Gender Studies, and Students

> First and foremost, the problem of oppression is a problem of violence. The violence may be crude or subtle; often it is both . . . those who monopolize and benefit from violence find it convenient to obfuscate and mystify the meaning and reality of violence. They enlist the services of religion, the law, science, and the media to confound and bewilder even the oppressed who otherwise would recognize that the social order is founded on and permeated by violence . . . this pervasive and structural violence is often masked and rationalized as the natural order of life.[54]

Liberation from mystification, violence, and oppression requires spaces to develop, think, and explore. Ethnic Studies and Women and Gender Studies have been able to create those spaces, however partial and imperfect, that function as a relatively "safe home" for many oppressed and marginalized students in higher education, as well as attracting students from dominant groups, despite the destabilizing and sometimes conflict-ridden external and internal forces noted earlier. ES/WGS, and their related entities like women's centers and research institutes, serve as important sites for students' projects of discovery and recovery—their cultures, histories, and themselves, in their homes, communities, and the wider world. I contend that the three most foundational impacts on students' personal and intellectual development through ES/WGS are their identity, voice, and agency.

Identity

According to Bulhan self-consciousness, a facet of existence, "is born of desire directed toward another human—namely, the desire for 'recognition' . . . the desire to have others affirm your values as theirs" and others' recognition "confirms one's self-worth, identity, and even humanity."[55] Further, he argues that "the highest ideal and most authentic self-validations derives from mutual and reciprocal recognition."[56] ES/WGS provide a site for the ongoing study, reconceptualization, and reconstruction of people's identities, typically in relation to changes outside the academy. For example, since "9/11" in the United States, "Arab" and "Muslim" have become synonymous for "terrorists" in all too many circles, with people so identified and classified facing the kind of hostility and violence that Bulhan described. Similarly, those who challenge the male–female gender binary face harsh questions and treatment from others and from institutions that uphold and require gender conformity and heteronormativity. In response, often initiated by the most affected students, new discussions and understandings are emerging outside and inside the classroom to benefit those directly affected as well as all the rest.

The spaces provided by ES/WGS courses, programs, and departments offer valuable opportunities for students to be recognized by others like them, and unlike them, to confront the challenge, confusion, dismissal, and maligning of students' identities especially as experienced in U.S. educational institutions. The following comments from students and a parent are illustrative:

> It's very important to have a sense of validation around experiences. Ethnic studies and women's studies reinforce that the personal is political (and vice-versa). Without this understanding people are in danger of isolation, confusion, self doubt, depression and much more. (Miranda Writes, personal communication, 2014)

Native American elder Red Haircrow reports the following:

> I think it is important they thrive as so many of our kids were receiving bullying, mockery and harassment in school, from elementary up to college age because of their native origins. Often school staff was dismissive of their concerns and the negative behavior towards them. Some expressed the fact they had begun to deny their heritage just to get by, or laughed at the jokes even if they were hurting inside. When they came together with other native students and learned about their cultures and peoples as an extended family, and supportive of what most of their parents were teaching them, most began to feel proud to be native in a positive way. (Red Haircrow, personal communication, 2014)

Voice

Student's voice in classrooms entails raising questions, expressing one's own ideas, challenging ideas of teachers and other students, and being willing to listen to others' voices. It also means being multilingual: having fluency in the languages of one's home, one's culture, and the academy where students engage and learn. Voice, however, is more than simply the act of speaking and being heard. It is a "linguistic marker"[57] of power, privilege, and oppression that sometimes identifies and marks the speaker, narrator, or writer as a member of a certain race, class, ethnicity, gender, sexuality, and other ascriptions and identities. Re(gaining) voice and discovering various ways to "speak" in ES/WGS spaces counteract the "silencing" so poignantly documented by numerous writers such as James Baldwin,[58] Gloria Anzaldua,[59] and Toni Morrison.[60]

> I initially took the studies out of curiosity and to satisfy liberal arts requirements for a well rounded education. As I became immersed in the coursework at the graduate level . . . I began to recognize the value of reading about multiple perspectives and hearing multiple voices, particularly those who have been pushed to the margins or overlooked in our social structures. What do these perspectives offer our world? What can these voices bring to our society and our world to make it a better place for greater social justice? When any group or groups are disadvantaged, our entire society and world lose out on their potential contributions. (Gloria Bravo Gutierrez, personal communication, 2014)

Agency

Agency is an individual and collective capacity to act and be actors in the world, rather than only be acted upon. Agency is to exercise self-determination. Consciousness and intentionality, along with identity and voice, constitute agency. Consciousness is a person's ability to reflect on his or her relations to and behavior and bearing in the wider world, and to observe the various and changing perspectives through which he or she faces reality.[61] Consciousness is often a complex combination of contradictory ideas, beliefs, and behaviors that may accommodate or resist the social reality of an individual's life, and sometimes the dialectic of accommodation and resistance creates tensions, resulting in moments of insight or mystification and magical thinking that enable or prevent the individual from seeing their reality clearly.[62] Intentionality concerns will, motivation, desires, and expectations that challenge the normative directives and mandates promoted by the state and the dominant structures and forces that shape societies.[63]

> My studies prepared me for life in a way that other majors don't and completely changed the way I think, watch TV, watch the news and interpret situations and experiences. For those who doubted the path I took, I can honestly say that every job I've ever had was because of what I chose to study. I don't work in academia and my two cents to academics would be to continue to bridge and strengthen the gap between academia and the real life applications and benefits of women's studies and ethnic studies. (Su Jin Lee, personal communication, 2014)

A core goal of ES/WGS is to support students' development in all three capabilities.

Just as ES/WGS face divisions and contradictions, students enrolled in ES/WGS experience conflict.

> I believe that as a woman of color that often my experiences with oppression have been experienced through the lens of race rather than gender. I have only experienced discrimination as a woman once. So taking classes and examining issues that women face helped open my eyes to issues that I probably would not have thought twice about. I think the issues or challenges with gender studies and feminism is that often it is discussed as though women are a monolithic group. And for me that is careless in that it ignores the struggles and challenges that women of color face. I also have observed that a lot of blame has been placed on men, which they do deserve a large share of the blame, but I feel that women need to accept some blame as well. In my life, most of the people who have encouraged and mentored me have been men. (Michaella Rey, personal communication, 2014)

Others never enroll for myriad reasons and some probably for reasons similar as the one reported here:

> I have never taken such studies, and here's why. The descriptions of the classes were hyper militant and did not appear to include future forward, supportive language. I have always been curious about women's studies, but only in how innovation and forward movement will occur in a way that is attainable and sustainable. (Colette Street, personal communication, 2014)

A foundational goal of ES/WGS is to teach students to *understand* their lives and the world around them in ways that will enable them to incorporate new understandings into their moral framework, a form of transformational learning, not just to know things intellectually and for technical applications such as in their jobs. This goal is built on the premise that such learning is necessary for the development of consciousness and agency and to be individual and collective agents of social change. However, as the preceding quote suggests, how do ES/WGS educators invite skeptical or hesitant students who would not even consider enrolling in our courses and, if they do, engage them in ways that will inspire possibilities and build confidence that their efforts can make a difference?

Critical Ethnic Studies and Women and Gender Studies and the Politics of Possibility[64]

The current seismic shift in the nature and purpose of higher education in the United States to advancing corporate agendas and the deteriorating social, political, and economic conditions for the largest segments of the world's peoples require generating possibilities for creative, imaginative, and effective collective and individual actions, locally, nationally, and transnationally, aimed at effecting progressive social change. What roles can and should ES/WGS play in doing so? As this chapter has shown, ES/WGS face formidable external and internal challenges in continuing to advance a progressive social change agenda. Nonetheless, as Sandra Harding asserts, higher-education institutions constitute a "fortuitous site" for training progressive student knowledge-producers and progressive social actors, host "truly multicultural student bodies with deep connections into most U.S. subcultures," and are a "rare site of possible meaningful political discussion in a surrounding world where such possibilities have been severely deteriorated in recent decades."[65] There do exist powerful, specific examples of Harding's fortuitous sites created by ES/WGS faculty and students:

> The Critical Ethnic Studies Association (CESA) aims to develop an approach to scholarship, institution building, and activism animated by the spirit of the decolonial, antiracist, and other global liberationist movements that enabled the creation of Ethnic Studies, and which continues to inform its political and intellectual projects. We seek to move away from current critical deadlocks, to counteract institutional marginalization, to revisit the political ideas that precipitated ethnic studies' founding moment within the US academy, and to create new conversations. (https://criticalethnicstudies.org/content/about)

The Democratizing Knowledge (DK) Project: Developing Literacies, Building Communities, Seeding Change . . . focuses on producing transformative knowledges and collectivities with the purpose of contributing to the growth of inclusive publics in higher education, in the workforce, and in the larger polity nationally and globally. A group of critical scholars from interdisciplinary programs and departments developed DK with the primary purpose of confronting white privilege, hegemonic masculinity, heteronormativity, and colonial heritages. (http://democratizingknowledge.syr.edu/)

The Critical Ethnic Studies Association (CESA) and Democratizing Knowledge Project (DK) are two formations challenging the deeply problematic results of institutionalization and legitimation of ES/WGS, such as an elitist, canonical orientation and the disassociation from the communities surrounding the institutions. Growing out of a recognition of the limitations of and contradictory, sometimes hypocritical, nature of some current aspects of ES/WGS, CESA and DK represent a dedicated effort to revitalize to face both the internal and external challenges described earlier in this chapter.

Critical Race, Gender and Sexuality Studies (CRGS) is an undergraduate program focused on the critical examination of race, class, gender, sexuality, dis/ability and nation as intersecting categories of identity, oppression and resistance. As a community of scholars, teachers and learners from the interdisciplinary fields of ethnic studies, women's studies and multicultural queer studies, we aim to create a just and sustainable world by analyzing systems of inequality and strategies for resistance. Our critical approach is intersectional and comparative; our focus is local, national, and transnational. This knowledge engenders transformative practices in research, creative work, and community activism. (http://www.humboldt.edu/crgs/)

The Critical Race, Gender, and Sexuality Studies at Humboldt State University in Northern California, founded in 2010, is an example of possibilities when the values, purpose, epistemological foundations, and aims of CESA and DK are translated into practice: "Ethnic Studies, Women's Studies, and Multicultural Queer Studies at HSU have a history of collaboration emerging from our shared commitment to intersectional analysis, emancipatory education, and social justice. For years, faculty and students in ES, WS and MQS have worked to create an interdisciplinary, innovative, and rich program that builds on our shared commitments and approaches, while simultaneously retaining the important and unique identity of each academic field."[66]

Although it is too soon to know the impacts of Critical Race, Gender and Sexuality Studies on Humboldt State University and the surrounding communities, its existence demonstrates that certain kinds of institutional change—in this case the redrawing of conceptual and programmatic boundaries—are possible. Other examples include the Department of Ethnic Studies at Mills College in Oakland, California, staffed entirely by women of color faculty with a curriculum that "promotes critical thinking and creative analysis through comparative study of the social, economic, cultural, and environmental concern . . . examine[s] racial dynamics as they intersect with gender, sexuality, class, and nation . . . many courses focus on the unique experiences of women of color. . . . explores the transnational and diasporic dimensions of racial identities,"[67] and the Public Science Project of the Center for Human Environments at the Graduate Center at CUNY, where "PSP researchers began their work as a coalition of activists, researchers, youth, elders, lawyers, prisoners, and educators, launching projects on educational injustice, lives under surveillance, and the collateral damage of mass incarceration. Most of these projects have been situated in schools and/or community-based organizations struggling for quality education, economic opportunities, and human rights. Knowledge-sharing research camps set the stage for most of this work, designed to bring together differently positioned people around a common table to design and implement the research."[68] It is hoped that these and other examples will inspire others to move similarly toward curricula and projects that are potentially transformative and committed to education for liberation and progressive social change.

The Politics of Possibility

Creating the kinds of changes suggested in this chapter requires ES/WGS faculty and constituents to generate principles of organization and movement-building that embody the core values of ES/WGS, most especially relevance and community roots, alongside related curricular innovations. These include drawing and redrawing permeable, moveable boundaries and borders; committing to a progressive "relational practice"; and developing imaginations that will enable visioning a democratic, just, and generative society.

Boundaries and Borders

The politics of possibility requires the redrawing of boundaries and borders that demarcate identities, fields of study, and distances between the college and university and community, as the very nature and purpose of such demarcations are interrogated. Are they to determine constituencies? To articulate important theoretical perspectives? To provide a sense of certainty? Or a starting point for conversation, teaching, research, building alliances? How permeable ought they be? What pitfalls need to be considered to prevent reinscribing and enshrining the kinds of boundaries and borders that exclude, shame, trivialize, and even demonize both insiders and outsiders, that canonize certain bodies of knowledge and methodologies, and that articulate and wield individual and institutional power as have been constituted historically?

To the extent that ES/WGS are identity based, the question of what kind of identities could serve as the basis for social movements and progressive social change is salient. Sandra Harding's notion of "sociological identities" is the result of "an account of processes of identity formation that are historically specific, to this time and place, without being completely determined by social structures. And, an account of subjects—collective identities—that are capable of transforming society and history."[69] Sociological identity can lead to "transformative identities" which, she argues, ought to be the basis of future social movements for progressive social change.[70]

Relational Practice

Sturdy, meaningful connections to local communities and transnational sites of struggle will help ensure the possibility of ES/WGS remaining relevant and current in an era of dramatic, seemingly instantaneous, deterioration in social, political, and economic conditions. These kinds of connections will provide opportunities for students, faculty, and people in the community to learn and teach together, to engage in analyses of material realties as "grounded, particularized analyses linked with larger, even global, economic and political frameworks,"[71] in other words, "in the real world." True connections will require meaningful engagements among multigenerational, transnational, and diverse groupings as one starting point and historicizing the current events and future possibilities by reaching into deep wellspring of knowledges brought by such groupings and "not just through oppression but in terms of historical complexities and the many struggles to change these oppressions"[72] thereby shaping Chandra Talpade Mohanty's notion of a "common context of political struggle."[73]

Consistently practicing and living the politics of possibility will require a "relational practice,"[74] which, by definition, is congruent with the progressive values espoused and a just future envisioned. Extrapolating from Fletcher's work, I argue that all the spaces named in this chapter—ES/WGS departments and programs, student organizations, research institutes, and community-based sites—are potential sites for individual and collective growth and development if and because they are founded on an expressed commitment to connection. Hence, the sites are potentially one very powerful place for Jean Baker Miller's "growth-in-connection" theory underlying Fletcher's work to be realized.[75]

Relational practice requires reconceptualizing practices and values typically disparaged in masculinist, individualistic, and goal-oriented academic settings specifically and U.S. dominant culture more generally, as necessary skills and ways of being for liberatory and transformative organization- and community-building. These include empathy, vulnerability, connection, and ability to listen deeply beyond spoken words, for instance. When consistently practiced, vulnerability allows us engaged in transformative learning or organizational-change work to identify contradictions often the result of structural inequalities and to examine our own complicities within the structures, for example. Such relational practice supports the growth-in-connection, which is foundational to establishing and maintaining the sturdy connections necessary for enduring alliances and solidarities within and across borders.

Imagination and Vision

Finally, at the core of the politics of possibility is ensuring that we, teachers, move beyond analyses to boldly and vividly imagining and envisaging a truly just and secure society. One of the most common laments and frustrations among students especially is that ES/WGS faculty and curricular content bear mostly, or only, "bad news" and criticism, whereby students suffer from "paralyses of analysis" that result in intertwined feelings of overwhelm (It's too big a problem . . .) and powerlessness (Nothing can be done . . .) and that blunt and undermine personal and collective agency. Students often ask us, "What other ways can we do things? Isn't what we have (in the United States) the best there is?" Maxine Greene eloquently captures these points when she states that the "general inability to conceive a better order of things can give rise to a resignation that paralyzes and prevents people from acting to bring about change. An accompanying sense of personal and communal efficacy may submerge people in the given, in what appears impervious to protest and discontent."[76]

To immerse in learning and understanding but not become submerged in powerlessness and despair demands being able to imagine multiple material realities, perspectives, and subjectivities that "will disclose multiple aspects of a contingent (not self-existent) world . . . to see beyond what the imaginer has called normal and 'common-sensible' to carve out new orders in experience. Doing so, a person [or a collective] may become freed to glimpse what might be, to form notions of what should be and what is not yet . . . and at the same time remain in touch with what presumably is."[77]

That is the promise of Critical Ethnic Studies and Women and Gender Studies 45 years on, in the 21st century.

Notes

1. Young 2011, pp. 39–65.
2. Bulhan 1985, p. 124.
3. Freire 1973, p. 62.
4. Elliott 1983, p. 111.
5. Young 2011.
6. Freire 1973, p. 68.
7. Mills 1959.
8. Giroux 1983. See also Giroux 1987, pp. 331–333
9. Labaree 1997. See also, for example, Giroux 1980.
10. Tyack 1974.
11. A lengthy discussion of the Progressive Era in education is beyond the scope of this chapter. However, it should be noted that the period spanned nearly 100 years, from just after the Civil War to the early 1950s, and included several philosophical positions. For more details, see, for example, Counts (1932), Cremin (1961), Dewey (1916), and Rugg (1947).
12. See, for example, Du Bois (1903), Washington (1903), Solomon (1986), and Wood (1981).
13. See, for example, Bowles and Gintis (1976) and Illich (1971).
14. Giles 1972, p. 1.
15. Karenga 1982, p. 18.
16. See Carson (1981) and Zinn (1964/2000).
17. Karenga 1982, p. 29.
18. Brisbane 1974.
19. Du Bois 1896.
20. Woodson 1933.
21. Biondi 2012.
22. Butler 1981, p. 2.
23. Evans 1979.

24. Chamberlain 1988, p. 138.

25. Ibid., p. 136.

26. Ibid., p. 138.

27. Kirk and Okazawa-Rey 2013.

28. Frankfurt Research Center for Postcolonial Studies.

29. Fenderson, Stewart, and Baumgartner, 2012.

30. Ahmed 2012, p. 12.

31. See, for example, Bunch and Pollack (1983), hooks (1994), and Schuster and Van Dyne (1985).

32. Retrieved from http://www.fmsproject.cornell.edu.

33. Gutiérrez y Muhs et al. 2012.

34. Liptak 2014.

35. Delgado 2013.

36. Lee, Menkart, and Okazawa-Rey 1998.

37. Okihiro 2010. See also, for example, Hu DeHart 1993.

38. Combahee River Collective 1978.

39. Alcoff and Mohanty 2006, p. 2.

40. Ibid.

41. Okihiro 2010.

42. http://science.jrank.org/pages/11660/Women-S-Studies-Controversies.html.

43. Bell-Scott, Hull, and Smith 1993.

44. http://science.jrank.org/pages/11660/Women-S-Studies-Controversies.html.

45. "Research Justice: Decolonizing Knowledge, Building Power."

46. Omi and Winant 1994.

47. Ferguson 2012, p. 33.

48. Lisa Lowe quoted in Ferguson (2012, p. 35). For more discussion of Lowe's point related to women and gender studies, see, for example, Messer-Davidow (2002).

49. Steck 2013, pp. 66–83.

50. Lieberwitz 2002.

51. Thorsten Veblen quoted in Steck 2013, p. 72.

52. Steck 2013, p. 72.

53. Fromm and Kem 2000, p. 50, quoted in Osei-Kofi 2003.

54. Bulhan 1985, p. 121.

55. Ibid., p. 103.

56. Ibid.

57. Christensen 2011.

58. See, for example, Baldwin 1953/2013.

59. See, for example, Anzaldua 1987/2012.

60. See, for example, Morrison 1973/2003.

61. Green 1983, pp. 168–184.

62. Ibid.

63. Gramsci 1971.
64. Term adapted from Olson and Worsham (2007).
65. Harding 2006, pp. 246–263.
66. Retrieved from http://www.humboldt.edu/crgs/ on August 15, 2015.
67. Ethnic Studies Department, Mills College.
68. Graduate Center of CUNY, Public Science Project.
69. Harding 2006, p. 255.
70. Ibid.
71. Mohanty 2003, pp. 499–535.
72. Ibid. p. 501.
73. Mohanty Cartographies of Struggle, p. 7.
74. Fletcher 2009.
75. Ibid.
76. Greene 1995.
77. Ibid., p. 19.

Bibliography

Ahmed, Sarah. 2012. *On Being Included: Racism and Diversity in Institutional Life.* Durham, NC: Duke University Press.

Alcoff, Linda, and Satya Mohanty. 2006. "Reconsidering Identity Politics: An Introduction." In *Identity Politics Reconsidered,* eds. L. Alcoff, M. Hames-Gracis, S. Mohanty, and P. Moya. New York: Palgrave.

Anzaldua, Gloria. 1987/2012. *Borderlands/La Frontera: The New Mestiza.* San Francisco: Aunt Lute Books.

Baldwin, James. 1953/2013. *Go Tell It on the Mountain.* New York: Knopf.

Bell-Scott, Patricia, Gloria Hull, and Barbara Smith, eds. 1993. *But Some of Us Are Brave: All the Women Are White, All the Blacks Are Men: Black Women's Studies.* New York: The Feminist Press.

Biondi, Martha. 2012. *Black Students, Black Studies, and the Transformation of Higher Education: The Black Revolution on Campus.* Berkeley: University of California Press.

Bowles, Samuel, and Herbert Gintis. 1976. *Schooling in Capitalist America: Educational Reform and the Contradictions of Economic Life.* New York: Routledge and Kegan Paul.

Brisbane, R. H. 1974. *Black Activism: Racial Revolution in the United States, 1954–1970.* Valley Forge, PA: Judson Press.

Bulhan, Hussein Abdilahi. 1985. *Frantz Fanon and the Psychology of Oppression.* New York: Plenum Press.

Bunch, Charlotte, and Sandra Pollack. 1983. *Learning Our Way: Essays in Feminist Education.* Trumansburg, NY: Crossing Press.

Butler, Johnnella. 1981. *Black Studies: Pedagogy and Revolution; A Study of Afro-American Studies and the Liberal Arts Tradition through the Discipline of Afro-American Literature.* Lanham, MD: University Press of America.

Carson, Clayborne. 1981. *In Struggle, SNCC and the Black Awakening of the 1960s.* Cambridge, MA: Harvard University Press.

Chamberlain, Mariam K., ed. 1988. *Women in Academe: Progress and Prospects.* New York: Russell Sage Foundation.

Christensen, Linda. 2011. "Finding Voice: Learning about Language and Power." *Voices from the Middle* 18 (3): 9–17.

Combahee River Collective. 1978. "A Black Feminist Statement." In *Capitalist Patriarchy and the Case for Socialist Feminism,* ed. Z. Eisenstein. New York: Monthly Review Press.

Counts, George S. 1932. *Dare the School Build a New Social Order?* New York: John Day.

Cremin, Lawrence. 1961. *The Transformation of the School: Progressivism in American Education 1876–1957.* New York: Vintage.

Critical Race, Gender, and Sexuality Studies, Humboldt State University. http://www.humboldt.edu/crgs/.

Delgado, Richard. 2013. "Precious Knowledge: State Bans on Ethnic Studies, Book Traffickers (Librotraficantes), and a New Type of Race Trial." *North Carolina Law Review* (June) 91 (5): 1513–1553.

Democratizing Knowledge Project, Syracuse University. http://www.democratizingknowledge.org/uncategorized/democratizing-knowledge-project/.

Dewey, John. 1916. *Democracy and Education: An Introduction to the Philosophy of Education.* New York: Macmillan.

Dong, Harvey. 2009. "Third World Liberation Comes to San Francisco State and UC Berkeley." *Chinese America: History and Perspectives* 95–106, 157. http://search.proquest.com/docview/207440100?accountid=13802.

DuBois, W. E. Burghardt. 1896/1999. *Suppression of the African Slave-Trade to the United States of America: 1638–1870.* Mineola, NY: Dover Publications.

DuBois, W. E. Burghardt. 1903. The Talented Tenth. *The Negro Problem: A Series of Articles by Representative American Negroes of To-day.* New York: James Pott and Co.

Elliott, John. 1983. "A Curriculum for the Study of Human Affairs: The Contribution of Lawrence Stenhouse." *Journal of Curriculum Studies* 15 (2): 105–123.

Ethnic Studies Department, Mills College. http://www.mills.edu/academics/undergraduate/eths/.

Evans, Sara. 1979. *Personal Politics: The Roots of Women's Liberation.* New York: Alfred A. Knopf.

Fenderson, Jonathan, James B. Stewart, and Kabria Baumgartner, eds. 2012. "Expanding the History of the Black Studies Movement." *Journal of African American Studies* 16: 1.

Ferguson, Roderick A. 2012. *The Reorder of Things: The University and Its Pedagogies of Minority Difference.* Minneapolis: University of Minnesota Press.

Fletcher, Joyce. 2009. *Disappearing Acts: Gender, Power, and Relational Practice at Work.* Cambridge, MA: MIT Press.

Frankfurt Research Center for Postcolonial Studies. http://www.normativeorders.net/en/component/content/article/289.

Freire, Paulo. 1973. *Education for Critical Consciousness.* New York: Seabury Press.

Freire, Paulo. 1985. *The Politics of Education: Culture, Power, and Liberation.* South Hadley, MA: Bergin and Garvey.

Fromm, Jeffrey A., and Todd V. Kern. Fall 2000. "Investment Opportunities in Education: Making a Profit While Making a Difference." *Journal of Private Equity* 3 (4): 38–51.

Future of Minority Studies Project, Cornell University. http://www.fmsproject.cornell.edu.

Giles, Raymond H. 1972. *Black Studies Programs in Public Schools.* New York: Praeger Publishers.

Giroux, Henry. 1980. "Critical Theory and Rationality in Citizenship Education." *Curriculum Inquiry* 10 (4): 329–366.

Giroux, Henry. 1983. *Theory and Resistance in Education.* South Hadley, MA: Bergin and Garvey.

Giroux, Henry A. 1987. "Liberal Arts, Public Philosophy, and the Politics of Civic Courage." *Curriculum Inquiry* (Autumn) 17 (3): 331–333.

Graduate Center of CUNY, Public Science Project. http://www.gc.cuny.edu/Page-Elements/Academics-Research-Centers-Initiatives/Centers-and-Institutes/Center-for-Human-Environments/Research-Sub-Groups/Public-Science-Project-%28PSP%29.

Gramsci, Antonio. 1971. *Selections from the Prison Notebooks of Antonio Gramsci,* Ed. and trans. Q. Hoare and G. H. Smith. New York: International Publishers.

Greene, Maxine. 1983. "Curriculum and Consciousness." In *The Hidden Curriculum and Moral Education,* eds. H. Giroux and D. Purpel (pp. 168–184). Berkeley, CA: McCutchan.

Greene, Maxine. 1995. *Releasing the Imagination: Essays on Education, the Arts, and Social Change.* San Francisco: Jossey-Bass.

Gutiérrez y Muhs, Gabriella, Yolanda Flores Niemann, Carmen G. González, and Angela P. Harris, eds. 2012. *Presumed Incompetent: The Intersections of Race and Class for Women in Academia.* Logan, UT: Utah State University.

Harding, Sandra. 2006. "Transformation vs. Resistance Identity Projects: Epistemological Resources for Social Justice Movement." In *Identity Politics Reconsidered,* eds. L. Alcoff, M. Hames-Garcia, S. Mohanty, and P. Moya (pp. 246–263). New York: Palgrave.

hooks, bell. 1994. *Teaching to Transgress.* Boston: South End Press.

Hu-DeHart, Evelyn. 1993. "The History, Development, and Future of Ethnic Studies." *The Phi Delta Kappan* (September) 75 (1): 50–54.

Illich, Ivan. 1971. *Deschooling Society.* London: Marion Boyars Publishers.

Karenga, Maulana. 1982. *Introduction to Black Studies.* Los Angeles: University of Sankore Press. Kirk, Gwyn, and Margo Okazawa-Rey. 2013. *Women's Lives: Multicultural Perspectives.* New York: McGraw Hill.

Labaree, David F. 1997. "Public Goods, Private Goods: The American Struggle over Educational Goals." *American Educational Research Journal* (March 20) 34 (1): 39–81.

Lee, Enid, Deborah Menkart, and Margo Okazawa-Rey. 1998. *Beyond Heroes and Holidays.* Washington, DC: Teaching for Change.

Lieberwitz, Risa L. 2002. "The Corporatization of the University: Distance Learning at the Cost of Academic Freedom?" *The Boston University Public Interest Law Journal* (Fall) 12 (1): 73.

Liptak, Adam. 2014. "Justices Back Ban on Race as Factor in College Entry." *New York Times, NY Edition* (April 23), A1.

Messer-Davidow, Ellen. 2002. *Disciplining Feminism: From Social Activism to Academic Discourse.* Durham, NC: Duke University Press.

Mills, C. Wright. 1959. *The Sociological Imagination.* New York: Oxford University Press.

Mohanty, Chandra Talpade. 1998. "Cartographies of Struggle: Third World Women and the Politics of Feminism." In *Third World Women and the Politics of Feminism*, eds. Chandra Mohanty, Anne Russo, and Lourdes Torres (pp. 1–51). Bloomington, IN: Indiana University Press.

Mohanty, Chandra Talpade. 2003. "'Under Western Eyes' Revisited: Feminist Solidarity through Anticapitalist Struggles." *Signs* 28 (2): 499–535.

Morrison, Toni. 1973/2003. *Sula.* New York: Alfred A. Knopf.

Okihiro, Gary Y. 2010. "The Future of Ethnic Studies: The Field Is under Assault from without and within." *Chronicle of Higher Education* (July 4). http://www.chroniclecareers.com/article/The-Future-of-Ethnic-Studies/66092.

Olson, Gary A., and Lynn Worsham. 2007. *The Politics of Possibility: Encountering the Radical Imagination.* Boulder, CO: Paradigm Publisher.

Omi, Michael, and Howard Winant. 1994. *Racial Formation in the US: From the 1960s to the 1990s.* New York: Routledge.

Osei-Kofi, Nana. 2003. "In the Image of Capital: The Making of the Corporate University." PhD dissertation, The Claremont Graduate University UMI Dissertations Publishing 3086756.

"Research Justice: Decolonizing Knowledge, Building Power": A conversation with Angela Davis, Jason Ferreira, and Chief Caleen Sisk, April 4, 2014. National Ethnic Studies Association annual conference, Oakland, CA. http://www.datacenter.org/event-video-and-photo-album-released-research-justice-decolonizing-knowledge-building-power/.

Rugg, Harold. 1947. *Foundations of American Education.* Yonkers-on-Hudson, NY: World Book.

Schuster, Marilyn, and Susan Van Dyne. 1985. *Women's Place in the Academy: Transforming the Liberal Arts Curriculum.* Totowa, NJ: Rowman and Allenheld.

Solomon, Barbara M. 1986. *In the Company of Educated Women.* New Haven, CT: Yale University Press.

Steck, Henry. 2013. "Corporatization of the University: Seeking Conceptual Clarity." *Annals of the American Academy of Political and Social Science* (January) 585, Higher Education in the Twenty-First Century: 66–83.

Tyack, David. 1974. *The One Best System: A History of American Urban Education.* Cambridge, MA: Harvard University Press.

Washington, Booker T. 1903. "Industrial Education of the Negro." *The Negro Problem: A Series of Articles by Representative American Negroes of To-day.* New York: James Pott and Co.

Wood, George Harrison. 1981. "Schools, Social Change, and the Politics of Paralysis." PhD dissertation, University of Illinois at Urbana-Champaign.

Woodson, Carter G. 1933. *Mis-education of the Negro.* Washington, DC: Associated Publishers.

Young, Iris Marion. 2011. "Five Faces of Oppression." *Justice and the Politics of Difference.* Princeton, NJ: Princeton University Press, pp. 39–65.

Zinn, Howard. 1964/2000. *SNCC: The New Abolitionists.* Boston, MA: South End Press.

Chapter 15

Race and Antiracist Practices: The Problem of Decolonization

George J. Sefa Dei

Introduction

This chapter espouses anti-racism education while making a conceptual link with colonialism, colonizing relations of schooling and the project of decolonization. In redefining antiracist practice, the chapter takes up Indigeneity and decolonization as international categories. I argue that the potency of antiracist work as a tool for transforming the school system can be realized only when practitioners know how to critically understand and critique the global structure of white colonization. Furthermore, practitioners need to be equipped to see and critically engage the enduring presence of white colonization in contemporary society. The effect of colonization on racialized/colonized/Indigenous bodies is real and felt at a number of interstices. This chapter briefly highlights these intersections of difference: race, gender, class, sexuality, and (dis)ability for anti-racism. In the final section there is a related discussion on transforming anti-racism education to include broader questions of colonial settlerhood in the specific context of the North American experience. In my discussion, I bring a particular reading to race and anti-racism as about colonial and anticolonial knowledge production. Clearly, anti-racism is more than theory; it is fundamentally about action and practice. However, I take the position that we need to understand the philosophy behind our practices in order to bring sincerity to politics. For example, the seeming prestigious social positions held by racialized bodies in the academy are volatile. This becomes apparent when we produce knowledge that seeks to challenge rigid institutional traditions. Implicitly, we are expected to exercise care and caution when speaking out differently. We share a basic humanity with a longing for love, dignity, respect, and so on. It is important to evaluate colonial and colonizing narratives about the "human" and who this subject is in order to understand larger questions of identity and knowledge production that inform ongoing conversations about our common humanity. The problem of liberal democracies today is the claim of fighting for individual rights and promoting equal opportunities for all mired within contexts of racism, colonization, and social oppressions.

Recently, I was at a public talk by a visiting African scholar who cautioned about the way we engage Indigenous knowledge and what it means for knowledge production. She asked us to think about what African Indigenous knowledge has to do with modern airplanes that allow one to fly from say a part of the African continent to a North American destination? Frankly, I was floored by this question because of what to me appeared to be an implicit assumption that modernity is simply through Western (science) scholarship. Upon deep reflection, I could see why the scholar was asking us to think through the question in the first place. We have all been schooled to think everything about "progress" as due to Western modernity. I see this mind-set as the uphill task of decolonizing contemporary education and to begin to think through different imaginings and possibilities of shared, collective, and accumulative dimensions of knowledge. The particularity of the Western experience has often masqueraded as the universal experience and is often presented as "scientific outlook."[1] What constitutes truth is not outside the determinants of power. Certainly, Africa has a rich intellectual tradition. Our Indigenous knowledges about mathematics, geometry, science, and technology have contributed to a global knowledge of science. Yet the colonial narrative or script has been written to disengage, devalue, or erase such contributions.

Consequently, I take as an entry point to this discussion the assertion that the problem with (contemporary) education is that it is still colonial and colonizing of learners alongside their myriad experiences, histories, cultures, and identities. Education has failed to affirm identities (race, class, gender, sexuality, disability, etc.) in everyday classroom pedagogies, instruction, and texts. And yet such grounding is vital in any meaningful politics of equity and social justice in education. Power is a global discourse. Power is embedded in the geopolitics of knowledge production about race, circulation of ideas, and the discourse pertaining to European colonialism, Indigeneity, and decolonization.[2] There are dialogues about power and knowledge that bring to the fore possibilities of counter-perspectives in subverting hegemonic practices. This creates a greater need for counterhegemonic, emancipatory, democratic strategies in education. At the global level, survival of colonized, racialized, and Indigenous peoples is part of the everyday anticolonial struggles/politics of decolonizing education (e.g., school curriculum, texts, and pedagogies). Da Costa has a point in asserting that "racism, white supremacy, and anti-Blackness [and Indigeneity] together constitute a hemispheric question"[3] that can only be partly resolved through decolonized educational practices.

Notwithstanding open denials, race is of critical importance. It shapes the identities and life chances of racialized, colonized, and Indigenous bodies in our communities. In order to survive, bodies have to resist. Race and racism through time have embodied particular histories of resistance to the hierarchical arrangements based on skin color and other phenotypical characteristics. Racism destabilizes our imagined order, peace, and happiness.[4] Throughout human history racist and racial ideologies have persisted to account for human differences and to justify unequal treatment of groups. We have never gone beyond race and this makes a mockery of claims of the "post-racial" context. Today, a "post-racial ideology exists in diverse, yet analogous forms, all sharing a rhetoric of racial progress amid systemic racial hierarchy."[5] Any critical analysis of post-racial ideology "reveals the ways in which post-racial discourses and practices persist even amid varying levels of societal recognition of racism and state implementation of ethno-racial policies."[6] The body politics of schooling and education is deeply racial. Within our schools, colleges, and universities, existing structures, policies, and mechanisms of educational delivery use "white codes" for business. What we have to continually contend with is a "body of knowledge, ideologies, norms, and particular practices that have been constructed over the history of Europeans with roots in colonialism."[7] In effect, Euro-American schools are "white in character, in structure and in culture." One of the many problems with this is that it perpetuates Western ideology as supreme and universal. This is suffocating for racialized/colonized/Indigenous bodies and makes it "difficult to conceptualize alternatives to them."[8]

Race is real and the problem of racism cannot be minimized by denying its existence. Color-blind politics of the 1980s is still with us, and claims of racial innocence quickly comes up when people are called upon to own up to their racist practices.[9] There is a push toward a "race-neutral universalism" that also authorizes and justifies the social retreat from race,[10] further allowing us "to repress, . . . passively accept, and justify [and/or ignore the debilitating effects of] social hierarchies," especially those based on race.[11] In employing an antiracist discursive lens[12] to this discussion I ask: what do race, racism and colonization have in common? A very easy answer is to say they all are about power and social oppression. But I would complicate this response and insist that, in fact, what they all share is a need to decolonize our cultural knowings and ourselves. The politics of decolonization is very central to anti-racism and antiracist practice. However, I would bring a different read on decolonization and anti-racism, one that moves beyond the slippery slope of simply critiquing oppressed bodies' advocacy for anti-racism as limiting with our understanding of what it means to pursue this work on settled lands. Decolonization is an international category. While I do not dismiss the importance of questioning what masquerades as "anti-racism" on settled Indigenous lands, I am also mindful of the taints of anti-blackness in Indigenous resurgence that goes with calls to "decolonize anti-racism." When and how do African peoples who have been Indigenous on their own Lands and compelled to migrate through either enslavement or the geopolitics of global political economies become "settlers of color"?[13] Citizenship is not just a paper/theoretical recognition of rights. It should be about distribution of social rewards and benefits, as well as responsibilities that flow from one being able to develop a sense of belonging, a sense of having a stake in a place and feeling welcomed. If the harsh realities of racialized bodies and so-called immigrants in Euro-American contexts have any lessons, they teach that we must interrogate, trouble, and refuse to work with Eurocentric definitions of citizenship. Notwithstanding the "benefits" of citizenship, there are also notable profound limitations in speaking of citizenship for colonized body given our experiences in Diasporic contexts.[14] I welcome and respect the diverse intellectual gaze we each bring to our work fighting for equity and justice. I have chosen to train my intellectual gaze on colonial whiteness that emerged from Europe's colonization of the "Other."

Expanding and Deepening the Imperative of Decolonization

There are key concepts that help ground a discussion of anti-racism for contemporary times. While the chapter is located within the Euro-Canadian/American context, it seeks to make broader global linkages. It moves discussions beyond Canada and U.S. centric. Long ago[15] I defined anti-racism as an action-oriented educational strategy to address questions of race and racism and the intersections with gender, class, sexuality, disability, and sites of power and social difference. I insisted on putting a focus more on action beyond the dialogue. Anti-racism contends that we can only see the full effects of race and racist practices in their imbrication with class, gender, sexuality, ability, and so on. Anti-racism espouses the saliency of race and the coloniality of whiteness in distributing rewards and punishment in society. Anti-racism uses the entry point of race to understand the complexities and interstices of social oppressions. It argues that notwithstanding the contested and fluid nature and contextual variations in our understanding of race, the concept is real given its material and political consequences and effects. It is racism that makes race real. Racism as a social practice of power uses assigned racial markers, distinctions, and hierarchies to distinguish among groups.

While racism is a conspicuous feature of Euro-modernity, its roots go back to European supremacist ideology that was passed on as "a pseudo-scientific ideology."[16] Since then racism has always spoken to particular "arrangements, relations, activities, representations, exploitations, domination and violence."[17] An understanding of colonialism and decolonization is critical for the theoretical foundations of anti-racism education. The concepts of colonization/decolonization as they relate to race and antiracist policies in North America and globally are about understanding the complex histories and trajectories of imperial relations, conquest, and subaltern resistance in education. Education is important both from what it does to you (the learner) and from what it does for us (learners). Colonial education has caused much damage and the only way to repair and heal wounded souls (learners) is through a decolonial/anticolonial resistance using the different tools of education. These tools are not just the "master's tools."[18] They are different tools. The sad fact is that so many perpetrators (educators and others) and "victims" (learners and others) do not even recognize the hurt or wounded souls. We still have far ways to go in acknowledging and accepting the place for different tools of and for resistance in education.

Colonialism has been much discussed in the literature.[19] Suffice to say that colonization (as the process of colonizing the Other) was the imperial occupation or annexation of Indigenous peoples and their Lands. It led to the imposition of European cultural values and social structures, including economic institutions and systems of governance of Indigenous peoples' lands and territories. Colonization also led to the imposition of Western European educational systems supplanting Indigenous forms of education. Such imposition disrupted or destroyed local cultures, politics, languages, spiritual beliefs, and practices, the effects of which are still being felt today. This was the case in the Americas, Africa, and the Turtle Island (now Canada). In Canada there is the all-familiar case of residential schools where Aboriginal children were separated from their families, raised in isolated reserves where they were taught the colonizers' sociocultural and political values, and forced to disconnect from Indigenous culture and the teachings of the Land.[20] For Aboriginal parents, students, and communities, their skepticism and suspicion of schooling is borne from their experiences and knowledge of the effects of residential schools and cultural genocide on their lives. This is a problem for historically marginalized students and communities everywhere.

In Africa, European colonization came with Western formal schooling, which taught Indigenous Africans the values of Europe and how to become "Europeans" (in thought and action) in their own Native places.[21] African learners were hardly taught their local culture and to speak the native language in school was an offense.[22] This history of forced European occupation was violent and brutal. It led to material, physical, and social damages or "death," and as well had far-reaching emotional, spiritual, and psychological destruction of Indigenous peoples.[23] Colonialism and racism worked in tandem reinforcing each other.[24]

Colonialism promoted racism globally by working with a restrictive definition and understanding of the "human" and humanhood. The human subject was all about the Anglo-Saxon subject. This subject became the archetype of humanity. Africans and other non-Europeans were less than human. Colonialism also privileged or superiorized the culture, language, and technology of the European, as well as his social values and norms. Furthermore, it carved a different nationality very exclusive of other peoples' social and material realities and conditions. Different colonial arrangements were enforced and reinforced in the context of the dominant and subordinate group relations. Human groups (races, cultures, etc.) were positioned in hierarchical relations with each other. These different racisms were pursued within arrangements of culture, religion, language, ethnicity, and class, and in these contexts it was possible for racisms to exist without strictly assigned races. But with time it has been the nature and extent of the myriads racisms that, as has been already noted, have actually made race real.

It must be reiterated that in situating colonialism at the center of a critique of the Euro-American school system, I am bringing a broader understanding to "colonial." Colonial relations are ongoing and not restricted to formal European colonial occupation of Indigenous peoples' Lands.

Colonial is beyond "foreign" and "alien" to anything that is "imposed and dominating."[25] Structures and systems of imposition and domination can be along lines of race, gender, class, (dis)ability, religion, language, and so on. Colonial hierarchies of schooling structured along lines and sites of social difference (race, gender, class, sexuality, etc.) have continued with the "formal end" of European colonialism. Colonial relations of schooling are everywhere looking at our current educational systems (e.g., hierarchies of knowledge, whose knowledge counts, whose knowledge is seen as valid, and the ways the reward structures of the academy). These colonial and colonizing relations are in themselves very oppressive, and they end up creating and reproducing social inequities in the educational system.

The material and discursive aspects of teaching, learning, and administration of education (that is the concrete realities and practices of educational delivery) in colonial and colonized contexts were effected through the perceived "disembodied presence" (i.e., bodies without identities) of educators and learners. In Africa and elsewhere we know colonial schooling did not cultivate in young Indigenous learners a counter-perspective necessary to challenge and subvert the dominant Westocentric/Eurocentric education.[26] For young learners to think contrary to the dominant paradigm was an intellectual heresy and offenders were actually not "intellectuals." To be able to mimic dominant theories and paradigms, to become oblivious to one's own cultural ways of knowing, and to fail to link our cultural, racial, gender, sexual, and spiritual identities to knowledge production were worthy of commendation. In Indigenous contexts the coloniality of Western schooling offered a theoretical structure of oppression rooted in relations of domination producing in young learners a disinterest in Indigenous perspectives, practices, and conditions. The devaluation, negation, and erasure of Indigenous ways of knowing assisted in the project for further dehumanizing colonized and oppressed peoples. This has been a human travesty.

Given the coloniality of Western education it is important for us to understand that decolonization cannot happen solely through Western science scholarship. This is because Western science has been part of the problem of objectifying and colonizing the Indigenous experience, discounting subaltern histories and non-Western knowledges and epistemes deemed not "scientific" or "scholarly enough" by Western standards. My critique is not an outright dismissal of the merits of Western science knowledge. There is something worth engaging and reading about such scholarship. For one thing our engagement can only sharpen our minds to ask more critical questions. I am asking us to be critical of the ways particular bodies of knowledge have assumed universality at the expense of other ways of knowing. There is a coloniality of Western science. History has always been a tool of colonization. We must continually question what is presented to us as "objective truth" and "history."

Given the colonial hand we have been dealt, the Indigenous, racialized, and the colonized scholar cannot be anything but anticolonial. We must be engaged in the project of decolonization for our own intellectual survival. We cannot afford to move further and further away from intellectualism although it has limits. Our intellectualism must be coupled with a degree of progressive politics. This decolonization is about an awareness of past, present, and future existence. It is a process of gaining a critical consciousness (through education) of self, body, mind, spirit, and soul and the community in order to challenge imperial structures of (Western) schooling. Decolonizing is about challenging the power entrapments of social privilege acquired on the basis of domination over others. In terms of pursuing decolonized education, the goal is to teach that coming to know is not simply an intellectual activity but a holistic engagement of the mind, soul, spirit, and body as experiences in place, time, culture, and history and within particular identities. Such decolonization is also about beginning to unlearn and learn, and understanding oneself in relation to the material and discursive and political practices of schooling.

In an excellent dissertation theorizing a "transformative pedagogical encounter" and "the significance of real bodies in real places," Kerr[27] notes that colonial education provided a "codified and disciplinary way of going about schooling" and was also "specifically directed toward the epistemological assumptions that lay unexamined therein." She argues colonizing education is one "managed through [a] codified approach without concern for local context and the real bodies in educational relationships"[28] and that underlying assumptions of colonial education "also reveal an epistemological move that obscures the body and place of potential oppressor and oppressed, and thus creates conditions for social inequity."[29]

Clearly, it is the destruction brought forth by colonialism that makes decolonization imperative. Fanon[30] long argued that there are many paths to decolonization and decolonization is always a violent and treacherous phenomenon. Decolonization is not an arrival point in history, but a historical ongoing process, which "engages with imperialism and colonialism at multiple levels."[31] Decolonization calls for an authentic and honest commitment to anticolonial and antiracist projects. Decolonization is not about mainstreaming practice. Decolonization projects cannot seek for legitimation and validation from the oppressor's domain. If decolonization is about developing a critical consciousness of one's self, place, history, identity, culture, and politics, then it requires that claiming "Indigenous" is a project of decolonization. Consequently, all projects of genuine decolonization require "Indigeneity." Cheikh Anta Diop[32] also reminded us that decolonization means "abandoning all reflexes of subordination." Similarly, black consciousness theorist Steve Biko asserted, "The most potent weapon of the oppressor is the mind of the oppressed."[33] Decolonization is about freeing the mind, body, soul, and spirit from colonization and oppression. Such take on decolonization is vitally important for all educators and learners to understand.

As far as schooling and education is concerned, decolonization is about building new collaborative futures. In the Euro-American schooling when decolonization is engaged to threaten, subvert, and replace colonial spaces, there are certain risks especially (but not exclusively) for the racial minority scholar. For example, how do we intellectually de-escalate mounting intensities that will no doubt come as white spaces become threatened and the Western frame of reference is either questioned or pressed against its traditional dominance? How do we ensure that the displacement and the resulting tension by white body do not land upon other bodies unjustly as it has always been (e.g., pitting Aboriginal and African Indigeneity against each other)? How do we come to think and understand ourselves as racial beings implicated in colonial (settler) relationships in the academy?

Decolonization and the Antiracist Implications

The implications of understanding the dialectic of colonialism and decolonization are to offer an anticolonial reading of the concept of *racism as* emerging from conventional understandings of the technologies of race that is discursively, politically and culturally, (re)produced to legitimize particular sociopolitical arrangements. The impact of colonization has been such that certain knowledges have been denied, subjugated, or dismissed as irrelevant to understanding the human experience. The history of colonial racism and our implications have added to race and racism becoming "difficult" subjects to discuss. Many educators and schools have tended to avoid critical discussions of race and racism. Race is often seen as controversial or "taboo subjects."[34] Given that racism is real, educators need to teach all students about race and, particularly, offer ways to assist young learners to grapple with the effects of racism on their lives and experiences. Racism affects both the racialized and the perpetrator of oppression. We must confront this fear of being candid about race and racism. The fear prohibits any meaningful discussion and action. A failure to see racism and colonialism as part of the institutional fabric of our communities and therefore as something to be seriously dealt with has contributed in no small measure to racialized and Indigenous bodies becoming deeply skeptical of schooling and education. This happens all the time. Racialized parents and communities learn NOT to trust the school system and we (e.g., teachers) are accused of not caring! Racialized and Indigenous learners and their communities are often pathologized as the source of the problems of schooling (e.g., youth disengagement from school, low academic achievement). Historically, discourses of cultural and cognitive deficiency are often attributed as the cause of students' educational problems. This is argued instead of examining the institutional structures of educational delivery (e.g., curriculum, texts, learning and pedagogical styles).[35] It is important for educational research to examine how different communities experience education and what their thoughts are about schooling. What do we understand about and how do we understand our students and ourselves in relation to the racialized, gendered, and class configurations of schooling and education? What does it mean to bring embodiment to schooling and education processes? Research must also explore how local communities (racialized/Indigenous) provide education to youth and tap into that wealth of knowledge toward improving educational outcomes for all youth. Clearly, there are culture-specific approaches to learning and teaching. Oftentimes, what is presented as Indigenous or culture-specific learning styles are in fact learning styles appropriate for all students.

In his essay on "Im/Plausible Deniability: Racism's Conceptual Double Bind," Barnor Hesse points out that one of the current seductions in intellectual praxis is the attempt to foreclose "subaltern anti-colonial critiques centred on Western Imperialism."[36] The author notes the different and privileging conceptualizations of racism have has been taken up in dominant social science scholarship (e.g., the hegemonic Eurocentric construction of racism as opposed to the subaltern anticolonial, understandings of racisms). It is important for us to pay attention to an understanding of race, racism, and anti-racism within the anticolonial paradigm. Such paradigm centers colonialism and ongoing colonizing relations. Racism is not a problem of the past. It has historical and continuing presence in human society. We cannot understand colonial racism without references to "Atlantic slavery," "European colonialism," "whiteness," and its colonial logics, "Eurocentrism" or "Western imperialism."[37] Some of us may know this for a fact in one way, yet we deny it in another way when called upon to act on our privileges.

Clearly, there are limited discourses in liberalism to offer critical understandings of continuing racial oppression and the necessity to pursue antiracist change in a way that centers structural questions of power, privilege, and resource sharing. Discourses such as social justice for all and "color blindness" may appeal to our moral instincts and become seductive. But these discourses are dangerous because of their obfuscation of power differentials and the implication of this on marginalized bodies in our communities. The pathology of color blindness is at the heart of race denial and racism. Counter models of social justice should be about targeted responses along lines of race, gender, disability, class, sexuality, language, and Indigeneity. One size fits all does not work. Some of the models may recognize the severity of issues for certain bodies, the historic fact of injustices structured differently for groups, the recognition that we all do not start from an equal footing, and the knowledge that certain groups have corrupted history to create, enforce, and sustain their dominance over others. In effect history and science have and continue to be tolls of domination. Any meaningful approach to social justice would have to recognize these facts and pursue multiple levels of responses, including targeted response. Such targeted response to problem solution would not mean treating people unequally or unfairly. Social justice approach that accords power and privilege differently to groups is problematic and must be distinguished from social justice approaches that respond to historic inequalities and inequities. Put together, we must be responding to and not reapportioning injustice.

The unique experiences of racialized, colonized, and Indigenous bodies in the white colonial encounters reveal the structural dimensions of racism and colonization for different bodies. The perceived sub-humanity of African bodies has long been part of the antiracist struggles. Citing Aime Cesaire, Hesse notes that the "thingification" of particular racialized, colonized, and Indigenous bodies has always been "a constitutive dimension of European colonialism across the world."[38] Antiracist approaches that target their responses to affirming the humanity of the African, colonized and Indigene, working to remove inequities, to empower these groups and create a level playing field is not a politics of privilege for the groups in question. To ask the dominant to cede power and its unearned privileges in the service of a common humanity is not subjecting the dominant to social injustice.

I have steadfastly held on to the position that asserts the saliency of race in my antiracist work.[39] This is because anti-racism is and should foremost be about race and racism. But this strategic understanding of the saliency of race is political (not a hierarchy of oppressions), an awareness of how race can be a difficult subject for the dominant because it is about power, privilege, and oppression. Race is the one thing we least want to cast our gaze on. There is a silence and a discomfort in speaking race. We only wish the problem of race and racism would "go away" somehow and are unwilling to do something concrete about it. Rather than being frank, we engage in intellectual gymnastics and foot dragging on race. We argue needlessly that race is meaningless, lacks intellectual validity, is complex and changing, and so on. These are exhausting exchanges for some of us. In fact, many times, particularly, those privileged by race conscript this idea of messiness, fluidity, and fussiness of race to deny questions of white accountability. Interestingly, it is easy to understand class as a salient feature of society while race or gender is not. Why do we experience this discomfort about race? What are we afraid of in not having an open, honest, and frank discussion about race? Why do we simply want to wish it away? For the dominant, any critical approach to these discussions will have to center power and privilege. This is what race is about.

While using race an entry point in antiracist work, we must also advocate for the fusion of race and social difference. Today the globalization of racism within a global capitalist modernity has made it imperative that we pursue anti-racism education within the lens of the interstices of difference (gender, disability, sexuality, class, etc.). The struggle against racism is also a struggle against internal(ized) colonization among social groups in the ongoing capitalist relations of production and accumulation of wealth through imperialism or corporate capital. In this historical moment, fighting racism is also a struggle against Euro-modernity and corporate greed. Therefore, incorporating a prism of transnational anticolonialism and the interstices of difference in the antiracist struggle provides a more profound understanding of how social oppression is mediated through race, gender, class, sexuality, (dis)ability, language, and culture. We are oppressed simultaneously through race, gender, sexual, and class intersections. The economic, political, and social position of racialized bodies in contemporary society requires the development of racial, gender, sexual, and working-class consciousness. Anti-racism calls on oppressed and dominant groups to discuss and reflect collectively on our respective positioning with the economic, social, and political structures and conditions of everyday existence. We must seek to understand the ways structured relations of power collude with systems of oppression and the interstices of race, class, gender, sexuality, and (dis)ability to sustain, as well as resist white supremacist logics and dominance. This is a tall order but so necessary if we are to make progress.

Re-colonial relations continue to perpetuate systemic, group, and institutional as well as individualized forms of oppressions. These oppressions are intersected by race, class, gender, sexual, and (dis)ability. However, it is not enough to understand, for example, how class-based oppressions intersect with racialized, gendered, and sexualized forms of oppression. We need to also use such knowledge to transform our communities. Transforming communities will bring lasting change. Racism and white supremacist logics function at institutional, group, and individual or personal levels to sustain the economic, political, and social domination of colonized, Indigenous, and racialized bodies. We are often caught in an unnecessary bind around shared experiences and similarities of experiences. Our experiences may be shared/linked/connected but they are not similar. We can speak of shared experiences while at the same time recognizing the uniqueness of these experiences for groups. It is not one or the other but interconnections of similarities and differences. A clear case is when we speak about the experiences of racism for black men and black women and intersectional analysis becomes very useful. While there are clearly unique experiences (e.g., when we see the case of gender oppression of black/African, Asian, or Indigenous women within a capitalist economy), the social position of the black female can be understood only in terms of how race intersects with gender, class, sexuality, (dis)ability, culture, and power. Black women experience oppressions not simply due to their working-class, race, or gender positions but through the confluence of race, gender, class, sexual, and (dis) abled difference. It is this confluence that Collins[40] long ago discussed as the "matrix" or the simultaneity of oppressions.

The question of subject positionality and social location is significant in antiracist praxis. Position and identity both inform knowledge and coming to know. Many scholars have long argued that gender, race, class, sexuality, (dis)ability, and other aspects of identity are relations of power, as well as "markers of relational positions rather than essential qualities."[41]

When we critically examine the position of the black woman in history and in contemporary contexts, one can contend that the displacement of black women's social position and status is very much connected to the emergence of a (white) patriarchal capitalist economy. The picture is made clear through a critical understanding of the interstices of difference, that is, how race, class, and gender, for the most part, have intersected through human lived experiences. This has been personal learning and intellectual growth for me in my work on "integrative anti-racism" (Dei 1996).

In pointing to the requirements of the interstices of difference for collective antiracist work, I will borrow from Stacey Papernick's paper in which she also uses the pioneering work of Claudia Jones reiterating that for black women "experiences of racialized economic oppression are not a necessary part of their identity but rather the way in which they experience gender, race and class in the social and political realm determining their economic reality."[42] Papernick drawing on Claudia Jones's pioneering theorizing reiterates that black women "experience gender oppression under patriarchy and can unite with White women in resistance to barriers created in the labour market as a result of sexism; however, under capitalism they must work in solidarity with Black men to challenge racism in the economic system."[43] This underlines an important basis for solidarity politics as we cannot intellectually, materially, politically, and emotionally separate "class struggle and anti-imperialism from Black women's daily oppressions."[44] Because black women are further limited by the means and the relations of production based on gender and race, their oppression goes beyond class oppression. We cannot deal with one oppression and leave the others intact. Current antiracist struggles must grasp the true meaning and implications of the complexity of social existence to work for social change even while upholding the centrality of race in antiracist work. It is not a contradiction. We can bring the same lens to how we look at the effects of ableism on bodies of color. Disabled black, working-class women face compounded oppressions given that they contend with the ways gender, race, and disability intersect to oppress beyond class exploitation. The lessons of black women compounded with oppressions within a capitalist modernity must inform antiracist practice. Without such a unified and collective (racial, sexual, gender, [dis]ability, and working class) resistance, capitalism cannot be transformed. Of course, such collective resistance will have to grapple with the question of power embedded in these social categories of identities and identifications in order not to reproduce the very things being contested.

To understand the interstices of difference we must always couple our analysis with individual as well as collective agency and resistance. It will be a limiting reading to see the existence of the oppressed strictly through the lens of oppression. Black women's social life cannot be comprehended solely through oppression and marginalization. There is the question of empowerment and "agential power." We must read resistance into the social life/existence of the black female and not see black women in history through a restrictive Eurocentric lens that presents them as being acted upon continually. This is important given the persistence of a very lazy reading of the black/African woman experience as perpetually oppressed and dominated. The experiences of black/African and in fact Indigenous women offer significant lessons in history to inform antiracist struggles. We know that through history African women have held relatively higher economic status positions in society with political influence. A clear case is the matriarchal communities of West Africa where women have been head of households with access to land and the distribution land wealth in society. In Indigenous communities, motherhood and mothering as "human production" was highly valued as part of "commodity production." These are lessons that speak about black and Indigenous women's power, agency, and resistance in history.[45] Quoting Johnston's work Papernick (2013) points out the active participation of these women in property control was "relatively higher in the family than that of European women."[46] To reiterate, it needs to be understood that the displacement of black women's social position and status is very much connected to the emergence of a patriarchal capitalist economy. But capitalism has always needed structural, systemic, and individualized racism and gender oppression to maintain its socioeconomic benefits. Racism and capitalism have been inseparable. Capitalism not only creates inequities; it depends on social inequality for its very survival. Race-based oppression supported and reinforced white supremacy in the capitalist labor market and has subsequently only exacerbated the subordination of black women in society. Today this subordination has intensified as gender- and race-based oppression continue to limit black women's access to paid employment, education, and health.[47]

The Question of Colonial Settlerhood

I am aware that I am raising a question that has been discussed by a number of scholars with shifting stances and is still germane to the current discussion because to the tendency for some Black, racialized and minority scholars to fall into the seductive trap of uncritical acceptance of our "settler" status.

I end this discussion with an important reflection on anti-racism for contemporary times. I raise a key question: what does it mean to see ourselves as racialized beings implicated in colonial settler relations? I will work with the saliency of anti-black/African racism and the limits of decolonizing approaches that simply collapse the African experience into the white colonial-settler discourse. Over the years I have reflected on my own work on anti-racism in the context of critiques by Aboriginal scholars to decolonize antiracist practice in Canada.[48] I agree that my situatedness and location on Turtle Island (Canada) highlights a need to transform anti-racism education to include broader questions of colonialism and colonial settlerhood in the context of the North American experience.[49] It is also important for us to be able to articulate the specificities of colonization and racism for different racialized groups and to acknowledge our respective roles and responsibilities in fighting and resisting colonial and racial oppressions. So I ask: what does it mean to see ourselves as racialized and radicalized beings implicated in colonial settler relations? I do not think for the black/African antiracist worker/scholar the answer simply rests on a prior recognition that we are "settlers" (of color)[50] (Amadahy and Lawrence, 2009). As already mentioned elsewhere (Dei 2014), I have voiced a different reading to such characterization. It is at best very divisive and for black bodies we can see a taint of anti-blackness in such characterization even if well-meaning and intended to generate critical discussions. More important, such characterization only helps derail a collective antiracist/ anticolonial project for racialized, colonized, and Indigenous peoples. When do we get to speak of a collective and/or collective experience? Are we so differentiated that it renders the notion of a "collective experience" meaningless? Herein lies the challenge confronting and also informing criticisms of "multicultural education." I believe we can speak of a collective without implying we are all the same or without differences. I have very often wondered how dominant groups hang on to ideas of differences and differentiation (e.g., conscripting idea of fragmented communities and experiences) when it suits their interests to deny responsibility and accountability.

Collective experience while not singular does not also absolve us of implications and responsibilities. To be implicated in colonial settlerhood is different from being a settler for black and racialized bodies in white colonial spaces. As I navigate around some of these challenges and responsibilities in my own antiracist work, I still want to articulate a saliency of anti-black/African racism (as a political project informed by who I am) because I feel a failure to acknowledge this further limits the discourse of decolonizing approaches that simply collapse the African experience into the white colonial-settler discourse. In broadening the debate on race and racism by redefining antiracist practice we must therefore be able to take up Indigeneity and decolonization as international categories. It is only through a critical understanding and structural critique of whiteness and the profound consequences that (white) colonial and colonizing projects have on racialized/colonized/Indigenous bodies that antiracist work can transform our institutions, specifically the secondary schools, colleges, and universities. The problem about whiteness is that so many white people struggle to articulate what this even is, let alone how it affects others. Whether this is an "avoidance strategy" or a genuine search for knowledge, it must be acknowledged that a critical understanding and action on the privilege of whiteness is central to antiracist and anticolonial work.

Black presence is Canada is not solely about a search for citizenship. The history of black presence in Canada as read through the transatlantic slave trade, human trafficking of today, Nova Scotia of the 1600s, escaping violence, and oppression that is expressed bodily in southern parts of the world through the colonial apparatus in its contemporary transmutation show complexity. Black/African bodies are either forced or enticed to be here not because we want to be a colonizer or steal Land from another Indigenous community. Black/Africans know too well the effects of land loss on the psychocultural, psychophysical, psycho-emotional, language, and spiritual levels of social existence and, in particular, the deep disruption to the experience and expression of Indigeneity.

As noted in Dei[51] (2014), Canadian citizenship is a colonial apparatus and so I understand why participation by any community can be conceptualized as being implicated in the colonial project. However, citizenship is a nation-based project that is also not pursued for nationhood by everyone. There are many reasons for black/African peoples being in Canada. Even the "choice" to be in Canada is complicated by the context from which the black/African body emerges. It is not simple assertion of desire. In the United States, the black body is not questioned about where one is from because racism is not denied in the same way or to the same degree as in Canada. In the United States there is a sense of "you are here because I am here . . . and, of course you have to be here for me!" In Canada it is "I am here because of you but I am not clear on why." There is a soft tension of denial that can be easily compartmentalized and disavowed.

Any claims black/African Canadians are making are not to Land but to humanhood. As an African by birth I know too well that African countries continually experience depletion economically and psychoculturally because of incessant struggles to survive. This struggle is not left in some parts of Africa when a person moves on to live in another land (e.g., Turtle Island/Canada). This ongoing struggle is impossible for the black/African to ignore and it is not the intent when moving away. The effects of the struggle/colonization are an emotional luggage for the black/African and is carried and embodied no matter where a person Indigenous to Africa may be. This psychocultural trauma continues in a new form in Canadian society and Africanness is not something that can be escaped and it is not what the African comes to Turtle Island/Canada for. In Canada/Turtle Island, the black experience is still about struggles and resistance, not benefits. Clearly, in our world today tensions are emerging between racialized, colonized, and Indigenous bodies and communities because of the amplification of neoliberalism in Canada and globally and the resource issues that emerge from this and the desires of Canadian nation-state. These tensions are produced and/or manufactured to serve the neoliberal interests and to suppress the emergence and radicalization of the Indigenous body and voice. The black/African struggle and active resistance against the colonial, the white body, and space is relevant for the global Indigenous population and not only for the black/African body.

It should be a larger struggle for Indigeneity for all and, of course, more closely a pursuit for transformative justice for the indigenous population across all oppression interstices. For the black/African body, anti-black and antiracist practices have a particular historical framework, praxis, and language, which is an acknowledgment of location and intimacy with collective experiences.

It is important, therefore, for us to engage some questions in our antiracist work: Is there one model of antiracist and anti-oppression work? Can we embrace different models that emerge from different contexts and that collectively resist in particular ways against the gross and totalizing expression of the colonial to weaken it at multiple sites? How can we pursue such strategies to strengthen each other in the goal of decolonizing space, our psyche, and relationships? I will urge that we return to Indigeneity and embrace differences to support and strengthen the collective interests of thorough delinking of the colonial through the relationships that are being produced or have been produced to serve whiteness, its space and dominance, power, and capital. We cannot afford to be distracted; it is and has been a powerful colonial tactic.

Conclusion

I end this discussion pointing to what in my reading constitutes the five areas for response in the goal to transform schools to serve the needs of all students. First is the question of Indigeneity and decolonization, as this has implications for producing counter knowledges to subvert the dominance of colonial education for our young learners. Indigeneity and decolonization must be pursued as international categories for all learners. Second, the high cost of education is keeping more and more learners from racial, working-class backgrounds outside our educational system. We cannot afford to lose these bright minds. Something needs to be done to address the problem, and this must be a key aspect of anti-racism. This necessitates that we engross anti-racism in broader questions of class and economics. Third, our world today is about difference. Difference not only is a site of strength but offers huge possibilities. Educators need to address questions of justice, equity, and schooling to ensure that excellence is not only accessible but also equitable for all groups and communities. There has to be a solution-oriented approach to engage difference as part of the equity and social justice debate. Fourth, there is a need for empowered local communities to have a voice in the delivery of education. This is critical for the survival of the collective. Antiracist education must therefore focus on local empowerment. How do we make our communities strong enough to articulate their issues of concerns and how do we come to hear and act on these voices of concern from our varied communities? Fifth is the related challenge of making our schools truly inclusive. Notwithstanding the hard work of a number of Canadian/North American educators, our schools still face the challenge of youth disengagement from school. This problem may be alleviated by the development of an inclusive, antiracist curriculum that promotes alternative, non-hegemonic ways of knowing and understanding our world. The solutions will come from concerted efforts by all stakeholders. However, there is particular responsibility placed on schools and educators to come up with effective measures to ensure that all students receive education and actualize their dreams and hopes for a better future. I believe a critical approach to inclusive schooling where students' identities, histories, cultures, and knowledge are acknowledged, valued, and responded to within a multicentric, anticolonial educational prism holds possibilities for educational transformation for all learners.

In teaching anti-racism education one must be prepared to encounter resistance. There is going to be those who would question the gaze on colonialism and whiteness as a metanarrative in a Canadian classroom. They will make all the usual arguments (colonialism is not black and white; whites are not monolithic; whiteness is demarcated by class, gender, sexuality, (dis)ability, ethnicity, etc.; and even question what privilege is, let alone white privilege, etc.). In an e-mail correspondence to me, recently a former master's student now doing her doctorate at another institution wondered: Why is that after decades of antiracist and critical race scholarship we seem to have completely forgotten about all of this work? It's "really demoralizing," she said. But "anyway, I am e-mailing to say thank you for continuing to do the work that you do. Too many people are comfortably asleep in this world" (Nketiah, personal correspondence, 2014).[52] Well said. Maybe we all have been sleeping long enough. It is time for us to wake up.

Acknowledgments

I would like to thank the students of the Ontario Institute for Studies in Education of the University of Toronto (OISE/UT); Rosalie Griffith, for sharing notes on some of the current challenges of the Ontario school system with me; Kate Patridge and Chizoba Imoka, for reading and commenting on drafts of the essay; and Yumiko Kawano, for some technical and editing work as well. I also thank the reviewers of the chapters for their comments.

Notes

1. Hesse 2004, p. 22.
2. Hale 2005, pp. 10–19; Smith 2012.
3. Da Costa 2014a, p. 15.
4. Ahmed 2010; Da Costa 2014b, p. 8.
5. Da Costa 2014a, p. 1.
6. Ibid., p. 2.
7. Baffoe, Asimeng-Boahene, and Ogbuagu 2014, p. 13.
8. Ibid., p. 15.
9. Bonilla-Silva 2010; Cho 2009, pp. 1589–1649; Wise 2010.
10. Cho 2009.
11. Da Costa 2014a, p. 7, citing Vargas 2004.
12. Dei 2013.
13. Amadahy and Lawrence 2009.
14. Dei, forthcoming.
15. Dei 1996.
16. Hesse 2004, p. 22.
17. Ibid., p. 24.
18. Lorde 1983, 1984.
19. Benita 1995, pp. 36–44; Fanon 1963, 1967; Loomba 2005.
20. Cardinal 1969.
21. Busia 1969; Fafunwa and Aisiku 1982; Sifuna 1990.
22. Adjei and Dei 2008; wa Thiong'o 1986.

23. Abdi and Cleghorn 2005.
24. Aujla 2000, pp. 41–47.
25. Dei 2000, pp. 111–132; Dei and Asgharzadeh 2001, pp. 297–323.
26. Abbam 1994, pp. 1870–1871; Abdi and Cleghorn 2005; Battiste 1998, pp. 16–27.
27. Kerr 2013, p. 10.
28. Ibid.
29. Ibid.
30. Fanon 1967.
31. Smith 1999, 2012, p. 21.
32. Diop 1974.
33. Biko 1978.
34. Tatum 1992, 2008.
35. Valencia 1997.
36. Hesse 2004, p. 9.
37. Ibid., p. 11.
38. Ibid., p. 19.
39. Dei 1996.
40. Collins 1991; 1993, pp. 25–45; 2004.
41. Alcoff 1988; Maher and Tetreault 1993.
42. Papernick 2013, p. 6.
43. Ibid.
44. Davies 2008, p. 7, quoted in Papernick 2013.
45. Amadiume 2008; Bambara 1970; Oyewumi 1997.
46. Johnson 1985, p. 13.
47. Papernick 2013.
48. Amadahy and Lawrence 2009; Lawrence and Dua 2005, pp. 120–143.
49. Simpson, Nanibush, and Williams 2012; Smith 2012; Talor 2011.
50. Amadahy and Lawrence 2009.
51. Dei 2014.
52. Nketiah 2014. Personal e-mail correspondence. April.

Bibliography

Abbam, Charles Moses. 1994. "Developing Education." *West Africa* 4022: 1870–1871.
Abdi, Ali A., and Alie Cleghorn. 2005. *Issues in African Education: Sociological Perspectives.* New York: Palgrave Macmillan.
Adjei, Paul Banahene, and George J. Sefa Dei. 2008. "Sankofa: In Search for Alternative Development Paradigm for Africa." In *Decolonizing Democratic Education: Trans-disciplinary Dialogue,* eds. Ali A. Abdi and George Richardson (pp. 173–182). Rotterdam/Taipei: Sense Publishers.
Ahmed, Sara. 2010. *The Promise of Happiness.* Durham: Duke University Press.

Amadahy, Zainab, and Bonita Lawrence. 2009. "Indigenous Peoples and Black People in Canada: Settlers or Allies?" In *Breaching the Colonial Contract*, ed. Arlo Kempf (pp. 105–136). Rotterdam, Netherlands: Springer.

Amadiume, Ifi. 2008. "African Women's Body Images in Postcolonial Discourse and Resistance to Neo-Crusaders." In *Womanhood: Images, Icons, and Ideologies of the African Body*, ed. Barbara Thompson (pp. 49–69). Hanover, NH: Hood Museum of Art, Dartmouth College in association with University of Washington Press.

Aujla, Angela. 2000. "Others in Their Own Land: Second Generation South Asian Canadian Women, Racism, and the Persistence of Colonial Discourse." *Canadian Women Studies* 20 (2): 41–47.

Baffoe, Michael, Lewis Asimeng-Boahene, and Buster C. Ogbuagu. 2014. "Their Way or No Way: 'Whiteness' as Agent for Marginalizing and Silencing Minority Voices in Academic Research and Publication." *European Journal of Sustainable Development* 3 (1): 13–32.

Bambara, Toni Cade. 1970. *The Black Woman: An Anthology.* New York: Washington Square Press.

Battiste, Marie. 1998. "Enabling the Autumn Seed: Towards a Decolonized Approach to Aboriginal Knowledge, Language, and Education." *Canadian Journal of Native Education* 22 (1): 16–27.

Benita, Parry. 1995. "Problems in Current Theories of Colonial Discourse." In *The Post-colonial Studies Reader*, eds. Bill Ashcroft, Gareth Griffiths, and Helen Thiophene (pp. 36–44). New York: Routledge.

Biko, Steve. 1978. *I Write What I Like.* London: Bowerdean Press.

Bonilla-Silva, Eduardo. 2010. *Racism without Racists: Color-Blind Racism and the Persistence of Racial Inequality in the United States.* Lanham: Rowman & Littlefield.

Busia, Kofi Abrefa. 1969. *Purposeful Education for Africa.* Mouton: The Hague.

Cardinal, Harold. 1969. *The Unjust Society.* Vancouver: Douglas & McIntyre.

Cho, Sumi. 2009. "Post-racialism." *Iowa Law Review* 94: 1589–1649.

Collins, Patricia Hill. 1991. *Black Feminist Thought.* New York: Harper Collins.

Collins, Patricia Hill. 1993. "Towards a New Vision: Race, Class, and Gender as Categories of Analysis and Connection." *Race, Sex and Class* 1: 25–45.

Collins, Patricia Hill. 2004. *Black Sexual Politics: African Americans, Gender, and the New Racism.* New York: Routledge.

Da Costa, Alexandra. 2014a. "Confounding Anti-racism: Mixture, Racial Democracy, and Post-racial Politics in Brazil." *Critical Sociology*: 1–19. Published online January 31.

Da Costa, Alexandra. 2014b. "The (Un)Happy Objects of Affective Community." *Cultural Studies*: 1–23. doi: 10.1080/09502386.2014.899608. Published online March 25.

Davies, C. B. 2008. *Left of Karl Marx the Political Life of Black Communist Claudia Jones.* Durham, NC: Duke University Press, 2008, p. 38, quoted in Stacey Papernick, "The Impact of Claudia Jones's Theoretical Perspective," 7.

Dei, George J. Sefa. 1996. *Anti-racism Education in Theory and Practice*. Halifax: Fernwood Publishing.

Dei, George J. Sefa. 2000. "Rethinking the Role of Indigenous Knowledges in the Academy." *International Journal of Inclusive Education* 4 (2): 111–132.

Dei, George J. Sefa. 2013. "Reframing Critical Anti-racist Theory (CART) for Contemporary Times." In *Contemporary Issues in the Sociology of Race and Ethnicity: A Critical Reader*, eds. George J. Sefa Dei and Meredith Lordan (pp. 1–14). New York: Peter Lang.

Dei, George J. Sefa. Forthcoming. "Why Do That Dance: Collapsing the African Experience into the White Colonial Settler Discourse." In *Black Studies and Critical Thinking*, ed. Rochelle Brock.

Dei, George J. Sefa, and Alireza Asgharzadeh. 2001. "The Power of Social Theory: Towards an Anti-colonial Framework." *Journal of Educational Thought* 35 (3): 297–323.

Diop, Cheikh Anta. 1974. *African Origin of Civilization: Myth or Reality*. Chicago: Lawrence Hill.

Fafunwa, A. Bobs, and J. U. Aisiku. 1982. *Education in Africa: A Comparative Study*. London: George Allen & Unwin.

Fanon, Frantz. 1963. *The Wretched of the Earth*. New York: Grove Press.

Fanon, Franz. 1967. *Black Skin, White Masks*. New York: Grove Press.

Hale, Charles R. 2005. "Neoliberal Multiculturalism." *Political and Legal Anthropology Review* 28 (1): 10–19.

Hesse, Barnor. 2004. "Im/Plausible Deniability: Racism's Conceptual Double Bind." *Social Identities* 10 (1): 9–29.

Kerr, Jeannie. 2013. "Pedagogical Thoughts on Knowing Bodies: The Teacher Educator Encounters the Elder and the Phronimos." Unpublished PhD dissertation, University of British Columbia.

Lawrence, Bonita, and Enakshi Dua. 2005. "Decolonising Anti-racism." *Social Justice* 32 (4): 120–143.

Linda, Alcoff. 1988. "Cultural Feminism vs. Poststructuralism: The Identity Crisis in Feminist Theory." *Journal of Women in Culture and Society* 13 (3): 405–436.

Loomba, Anita. 2005. *Colonialism/Postcolonialism*. New York: Routledge.

Lorde, Audre. 1983. "The Master's Tools Will Never Dismantle the Master's House." In *This Bridge Called My Back: Writings by Radical Women of Color*, eds. Cherie Moraga and Gloria Anzaldua (pp. 98–106). New York: Kitchen Table Press.

Lorde, Audre. 1984. *Sister Outsider*. Berkeley: The Crossing Press.

Maher, Frances A., and Mary Kay Tetreault. 1993. "Frames of Positionality: Constructing Meaningful Dialogues about Gender and Race." *Anthropological Quarterly: Constructing Meaningful Dialogue on Difference: Feminism and Postmodernism in Anthropology and the Academy Part 2* 66 (3): 118–126.

Oyewumi, Oyeronke. 1997. *The Invention of Women: Making an African Sense of Western Gender Discourses*. Minneapolis: University of Minnesota Press.

Papernick, Stacey. 2013. "The Impact of Claudia Jones's Theoretical Perspective on Marxist Feminism: The Intersectional Oppression of Black Woman in the United States in the Post-Depression Era and in Ontario in 1990 in the Nursing Profession." Unpublished Course Paper.

Sherwood, Marika. 1999. *Claudia Jones: A Life in Exile.* London: Lawrence & Wishart.

Sifuna, Daniel Namusonge. 1990. *Development of Education in Africa: The Kenyan Experience.* Nairobi: Initiatives.

Simpson, Leanne, Wanda Nanibush, and Carol Williams. 2012. "The Resurgence of Indigenous Women's Knowledge and Resistance in Relation to Land and Territoriality: Transnational and Interdisciplinary Perspectives." *Intensions, Fall/ Winter* 6: 1–7.

Smith, Andrea. 2012. "Indigeneity, Settler Colonialism and White Supremacy." In *Racial Formation in the Twenty-First Century,* eds. Hosang Daniel Martinez et al. (pp. 66–90). Berkeley: University of California Press.

Smith, Linda Tuhiwai. 1999. *Decolonizing Methodologies: Research and Indigenous Peoples.* New York: Palgrave.

Talor, Malanie Benson. 2011. *Reconstructing the Native South: American Indian Literature and the Lost Cause.* Athens: University of Georgia Press.

Tatum, Beverly Daniel. 1992. "Talking about Race, Learning about Racism: The Application of Racial Identity Development Theory in the Classroom." *Harvard Educational Review* 62 (1): 1–24.

Tatum, Beverly Daniel. 2008. *Can We Talk about Race: Another Conversation in an Era of School Resegregation.* Boston: Bacon Press.

Valencia, Richard R. 1997. "Conceptualizing the Notion of Deficit Thinking." In *The Evolution of Deficit Thinking: Educational Thought and Practice,* ed. Richard R. Valencia (pp. 1–12). Oxon: RoutledgeFalmer.

Vargas, Joao H. Costa. 2004. "Hyperconsciousness of Race and Its Negation: The Dialectic of White Supremacy in Brazil." *Identities* 11 (4): 444.

wa Thiong'o, Ngugi. 1986. *Decolonizing the Mind: The Politics of Language in African Literature.* Portsmouth: Heinemann.

Wise, Tim. 2010. *Colorblind: The Rise of Post-racial Politics and the Retreat from Racial Equity.* San Francisco: City Light Books.

Chapter 16

Living with the Dark and the Dazzling: Unlearning Racism

Joan T. Wynne

"The United States is a racist country and because of that, I, as a white person, am the beneficiary of power and privileges that have an adverse effect on citizens of color."[1] I have begun opening presentations I make to any audience, at national conferences or in university classes, with that sentence, one that a young writer for *The Nation,* Mychal Denzel Smith, has persuaded me is a necessary starting place for any white person who wants to unravel racism in our society.

Because of my lifelong journey of "un-learning" racism, I find his sentence to be essential and pertinent also to my writing for this book. The sentence reminds me that a Southern white woman, creating a chapter on the impact of racism on the college experience of black students, seems arrogant and a bit preposterous. So before I can address the topic, I must admit that anything I say comes tempered by the reality that I can never fully understand the impact of racism on these students. I can read and cite the research about it. I can do my own research about it. I can observe it in my classrooms; but because of my unearned power and privilege, I can never really know it as my African American and black students do. In this chapter, though, I will describe what I do know in hopes it might be valuable to practitioners, especially to people who look like me and who care about eliminating racism—not only to better teach black students but also to rid ourselves of the pathology that we, not African Americans, have carried within our national DNA for centuries.

The late singer and stalwart activist, Pete Seeger, once said in an interview, "The key to the future of the world is finding the optimistic stories and letting them be known."[2] I intend to do just that. Yet, before telling those stories, I'm driven to depict another facet of our dilemma. That, for me, has been crystallized by the words of another activist, Bryan Stevenson, director of the Equal Justice Initiative. When he spoke for TED.com, Stevenson said, "It's that mind-heart connection that I believe compels us to not just be attentive to all the bright and dazzling things but also to the dark and difficult things."[3] I, too, believe that to fully understand the optimistic stories, we all, first, must wrestle with the "dark and difficult things." Thus, the beginning of this chapter addresses my observations of the negative consequences of the dominant culture's institutions on black students. Later the "brighter" stories emerge, illustrating the philosophy and pedagogy that I have found effective in creating environments that support the intellectual achievements of black students. And within those stories, I include the words and wisdom of African American and other students who have informed my exploration of the dilemma.

The Dark and Difficult

Because I now live in Florida where within an 18-month span, two unarmed black teenage boys were murdered—one, Trayvon Martin, for walking while black in a mostly all-white neighborhood, and another, Jordan Davis, for playing loud music in a car—I am more dedicated than ever to understanding how racism plays a part not only in the mis-education of our African American children but in the mis-education of our Anglo children who are schooled to become adults who "can stand their ground" to murder black boys or who can serve as masters of judicial systems that legitimize these murders.

So as I wrote this chapter, I hoped to explore the kind of schooling needed for white Americans to stand up not only for quality education for the nation's children but also for protecting the lives of all children. Racism is a blight on this nation, and a blight on any intellectual who sits silently as his or her black students' very lives are daily threatened. That threat never seems more clearly stated than in the words of Ella Baker, who said: "We who believe in freedom cannot rest, until the killing of Black men, Black mothers' sons is as important as the killing of White men, White mothers' sons."[4] Those words constantly challenge me to dig deeper, to explore abusive schooling more urgently, whenever I write about the education of black students and, indeed, about the education of any mother's child. For, all of our children are at stake at different levels—those who are being victimized by demoralizing education and violence and the souls of those whose education is so severely distorted that many later become either the perpetrators or the protectors of violence against black children. If not addressed in the classroom, the tentacles of white supremacy, that strangle the K-16 system of public and private education, leave no one undiminished by the destructive powers of the dominant culture. And the dearth of disciplined discussion about it allows and encourages a divisive nation.

Civil rights icon and president of The Algebra Project, Bob Moses, in a keynote address at a public forum explained the dire consequences of bad education for our black, brown, and white, poor children. During his address, Moses reported,

> The Southern Educational Fund looked at a 40-year period from 1970 to 2010 and asked the question who gets a B.A.? Not who goes to college, but who gets a B.A.? They answered it in terms of the quartiles, the top economic quartile and the bottom economic quartile. In 1970, 40% of the top economic quartile got their B.A.s. Forty years later 80% received it. It doubled over this 40-year period. In 1970, 7% of the bottom quartile got B.A.s. *Forty years later in 2010, only 9% of the bottom quartile graduated from college.*[5]

With that grim 40-year record of sorry education delivered to our students at the bottom, can we continue to pretend that we are a democratic nation that offers quality education to all its people? Or will we continue to blame the victims for this travesty of unequal opportunity?

In other chapters in this book, K-12 racist realities are addressed, especially the horrific criminalizing of our young children, paving the way for a corporate school-to-prison pipeline. So my chapter will not primarily address K-12. Yet I must share here one of the more shocking statistics, that I only recently discovered. A Department of Education report in March 2014 declared that "Black children represent 18 percent of preschool enrollment, but 42 percent of the preschool children suspended once, and 48 percent of the preschool children suspended more than once."[6] Really? Suspending virtual toddlers? What is wrong with a nation that cannot deal with three- to five-year-olds? And what kind of nation keeps the doors open to preschools that don't know how to nurture or discipline children who not too long ago have just learned to talk and walk? But still a stunning silence exists in mainstream corridors of this country about the exploitation of our children of color.

With these kinds of child abuse, institutionalized racism is crucial to any legitimate study of quality education for all children. Moreover, these debacles in K-12 severely impact the opportunities for African American students to attend and succeed in college, long before they are of age to enroll. Recently, California published a snapshot of its state's manifestations of systemic racism on black students in its universities:

- Blacks have the lowest completion rates for freshman and transfer students at all three higher education segments: community colleges, California State University and the University of California.
- Black students are more likely than any other group to attend college without ever earning a degree.
- The achievement gap between Blacks and Whites earning a bachelor's degree or higher has narrowed by only a percentage point over the last decade. In 2011, about 24% of Black adults had obtained a bachelor's compared with 41% of Whites. [Opportunity gap, not achievement gap, probably more aptly describes this dilemma.]
- Black students appear to have been disproportionately affected by policy decisions such as the state ban on affirmative action in education and budget cuts in recent years that resulted in significant declines in enrollment at community colleges and Cal State campuses.
- Reluctance on the part of policy makers and educators to tackle racial disparities head-on is one factor in the persistent gaps, said Michele Siqueiros, executive director of the Campaign for College Opportunity.
- "I've come to be more convinced of an inability to really address these issues more openly in a way that forces state policy makers to come up with ideas and colleges to find solutions," Siqueiros said. "Especially after the ban on affirmative action, we don't feel comfortable talking about race and nothing really happens."[7]

So where do we go from here? How do we more effectively consider the dark and difficult in order to integrate our sense of humanity into the "bright and dazzling"?

Focus Groups

Thinking about that challenge propelled me to first elicit the wisdom of my black students, hoping to also raise their voices for publication. Sixty-seven percent of the students in the university where I now teach are Hispanic/Latino students. But many of my black students come from the Caribbean Islands—Cuba, Trinidad, Jamaica, Haiti. Some are African American. However, because of scheduling conflicts (two months to finalize respondents' available dates), and because of a fear of some students that this confidential conversation might somehow, by some participant, be revealed, only seven students joined the focus groups. Their fear of disclosure reminded me of the treacherous terrain that many of our students travel. Finally, though, four of the seven students who were able to participate in focus groups were black students from the Caribbean and three identified themselves as African American. Some were still attending my present university; some had attended Primarily White Universities (PWI) in other parts of the state.

James Baldwin once insisted that "while the tale of how we suffer and how we are delighted and how we triumph is never new, it must be heard. There isn't any other tale to tell, it's the only light we've got in all this darkness."[8] Guided by his perspective, I invited the focus students to share their stories of navigating the university system. I wanted to hear their insights about the challenges of dealing with covert and/or overt racist behavior and attitudes while attempting academic success in a PWI. Though this university is considered a minority institution, the majority of its Hispanic/Latino population describes themselves as white Hispanic and in the particular city where most of them live, they hold power and privilege that doesn't exist for them elsewhere in the state. Therefore, many of the Hispanics in classroom discussions originally report that they never think about themselves as victims of racism.

Though, like Beverly Tatum, president of Spelman College, I believe the darkness of racism and its consequences in schools are all around us. It's the elephant in the classroom that no one wants to talk about out loud. And, like Baldwin, I think the stories of those who suffer racism in our schools must be heard. They must be heard over and over until the nation commits to reckoning with its 400 unrelenting years of bloody, racist history. As a developing democracy, to move forward from the darkness of that history into the light of redemption may lie in our willingness to listen deeply and well and to learn from the collective stories of "suffering, delight, and triumph."[9]

Therefore, my goals for initiating these focus groups were

(1) to explore the dynamic of and discoveries from intentional conversations among those who have experienced overt and/or covert racism in schools and universities;

(2) to listen for any mention of schisms that often occur between African Americans and Caribbean blacks in my classroom and in many U.S. urban universities;

(3) to learn from students' stories of specific challenges they have faced that I may not have recognized as a professor from the dominant culture.

Conversations involving the two focus groups began with the same guiding question: Can you describe any specific challenges that you faced because of overt or covert racism in your university experience?

Emergent Themes

Four themes seemed to evolve throughout the dialogue among respondents in both focus groups: isolation, struggles to name racism, exhaustion from playing expected roles, and schisms between black cultures.

Isolation

Often in the conversation, the sense of isolation was addressed, an isolation that black students felt as a consequence of being in a PWI, where no one, professors nor students, assumed a responsibility to reach out to them. As one respondent explained about being in a classroom, "And so it seemed like you were just kind of by yourself, just doing your own thing. Everybody would kind of group up together, people that weren't Black or whatever, and you would just kind of be sitting there on your own."

One of the doctoral candidates told the story of being at an educational conference, sitting in a restaurant talking to two white female participants. While she sat with them, a white male later joined their table, spoke, and looked directly at the other women, yet never acknowledged her presence, as though she were invisible. The other women shifted their attention to him and never again spoke to her. Similar stories were cited by all seven focus participants, explaining that this isolation happened in classrooms, in cafeterias, at social events, at professional meetings, and so on. However, the participants' stories of determination to forge ahead and, indeed, achieve, might startle those who see these students only as victims, or incapable of academic achievement, or too sensitive about racism, or worse, somehow guilty for the nation's institutionalized racism.

Struggles to Name It

Yet, in the opening of each dialogue, an unexpected response emerged in the group. The respondents seemed initially somewhat unconscious of racist attitudes or behaviors at the university. It took the telling of many stories among them to unravel the obvious. As one student explained, "Because it hasn't been so overt, it is hard for me to think of an incident." When stories began to unfold in the conversation about specific encounters they had experienced when relating to white professors and students or white Hispanic/Latinos either at the university or at their employment, all respondents initially used expressions like "I don't think this was racist; it may have just been ignorance."

One of the students' reflections of an experience during her undergraduate program explained her struggle to understand the motivation of the advice of her Anglo professor/advisor:

> For the dietitian program you put in bids for an internship . . . So you pick your three and you pray that you get into one of those three. Okay. And so to the professor, I was like well this place gives a voucher so you get a certain amount of money every month. She kept saying, "No, no, don't pick that one. . . . You're definitely not going to get into that one." Okay. Well, what about this one? "No, no, no don't do that one." And you know you're thinking that the professor knows best but then kind of in the back of your head you're like is she being racist? You're not really sure because this is a person that's above you . . . your professor that you've been with for the last year. So you're like well, I guess I'm just going to pick these three that she thinks are the only ones I can do—not really knowing if, maybe, I could have done one of my first three choices. . . . Maybe it was racism. Maybe it's not. I still really don't know. I kind of feel like maybe it was though.

Another student told a story about white students from her high school whom she knew well, but who once on the same PWI campus with her, went their separate ways and never befriended her again. She commented that she didn't "know if this would be called racism, but I never had any White friends approach me in college." Later she told a story of being one of three black students in a majority "white Hispanics" graduate course, where students were encouraged to complete research projects with others who were interested in the same research topic. She said that the three black students remained alone in their group with no one else gravitating toward their research. Again, she said she assumed the Cuban Americans still were uncomfortable working alongside black students but insisted it might have been for other reasons. She seemed unwilling to suggest that the reason could be an unconscious undercurrent of racist "othering" by those students.

The student's ambiguity about how to describe a reality that society denies exists echoed previous comments from other black students in my classrooms after they finish reading *Other People's Children*.[10] In the 16 years, I've been using that book in courses, most of my black students react similarly to it. Each, using different words or phrases, confirms what one PhD student succinctly remarked, with tears rolling down her cheeks, "I thought I was crazy until I read her book. She says what I have been feeling all of my life, but I thought I was crazy." The waltz forced on black students to dance around covert racist attitudes and behaviors sometimes makes them feel schizophrenic. They want to achieve in college. Indeed, their families expect them to. Yet these barriers to experiencing a "typical college life" often make black students question their judgment of reality, sometimes making them feel "crazy."

One respondent explained, "You don't know what that is so you question yourself. . . . you've come from a school where everyone is Black and all of the teachers around you are Black, and the administration is Black. So you don't know what racism is. You've seen it on TV. You've heard about it before but to actually experience it in a White college . . ."

A graduate student suggested, "There's an undercurrent working behind the scenes all of the time that we have kind of figured out it's there. We don't see it exactly but we also know that you have to do certain things when you navigate that current. So even if you don't see the current happening . . . you know you've got to perform better. You have to be sure everything is on the up and up."

In one group session, respondents discussed how they often ignore or mentally question assumptions that other cultures make about them, whenever black students are in a room with predominantly white people. One PhD student/respondent suggested:

And it's more micro aggressive, I guess. . . . Not only am I here for some of my degree, but I'm working here. And a lot of times I walk into a room, and I just feel this automatic assumption arises that "you don't know as much as we do." And I look around as to who else is in the same position as I am, and I think I can count on one hand how many Black descended individuals who are ITs [Instructional Technicians]. So I just wonder a lot of times with them, are you presuming that I don't know this because I'm Black? Or are you just presuming I don't know this because I don't know it . . . I look at my resume and I'm like, well, I think I pretty much accounted for what I know. And, I think, you guys have tested me enough by now. You still shouldn't be looking at me and wondering those types of things as to what it is I'm capable of. So I experienced more that than anything else on this campus.

Another respondent, who also works at the university, explained a further dimension of work experiences for blacks in a white environment:

> I probably wouldn't call some of the things that I've experienced racism per se. . . . What I think in terms of experience here, what I've noticed for myself, my assistant is Hispanic, White Hispanic. And I know whenever we go out together if we have an appointment to go someplace to a meeting they assume she is Dr. _____. Or if we're both in my office and we're expecting someone to come in, they assume that she is Dr._____, although I'm behind the desk, and she's sitting in front of me. So I find it very interesting.

Her comment suggests the convolutions that students mentally juggle as they try to navigate a system where institutional racism pervades, yet is always masked as the victim's problem, not an institutional structural trap.

Nevertheless, in both focus groups, as the conversations evolved, tales of overt racism unfolded, but most were instances that had happened at PWI's that they had previously attended in another part of the state. One respondent mentioned, "And so the newspaper there, the cartoonist did this little cartoon with Condoleezza Rice and Kanye West and basically painted them monkeys." Another student reported the unabashed and pervasive flying of Confederate flags on homes and cars in another city in the state. Many, however, cited instances of racist pictures or discussions on Facebook pages of white students with whom they now attend classes. Several mentioned their surprise when their white peers "befriended" them on Facebook yet sooner or later posted unmistakable, racist comments: "Sally is always nice to me and stuff. But then I look on her Facebook page and she's got some racist monkey picture of Obama and I'm like, 'Man, I never would have thought Sally was thinking like that.'" Another respondent commented, "I don't know. It seems like social media to me is helping to refuel racism."

Nevertheless, in an e-mail, sent after her participation in the focus group, a respondent unknowingly corroborated my observation of the respondents' struggles to clearly identify racism. She remarked, "Throughout the conversation we reflected on multiple incidents and wrestled with being able to say it was covert, overt or simply racism at all. As college students we experienced both types of racism, weathered all of the side effects and still could not name or simply call it out. If we can't name it, how can we change it?"

Exhaustion from Playing the Role of Hostess

In one focus group, the metaphor of hostess, one also introduced in bell hooks's text, emerged as a thread to explain the mainstream culture's implicit expectation of the chief role of black students, and black people in general, whenever they are in the room with white Americans.

Respondent A: But that every time you go to a new group there is that constant need to prove yourself. . . . Yeah, it does a toll emotionally as far as being tiring because then once you realize ain't nobody else hosting. Nobody else cares about what they say to people around here why should I care about what I say?

Respondent B: Right. And it's tiring, right . . . the fact that sometimes you're put in the position to make people comfortable. Yeah, it is like being the hostess. I have to make you comfortable so you can be comfortable with me. That's tiring. So it's like you're at a party and you have to host everybody. That would be tiring. I mean you want to be a guest. You want to be a guest. So that sometimes you do and sometimes you don't, I'm not tired today. Other times I'm tired, but I'm not doing it today, so I'm not hosting, I'm a guest.

Respondent A: And that's when problems usually start.

Respondent B: Right. Who does she think she is? She thinks she belongs. I mean no one is saying this, but the look is like, "Oh she looks comfortable here. Why is she so comfortable here?" Because you know what I'm a guest today. I'm not hosting.

(Group Laughter)

Respondent C: I'm telling you we can't have a day off.

Respondent B: No. And then people wonder why people are so comfortable, and they let their hair down with people from their own cultures—because [when you're with your own culture] you don't have to host. We all are guests. But we need to be able to intermingle with other cultures as guests, not a host and a guest, a host and a guest, a host and a guest.

Respondent A: How can we all get invited to the party? . . . And leave somebody else to host? Or why have a host at all? Let's just all show up.

The act of hosting (a flip of the use of the metaphor by hooks), of having to make everyone else feel comfortable in a room, seemed to speak to the mainstream notion that blacks should not show competence nor aloofness, irritation, and certainly not anger. To the contrary, the unspoken and maybe unconscious notion is that blacks should continue to take care of people, as they for centuries in the South were demanded to do. This unconscious yet structural racist belief system continues to wear many black students down, to make them "tired."

Schisms between Black Cultures

During the focus groups, subtle tensions surfaced between those who identified more with African American culture and those who identified primarily with a Caribbean Island culture. In each group, students acknowledged those tensions existed at the university and in the city. Exploring some of the assumptions that created the divisions shaped a great deal of the conversation. At Morehouse College I had noticed the same division between African American students and students and professors from various countries in Africa. In her book, *Teaching Community: A Pedagogy of Hope,* hooks explains: "Dominator culture has tried to keep us all afraid, to make us choose safety instead of risk, sameness instead of diversity."[11] That fear and practice bubbled up in each focus group around attitudes of Caribbean and African Americans toward each other.

An African American student explained: "That's kind of what we were talking about earlier about Caribbean's not associating themselves with African-Americans. Like oh, no I'm not African-American, I'm Haitian. I'm not African-American, I'm Jamaican. So it's like still separating ourselves while we should be cohesive."

One respondent explained her epiphany as a Jamaican-born student who attended K-16 schools in Florida:

> My family is Jamaican and I was taught you are not African-American and neither do you want to be African-American. You want to make sure that folks know that you're Caribbean; you're Jamaican; you're other. And, of course, I think going to—U definitely snapped it out of me because when people looked at me and they left two seats empty they weren't saying, "Oh there's the Jamaican girl." No, they're thinking, "Oh she's Black. She's got a big afro; we don't want to sit next to her" . . . that's a conversation on a whole that we need to have more as a people and what does it mean to actually be Black in America period. Like I said, after seeing myself for 12 years of schooling here as a Jamaican, and socializing only with Jamaicans, I experienced a rude awakening when I attended—U. That's when I began to identify myself differently, as a Black woman . . . devoted to the struggle.

In the other focus group, a Caribbean student explained, "You hear all of the bad things about African-Americans, they're lazy. They don't want to work. They use public assistance, blah, blah, blah. I'm going to be honest with you, we come with those thoughts. We come with those thoughts . . . What we didn't understand is the structure of racism because we didn't have a structure of racism where we came from that impeded our development. So we didn't get it. And I didn't get it either . . . I don't think my parents even got it yet."

Later, the same respondent commented, "Yes, sometimes between African-American and immigrant Blacks there's some kind of division. . . . Like we're potentially better or we think we're better than other Blacks, especially African-Americans, right. But I think it's not about being better. I think it's just the fact that we're coming from an environment that's all about you ethnically. You've seen everyone who is powerful, doctors, lawyers, nurses, everybody is Black, and I really don't see that in this country. So [unlike African Americans] I'm not yearning to see it because I've seen it before."

Several respondents suggested that student clubs that designated themselves as a specific ethnic culture such as Jamaican or African American or Bahamian further complicated this issue of separation among black students.

Yet, during these portions of the conversations, everyone seemed baffled by the oppressive behavior of white Hispanics/Latinos when interacting with black students. All respondents insisted that whether they were from the islands or from America, if they were black, the Hispanic culture did not accept nor befriend them. Whenever sharing scenarios about the deliberate choice of "white" Hispanic/Latino peers or professors to avoid them, the black students all seemed to wonder what one respondent voiced, "How could you be participating in the very thing that other people are imposing on you?" Many insisted that they had heard Hispanic/Latino peers mention the shock of oppressive attitudes and behaviors they experienced when traveling outside the city into other parts of the state. The respondents suggested that the city seemed to provide a protective cocoon for its Hispanic/Latino population, and unless white Hispanics traveled beyond the city's boundaries, they were unable to see themselves as caught in the vice of hegemony. One of the focus participants insisted, "If they could just understand that if we all stood together, stood united, we could seriously change this system that oppresses all of us."

The Optimistic Stories—What Works

A week after the dialogue, a couple of respondents, when seeing me in the elevator, mentioned that they had continued to talk about the conversations from the focus group. They asked if we might reconvene, maybe meet with other students, and continue the conversation. They also mentioned that they had experienced a few epiphanies as a result of the dialogue about racism. We agreed to meet during the fall semester and talk again about how we might fit future dialogues into their busy university schedules. I also asked if they might e-mail a sentence or two describing those epiphanies. The following are their e-mailed responses:

Epiphanies

E-mail Respondent 1: A dialogue about racism can be difficult to have, considering in America we live in it constantly. It is often such a complex issue that it cannot be separated from everyday life. It can be blatant and obvious, but most of the time it is subtle and unclear. From the discussions I began to understand more about how I navigate the world—I recognize covert racist actions may be happening around me, but I do not give it much thought. If I do, it is often in the form of counter narrative stories that I run down as a list of why this action may have occurred. Often after reviewing the counter narratives list, it does come back down to "probably because I am Black." The dialogue discussion also provided me, a Black American, with some of the perspectives of Caribbean Blacks living in the U.S. The notion of cultural capital that Caribbean people gain from growing up in a society that is predominantly Black helped me understand what is often perceived by Black Americans as a "better than you" persona; it is simply a greater amount of cultural capital they are ingrained with from living in a society where they are not told they are "less than."

E-mail Respondent 2: Basically, the dialogue reminded me how "targeted" my social identities (race, gender, etc.) are here . . . and how psychologically exhausting it is to be a Black-female-professional or simply a human being in the U.S. This exhaustion, I think results in racial/ethnic minorities becoming hypersensitive to their environment, as a defense mechanism, to combat this racial-psychological warfare that exists in the U.S.

E-mail Respondent 3: Because of the dialogue I did remind myself that I have a voice; that I do not have to be bound by the contingencies or the constructs that others create for me. Nor do I need to subject myself to the one I created for myself. So, for that . . . I sincerely thank you!

These comments as well as the dialogue in both focus groups seemed to echo the concerns of many of my African American and black students during the 12 years of teaching at the present university. Rereading the transcripts from this dialogue has helped me rethink my pedagogy and assumptions about tensions between students here. Reading the respondents' e-mails reminded me that, as Baldwin suggests, having space and time to tell the "tales" of struggle and triumphs around the issues of racism might be a necessary journey for many of our black students at the university. And because such a space and time happens so rarely in classrooms, I've committed to cocreate with interested students a professional learning community where black students can come together once or twice a month and address these issues by telling their stories.

Yet, having worked with black students at a number of universities, the conversations during the focus groups offered no surprises about the racist culture in PWIs. Except when teaching at Morehouse, I have witnessed institutionalized racism on every plantation where I have taught. The surprise for me at PWIs has always been not the abuse of students of color but mainstream professors' unconsciousness of that abuse and of the hegemonic structures that undergird their own university life. My students have consistently validated this observation when they, during and at the end of my courses, challenge the nature of their college education with comments such as, "Why am I a graduating senior, and I have never engaged in conversations about racism and classism in any other courses?" or "I'm at the end of my Master's Program, and no other class has ever addressed issues of justice."

Thus, the dialogue with the focus groups seemed an affirmation of the practices and curriculum used in my classrooms. Both investigate the impact of institutionalized racism, classism, sexism, homophobia, and so on, on education. Like Paulo Freire,[12] I believe that education is never politically neutral; it either supports the status quo or encourages transformation of our worlds. Included in that belief is the notion that anything we want to change must be addressed intentionally and directly within the classroom. If we don't name it, it sits there in defiance. Moreover, confronting justice issues can lead toward eliminating the structures that diminish our marginalized students and that also trap mainstream students into destructive notions of white supremacy, mocking the nation's dreams of democracy.

Due largely to my experiences at Morehouse College and to my African American mentors, who have over 30 years modeled for me a different way of being and of teaching in a compromised world, I have over the past 30 years developed course content and practices that many students have evaluated as successful. They claim the curriculum and the pedagogy have raised their consciousness about hegemony and have paved a road for them to become better teachers in their public school classrooms. Like bell hooks, I believe that "moving through fear, finding out what connects us, revelling in our differences; this is the process that brings us closer, that gives us a world of shared values, of meaningful community."[13]

One of the college's Cuban American graduate students, who was graduating from her master's program at the university that semester, when responding to an assigned reading in one of my courses, posted the following on the online discussion site:

> The process of unlearning racism is a mind blowing experience. From the readings I've begun to realize the hidden truths about the way I treat some of my students. I had never considered myself racist in the past and yet like the teachers from this article, I would have never known the harm I was causing without taking a course like this and realizing I had to take a deeper look at my actions and thoughts. I know I still have a lot to learn but I have begun to see a change in my attitude towards my students and parents. I think that all teachers' especially new teachers coming into the classroom should be required to take a course like this . . . teachers are never truly prepared of how to deal with our underlying attitudes about students and parents. . . . I have lived it as a teacher in an urban school. In a city like _____where almost all the schools have such diverse populations of students, why is it that undergraduate students are not required to take an Urban education course? The article also states, "The teacher loses sight of her own power to teach all children, and she, unconsciously, sends messages to her students that they are unteachable" . . . as an experienced teacher, I have been there as well and these types of courses are the ones that readjust our thinking and remind us that we are not "just" teachers.

Her comment is typical of other student responses about awakenings in these courses versus their disappointments in the curriculum of other college courses. However, I take little credit for these transformations because my content and practices come not from my own wisdom but the wisdom of my African American mentors. They have deeply influenced my research and teaching.

Because of the work and mentoring of Asa G. Hilliard III, I began to consider that no matter what I taught, I must address the hegemonic structures, policies, and practices of schooling, that it was not enough for me to discuss with my preservice and in-service students the "how" of teaching, but I must also consider the "what" of teaching. Consequently, I integrate into all of my courses a historical perspective of how race was and is still being lived in America in order to invite my students into the struggle to liberate themselves and their students from the destruction of hegemonic systems.

From Lisa Delpit, I learned the language to address issues of power and privilege that manifest themselves in schools and that cripple the achievement of our black, brown, and poor students in K-16 public and private schools. From observing her leadership style, I learned the value of deep listening to the "other"; of believing in the brilliance of every mother's child; of exposing white students to the reality that white supremacy diminishes us all; of how to turn my anger toward racism into more creative, exploratory conversations; of understanding the value of humor and laughter while resisting hegemony; and of taking no one too seriously, especially myself.

From Bob Moses, I discovered the value of investigating the nation's historical records and the organizing tools of the Southern Freedom Movement to teach the power and intellectual capacity of the people pushed to the bottom of society's academic and economic ladder. Through him, I learned the wisdom of Ella Baker and Fannie Lou Hamer who believed that the people at the bottom often offered the most ingenious ideas. And through Moses, I realized that my responsibility included teaching teachers how to allow space and time for students at the bottom quartile to wrestle with abstractions and to use their language, not their oppressors, to demystify mathematical and interdisciplinary concepts, process, and design. From Moses I also learned the "demand" side of education—that the children at the bottom, through disciplined study, must earn their right to become insurgents, to demand what the country says they don't want, a quality education; that advocacy is useful, but ultimately, significant change will come only when those at the bottom demand their constitutional rights as "constitutional people."[14]

From Theresa Perry, I learned the imperative of teaching the "counternarrative" to the nation's story of the history and education of African Americans.[15] Because of her retelling the history of African Americans' passion for education, I began to flip the image of African Americans from victims to liberators, engaged in a 400-year-old struggle to educate themselves and to free the nation from oppressive policies and practices. Teaching that historical context in classrooms seems to create possibilities for a liberation journey for the teachers I teach and for the students they teach.

Pedagogy

For decades, I have designed practices that can mirror anti-hegemonic content. Instead of a "sage on stage" methodology, my courses offer student-centered, participatory engagement with each other, with me, and with the content. These practices are validated in most research about sound pedagogy for the teaching and learning of new ideas and skills. Nevertheless, these strategies primarily interest me as an intentional challenge to that which buoys authoritarian power in the classroom. Yet, at the same time, I insist that no one is force-fed any belief system or ideology, most especially my own. Refuting hegemony demands a delicate and disciplined dance of avoiding proselytizing and of honoring the organic nature of individual intellectual discovery. It demands a tolerance for ambiguity, for nuance, for living the question instead of the answer.

Circles as the Primary Instructional Structures

Typically at the university, most classrooms are set up with rows of desks facing the front of the room. On the first day of every class, before I introduce myself, I ask if anyone has ever heard the word "hegemony." Most often the collective answer is "no." After I explain what the word means, we explore the alignment of their desks as a hegemonic structure. Then, we move the desks into a circle, while discussing the issues of power that the two distinct physical structures symbolize.

Afterward, we introduce ourselves as peers in the teaching/learning process, though I admit during this portion that the power of the letter grade demanded by the university, students, and parents hands the professor an unequal tool of power—(later in the course, we explore how to banish or transform this evaluative, subjective "sorting" tool). We continue by discussing mutual course expectations—what we each hope to learn; what must happen in the class for them and me to feel that the class time has been well spent.

Collaborative Learning and Teaching

To counteract institutionalized isolation, self-aggrandizement, and unhealthy competition, I introduce the value of collaboration in intellectual explorations. Time is spent inviting students to complete a Group Process form that addresses their past experience with groups, their frustrations, the expectations for each member's participation, the strengths each brings to the group, and what must happen for the group experience to be valuable for them. After completing the form, students create groups of five, charged to include people from unfamiliar cultures. Groups then are asked to go anywhere inside or outside the classroom for 20 minutes and discuss their questionnaires and create a group name. Afterward, groups report their experiences to the class, discussing roles that can lead to high-performing teams.

Because in most cultures, "breaking bread" together is a sacred ritual that helps create community, an out-of-class assignment is to dine together with their small group while discussing the theme of their collaborative research projects, data collection and analysis, and responsibilities of each researcher. Also because I believe this ritual is significant for creating community, I bring food to share each session. Our last class is spent sharing dinner at my home.

Written Responses to Selected Readings

The content of the course is partially grounded in the readings that require written responses posted on an online site, where participants can offer feedback. Their guidelines for the responses are to consider these questions: Which ideas seem compelling and why? Which ideas made them uncomfortable and why? What questions arose as a result of the reading? This practice of writing and response seems to foster the growth of their critical thinking skills, deepens their knowledge of issues, and supports the philosophy that their classmates' responses to their ideas are as significant as the professor's. They are also asked to recommend articles that they feel are pertinent for us to read concerning the issues being studied.

Music

From teaching in high school, at Morehouse College, and studying the Southern Freedom Movement, I learned that music is an integral part of the African culture.[16] A number of studies also indicate that the use of music effectively facilitates the discussion of difficult concepts and skills.[17] To create a welcoming space for all cultures as well as to use effective tools to study abstractions, I share music whose themes I believe relate to concepts we are exploring. Later students bring their music to explain concepts being investigated. Students repeatedly insist that music helped them better explore and remember theories like "critical race theory" or "culturally responsive pedagogy."

Videos

To keep ideas current, and because we live in a digital age, I include videos that are relevant to many issues being studied, from educational sites, Youtube.org, and TED.com. Videos like Howard Zinn's, *the People Speak,* have become a staple in my curriculum. Within such videos, students can learn the variety of freedom struggles in this country and can begin forming their own sense of social agency. The videos are always followed by open-ended questions that students consider with their small groups. They continuously evaluate the videos, suggesting the "good, bad, and ugly" of each.

What Worked? What Did Not Work?

The last 5 minutes of each session is devoted to the students anonymously writing what activities or discussions worked for them and what did not work. This evaluation helps us understand that teaching/learning is a continuous cycle of success and failure and that my growth as a professional is tied to their honest reflection on how the class either facilitated or hindered their learning. This mechanism, I believe, reminds me and my students to see ourselves more clearly as peers in the struggle for truth.

Mantra at the End

From studying African-centered curriculum and practices, I became a believer in the power of affirmations. Because that and studying the Southern Freedom Movement convinced me of the value of community building in educational spaces, I end all sessions, with us standing in a circle, repeating the mantra, "None of us is as strong as all of us." On the first day, I explain the history of choosing to end my classes with the mantra, what standing in solidarity might mean for us as educators and for dismantling hegemony. Thereafter, I invite students to volunteer to lead the mantra at the end of sessions. I've also experimented by asking students to create mantras. One student's creation that I particularly liked was "None of us is free until all of us is free." But students most often later choose to end the class with the same mantra we used on the first day. Many students have reported that they later have used this mantra in their K-12 classrooms.

Conclusion

This may be the last time, a spiritual sung during the Southern Freedom Movement, still compels me to understand the sacred nature of each moment of instruction.[18] The power of that song and that moment in time in the building of this nation remind me of how fragile the experience of building community is. It reminds me that each semester probably is the last time that my students and I are together, exploring the depth of oppression and the breadth of possibilities for transformation. So each classroom moment must be grounded in the integrity of discovery, a willingness to explore the unknown. Philosopher Martha Nussbaum indicates that this kind of exploration "says something very important about the human condition of the ethical life: that it is based on a trust in the uncertain and on a willingness to be exposed; it's based on being more like a plant than like a jewel, something rather fragile, but whose very particular beauty is inseparable from its fragility."[19] Because of this ethical conundrum of beauty and fragility, maybe no classroom moment should be corrupted by the tyranny of grades, of sorting students, of rigid adherence to syllabi or bell curves or boring lectures. And possibly, the space and time for story—for expressing feelings of isolation and cultural separation, time for tales of victimization and liberation along with confessions of denial ultimately can help us effectively juggle the dark and the dazzling.

Who knows—if we have the courage to face our collective stories, they may lead us toward a recognition of what poet, Mary Oliver, proclaims, "Whoever you are, no matter how lonely, the world offers itself to your imagination, calls to you like the wild geese, harsh and exciting—over and over announcing your place in the family of things."[20]

Notes

1. Smith 2014, p. 1.
2. Poreles 2014, p. A20.
3. Stevenson 2012.
4. Ransby 2003, p. 335.
5. Moses 2014.
6. Civil Rights Data 2014.
7. Rivera 2013.
8. Baldwin 1995.
9. Tatum 1997.
10. Delpit 1995.
11. hooks 2003., p. 197.
12. Freire 2001.
13. hooks 2003, p. 197.
14. Moses 2014. ETS keynote.

15. Perry, Steele, and Hilliard 2004.
16. Wynne 2002.
17. Gardner 2008; Moffett and Wagner 1991.
18. Freedom Song, DVD, 2000; *This may be the last time*, 1961.
19. Nussbaum 1989, p. 448.
20. Oliver 1986.

Bibliography

Baldwin, James. 1995. *Sonny's Blues*. New York: Penguin Books Ltd., p. 87.

Canfield, Becvar, and Brian Canfield. 1997. *Group Work: Cybernetics, Constructivist, & Social Constructionist Perspectives*. New York: Love Publishing Co.

Civil Rights Data Collection. 2014. "Data Snapshot: School Discipline." U.S. Department of Education Office for Civil Rights. March. Accessed June 16, 2014. http://www2.ed.gov/about/offices/list/ocr/docs/crdc-discipline-snapshot .pdf.

Delpit, Lisa. 1995. *Other People's Children: Cultural Conflict in the Classroom*. New York: The New Press.

Delpit, Lisa. 2012. *Multiplication Is for White People: Raising Expectations for Other People's Children*. New York: The New Press.

Delpit, Lisa, and Joanne Dowdy, eds. 2002. *The Skin That We Speak: Thoughts on Language and Culture in the Classroom*. New York: The New Press.

Freedom Song. 2000. AlphaVille with Carrie Productions, Danny Glover. TNT. DVD.

Freire, Paulo, and Donaldo Macedo. 2001. *Literacy: Reading the Word and the World*. London: Routledge.

Gardner, Howard. 2008. *Multiple Intelligences: New Horizons in Theory and Practice*. Boston: Basic Books.

Harding, Vincent. 1990. *Hope and History: Why We Must Share the History of the Movement*. Maryknoll, NY: Orbis Books.

Harding, Vincent. 1997. *We Changed the World: African Americans 1945–1970*. New York: Oxford University Press.

Hilliard, A.G., III. 1995. *The Maroon within Us: Selected Essays on African American Community Socialization*. Baltimore, MD: Black Classic Press.

Hilliard, A.G., III. 1998. *SBA: The Reawakening of the African Mind*. Gainesville, FL: Makare Publishing Co.

Hilliard, A.G., III. 2014. "What Do We Need to Know Now?" *Rethinking Multicultural Education: Teaching for Racial and Cultural justice*, ed. Wayne Au (pp. 25–38). Milwaukee, WI: Rethinking Schools.

hooks, bell. 2003. *Teaching Community: A Pedagogy of hope*. New York: Routledge, p. 33.

Hsieh, Steven. 2014. "Jury Fails to Reach Verdict on Murder Charge in Michael Dunn Trial." *The Nation* (February 15). Accessed June 16, 2014. http://www.the nation.com/blog/178370/jury-fails-reach-verdict-murder-charge-trial-michael-dunn.

Moffett, James. 1988. *Coming on Center: Evolution of English Education.* New York: Boyton/Cook.

Moffett, James, and Betty Wagner. 1991. *Student Centered Language Arts K-12.* New York: Heinemann Publishing Co.

Moses, Bob. 2014. Unpublished Keynote Address. Educational Testing Service Institute for Student Achievement. June 30.

Moses, Robert, and Charlie Cobb. 2001. *Radical Equations: Civil Rights from Mississippi to the Algebra Project.* Boston, MA: Beacon Press.

Nussbaum, Martha. 1989. "Interview." In *Bill Moyers: A World of Ideas,* ed. Betty Sue Flowers (p. 448). New York: Doubleday Dell Publishing.

Oliver, Mary. 1986. "Wild Geese." *Dream Work.* New York: The Atlantic-Monthly Press-Grove/Atlantic, Inc., p. 6.

Palmer, Parker. 2007. *The Courage to teach: Exploring the Inner Landscape of a Teacher's Life.* San Francisco: Jossey Bass.

Perry, Theresa, Claude Steele, and Asa G. Hilliard, III. 2004. *Young Gifted and Black: Promoting High Achievement among African American Students.* Boston, MA: Beacon Press.

Poreles, Jon. 2014. "Pete Seeger, Champion of Folk Music and Social Change Dies at 94." *The New York Times* (January 29), A20.

Ransby, Barbara. 2003. *Ella Baker & the Black Freedom Movement: A Radical Democratic Vision.* Chapel Hill: The University of North Carolina Press, p. 335.

Rivera, Carla. 2013. "Black College Students Face Persistent Gaps." *LA Times* (December 5). Accessed June 16, 2014. http://articles.latimes.com/2013/dec/05/local/la-me-ln-college-blacks-20131205.

Robles, Frances. 2012. "A Shooting in the Neighborhood." *The Miami Herald* (Broward & Keys edition) (March 16), A2.

Smith, Mychal D. 2014. "White People Have to Give Up Racism." *The Nation* (February 14), 1.

Stevenson, Bryan. 2012. "We Need to Talk about an Injustice." TED.com, March. Accessed March 17, 2014. http://www.ted.com/talks/bryan_stevenson_we_need_to_talk_about_an_injustice.html.

Tatum, Beverly. 1997. *"Why Are All the Black Kids Sitting together in the Cafeteria" and Other Conversations about Race.* New York: Basic Books.

This may be the last time, Old Negro Spiritual sung in African American churches but originally recorded by the Staple Singers in 1961, and often sung later by the Student Non-Violent Coordinating Committee youth when leaving meetings during the years of the Southern Freedom Movement. Sung recently at Freedom Summer 50th Anniversary Congress, June 29, 2014.

Weimer, Maryellen. 2002. *Learner-Centered Teaching: Five Key Changes to Practice.* San Francisco: Jossey Bass.

Wynne, Joan T. 2002. "We Don't Talk Right. You Ask Him." In *The Skin That We Speak: Thoughts on Language and Culture in the Classroom,* eds. Lisa Delpit and Joanne K. Dowdy (pp. 215–216). New York: The New Press.

Wynne, Joan T. 2005. "Education, Liberation, and Transformation: Teaching African American Students within a Context of Culture." In *Instructing and Mentoring the African American College Student: Strategies for Success in Higher Education,* eds. Louis Gallien and Marshalita Sims Peterson (pp. 101–121). Boston, MA: Pearson Education, Inc.

Wynne, Joan. 2012. "Grassroots Leadership: Leading by Not Leading." In *Confessions of a White Educator: Stories in Search of Justice and Diversity,* eds. Joan T. Wynne, Lisa Delpit, and Ron E. Miles (pp. 228–239). Dubuque, IA: Kendall Hunt Publishing Co.

Zinn, Howard. 2010. *The People Speak* DVD. A&E Home Video.

Index

Note: Page numbers in **bold** indicate a table on the corresponding page.

About the Editor and Contributors

Editor

Lillian Dowdell Drakeford, PhD, is retired from the Dayton Public Schools, Dayton, Ohio, where she served as a teacher of the deaf and hard-of-hearing, intervention specialist for children with special needs, curriculum and instruction intervention coach, high school assistant principal, and associate director of curriculum and instruction. Dr. Drakeford completed a bachelor's degree in education of the hearing impaired from the School of Speech at Northwestern University and a master of education degree in curriculum and supervision from Wright State University. She holds a doctorate in leadership and change from Antioch University.

Contributors

Anthony Ash is a doctoral student in the Curriculum and Instruction, Urban Education program at UNCC. He spent six years teaching middle and secondary science. As a graduate student, Anthony taught undergraduate teacher education courses and currently works as a research assistant in the Center for STEM Education at UNCC.

Anthony Collatos is associate professor of education within Pepperdine University's Graduate School of Education and Psychology. His research involves urban education, the sociology of education, college access, and teacher education. He directs multiple programs that empower urban youth, families, and educators to challenge existing policies/practices of educational inequity.

Duane L. Davis, BS, MA, EdD, is a native of Toledo, Ohio. He earned his bachelor of science degree in biology at Morehouse College in Atlanta,

Georgia, and returned to Toledo to begin a career in public education as a science teacher for the Toledo Public School system. Dr. Davis has completed a master of arts degree in guidance and counseling and an educational doctorate in educational leadership from Bowling Green State University with a dissertation concentration on African American adolescent identity development. He has served as a middle-school guidance director, high school assistant principal, and principal. Retired since 2013, Dr. Davis currently serves as senior pastor at Shorter Chapel African Methodist Episcopal Church in Greenfield, Ohio.

John E. Fife is associate professor of psychology at Virginia State University. He is the PI on an NSF-funded grant entitled "Attenuating STEM Test Anxiety: A Role for the Meditative, Meta-cognitive and Media Technology Interventions." Dr. Fife's research focuses on preparing STEM to thrive within the university context.

Steve Grineski teaches educational foundations at Minnesota State University Moorhead and serves as liaison between the MSUM Teacher Education and local Alternative Education programs. Recent books include with Julie Landsman and Robert Simmons, *Talking about Race: Alleviating the Fear,* and *"We Were Pretty Darn Good": A History of Rural Education.*

Toni S. Harris has her PhD in counseling psychology from Virginia Commonwealth University. Dr. Harris is associate professor in the Department of Psychology at Virginia State University. Her research examines how familial factors influence African American children's cognitive and physical outcomes.

Laura M. Harrison is assistant professor in the Counseling and Higher Education Department at Ohio University. She is the coauthor of *Advancing Social Justice: Tools, Pedagogies, and Strategies to Transform Your Campus* (Jossey-Bass). Her forthcoming book *Alternative Solutions to Higher Education's Challenges: An Appreciative Approach to Reform* (Routledge) will be available in 2016.

Oliver W. Hill Jr. is professor of psychology at Virginia State University. Dr. Hill is an experimental psychologist specializing in studying cognition. Hill received his undergraduate training at Howard University in

Washington, DC, and his PhD from the University of Michigan. He is particularly interested in fostering the concept of quality education as a civil right.

M. Francine Jennings, a former public school teacher, serves as national faculty of arts integration for Lesley University in Cambridge, Massachusetts. With experience as a performing artist, teaching artist, and arts integration consultant, she has designed and implemented numerous arts-based workshops in the areas of social justice, diversity, and teacher leadership. Currently a training consultant with the United Negro College Fund, she holds a doctorate in educational leadership from Virginia Polytechnic and State University in Blacksburg, Virginia.

Candice Jimerson-Johnson has joyfully served 19 years in education as a teacher and administrator. Her experiences in public, private, urban, and suburban schools in The Midwest, New England, and South have developed in her a depth of knowledge of the U.S. educational system that few can boast.

Julie Landsman taught in Minneapolis Public Schools for 25years. She has written and coedited numerous books, including *A White Teacher Talks about Race, Growing Up White,* and *Basic Needs: A Year with Street Kids in a City School.* She has taught at Carleton College and Hamline University. She trains teachers in cultural competency and social justice.

Christine Brigid Malsbary is a critical anthropologist of education whose scholarship concerns issues related to equity, language, race, and learning in transnational urban contexts of new immigration. Her work has been published in such journals as the *International Journal of Qualitative Studies in Education* and *Anthropology and Education.* Currently, Malsbary is visiting professor at Vassar College and a recipient of the 2014–2015 NAE Spencer Postdoctoral Fellowship.

Margo Okazawa-Rey currently is on the faculty of the School of Human and Organizational Development at the Fielding Graduate University and professor emerita at San Francisco State University. Dr. Okazawa-Rey's teaching, research, and activism are grounded in her experiences as a founding member of the Combahee River Collective, who articulated a theory of intersectionality in "A Black Feminist Statement" in the 1970s. She received a doctorate in education from the Harvard Graduate School of Education in 1987.

Tema Okun has spent over 30 years working for social justice, most recently as a lead trainer with a dRworks, a collaborative working on and for race equity. She holds a doctorate in curriculum and instruction with a specialization in cultural studies and has taught in undergraduate and graduate classrooms, most recently as faculty in the Educational Leadership Department at National Louis University in Chicago. She is the author of the award-winning book *The Emperor Has No Clothes: Teaching about Race and Racism to People Who Don't Want to Know* (IAP, 2010) and is currently engaged in a community-based research project on the history of the race construct.

Melissa Pearson is assistant professor of English at Claflin University. Dr. teaches composition and African American Studies. Her research interests are in African American feminist rhetoric, First-Year writing, and writing pedagogy. Since earning the PhD in rhetoric and composition from the University of South Carolina, she continued to strengthen her breadth of knowledge as a graduate of HERS Women Higher Education Leadership at Bryn-Mawr College and the Composition Research Seminar at Dartmouth College.

Jeffrey O. Sacha is a Haynes Fellow and a PhD candidate in sociology at the University of Southern California. His research explores the ways that extracurricular experiences impact students differently across race, class, and gender. In his free time, he also runs a free community boxing gym in Los Angeles.

George J. Sefa Dei is professor of social justice education at the Ontario Institute for Studies in Education of the University of Toronto. He is the director for the Centre for Integrative Anti-Racism Studies at the University of Toronto. His teaching and research interests are in the areas of anti-racism, minority schooling, international development, anticolonial thought, and Indigenous knowledges systems. He has published extensively on minority youth education, anti-racism, Indigenous philosophies, and anticolonial thought. In June 2007, Professor Dei was installed as a traditional chief in Ghana, specifically as the Adumakwaahene (and Gyaasehene-elect) of the town of Asokore, in the New Juaben Traditional Area of Ghana. His stool name is Nana Sefa Atweneboah I.

Carolyn M. Shields is professor at Wayne State University in downtown Detroit where her academic focus is transformative educational leadership, democracy, and social justice. Her scholarly contributions include 11 books, over 100 articles, and numerous chapters and international presentations, for which she has received several awards, including lifetime achievement awards.

Christine Stroble, PhD, is assistant professor in the School of Education at Claflin University. She earned her doctoral degree from the University of North Carolina at Charlotte. Her research interests include schooling for pregnant and parenting students and low income, minority students; and preparing preservice teachers to use a culturally relevant pedagogy.

Cheryl P. Talley teaches in the Behavioral and Community Health Sciences program at Virginia State University. Dr. Talley's research examines the role of affective neuroscience in elucidating the mental, emotional, and spiritual factors that lead to high academic achievement, as well as the beliefs and behaviors that promote health and resilience.

Greg Wiggan is associate professor of Urban Education, adjunct associate professor of sociology, and affiliate faculty member of Africana Studies at the University of North Carolina at Charlotte. His research addresses urban education and urban sociology in the context of school processes that promote high achievement among African American students and other underserved minority student populations. In doing so, his research also examines the broader connections between the history of urbanization, globalization processes, and the internationalization of education in urban schools. His books include *Global Issues in Education: Pedagogy, Policy, Practice, and the Minority Experience; Education in a Strange Land: Globalization, Urbanization, and Urban Schools—The Social and Educational Implications of the Geopolitical Economy; Curriculum Violence: America's New Civil Rights Issue; Education for the New Frontier: Race, Education and Triumph in Jim Crow America 1867–1945; Following the Northern Star: Caribbean Identities and Education in North American Schools;* and *Unshackled: Education for Freedom, Student Achievement and Personal Emancipation.*

Joan T. Wynne, PhD, directs the Urban Education Master's Degree Program at FIU. Her newest text, "Confessions of a White Educator: Stories in Search of Justice and Diversity," explores what works and doesn't work in public education. Her recent research concerns the visionary curriculum and pedagogy of the Algebra Project and the Young People's Project, organizations rooted in American history and grassroots communities.